The Mightiest Magpies

THE MIGHTIEST MAGPIES

MICHAEL ROBERTS
with Glenn McFarlane

MICHAEL JOSEPH
an imprint of
PENGUIN BOOKS

Contents

Foreword by Michael Malthouse — vii
Progress and the Premiership — ix

Year	Title	Page
1896	**The first flag**	1
1902	**Revolution**	21
1903	**Back to back**	39
1910	**Floreat Pica**	57
1917	**Sacrifice and success**	73
1919	**Order restored**	87
1927	**Whatever it takes**	101
1928	**Band of brothers**	121
1929	**The Machine**	141
1930	**Mission accomplished**	163
1935	**Rebuilding the Machine**	185
1936	**Validation**	203
1953	**A very Collingwood flag**	219
1958	**Destiny**	247
1990	**Breaking the drought**	275
2010	**Side by side**	307

Collingwood premiership players — 338
Acknowledgements — 339

MICHAEL MALTHOUSE

Foreword

I have been very fortunate to be involved in VFL/AFL football for more than 40 years, and there is no greater achievement, and of course no better feeling, than winning a premiership. And that applies whether you're a coach, a player, an administrator or a fan. It's what we play for, what we coach for, what we all strive for.

Collingwood has experienced the heartbreak of losing grand finals and has built a reputation for sticking together 'side by side' through the lean times. It's what makes winning a premiership so special.

You can't fluke a premiership. You don't just fall into a grand final. It takes a touch of luck and years of hard work and planning to even get in a position to challenge for a premiership. That's why every premiership is memorable. Every premiership has a remarkable tale to tell.

Collingwood has enjoyed plenty of premiership success over the years, but what history – and this book – tells us is that premierships are not easy to win. Each one is different in its own way, but every one of them has been hard earned. And that means every flag deserves to be celebrated and remembered not just for a few months, but forever.

That's what this book does, and in wonderful style.

I've been lucky to be involved in just a few Premiership victories along the way, and I'll cherish those memories and feelings forever. I know many of you reading this book will feel that way about Collingwood's historic flag in 2010, and perhaps also the extraordinary victory in 1990. Many will remember fondly the incredible 1958 win against all odds. Witnessing the response to our success in 2010, seeing how it brought people together, understanding what it meant to so many people has only reinforced how special such moments are to everyone associated with this great club.

I'm proud to have helped the Collingwood Football Club add to its tally of premierships. It is a great club, with an extraordinary history and the most passionate fans of any club. Long may it reign!

Michael Malthouse
Senior coach, Collingwood Football Club

PROLOGUE

Progress and the Premiership

When the Collingwood Football Club was born, in 1892, one of the mottos its founders employed was 'Progress and the Premiership'. Sure, that wasn't exactly an inspirational, 'Eat 'em Alive' kind of motto, but it did neatly sum up the fledgling club's aims. And while few doubted that the new club would indeed make progress – even then, what would come to be known as the Magpie Army was a factor to be taken seriously – nobody outside the club's founding fathers seriously thought that Collingwood would be in a position to challenge for a premiership for many, many years.

This was, after all, a club that came out of one of the poorest, most derided suburbs in Melbourne, a place where not many people wanted to live. It might not have been slum territory, but it was not far off. Collingwood the suburb was lampooned, its residents derided – so much so that the football team was briefly nicknamed 'The Purloiners' by rival fans and even the media during the 1890s. So when Collingwood took its place in the state's premier football competition, the 15-year-old Victorian Football Association (VFA), alongside long-established clubs such as Melbourne, Geelong, South Melbourne, Carlton and Essendon, it wasn't considered a serious threat. Most footy people thought Collingwood would be simply making up the numbers.

But that isn't what the club, or its fans, believed. Collingwood people did not have much in their lives to cheer about in those days, so the formation of their own football club was a matter of great civic pride, and they were determined it would succeed. This pride was in fact the driving force behind the club's creation, in particular the desire to match fierce neighbourhood rival Fitzroy. The Roys had their own senior football team, so why shouldn't Collingwood? There would be commercial benefits, too, but they were really a fringe benefit: the club's creation was driven largely by the desire to raise the standing and dignity of the suburb and its residents.

One thing that stood out about Collingwood, even in its earliest days, was the strength and passion of its supporter base. More than 16,000 turned out to the club's first ever game in May of 1892 – a staggering number for the time. Membership hit 400 in its first season, giving the club the highest membership level in the VFA. And all this despite the onset of a depression that hit poor suburbs like Collingwood harder than most. Unemployment was rife, and those who did have jobs found their wages falling. It's difficult to imagine a worse environment in which to launch a new sporting club: many clubs folded or went into temporary abeyance around this time. But Collingwood survived. It had a unique bond with its fans that could not be shaken, a bond that remains strong today.

So Collingwood had the support it needed to progress, to be a power. But the idea that the lowly Magpies could rival the big clubs on-field seemed fanciful. The team won only three games in its first season and finished equal bottom: dreams of a premiership must have seemed distant. Two men changed all that.

Although its origins lay in the old Britannia Football Club, Collingwood was essentially a new club. Many of the former Brits opted to join the more established Fitzroy, rather than the riskier option of a new club. That meant Collingwood's early playing list was a youthful bunch, full of spirit and determination but desperately lacking in leadership. This was a time when there were no coaches, and captains played a much more important role in directing on-field activities. Collingwood had no fewer than three skippers in its first year, and a fourth, Ken McPherson, was named for 1893. He, too, was gone within a few weeks – replaced by the man who would do more than any other to shape the club's early playing fortunes.

Bill Strickland was already an established star with Carlton when he came to Victoria Park. Broad-shouldered and strong-limbed, 'Strick' usually played in the centre or as a follower, and had come to be regarded as one of the finest players in the game. He was robust, durable, a good mark and a fine kick and loved playing aggressively. But he had fallen out with his club in a dispute over the captaincy, after which the Blues were happy to clear him. Collingwood beat several other clubs in the race for his services.

Strickland's arrival changed the playing culture at Collingwood. The young players now had an experienced and respected leader to look up to, and they followed his every direction. He instilled far greater discipline throughout the club, and focused on having the players combine as a team, rather than playing as individuals. More than 100 years later, Mick Malthouse might describe his approach as promoting 'teammanship'. Strickland was also fortunate in that his arrival coincided with a period of freakishly successful recruiting. Many of the players who would form the core of the Magpies' first three flags, including Charlie Pannam, Jack Monohan, Lardie Tulloch, Dick Condon and Fred Hailwood, joined in 1893 or 1894. On the field, Collingwood's stocks were definitely on the rise.

"PAST & PRESENT CHAMPIONS."
(11) W. STRICKLAND, 1882-89.
CARLTON FOOTBALL CLUB.

But it was a different story off-field. After the euphoria of its debut season, the impact of the depression hit Collingwood hard. Attendances in 1894 fell to roughly half what they had been two years earlier. Membership also fell, to below 300, though it remained the highest in the competition. The fans were still keen and enthusiastic, but they simply didn't have the money to support the club. The club was also deeply in debt – more than one thousand pounds at the end of 1894, a figure blown out by the costs of building a new grandstand at Victoria Park. On all the figures, the club appeared to be heading into a financial abyss.

Clearly, something had to change. And that change came in the shape of a new club secretary, Ern Copeland, who had been a clerk at the Metropolitan Gas Company. He took over at Collingwood for the 1895 season and immediately began to overhaul the club's finances. He borrowed from a local patron to repay some immediate debts, allowed season tickets to be paid by instalments, encouraged a more family-friendly feel at games and organised a series of major fundraising projects. These were generally social events (such as concerts, a cycling carnival at Victoria Park, fancy-dress balls) and had the dual benefits of not only raising significant funds but also bringing the club even closer to the community.

Copeland's financial makeover achieved remarkable results – and quickly. Most of the debts were paid off in just two years, while membership soared to just under 800. The club was back on the path to financial security. Just as importantly, Copeland also became Strickland's off-field ally in changing the culture of the club. Both were strong believers in the need for discipline, unity and the subservience of individual interests to those of the team. Those beliefs underpinned so much of the club's success in the decades that followed, and they were still at the heart of its rebuilding under Malthouse and Eddie McGuire more than 100 years later. By then the approach had a new name – Side by Side – but the principles were the same. And it all started back in those early, early days, when Ern Copeland and Bill Strickland turned the Collingwood Football Club around, and set it on the path to premiership glory. Lots of it.

CHAPTER ONE
1896

The first flag

'To start at the bottom of the ladder, and in five short seasons to achieve the top-most rung, is a performance for which Collingwood is entitled to high praise.'

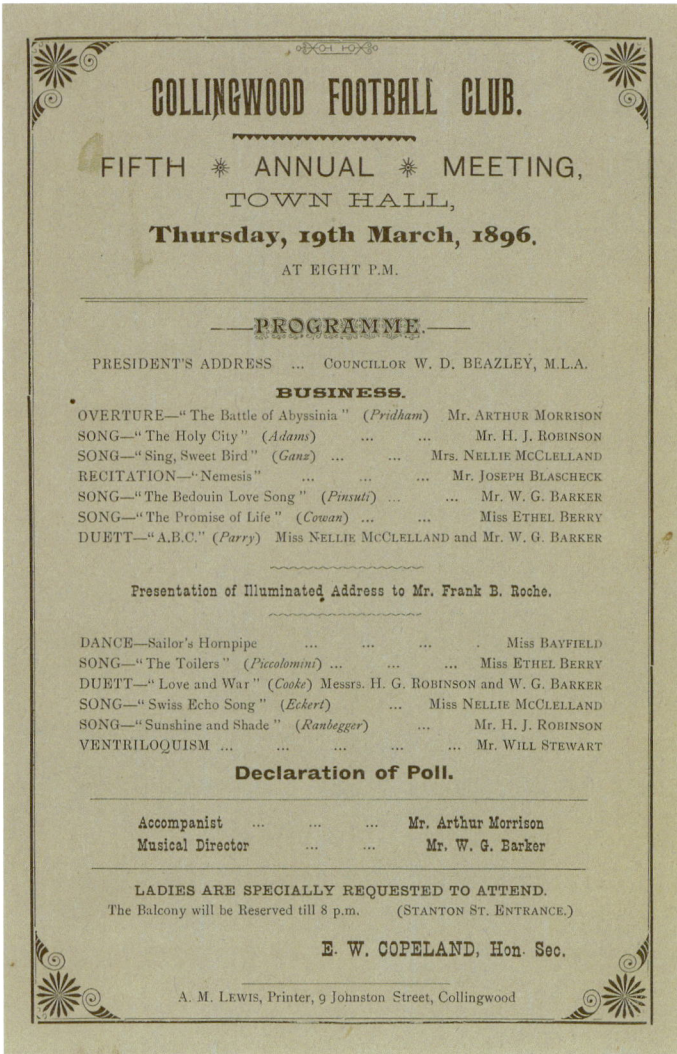

It is the evening of 19 March 1896, and the Collingwood faithful are gathering for the club's annual meeting. Collingwood get-togethers have by now become famous for their passionate, sometimes chaotic, atmosphere. Back in 1892, before the club even officially existed, a meeting called to endorse the club's creation resulted in the Collingwood Town Hall being packed so tight that many people couldn't get in and some, determined to see history being made, resorted to crawling through windows. A local parliamentarian, John Hancock, roused the crowd to fever pitch, predicting the club would soon win a premiership because 'the very name of Collingwood would strike terror into the hearts of opposing players'.

Three months after that chaotic February meeting, the club played its first game in the Victorian Football Association before one of the biggest crowds the VFA had ever seen. Two years later, with the suburb in the grip of a crippling depression, more than 1000 again packed out the Town Hall in a boisterous celebration of all things black-and-white that was, according to a local reporter, 'so light-hearted and bubbling over with enthusiasm that want of work and want of food, one would imagine, to be unknown in depression-ridden Collingwood'.

But tonight, the mood at the 1896 annual meeting seems a little different. Although the Town Hall is again packed out, the mood seems quieter, more gently optimistic. An air of expectation and quiet confidence pervades the evening, and the Magpie fans arrive talking excitedly about the season to come. They are entertained by a range of acts including ventriloquist Will Stewart, Miss Bayfield dancing the Sailor's Hornpipe and songs from Nellie

Action from the opening game of the 1896 season at Fitzroy, including a goal to Charger Hailwood.

McClelland and Ethel Berry, among others. From today's perspective, the idea of listening to W.G. Barker sing 'The Bedouin Love Song' hardly seems like the ideal way to inspire a football club to great heights. But this night it works a treat. The fans also like what they hear from a range of club officials, each of whom speaks optimistically about the season to come. A premiership, they note, is very much in the club's sights.

That optimism seems well-founded. After finishing equal last with three wins in 1892, the club had finished ninth with seven wins in 1893, eighth with eight wins in 1894 and then equal second with 12 wins behind Fitzroy in 1895. The Magpies were closing in on the rest of the competition – quickly.

Just how quickly became evident a few weeks later, when the season opened. The Collingwood players stood quietly at the Fitzroy Cricket Ground, watching fierce neighbourhood rivals Fitzroy unveil their 1895 flag and don the caps given to members of the premiership-winning team. They then immediately delivered a blistering first quarter of four goals to none. Even allowing for the strong breeze, it was an impressive statement of intent and all but ended

R. Condon

C. Pannam

J. Monaghan

the game by the first change. The Pies eventually won 6.8 to 2.4, sending a warning to the rest of the competition in the process.

That opening game provided a good indication of what was to come. The team won 12 of its opening 13 games, its only setback coming against Essendon in Round 4 (in the wake of which one Collingwood barracker, Bill Davis, was given a month in jail for using 'disgusting epithets' towards Essendon's 'Tracker' Forbes). Captain Bill Strickland, a legend at Carlton before crossing to Collingwood in 1893, was leading his players superbly, and playing with all the energy of his earlier years. Full-back Bill Proudfoot and centre half-back Jack Monohan formed a formidable combination in defence, Frank 'Charger' Hailwood was indefatigable in the ruck and Charlie Pannam was thrilling crowds with his brilliant dashes down the wing. Danny Flaherty and Harry Dowdell were providing great value as rovers and in the forward line, while Dick Condon starred around the ground and goalsneak Archie Smith was dangerous up forward. The team had developed a fine mixture of speed, skill and strength, and its high marking – where Monohan, Hailwood and even the smaller Condon shone out – drew constant praise.

Although the team's progress looked smooth on paper, the games were often tight. Behinds still did not count in a team's score in 1896, so a scoreline of 4.9

to 4.1, for example, was considered a draw. Low scoring was the norm – play was slow and crowded, ball movement even slower and kicking skills were often poor – so a team that was behind often remained in the contest by virtue of needing only one or two goals to square a game. Five of those 12 victories with which the Magpies started 1896 were achieved by just a solitary goal.

One of those victories was clouded in controversy. It came against Carlton, when the Pies narrowly avoided a draw after Wal Gillard scored a goal in the dying seconds, the bell ringing while the ball was in the air. Carlton protested to the VFA, claiming that the winning goal had been kicked some five minutes after time should have been called. The committee hearing the case met at the Young & Jackson Hotel a few weeks later and soon rejected the protest, noting archly that Collingwood's timekeeper had produced written notes taken during the match, while Carlton's official had relied on his memory 'which proved rather deficient'.

The following week saw a special 'charity weekend' at the MCG, where the four leading clubs took part in a mini version of a lightning premiership. Collingwood's involvement was limited, as it lost its 40-minute game against Essendon, but over 9000 people turned out to watch and the games raised around 180 pounds. The VFA used the matches to trial some innovations, much as the AFL has done in recent years with the NAB Cup. Two boundary umpires were on duty to throw the ball in, and a ball being returned from out of bounds did not have to touch the ground first before it was considered 'in play'. The VFA, keen to discourage scrimmaging around the goals, also decided to erect a bar *across* the goalposts for the games, requiring that all goals would have to be kicked over the bar to be counted. The first two innovations were warmly received (the latter one less so), and within a few weeks the rules governing boundary throw-ins had been changed permanently.

Early in July, on one of its bye weekends, the club embarked on its first ever mid-season trip. The players, officials and a number of fans gathered at Spencer St station early on Wednesday morning for a packed program: the team played a game against Bendigo on Wednesday afternoon, drove to Eaglehawk on

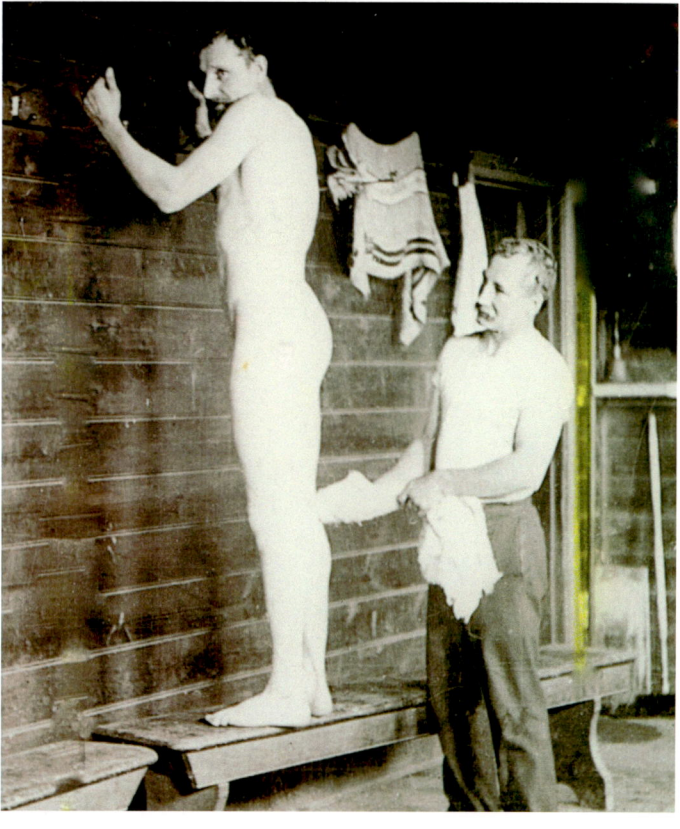

Star defender Jack Monohan gets a rubdown after training from trainer Wal Lee.

Thursday and played a local team that afternoon, and finished up with a third game in four days against a Ballarat team on Saturday afternoon.

In between there seem to have been plenty of high jinks, including any number of official welcomes and dinners (almost always featuring songs and recitals from the players), hilarious pranks such as short-sheeting of beds and the sprinkling of salt on sheets, as well as visits to local sights such as the Bendigo School of Mines, the New Chum Railway Mine, the gardens at Lake Wendouree and the Ballarat Woollen Mills. An internal club report noted that the Mills were particularly interesting to the group 'on account of the very large number of handsome young ladies at work there, who evidently took a pleasure in enlightening their visitors in the different processes the wool has to go through before it is ready to be worn.'

The travelling party returned to Melbourne on Saturday evening. The trip was a great success, and in today's terms would have been considered a highly successful team-bonding exercise. But the club, and indeed the suburb of Collingwood, benefited too. The club's internal report noted: 'It used to be thought that nothing good could come out of Collingwood, and as for a football team, that would be the quintessence of larrikinism trebly distilled. But by degrees that idea is being removed and in its stead a good opinion is spreading, and, to their credit be it said, our footballers have done a great deal towards it.'

How *Punch* magazine portrayed the violent attack on umpire Roberts at Arden Street.

Any thoughts of mid-season holidays were well and truly forgotten a couple of weeks later, when the team took on North Melbourne at Arden Street. North's home ground was a dangerous place in the 1890s, with crowd violence and hooliganism rife, but it was never wilder than on this Saturday, when spectators witnessed what *The Age* described as 'an abominable display of cowardice and brutality' and 'the most humiliating and disgraceful scene that has ever taken place in connection with football or any other sport in the colony'.

There were early signs of unrest, with a goal umpire threatened with a knife and a female North fan hitting field

W. PROUDFOOT

umpire Roberts (a former Carlton player) in the face at half-time. But that was nothing compared to what happened after the game. As the players left the field, the Pies having won by only a goal after a terrific contest, a mob of angry North fans descended on the umpire. A group of players from both teams, led by Collingwood's redoubtable defender Bill Proudfoot, gathered around the helpless Roberts and tried to protect him as the mob attempted to kick, bite and punch him, and strike him with sticks.

The ump eventually made it to the rooms beaten, bruised and completely exhausted – but he was lucky. *The Age*'s reporter noted that, had it not been for the pluck and strength of Proudfoot, 'there is every reason to believe that the umpire would have been killed'. Several of those involved in the mayhem, including a North Melbourne player, were knocked unconscious. Proudfoot, a police constable by profession, also suffered serious injuries, collapsing in the rooms after taking a fearful battering while protecting the umpire. North's reputation took a beating too, and, in the wake of a subsequent threat from umpires to refuse to officiate at games at Arden Street, the VFA banned matches at the ground for the rest of the season.

It wasn't until Round 14 in August that the Woodsmen's nine-match winning streak was broken, by Melbourne. Essendon, which had started the season with nine straight wins, was also faltering and lost its second match, this time to the season's other form team in South Melbourne. That left Collingwood, Essendon and South locked together at the top of the ladder in the race for the premiership, which in those days was determined not by a grand final or finals series, but simply by which team topped the ladder at the end of the season.

Collingwood and South met in Round 15 and produced a tense draw in front of the Governor of Victoria, while Essendon's slump continued when they went down to Melbourne on the same weekend. Round 16 was initially abandoned due to bad weather, but a week later the Pies trounced Essendon – the Same Old's third successive loss – leaving Collingwood and South six points clear with two games to play. The battle for the premiership was now a two-horse race.

The flag seemed to be heading for Victoria Park after the penultimate round of the season, when Collingwood thumped Carlton 9.15 to 1.3, and Fitzroy

---

The Age

On the crowd violence at the Collingwood v North Melbourne game at Arden Street:

Surging towards the gate they attacked [umpire] Roberts like so many fiends. He is a little fellow, but great hulking men struck viciously at him with sticks or clenched fists, and some of the brutes succeeded in tearing at his hair. Scores of fellows who could not get near enough to strike a blow or have a kick at the unfortunate little fellow's body incited the others to further brutality by their yells, while women disgraced their sex by screaming, 'Kill Him!'

belatedly reproduced its 1895 form to upset South. That left the Pies needing only a win or a draw at home against Fitzroy in the last game of the season to be crowned Premiers, and many fans confidently prepared for a major celebration at Victoria Park that day. Such confidence seemed justified: there were nine possible combinations of outcomes from the Collingwood–Fitzroy and South–Port Melbourne clashes in the final round, and only one of those – a Collingwood loss and a clear South victory – would necessitate a play-off to determine the season's champion team.

Unfortunately for Magpie fans, that is exactly what happened. In a final round full of high drama, South Melbourne defeated Port at Port and Fitzroy upset the Magpies' celebration plans at Victoria Park. It was no consolation that they went down in what was generally regarded as the best and most exciting game of the season. It was even more galling that they were thwarted at the last by – of all opponents – their most fierce local rivals. Scores were level at three-quarter time and the Pies dominated the final term, only to squander numerous chances and have one shot from 'Charger' Hailwood hit the post. In the end, the only goal of the final term came from Fitzroy's Jim Grace, and that was enough to break black-and-white hearts.

The VFA, Collingwood and South Melbourne now had a problem. With both clubs absolutely level on the top of the ladder (each side had 14 wins,

An unnamed Collingwood player out marks his South Melbourne opponent during the Round 15 drawn game.

three losses and one draw from their 18 games, Collingwood had kicked 86 goals to 85 and both had had 55 goals kicked against), a play-off would be necessary. This was, in effect, the first true grand final. The clubs had to agree on a venue, while it was up to the VFA to fix a date. But the Association still had four more matches to play: with 13 teams in the competition the fixture had to allow for byes, and also provided for several rounds of 'staggered' matches. This meant that eight more clubs – none of whom could get near South or Collingwood – still had to complete their seasons. So would the VFA be prepared to take the focus away from those four meaningless games and play the grand final the next weekend, or make Collingwood and South wait around for an extra week?

Most observers agreed that the latter course would be farcical. Follower in *The Age* summed up most feelings when he wrote: 'It would be quite unreasonable to keep 40 men in hard training for a clear week longer than is necessary.' The two clubs themselves agreed they wanted to play on the earlier Saturday (26 September), at the East Melbourne Cricket Ground, but many of the other clubs – especially those involved in games on the 26th – opposed the idea. On 22 September, the VFA ruled that the grand final would not be played until 3 October. Incredulous club officials demanded another meeting of the VFA delegates, but again they were thwarted – this time by a solitary vote. Collingwood and South Melbourne would have to wait.

South Melbourne was prepared to stick by its agreement and play the game on the 26th anyway, but Collingwood did not want to risk a possible premiership being rendered illegitimate. So the Pies spent that day engaged in a meaningless practice match against Eaglehawk to keep the players match-tuned. The players were frustrated, the officials angry and fans and media bemused.

The biggest loser, though, turned out to be the Victorian Football Association. There had been growing disquiet all year with the VFA. Many were critical of the way it was running the game, the quality of football itself came under constant attack, and attendances were falling. But its biggest threat came from its strongest clubs looking to form their own breakaway competition. Those clubs had become increasingly frustrated with the VFA's stewardship of the game and angry at proposed reforms for revenue sharing that would have favoured the smaller clubs. Collingwood was now considered one

PLAYER OF THE YEAR

Bill Proudfoot

When he wasn't busy protecting umpires from hordes of rampaging opposition fans, Constable Bill Proudfoot spent most of the 1896 season doing an equally good job protecting the Collingwood goal.

Proudfoot was a big, strong, hulk of a man who held down the full-back position for most of his 15 years in the black-and-white. He was one of the few ex-Britannia players who crossed to Collingwood, and he played in the club's first-ever game in 1892.

In 1896 he and Jack Monohan formed an almost impenetrable defensive combination for the Pies. Proudfoot wasn't quite as strong a mark as Monohan (then again, few were), but he was a glorious kick who regularly launched long drop kicks or place kicks from deep in defence to relative safety.

Proudfoot rarely put in a bad game in 1896 and at year's end he was presented with a diamond pin donated by a generous supporter. But, like his teammates, his real reward came from the premiership itself.

PLAYER OF THE YEAR

Bill Strickland

Before he joined Collingwood in 1893, Bill Strickland was regarded as one of the best all-round footballers of his time. But by the 1896 season, during which Strickland turned 32, most observers in football thought his best playing days were long behind him.

How wrong they were. Instead, season 1896 became for Strickland the kind of 'Indian summer' that most sportsmen only dream about. He played superbly throughout, and was judged by sportswriters to be one of the two outstanding players of the season (Melbourne's Fred McGinis was the other). His leadership, which had always been one of his strong points, rose to new levels.

The Australasian's Markwell, in voting Strickland his player of the year, said:

'This year he has not only shown his finest form, but has added to his great usefulness as a player the cool judgement and ability of a general. Despite playing with consistent brilliancy, he has unquestionably shown himself the most gifted commander of the day.'

Strickland capped his magnificent season with a best-on-ground performance in the grand final – together, of course, with his brilliant tactical moves. No one player did more to bring that first flag to Victoria Park.

of the power clubs, as much for its drawing power as its on-field success, and was eagerly courted by the dissidents.

The Magpies had, mostly, been supportive of the VFA. But the Association's scheduling of the grand final changed all that, and prompted Collingwood to turn its back on the competition. Club delegates were furious at the Association's first refusal to bring the game forward, and had warned it before the second meeting that failure to change the date would see Collingwood abandon its support for the VFA and instead throw in its lot with a new league. The VFA stuck rigidly to its ruling for 3 October and, as promised, Collingwood threw its weight behind the establishment of the soon-to-be-formed Victorian Football League. In a neat twist of timing, the famous meeting at which Collingwood, South Melbourne, Fitzroy, Essendon, Geelong and Melbourne decided to formalise their breakaway (Carlton and St Kilda were invited later) was held the night before the long-delayed final play-off match.

Less than 24 hours after that meeting, Collingwood and South Melbourne lined up at the East Melbourne Cricket Ground to decide which team would be crowned premiers for 1896 – with both teams knowing it would be their last match in the VFA. The delayed end to the season meant grounds would soon be turned over to cricket so the governing body ruled that, in the event of a draw, the teams would play extra time (two 10-minute periods either way) in order to ensure a result. Nick Maxwell might have approved.

Still, the prospect of extra time appealed to no one, for 3 October turned out to be a stinking hot day. The crowd of around 12,000 was healthy, but many more had been deterred by the clubs' decision to charge one shilling for entry – double the usual admission price.

Those who braved both the heat and the expense were treated to what one journalist described as 'one of the most exciting football matches which have been played during the annals of the game in Victoria'. South won the toss and decided to kick into the breeze, hoping that coming home with the wind would help make up for tiring legs. The Pies jumped away early, and had two goals on the board – to Jim Gregory and Richard Hall – before South had scored. South then hit back with two goals of their own, but a long drop-kicked goal from the mercurial Dick Condon, and another after the bell from Harry Dowdell left Collingwood with a four-goals-to-two lead at quarter-time.

Jack Monohan, one of the stars of the 1896 Grand Final, was captured on canvas flying for a mark.

It was a breathtaking start to the game. A six-goal tally was considered reasonable for an entire match: it was rare for it to be reached in one quarter. The Magpies looked in top form, and seemed to have South's measure across the field. Captain Strickland was dominating the midfield, Monohan and McDonald were strong in defence and the forwards looked threatening.

But everything changed in the second term. South dominated the game and peppered the goals but could add only 1.5, while the sum total of Collingwood's few forays forward was a solitary behind to small man Danny Flaherty, who hit the post. The Magpies still led by a goal at half-time, but Observer in *The Argus* noted that anyone tipping the result at this stage would have opted for South. This view, he wrote, was confirmed in the early part of the third term, when 'South's superiority seemed so pronounced that the game was apparently all over'.

What none of the onlookers knew, however, was that Bill Strickland had taken a huge risk during the half-time break. He had great faith that Collingwood's younger team would finish the game stronger than their rivals but, even so, had told his charges to 'take it easy' in the third quarter and conserve their energy for the last. For much of the third term it looked as if the players had followed his instructions too literally, for South again dominated and would surely have put the game beyond the Magpies' reach had they capitalised on their numerous chances. In the end they managed 2.3 to Collingwood's two behinds – enough to give the Southerners a one-goal advantage at the last change.

The Pies looked shot. South had the lead and all the momentum, with the boys from Victoria Park having managed just three behinds in two quarters of

The Magpies take a shot on goal during the grand final. Note the goal square stretching from point post to point post.

football. But Strickland then intervened for a second time. At the last change he urged his players to move the ball on at all costs, and make the most of what he believed was their superior fitness. 'Never let the ball out of play if you can help it, or you'll give them breathing time,' he told his men. He also pulled off a tactical masterstroke by moving centre half-back Jack Monohan into attack. The effect of both initiatives was immediate. Markwell in *The Australasian* wrote: 'No sooner had the ball been bounced in the concluding quarter than the Woodsmen set to work at a pace for which their adversaries had never given them credit, and three tremendous marks by Monaghan (sic), one of them the finest of the match, fairly electrified the crowd.'

Monohan's marks all resulted in place kicks on goal. All missed. But in an instant the tone of the game had changed. His marks 'caused perturbation amongst the Southern defenders', and the Pies began attacking incessantly. Collingwood players were no longer taking it easy but were finishing the game full of running, while their opponents suddenly looked tired. Right through the final term, the Collingwood war cry was 'Faster – make it faster!' Fans and officials shouted the words whenever the players came close enough to the fence to hear, and the players did likewise among themselves. South Melbourne simply couldn't keep pace, and were grimly holding on to their one-goal lead as the minutes ticked by.

Eventually the black-and-white onslaught proved too much, and 'Charger' Hailwood, a strong follower but an ungainly and unreliable kick, levelled the goals tally with a straight punt kick. Hailwood collided head-first with teammate William Callaghan while stooping to collect the ball soon afterwards, but even that couldn't stop the Collingwood charge. Just as extra time beckoned, Danny Flaherty was slung to the ground without the ball and awarded a free kick, then coolly steered home what proved to be the winning goal from close

Collingwood players race together to celebrate as the final bell signals that the Magpies have won their first premiership.

The Australasian

Markwell, on the popularity of the Magpie premiership

Their premiership is not begrudged them by teams below them on the list, nor by the football-loving public, who are only too pleased to find a comparatively new team taking the field. To start at the bottom of the ladder, and in five short seasons to achieve the top-most rung, is a performance for which Collingwood is entitled to high praise.

PLAYER OF THE YEAR

Jack Monohan

Few players in Collingwood's history have been able to match Jack Monohan's aerial skills. Stationed mostly at centre half-back, the strongly-built Monohan consistently thwarted opposition attacks with towering marks and long, booming kicks out of defence.

He was rarely, if ever, in better form than throughout 1896. Critics marvelled at the quality of his marking, with one from *The Sporting Judge* being moved to verse after yet another outstanding performance:

'It was Monohan, yes Monohan,
who took the blessed cake,
And hero of the forty is the
honour he must take,
For his play was really perfect
and his manner of the best,
Qualities so seldom shown
when one's put to the test.'

Like Strickland, Monohan also saved his best for last, ending his season with a stunning display in the grand final. His marking that day was described by one newspaper as 'rarely witnessed and never excelled', while Strickland himself said Jack's three marks at the start of the last quarter were the turning point of the game.

in. South pressed again in the final minutes but the Pies held on, the last shot from South's Windley coming after the bell but falling well short. In just its fifth season as a football club, the Magpies had won the flag. The players ran from the field exultant, to wild cheers from their fans.

But it wasn't only their fans celebrating. For what would probably be the only time in the club's history, a Collingwood premiership was popular with the general football community: the media, and many opposition teams and fans, were actually *happy* the relative newcomers to the VFA had won.

Strickland was, quite rightly, given much of the credit for Collingwood's triumph. 'There was no one in the match to be compared with Strickland, who, besides playing the hardest game on the side, managed his forces with consummate ability,' wrote Markwell in *The Australasian*. 'To him much more than any of his followers must be ascribed the securing of the premiership by Collingwood. His method of handling the team after half-time undoubtedly won the game for his side.'

Strickland himself thought of the flag as his finest moment in football. 'No team has worked harder, trained harder or played more unselfishly to win the premiership than the team I have had the honour of captaining,' he was reported to have said at a post-match function. 'I am very proud of the way this club has been received by the public of Collingwood, and the proudest day of my life was when our team walked off the East Melbourne Cricket Ground as Premiers.'

But if the credit for the victory was Strickland's, the glory was widely shared. The premiership sparked a wave of celebrations that would not be seen in the community again until the drought-breaking flag of 1990. Over 2000 people turned out to the victory celebration at the Town Hall. Other councillors and prominent supporters threw separate parties, smoke nights and banquets in the club's honour, as celebrations continued for the best part of a month. One local councillor was quoted as expressing mock concern that if the festivities continued for much longer, the club's doctor would be treating players for gout instead of accidents. Strickland told another function the players had been toasted so often he was 'getting out of wind in responding'. 'The Collingwood Football Premiers are having gay times,' reported one local newspaper.

1896: The first flag

Indeed they were. At one function held at the City Hotel in Johnston Street, they were presented with beautiful gold medals donated by Joseph Cross, the brother of one of the club's founders. Each of the players was called upon to respond, though one unnamed player apparently bolted rather than face the ordeal of public speaking. In all, the toasts and presentations involved no fewer than 80 speeches!

Local politicians took particular pride in the victory, and went into hyperbolic overdrive on its significance. The Mayor, Cr William Cody, said the footballers were a credit to the city and that 'their good conduct wherever they went did much to do away with the bad name Collingwood once enjoyed'. Another councillor, Edgar Wilkins, said the premiership win had 'done so much to lift Collingwood in the eyes of the world'. (Yes, he really said *the world.*) William Beazley, the club's president and also a Member of Parliament, said the club had done much to uphold the credit of football, for although they went in to win they also went in to play 'a pure and honourable game'. VFA secretary Thomas Marshall said 'no club played the game of football truer than Collingwood' and that this opinion was endorsed everywhere they played (except North Melbourne).

Everyone, it seemed, wanted to share and rejoice in the Magpies' success. That included at least one company – MacRobertson's, the makers of Pepsin chewing gum – that tried to cash in. Soon after the grand final, an ad for Pepsin appeared, consisting of a statement by the Collingwood players that read, in part: 'We certainly ascribe to the use of your Chewing Gum the credit mainly of our staying power and endurance in the field. We all chew Gum (Your Gum) and rely on it for exceptionally severe tussles and spins.' The players signed off: 'Unitedly thanking you for putting such a genuine article on the market, we subscribe ourselves, Gratefully Yours . . .'

The medal awarded to Collingwood's 1896 premiership players.

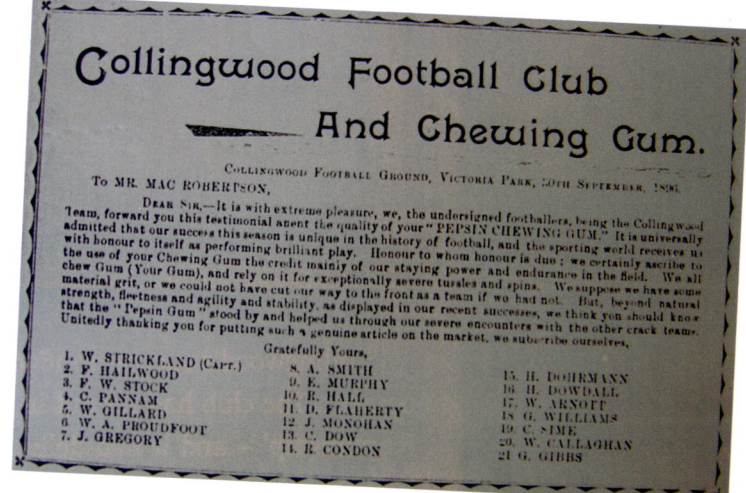

It was, quite possibly, one of the most heartfelt endorsements in the history of Australian sport. But behind the stiffly formal hyperbole lay one important fact: even in those difficult times, savvy companies had already spotted the potential advantages of being commercially associated with the Collingwood Football Club.

Collingwood's success in 1896 capped off a period of extraordinary development. The club had set out in 1892 under the motto of 'Progress and the Premiership' – and it had delivered on both promises faster than anyone thought possible. In just five short years the combination of a large and passionate supporter base, prudent financial management and on-field success had turned the club into one of the powerhouses of the VFA. Now it was to be a founding member of the breakaway competition. New challenges lay ahead, but the building blocks for success had been put in place. All that remained was for Collingwood to take the newly-formed Victorian Football League by storm.

DANNY FLAHERTY
GRAND FINAL HERO

Even today, it is every football-loving kid's dream to kick the winning goal in a grand final. That's a dream Danny Flaherty got to live out in 1896.

Flaherty had joined the Pies from Port Melbourne in 1893 and became a regular throughout 1894, 1895 and 1896 as a lively rover and small forward. He was well regarded but not one of the game's stars.

That all changed late in the 1896 Grand Final when he was slung to the ground by a South Melbourne opponent. He wasn't far from goal but the pressure was immense: somehow, he kept calm and kicked truly for the goal that gave Collingwood the flag.

Flaherty was the focus for many of the premiership celebrations. At one of the parties for the players he was presented with the match ball, silver-mounted on an ebony stand and encased in a glass dome. A toast and musical number were then performed in his honour.

Despite his grand final heroics, Flaherty didn't last much longer at Collingwood. He managed only four games in 1897, then left top-level football. Still, no Magpie fan of the era ever forgot his flag-winning contribution on that sunny October day in 1896.

PLAYERS

Player	Games	Goals
William Arnott	18	2
W Balfour	1	0
William Callaghan	19	0
George Calleson	16	2
Clarke	1	0
Dick Condon	18	8
George Davidson	1	0
Herman Dohrmann	12	3
Charles Dow	16	1
Harry Dowdell	17	7
Danny Flaherty	17	5
Flynn	1	0
Arthur Gibbs	13	1
Wal Gillard	18	13
Jim Gregory	9	4
Frank Hailwood	19	12
Richard Hall	19	12
Letcher	2	1
Robert McDonald	3	0
Jack Monohan	19	0
Edward Murphy	12	2
Charlie Pannam	19	0
Payne	1	0
Piper	1	0
Bill Proudfoot	19	0
E Ross	2	1
Charles Sime	4	1
Archie Smith	19	12
F Stock	15	3
Bill Strickland	18	0
Albert Tame	6	2
Lardie Tulloch	4	0
George Williams	19	0

Club Awards
Regular training awards to Arnott, Monohan, Smith
Gold watch presented to Bill Strickland
Leading goalkicker – Wal Gillard (13)

1896 SEASON

ROUND 1 May 2 Fitzroy Cricket Ground

Fitzroy **2.4** v **Collingwood** 6.8

Goals: Gillard 2, Hailwood, Smith, Dow, Hall

ROUND 2 May 9 Victoria Park

Collingwood 3.12 v Richmond **0.1**

Goals: Hailwood, Gillard, Tame

ROUND 3 May 16 Victoria Park

Collingwood 4.5 v South Melbourne **3.2**

Goals: Condon 2, Smith, Murphy

ROUND 4 May 25 East Melbourne Cricket Ground

Essendon **4.14** v Collingwood 2.5

Goals: Dowdell, Gibbs

ROUND 5 May 30 University Ground

Carlton **3.11** v **Collingwood** 4.8

Goals: Gillard, Hall, Dohrmann, Dowdell

ROUND 6 June 13 Victoria Park

Collingwood 4.4 v Melbourne **2.4**

Goals: Hailwood 2, Smith, Gregory

ROUND 7 June 20 Williamstown Cricket Ground

Williamstown **3.5** v **Collingwood** 4.3

Goals: Smith, Flaherty, Condon, Dowdell

ROUND 8 June 27 Corio Oval

Geelong **4.9** v **Collingwood** 5.7

Goals: Hailwood, Hall, Tame, Murphy, Gregory

ROUND 9 July 4 Victoria Park

Collingwood 3.12 v St Kilda **0.4**

Goals: Flaherty, Hall, Sime

ROUND 10 July 18 Western Oval

Footscray **4.5** v **Collingwood** 7.5

Goals: Condon 2, Hailwood, Gillard, Hall, Arnott, Letcher

ROUND 11 July 25 Arden Street

Nth Melbourne **4.4** v **Collingwood** 5.6

Goals: Hall 2, Hailwood, Gillard, Dowdell

ROUND 12 August 1 Victoria Park

Collingwood 8.5 v Geelong **5.2**

Goals: Stock 3, Gillard 2, Smith, Flaherty, Condon

ROUND 13 August 8 Victoria Park

Collingwood 6.6 v Port Melbourne **4.11**

Goals: Hailwood 2, Smith 2, Gillard, Dowdell

ROUND 14 August 15 MCG

Melbourne 6.8 v Collingwood **4.3**

Goals: Gillard 2, Hailwood 1, Gregory

ROUND 15 August 22 Lakeside Oval

Sth Melbourne **3.10** v Collingwood **3.5**

Goals: Smith 2, Calleson

ROUND 16 September 5 Victoria Park

Collingwood 6.8 v Essendon **3.4**

Goals: Hall 3, Smith, Calleson, Ross

ROUND 17 September 12 Victoria Park

Collingwood 9.15 v Carlton **1.3**

Goals: Gillard 2, Hailwood, Smith, Flaherty, Hall, Condon, Dohrmann, Arnott

ROUND 18 September 19 Victoria Park

Collingwood 3.8 v **Fitzroy** 4.4

Goals: Smith, Dohrmann, Dowdell

1896 FINAL

LADDER			(before the play-off match)	
Team	W	L	D	Pts
Collingwood	14	3	1	58
Sth Melbourne	14	3	1	58
Essendon	14	4	0	56
Fitzroy	12	6	0	48
Melbourne	12	6	0	48
North Melbourne	8	9	1	34
Port Melbourne	7	8	3	34
Williamstown	7	8	3	34
Footscray	5	10	3	26
St Kilda	6	11	1	26
Geelong	4	11	3	22
Carlton	2	14	2	12
Richmond	3	15	0	12

GRAND FINAL Oct 3   East Melbourne Cricket Ground

Collingwood	4.3	4.4	4.6	6.9
Sth Melbourne	2.1	3.6	5.9	5.10

Goals: Hall, Gregory, Condon, Dowdell, Hailwood, Flaherty
Best: Strickland, Monohan, McDonald, Gibbs, Smith, Flaherty, Hailwood
Umpire: J.J. Trait
Crowd: Approximately 12,000

Grand Final Team
B: A. Gibbs, W. Proudfoot, R. McDonald
HB: G. Williams, J. Monohan, C. Dow
C: C. Pannam, W. Strickland, W. Callaghan
HF: A. Smith, F. Hailwood, W. Gillard
F: J. Gregory, D. Flaherty, G. Calleson
R: H. Dowdell, F. Stock, R. Hall, H. Dohrmann, R. Condon

CHAPTER TWO

1902
Revolution

'Their system was simply perfect. They carried half-distance passing to a point of excellence that has seldom, if ever, been equalled in the history of Victorian football … no team in the competition will have a chance against them for the premiership.'

More than 40 Collingwood footballers and officials huddled together on the Melbourne docks, trying to keep out the bitter cold of the late June morning. It was the interstate match break in the 1902 season, and the Magpies were taking the opportunity to spend 12 days in Tasmania. Such trips had become hugely popular in the club's first decade: they provided great bonding experiences for the players, and were also considered something of a perk in what was still an amateur competition. A few matches had been organised against combined local teams for the Magpies' trip, but everyone knew they wouldn't be serious affairs. So, as the players boarded the steamer *SS Coogee*, they were simply looking ahead to a nice little mid-year holiday. What they couldn't have known was that they were about to revolutionise the way Australian football was played.

Collingwood's plans for domination of the newly-formed Victorian Football League had not quite gone to script. The team had entered the competition as reigning VFA Premiers but, despite regular finals appearances, hadn't been able to snare another flag. They had gone closest in 1901, finishing runner-up to a rampaging Essendon side. But they'd been well beaten in the season's final match, and it was obvious that work was still needed if the Pies were to match it with the best. Perhaps that's why, as one newspaper reported, there were rumours Collingwood players had begun training 'while the test cricket matches were still in progress!'

Nevertheless, hopes were high in the Magpie camp. Many of the heroes from the 1896 flag were still pulling on the black-and-white jumper each week. Champion defenders Bill Proudfoot and Jack Monohan continued to make life difficult for forwards, 'Charger' Hailwood was as tireless as ever in the ruck, Charlie Pannam remained dazzling and tricky and Lardie Tulloch, a bit-part player in 1896, had matured into a fine follower and outstanding captain. The squad had been further boosted by the brilliant Ted Rowell, who had joined from the goldfields of Kalgoorlie in 1901. Then, on the eve of the season, twins Ted and George Lockwood crossed from Geelong, where they

The Victoria Park ground as it looked around 1902, with a cycling track inside the fence and small gas lights in front of the grandstand.

had both been more than handy. The Pies also secured a VFA star in Henry Pears and an outstanding youngster from Northcote in Cornelius McCormack.

This was looking like a formidable Magpie outfit. The only real question mark for the Pies was the uncertainty over the enigmatic Fred Leach. Fast, strong and highly skilled, Leach was just about the complete footballer, and had been voted by some sportswriters as the best player in the VFL in 1901. But Leach was injury-prone and mentally fragile, missing many games with low-level injuries or illness, absenting himself mid-season to take a three-week holiday and retiring three times in his seven seasons. The second of those retirements came on the eve of the 1902 season when Leach declared he 'wanted to keep out of the bumps and bruises'.

There was action outside the football department, too. Membership had passed 1100, and by season's end would swell by a further thirty per cent. This prompted the club to provide 300 extra seats in the members' reserve, as well as raising and widening the banks around the ground so an estimated 30,000 fans could see games in comfort. The club also purchased eight automatic turnstiles 'to prevent crowding at the entrances'.

Above: **Dick Condon.**
Below: **Charger Hailwood in a marking contest against South Melbourne in the first game of the season.**
Opposite: **Ted Rowell gathers the ball against Essendon in 1902. Once he had it, his great speed made him just about impossible to catch.**

But the main reason the Collingwood faithful entered the 1902 season with a spring in their step was the return of the prodigal son, Dick Condon.

Condon was one of the most gifted players ever to don a Collingwood jumper. He played mostly as a rover or centreman and was renowned for his marking, agility and ball skills. He had an extraordinary ability to twist in the air while marking, so he could land and take off running in almost one movement. He was quick, with great kicking skills even on his wrong side – something that was highly unusual for the time – and possessed a fine football brain. Former teammate Eddie Drohan later described him as 'a footballing freak'. Thirty years after he retired, judges as hard to please as Jock McHale and Bill Strickland still rated him the best footballer they had seen.

But Condon was also a troublemaker. He had a rebellious temperament that was always getting him into hot water. In his earliest days at the club he was hauled before the committee for disobeying instructions from Strickland, his captain. In 1900, when he was captain himself, he was suspended for three weeks for abusing an umpire. Soon after his return, he came to blows with one of his own players at a three-quarter-time break. Later in the year he walked from the field in protest at what he considered to be poor umpiring and tried to take the team with him. The next week he lost the plot completely, abusing the highly regarded (though unfortunately named) umpire, Ivo Crapp, by yelling, 'Your girl's a bloody whore!'

PLAYER OF THE YEAR
Ted Rowell

That was too much for the VFL. The League suspended Condon for life, and Collingwood – heartily sick of his continued breaches of discipline – did nothing to support him. It took 18 months for the club to mellow its stance and, as the 1902 season approached, officials finally wrote in support of Condon's appeal for his suspension to be revoked. That seemed to be enough to sway the VFL's decision makers: in May, just as the season was getting underway, Dick Condon's life ban was lifted and he was free to return to the game.

Collingwood began the season with three comfortable wins in a row. But things threatened to fall apart after the Round 4 game against Fitzroy at Victoria Park. The 33-point loss on home turf was bad enough, but the misery was compounded when Ted Rowell became embroiled in a bribery scandal.

Rowell had taken the competition by storm since moving across from Western Australia the previous year. His blistering speed, strong marking and superb kicking made him a dangerous player, and he'd kicked 31 goals in his debut season, good enough for third place on the VFL goalkicking ladder. He had started 1902 in a similarly rich vein of form, kicking seven goals in the first three matches. But he had a shocker against the Roys at Victoria Park. *The Argus* described his performance as 'useless' and 'too bad to be true', saying that Rowell had failed the club when it needed him most. *The Age* said he was 'conspicuous for his most remarkable failure to render his team the slightest assistance'.

It had been a rare horror day at the office for Rowell, and that set suspicious tongues wagging. Rumours quickly swept the football world that he had taken a bribe to 'play dead' in the match. The

Seasons don't come much better than that enjoyed by Ted Rowell in 1902.

He was named by a number of different sportswriters as their 'Champion of the Colony' for the season, and jointly topped the VFL goalkicking list (33 goals) with Essendon's Albert Thurgood. He was twice chosen to play for Victoria, kicked the first goal of the grand final, and – more importantly – the one that broke Essendon's resistance in the final term, in what was overall a fine display in the game that matters most. He also ran at Stawell for the first time.

Throughout the season he played consistently outstanding football. Markwell, writing in *The Australasian*, wrote: 'I must credit him with having, with his pace, his fairness, his magnificent kicking, and especially with his accurate passing to his clubmates forward, done his team an immense amount of service.'

Magpie fans loved him, and showed they had quickly forgotten the unpleasantness of the mid-year bribery insinuations when they made him the focus of this ditty:
 'When Condon kick to Pannam,
 The crowd begins to howl
 But they really pull the fence down
 When it goes to Teddy Rowell.'

> **The SPORTING GLOBE**
>
> **Ted Rowell, writing about the players' time in Tasmania:**
>
> One morning we left the hotel in our football togs and boots, and drove out to the foot of Mt Wellington. A competition that we held there was a severe test of strength and stamina. It was a race to the top of the mountain and back, with a trophy to the winner. There was plenty of snow and the track was very primitive. It was tough going but Lardie Tulloch, our skipper, went like a mountain goat. He was the winner, and broke a record.

Collingwood committee suspended him while it investigated the rumours, but Rowell was so incensed that he resigned, citing 'ungenerous treatment by outside barrackers and the insinuations made'. Rowell said he had always given his utmost for the team and attributed his poor performance to several heavy falls and a knock to the head he'd received early in the game, incidents that were referred to in press reports at the time. He fronted the committee the next week and gave such a convincing presentation – backed by a statutory declaration – that the club unanimously accepted his explanation and exonerated him from any suspicion of not having done his best.

Rowell missed four matches while the whole sorry mess was sorted out, and returned to the team the week before he and his teammates gathered to board the SS Coogee. The Pies had struggled a little in Rowell's absence, narrowly getting home against the woeful Saints by a mere seven points, losing to Essendon, then beating both Carlton and South – the latter despite an extraordinary scoreline of 4.26. Essendon and Fitzroy were the competition's early pacesetters. It seemed like a good time for the Woods to regroup with a short break in Tasmania.

The Collingwood touring party (including Fred Leach, who had ended his 'retirement') landed in Launceston and played games both there and in Hobart against combined local teams. As expected, the games didn't provide any real challenges for the Magpies. They played against 21 locals in the first match, and five regular Magpies had to be dragooned into the opposition's line-up to make up the numbers in the last match. It was hardly surprising that the Magpies didn't take things too seriously. They began playing around, almost

Opposite: **The team before a game in Tasmania.**
Left: **The players during their race to the top of Mt Wellington. Skipper Lardie Tulloch is on the move, third from right.**
Below: **Two of the architects of the stab pass, Dick Condon and Charlie Pannam.**

toying with the home team, trying dinky, low, short kicks to their teammates, placed just out of reach of their opponents. The team's most highly skilled players – Condon, Leach, Pannam and Rowell – were responsible for starting this style of play, but it was just a bit of fun and nobody took too much notice.

The tourists returned to Launceston when the games and socialising were done to board the *SS Coogee* for the journey home. In a crazy bit of scheduling, they were due to arrive back in Melbourne on the morning of Saturday 5 July, and would have to promptly jump on a train to Geelong to play that afternoon. But choppy conditions in Bass Strait made the crossing a stressful one, and – more importantly – delayed the boat. As the *Coogee* slowly made its way to Melbourne it was looking more and more like Collingwood would miss the train and have to forfeit the game to the Pivotonians. So club secretary Ern Copeland stepped in, and convinced the *Coogee's* skipper to signal a request to Queenscliff for railway officials in Melbourne to delay the train. Remarkably, the message got through successfully and the railway bosses agreed. The players changed on the train on the way down, and had their rubdowns on-board too. The train made it into Geelong less than 10 minutes before the scheduled start time of 3pm, and the players went straight from the station onto Corio Oval – with about a minute to spare.

Most of the players were still suffering the after-effects of the sea voyage, not to mention the chaos of their late arrival at the ground. Geelong must have thought it was in for an easy ride, but the Magpie players, perhaps not feeling up to their normal game, decided to experiment with the short-passing tactics they'd been using in Tasmania. It worked so well that the Geelong players simply didn't know which way to turn. They lost by 40 points.

Collingwood and Essendon players give three cheers for the Governor of Victoria, Sir George Clarke, who was witnessing his first game of football. Sir George said later that he thought the game was 'a splendid exercise that is the training in the time of peace to make good soldiers in time of war'.

The Argus
On Collingwood's new style of play:

What served Collingwood best of all was the marvellous quickness with which they picked their own men and the certainty in passing to each other. In half-kicking their length was nearly always perfect and... when they saw one of their own men unguarded, they played to him with a low, quick, skimming kick which got there promptly.

Collingwood, buoyed by the early success, continued using their new style of play. The effectiveness of the tactics was further underlined in the next three weeks. The Pies first turned the tables on Fitzroy by 23 points, then belted St Kilda by a massive 117 points, before also defeating the other main flag threat in Essendon. The system was deceptively simple – each time a Collingwood player got the ball, a teammate would instantly run to space to allow the ball to be passed to him – but it baffled all their opponents. Beyond players running into space, the system also relied on precision and pin-point passing. Through this combination of low, zooming passes to leading teammates, Collingwood was able to move the ball systematically, quickly and with fewer instances of what now would be called turnovers. From today's standpoint it sounds simple, but in 1902 it turned football on its head.

Until this point, football had been a fairly static game. There were lots of packs and scrimmages, and movement of the ball was so slow that players at one end of the ground had been known to sit down and have a rest when the ball was at the other end. Players from some clubs, including Collingwood, still wore hats or caps, and would sometimes stop to pick them up when chasing after the ball. Players looked for teammates when passing, of course, but often with high, floating kicks to the general vicinity of a colleague, rather than the precision kicking that became the Magpies' trademark. This system brought a faster, much more strategic, approach to football. In effect Collingwood became one of the first clubs to introduce a defined game plan – so much so that one newspaper reported how the players would sketch out imaginary moves 'as if in a game of chess' in chalk on a blackboard in the Victoria Park dressing rooms. The club was years ahead of its time.

In 1902, however, the system simply gave Collingwood a huge advantage over its rivals. The Pies did not lose a game after returning from Tasmania, and finished the 17-round season on top of the ladder. They tuned up for the finals with a stunning 89-point thrashing of Geelong in the last game, with Henry Pears bagging seven goals.

The top four teams now prepared to play two semi-finals – first versus third and second versus fourth. Collingwood prepared for its semi-final against Fitzroy in supremely confident fashion. They could not have been in better form: 11 wins on the trot, and the week before the last-round demolition of Geelong they had smashed Fitzroy by nearly nine goals. Teddy Rowell was unstoppable with six goals.

'No praise could exaggerate the merit of Collingwood's triumph,' wrote Markwell in *The Australasian*. 'Their system was simply perfect. They carried half-distance passing to a point of excellence that has seldom, if ever, been equalled in the history of Victorian football, and the coolness and celerity with which they exchanged marks in all parts of the field . . . gave onlookers the impression that no team in the competition will have a chance against them for the premiership.'

Fitzroy, though, had other ideas. On the Thursday before the semi-final, Fitzroy players and officials concocted a plan designed to combat Collingwood's system. Every Roys player was given a man to mind, with instructions to stick to their opponents like glue. Special attention was to be paid to Rowell, who was in rare form. To the surprise of everyone outside Fitzroy HQ, the plan worked and the rank outsiders won by 16 points.

Skipper Lardie Tulloch (left) with teammate and good friend Matt Fell.

Alf 'Rosie' Dummett outmarks his opponent during the Magpies' 53-point win late in the season.

PLAYER OF THE YEAR — Charlie Pannam

Charlie Pannam was a Collingwood stalwart who played a key role in the club's first three premierships. But he rarely, if ever, played a more consistent season than in 1902.

Pannam was outstanding from start to finish on a wing, where his speed, ball skills and evasiveness made him a feared opponent. So, too, did his bag of 'sly tricks', which often exasperated umpires, opponents and rival fans. It all got too much for one of those fans at Fitzroy during the year, who gave Pannam a fearful spray. Pannam responded by jumping the fence to hit him!

But Pannam was more than just a brilliant flashy player who could get under the skin of the opposition. He was also resilient, as shown by the fact that in Round 15 he became the first player in VFL history to reach the 100-game milestone. And he was a renowned big game player – as he showed again with a grand final display that rivalled Frank Hailwood for best on ground.

This is where the benefits of being minor premiers kicked in. In the new finals system introduced that year, if the team that finished on top of the ladder lost either its semi-final or grand final, it could issue a challenge. In this case, that meant Fitzroy and Essendon, winners of the two semi-finals, would play off for the right to play the Pies in a grand final. Essendon won the final against Fitzroy, probably to the Magpies' relief, and so lined up against the Magpies in the premiership decider for the second successive year.

This was the first grand final to be played at the MCG, and more than 35,000 fans turned out – a huge crowd for the time. Those fans were stunned pre-match when news spread that Collingwood had left out champion centre half-back Jack Monohan. The defender had injured his leg in the semi-final against Fitzroy but was expected to be right for the grand final after a two-week break. At the last minute, however, Collingwood selectors decided not to take a risk with their injured star, believing he might not last the whole game. It was a huge loss for the Magpies

The early exchanges were fast and furious. Collingwood grabbed the first goal when Ted Rowell swooped on a loose ball after Essendon's 'Dookie' McKenzie had kicked into the man on the mark while trying to clear from defence. Soon after it looked as if the Same Old, as Essendon were known at the time, must surely score, when Billy Griffith's shot rolled towards goal while Magpie full-back Bill Proudfoot lay on the ground nearby. But the still prostrate Proudfoot

stretched out a hand and stopped the ball inches from the line, prompting huge cheers from the black-and-white hordes.

There was only a point in it at quarter-time, in Essendon's favour. The great Albert Thurgood, probably the best player in football at the time, was causing havoc for Collingwood's defenders, especially his direct opponent McCormack, and only some unusually wayward kicking stopped him having a greater impact on the scoreboard. At quarter-time, the injured Jack Monohan suggested that the Pies swing Fred Leach onto Thurgood. It was a left-field suggestion but it worked to perfection: Leach, supported by McCormack, gradually got on top of Thurgood and all but shut him out of the game in the second half, drying up Essendon's scoring power. That move proved to be the strategic masterstroke of the game.

Collingwood led by a single point at half-time, thanks mainly to Essendon's wasteful 2.7. That would seem like a good time for a stirring address from the skipper to rally the troops for a big second half, but instead there were incongruous scenes in the Magpie dressing room with ball manufacturer T. W. Sherrin choosing the moment to make a special presentation to the recently married Jack Monohan (he was given a brooch for his new wife). Only after a heartfelt thank-you speech from the injured defender did his teammates return to the field.

Both sides had trouble scoring in a fiercely contested third quarter that almost produced an unexpected casualty. A man selling peanuts, who had been casually crossing the ground at one end, had to scamper madly for the safety of the boundary line when the ball returned to his area far quicker than

Opposite: **Lardie Tulloch and Essendon's Hugh Gavin toss the coin.**
Above: **Charlie Pannam soars for a great high mark during the 1902 Grand Final.**
Below: **How** The Australasian **illustrated Bill Proudfoot's goal-saving heroics.**

Proudfoot (Collingwood) Saves the Goal.

Spectators even clambered into trees to get a perfect view of the goalmouth action.

he'd expected. As the quarter passed it quickly became clear that Collingwood had taken control, in general play if not yet on the scoreboard. Pears hit the post and missed another sitter before Rowell, lifting his game several notches, goaled, followed soon after by another to George Angus. Even so, the tightness of the contest meant that, when the Same Old pulled a goal back late in the quarter, they were just 10 points adrift at the final change.

The huge crowd was cheering and roaring madly as the final term began, and Essendon, with the aid of a slight wind, attacked incessantly for the first seven minutes but could find no successful route to goal. 'The crowd was in an ecstasy of delight and raged like the ocean in a time of storm,' wrote one journalist. Then a horrible turnover from the Same Old wingman, Edwin

Kennedy, resulted in a chain of Collingwood passes and a goal to Ted Lockwood. When Rowell was given a free kick shortly afterwards from a long way out, he sensed a chance to put the game beyond doubt. So he prepared and took a mighty place kick that seemed to hang in the air forever, into the wind. It had just enough to get over the goal line, prompting one fan in the press box to exclaim, 'It's there! It's there! By heavens it's there! That settles it. They can't catch us now.'

The observer was right: the Pies were home and hosed, adding a further two late goals for good measure, ending with a 33-point victory that looked far more comfortable on paper than it had been through most of the match. There were chaotic scenes of triumph in the dressing rooms afterwards, and Essendon captain Hugh Gavin made his way through the celebrations to pay tribute to the Magpies, saying simply that they deserved their victory and that the better team had won.

That they did so owed much to the magnificent defensive work of Fred Leach, Bob Rush, Bill Proudfoot and Cornelius McCormack, but also the brilliance of Charlie Pannam and John Allan on the wings. Skipper Lardie Tulloch and the ever-reliable Frank Hailwood worked manfully in the ruck, while Ted Rowell and Ted Lockwood were superb up forward, kicking three goals each.

PLAYER OF THE YEAR

Frank Hailwood

In a team full of highly skilled stars like Rowell, Condon, Pannam and Leach, it's instructive that one of the team's most valuable contributors in the premiership year of 1902 was an honest battler in the ruck.

Frank 'Charger' Hailwood was a tireless, gutsy worker who did a huge amount of grunt work for the Magpies over a long career. He was a star in the team's 1896 flag, and developed his game further in the years after that success. He worked hard to improve his ungainly kicking, and fortunately never lost his strong marking ability. Combine those skills with an unfailing willingness to subject his body to the regular bumps and clashes of ruck contests, and you have a player who was regarded as one of the best ruckmen in the game.

That reputation was enhanced throughout the year, and especially after a stellar performance in the grand final. More than one observer declared to be the best of any player on the ground. If a Norm Smith Medal was awarded in 1902, he might very well have won it.

By beating Essendon, Collingwood became the fourth team to win a flag in the six-year-old VFL. But they were the first to win in a style that changed the way the game was played. Just as it would be in 2010 after the success of the Collingwood 'press', the question was: how would their opponents respond? Fitzroy had already shown that an opposition side could counter the famed Collingwood system for one match, but could they, or anyone else, do so throughout a season? Back at Victoria Park, celebrations were quieter than they had been six years earlier. The system that brought science and strategy to football had already delivered one flag to the Pies but one flag was no longer enough. The club was hungry for more – and it set its sights on going back to back.

FRED LEACH
GRAND FINAL HERO

It's no surprise that Fred Leach had a major impact on Collingwood's victory in the 1902 Grand Final. What is surprising, however, is that he had that impact as a defender.

Leach was a brilliantly talented midfielder who was widely regarded as one of the best centremen in the competition. But he was also unconventional, wandering far and wide from the centre position – an approach that was considered risky at the time.

Leach was a roamer, and defensive skills were not his strong suit. Yet it was when he was moved to centre half-back on Albert Thurgood in the grand final that he changed the course of the game.

Leach played him shoulder-to-shoulder, going for the ball fairly and pitting his skills and athleticism against those of the Essendon champ. Leach won the duel convincingly. Thurgood had destroyed Collingwood in the 1901 Grand Final with three goals, but there was no repeat in 1902 – thanks to the defensive efforts of one of the Magpies' most attacking players.

PLAYERS

Player	Games	Goals
John Allan	17	8
George Angus	12	2
Alf Boyack	5	0
Bob Bryce	1	0
Dick Condon	16	17
Charlie Dow	4	0
Alf Dummett	18	0
Jack Farrell	6	2
Matthew Fell	16	3
Frank Hailwood	19	7
Jack Incoll	10	9
Arthur Leach	17	9
Fred Leach	10	0
Ted Leach	8	1
George Lockwood	15	2
Teddy Lockwood	17	29
Peter Martin	1	0
Con McCormack	18	0
Bill McCulloch	1	1
Jack Monohan	17	2
Leo Morgan	3	1
Harry Newbound	1	0
Charlie Pannam Snr	18	4
Henry Pears	16	22
Bill Proudfoot	17	0
Ted Rowell	15	33
Bob Rush	16	0
Archie Smith	4	5
Alby Tame	5	0
Lardie Tulloch	19	10

Club Awards
Training awards* to John Allan, Dick Condon, Alf Dummett, Frank Hailwood, Arthur Leach, Jack Monohan, Cornelius McCormack, Charlie Pannam, Lardie Tulloch.
*These awards included a suit of clothes by Treadway & Co, one guinea awards, half-guinea awards, a clock and a silver-mounted pipe.

Leading goalkicker – Ted Rowell (33)

1902 SEASON

ROUND 1 May 3 Lake Oval
Sth Melbourne **3.7.25** v **Collingwood 5.13.43**
Goals: Pears 2, Morgan, Rowell, Tulloch

ROUND 2 May 10 MCG
Melbourne **4.10.34** v **Collingwood 8.3.51**
Goals: Rowell 3, Condon 2, T Lockwood 2, Hailwood.

ROUND 3 May 17 Victoria Park
Collingwood 11.15.81 v Geelong **3.2.20**
Goals: Rowell 3, Tulloch 3, Hailwood, Incoll, A Leach, T Lockwood, Pannam.

ROUND 4 May 24 Victoria Park
Collingwood **3.4.22** v **Fitzroy 7.13.55**
Goals: G Lockwood, McCulloch, Pears.

ROUND 5 May 31 Junction Oval
St Kilda **5.5.35** v **Collingwood 5.12.42**
Goals: Incoll, T Lockwood, Monohan, Pears, Tulloch.

ROUND 6 June 7 Victoria Park
Collingwood **6.15.51** v **Essendon 11.10.76**
Goals: Condon 2, T Lockwood 2, Pears, Smith.

ROUND 7 June 9 Victoria Park
Collingwood 8.11.59 v Carlton **3.3.21**
Goals: T Lockwood 3, Smith 2, A Leach, Pears, Tulloch.

ROUND 8 June 14 Victoria Park
Collingwood 4.26.50 v South Melbourne **1.8.14**
Goals: Condon, Fell, T Lockwood, Smith.

ROUND 9 June 21 Victoria Park
Collingwood 7.19.61 v Melbourne **4.7.31**
Goals: Rowell 2, Allan, Condon, A Leach, T Lockwood, Smith.

ROUND 10 July 5 Corio Oval
Geelong **6.8.44** v **Collingwood 12.12.84**
Goals: T Lockwood 2, Condon 2, Rowell 2, Allan, Fell, Hailwood, Incoll, Pears, Tulloch.

ROUND 11 July 12 Brunswick St Oval
Fitzroy **6.9.45** v **Collingwood 9.14.68**
Goals: Condon 3, Rowell 2, Hailwood, Incoll, A Leach, Tulloch.

ROUND 12 July 19 Victoria Park
Collingwood 19.13.127 v St Kilda **1.4.10**
Goals: Allan 4, Pears 3, Rowell 3, Condon 3, A Leach 2, T Lockwood 2, Incoll, G Lockwood.

ROUND 13 July 26 East Melbourne Cricket Ground
Essendon **5.6.36** v **Collingwood 7.5.47**
Goals: Incoll 2, T Lockwood 2, Condon, Rowell, Tulloch.

ROUND 14 August 2 Princes Park
Carlton **2.3.15** v **Collingwood 7.10.52**
Goals: Farrell 2, Pears 2, A Leach, T Leach, Pannam,

ROUND 15 August 16 Victoria Park
Collingwood 12.12.84 v South Melbourne **5.14.44**
Goals: T Lockwood 4, Pears 2, Rowell 2, Allan, Condon, Fell, Hailwood

ROUND 16 August 23 Brunswick St Oval
Fitzroy **5.4.34** v **Collingwood 13.9.87**
Goals: Rowell 6, A Leach 2, T Lockwood 2, Angus, Pannam, Tulloch

ROUND 17 August 30 Victoria Park
Collingwood 16.16.112 v Geelong **2.11.23**
Goals: Pears 7, Rowell 3, Hailwood 2, Incoll 2, Condon, Pannam

1902 FINALS

LADDER

Team	W	L	D	For	Agst	%	Pts
Collingwood	15	2	0	1121	562	199.5	60
Essendon	13	4	0	885	625	141.6	52
Fitzroy	10	7	0	914	726	125.9	40
Melbourne	9	8	0	800	735	108.8	36
Sth Melb	7	10	0	700	704	99.4	28
Carlton	7	10	0	594	770	77.1	28
Geelong	7	10	0	702	914	76.8	28
St Kilda	0	17	0	490	1170	41.9	0

SEMI FINAL   September 6   MCG

Collingwood 6.12.48 v **Fitzroy 9.10.64**

Goals: T Lockwood 3, Rowell 2, Monohan

GRAND FINAL   September 20   MCG

Collingwood	1.2	3.2	5.5	9.6	(60)
Essendon	1.3	2.7	3.7	3.9	(27)

Goals: Rowell 3, E Lockwood 3, Pears, Allan Angus
Best: Pannam, Hailwood, F Leach, Allan, Rowell, McCormack, Tulloch
Umpire: Crapp
Crowd: 35,202 at the MCG

Grand Final Team
B: G. Lockwood, W. Proudfoot, M. Fell
HB: R. Rush, C. McCormack, A. Dummett
C: C. Pannam, F. Leach, J. Allan
HF: J. Incoll, E. Rowell, G. Angus,
F: H. Pears, E. Lockwood, A. Leach
Foll: F. Hailwood, L. Tulloch, R. Condon

CHAPTER THREE

1903

Back to back

'There is not much love between Fitzroy and Collingwood . . . Metaphorically, each city is thirsting for the gore of the other.'

A young Jock McHale in his playing heyday.

It is the eve of the 1903 season, and some of the best footballers outside the VFL and VFA have gathered at Victoria Park for the annual match between a combined team and the reigning Premiers. The smallish crowd includes the eagle-eyed Collingwood selectors, always on the lookout for new additions to the team. Just a few weeks earlier, a club committeeman had seen a wiry young man kicking a ball around a local timber yard and invited him down to try his luck. That same young man is in the combined team today – he has been playing with a Coburg side. He'd played in the corresponding game the previous year against Essendon, but had been rejected by the Same Old. He'd had an earlier trial at Collingwood, and been rejected there too.

Today, that young man, James McHale, is named at half-forward. But the captain of the combined team, former Magpie Billy O'Brien, swings McHale into the centre early in the game, where he finds himself pitted against the mighty Fred Leach. O'Brien knows that the Collingwood selectors want to see McHale in action, and figures there could be no tougher test than a direct one-on-one contest with one of the game's best midfielders. McHale rises to the challenge and plays superbly. As he leaves the field, club secretary Ern Copeland approaches the 20-year-old, shakes his hand and tells him he's just earned a spot on the club's senior list. A few weeks later, McHale is named in the Collingwood team for the opening game of the season against Carlton. The career of James 'Jock' McHale, the club's most famous and iconic figure, has begun.

But for now, all that mattered was that the Magpies had found another promising young player, at a time when they needed to boost their playing stocks. Outstanding ruckman Frank Hailwood had gone to Boulder City in Western Australia, while Archie Smith and Albert Tame had retired. John Allan, so important on the wing in the 1902 flag, would manage only two more games, while the mercurial Fred Leach would coax just a handful of matches from his broken-down body before retiring permanently mid-season.

The loss of Hailwood, in particular, was a body blow, and was said to be one of the main reasons the team lost its Round 1 game to the rapidly improving Carlton. The line-up had been further weakened by the absence of Fred Leach, Con McCormack and George Angus with colds, but it was still a disappointing way to start the premiership defence. McHale performed 'commendably' on debut and kept his place, but too many of his teammates were well below their best. The team's famed short passing game stuttered, kicking into gear only occasionally, and the players seemed to lack energy. Although the term hadn't been invented yet, it seemed for all the world as if the Pies started the season with a premiership hangover. It was a glum Lardie Tulloch who made his way to the Carlton dressing rooms post-match, telling them they had the best ruck division he'd ever

It speaks volumes for Jack Monohan's longevity that his eleventh year of senior football might very well have been his best.

Monohan had been a star for Collingwood in its first flag season of 1896, and especially on grand final day. Seven years later, and now 30, the linchpin of the Magpie defence turned in an even better season to help Collingwood to its third flag.

Monohan's defensive play was better than ever in 1903, especially his marking, which The Argus at one stage during the year described as 'a gift that neither age can wither nor custom stale'. A regular selection in Victorian sides since 1900, he was rewarded for his outstanding form in 1903 with captaincy of the state side – a huge honour for one who wasn't even captain of his club side.

Jack Monohan continued to show fine form in the following two seasons, and eventually clocked up 15 years of service – only the second Magpie to achieve the distinction – and 230 games in a magnificent career.

PLAYER OF THE YEAR
Ted Lockwood

WR Hamilton — Wood v Roy

When twins Ted and George Lockwood crossed to Collingwood from Geelong on the eve of the 1902 season, Magpie fans thought they'd be getting a couple of useful players.

That was certainly the case with George, who turned into a solid defender. But they got much more with Teddy, a clever forward with an uncanny knack of kicking goals when they were most needed. He did so 29 times in his debut season with the Pies, only four goals behind the joint VFL leading goalkickers.

He continued that form into 1903 and took his game to another level, slotting home 35 goals and grabbing the mantle of VFL leading goalkicker for himself. That included one of the team's four goals in both the semi-final and grand final. Added to the six he'd kicked in the two finals in 1902, it confirmed his reputation as a big game player.

Teddy Lockwood never quite scaled the same heights again as a player, but he'd played a key role in successive Magpie premierships. Not bad for a pick-up from another club!

seen. The Blues responded with three cheers for Collingwood 'and an extra special one for their leader'.

The mere thought of Carlton and Collingwood being friendly with each other is enough to make a current-day Magpie fan feel sick. But back in 1903 Collingwood regarded Fitzroy, not the Blues, as its fiercest foe. Indeed, the Magpies' intense rivalry with the Roys would prove to be the underlying story of the season. After all, the Maroons had been the only team to unpick the Collingwood system in 1902. And right down to the final seconds of the 1903 season they would remain the team most likely to deny Collingwood back-to-back flags.

The enmity between the two clubs had its roots in the days before the Collingwood team was formed. The suburb of Fitzroy was not much better off than Collingwood, but it thought itself superior, at least in part because it had its own football team. Fitzroy residents were keener than most to pour scorn on their neighbours, and the two suburbs were intensely competitive, arguing over everything from regional boundaries to the dumping of waste.

When Collingwood also formed its own football team, it offered the local community an opportunity to strike back against all those who derided them, and especially Fitzroy. No longer were suburban battles confined to town halls, or to the gangs that roamed the streets. Football now became a legitimised forum for the expression of a mutual loathing. A local newspaper, *The Observer*, summed it up

1903: Back to back

neatly in 1892: 'There is not much love between Fitzroy and Collingwood . . . Metaphorically, each city is thirsting for the gore of the other.' Matches between the two teams quickly became a highlight of each season. They attracted huge crowds and were usually rugged affairs both on and off the field, with players regularly having to be protected from angry spectators. As *The Argus* noted in 1897: 'If you don't get good football, you're bound to have bloodshed.'

The Collingwood–Fitzroy rivalry was further compounded by the fact that they were the dominant teams of the decade from 1895, winning the last two VFA premierships and six of the first nine within the VFL. So when the VFL decided it wanted to boost the development of the game by playing a match in Sydney in 1903, it made perfect sense to choose Collingwood and Fitzroy as the protagonists. This would be no exhibition match, either: the game would be played for premiership points.

Collingwood was quick to support the VFL initiative, but its members were not happy. They revolted at the annual meeting in March, angry that they were being denied the chance to see 'the most popular game of the season', and actually succeeding in passing a motion disapproving of the committee's decision. But the club ignored its members' disapproval, claiming they did not appreciate that the broader interests of the game were at stake.

The Round 4 game between Collingwood and Fitzroy was played at the Sydney Cricket Ground. The match is historic for many reasons, not the least because it was the first known game where players wore numbers on their jumpers, to help the enthusiastic crowd identify them. The game was a promotional success, with more than 20,000 turning out, but the Pies lost by

Above: **The program from the historic match in Sydney.**
Below: **Action from the game, with players wearing numbers on their jumpers for the first time.**

17 points, angering still further their members back in Melbourne. That made it two wins in a row for Fitzroy over Collingwood: clearly they remained the Woods' biggest challengers for flag honours. The Magpie players had plenty to think about when they stopped off at Rutherglen for a bit of R&R on their way back from Sydney – and they were already plotting their revenge for the return bout with the Roys in Round 11.

Rosie Dummett flies for a big mark in the match of the season against Carlton, which was attended by a huge crowd (below).

Before then, however, they had to face Carlton again in a game at Victoria Park that was promoted as the 'greatest battle of the season'. The Blues had already beaten Collingwood, Essendon and Fitzroy, so anticipation was high for a match that would decide second place on the ladder. And it turned out to be a game that – for once – lived up to the hype, so much so that one journalist described it as 'a spectacle such as has rarely been equalled in the history of Australian football'.

Collingwood jumped the visitors from the first bounce and piled on three goals before the Blues had caught their breath. Carlton managed to sneak one back but the Pies added a fourth just before the break and Victoria Park was rocking, with the Woods enjoying a comfortable 18-point lead. But the game turned 180 degrees in the second term, and only a late goal to Rowell kept the home side in front at half-time, by a mere two points.

If the first half had been good, the second was even better. Both teams traded goals, with Carlton hitting the

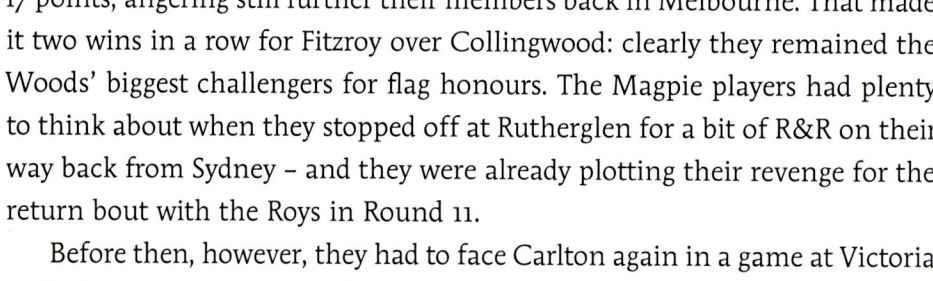

Ted Lockwood shows how a place kick works, bringing up full points against Carlton.

front through Webber, before the Pies reclaimed the lead with a brilliant snap from Ted Lockwood. As the crowd roared, the home team 'charged forward like a locomotive express on the down grade' and added another through George Green. But Carlton hit back with two more superb goals, separated by one from Condon that kept Collingwood in front by seven points at the last change. Henry Pears snapped a brilliant goal early in the last term and some home fans thought the game was just about theirs. But the Blues grabbed two majors in quick succession – ten minutes gone and there was only a point in it! Ted Lockwood gave the Pies a little breathing space with a fine goal from a place kick, and two more followed as Carlton, finally, tired. The margin in the end was 14 points, but it had been a titanic struggle. Carlton was a legitimate premiership contender.

Three weeks later, the Pies had to do it all again when Fitzroy came to Victoria Park in an atmosphere even more heated than usual. The home fans had been hungering to witness a contest against their arch rivals all season, and the loss in Sydney seven weeks earlier still burned. The spectators, according to *The Herald*, 'poured into the Victoria Park in huge swarms from all points of the compass . . . in cabs, in trams, trains, vans, carts of all sorts and on foot'.

Those spectators saw a Collingwood side run onto the field without the brilliant Fred Leach, who had retired during the week for the third and final time. But the biggest selection surprise was the appearance at full-back of a mysterious character called 'Wilson' who looked remarkably like veteran Bill Proudfoot. Proudfoot had been forced to retire after the game in Sydney when the Police Commissioner decreed that policemen were no longer allowed to play football, but the burly defender and the club obviously decided this game was big enough to justify a little low-level deception. Unfortunately, some careless journalists spoiled the ruse by using the name 'Proudfoot' in their match reports.

Early on, 'Wilson' and his fellow defenders were forced to work overtime,

The Australasian

How the press saw the game against Carlton:

No flaw was found in the game from first to last. The ball was handled and kicked in artistic style, high marking, running with the ball, accurate goal-getting, and all the details that go to make up perfect football were present in abundance. The spectacle was magnificent, and the closeness of the scoring until late in the day gave additional zest to a combat in which every possible feature of attractive football was portrayed at its best.

PLAYER OF THE YEAR
Lardie Tulloch

Lawrence Gideon 'Lardie' Tulloch was one of the key influences behind Collingwood's back-to-back flags – but you'd hardly have known it.

In a team full of big names, Tulloch was the quiet, inspirational leader who, as captain, had the full respect of all who played with and against him.

As a player he was a good, honest contributor, mainly playing as a follower but also proving handy up forward or in defence. But it was as a leader that Tulloch really shone. He was the perfect example of a good player who made a great captain. He played brilliantly throughout both 1902 and 1903, and led the team superbly. Markwell in *The Australasian* paid him this tribute:

'Tulloch, in his capacity as skipper and in the excellence of his football, has exercised a paramount influence upon the performances of the club. The undemonstrative Tulloch commands the obedience and respect of his team and the good opinion of players in other teams, for he is a thorough sportsman.'

Tulloch retired in 1904 and became an umpire, taking charge of the 1907 VFL Grand Final. That made him the only VFL/AFL player to have captained his team to a premiership and umpired a grand final.

as Fitzroy came hard at the home team and Collingwood got the jitters in front of goal. The Roys led by three points at quarter-time, and extended their lead with an early goal in the second. Magpie fans were starting to worry, but skipper Lardie Tulloch goaled, then set up another soon after to regain the lead. Rowell grabbed one with a long bomb set shot, and the Pies led by 10 at the long break. Two more goals to Rowell in the third quarter, another long bomb and a clever snap, gave the Woods 23 points of breathing space at the last change, and a dour last quarter saw the home team emerge with a 20-point win.

The most revealing thing about the victory was the way it was achieved. Collingwood stuck mostly to the system that had served it so well, but also showed a far greater willingness to adapt their game plan when needed. So when Fitzroy played tight and tough, Collingwood players were prepared to fight fire with fire and turn the contest into a scrap, rather than always trying for precision execution to teammates in the open. This Magpie win owed much more to grit than the artistry that had characterised their recent play.

The win saw Collingwood draw level with Fitzroy at the top of the ladder, and when St Kilda produced the upset of the season to defeat the Roys the following week, the Pies had top spot to themselves. They remained there until the end of the home-and-away season, despite a narrow squeak against Carlton in the penultimate game when the Blues' Mick Grace missed an easy late shot that would have given Carlton victory and Fitzroy top spot.

Instead it was Fitzroy who took on and comfortably beat Geelong in the first semi-final, while Collingwood once again faced up to Carlton. The Magpies were warm favourites but never played like it. The football failed to reach great heights in unpleasant windy conditions, and Collingwood could hardly get their system going at all. They managed only a solitary behind into the wind in the first quarter and were held scoreless in the third. But the Blues fared little better, and the game quickly became a fierce struggle that was, as one observer noted, 'as determined as if an empire was at stake'. The scoreboard reflected the tightness of the struggle, with Carlton leading 3.3 to 2.2 at three-quarter time. The Pies added two goals in the final term and that was enough – just – to get them over the line. The Blues had been the better side for most of the day, and fashioned three late chances to kick the goal that would have won the game, but couldn't capitalise. It was a mightily relieved group of Magpies who left the ground with a four-point win.

A Collingwood–Fitzroy match-up was the grand final most observers wanted: they had been the two best teams all year, had split their games during the season and the intense rivalry between clubs and fans ensured a fantastic atmosphere at the MCG. Another huge crowd of just over 32,000 piled in on a humid September day. *The Herald* reported that 'a glimpse into

Opposite: **Senior Constable Bill Proudfoot, aka 'Wilson'.**
Below: **Collingwood players enter the MCG for the grand final.**

Right: **Rival skippers Lardie Tulloch and Gerald Brosnan toss the coin for choice of ends.**
Below: **Fearless youngsters got the best vantage points possible.**
Bottom: **Action from the game.**

the teams' dressing rooms revealed men bubbling over with life and health and trained to the hour'. Everyone, it seemed, was ready to go. What followed was one of the most exciting grand finals of all time.

The mysterious 'Wilson' was again in the Magpie line-up, as he had been in the semi against Carlton, where his defensive efforts had helped save the game. The youngster Jim McHale was the only change from the semi-final team: he'd played 14 games in an outstanding debut season but was left out for the decider.

The early play was frenetic but error-strewn, as players from both sides seemed over-anxious and a little too keen to exert physical pressure, forcing the umpire to caution a handful of players. *The Argus* noted that the game was being played in a 'nasty spirit' and that players were frequently striking each other. Goals to Dick Condon and Ted Lockwood allowed the Pies to cling to a one-point lead at quarter-time, and the already exhausted players were seen sucking on oranges at the break to help them reclaim their energy.

Star goalsneak Teddy Lockwood holds on to a mark over his Fitzroy opponent in the grand final.

The second quarter was every bit as hard-fought as the first. The Magpie defence, led by the trusty combination of Proudfoot and Monohan, performed heroically in this term, keeping the Roys to a meagre three behinds. But the Pies could manage only a single goal themselves, through a clever snap from Jim Addison, playing just his third game. The Magpie system coughed and spluttered but never fully kicked into gear, and Fitzroy's physical counter-attack was turning the game into a ferocious battle. Collingwood led by just five points at half-time, and by four at the final change after a gruelling third quarter where neither team kicked a goal. Fitzroy in particular squandered a succession of chances.

The players by now looked all but spent, the combination of warm conditions and fiercely contested football having drained them of all strength. This game had never been pretty, and most of the second half was a real scrap. But Collingwood somehow found a way through the packs and scrimmages for Addison to grab his second goal and set up an 11-point lead which, in the

J. ADDISON

Below: **Ruckman Arthur Leach soars for a lovely left-handed tap, while captain Lardie Tulloch waits for the ball.**
Bottom: **The team takes a breather at three-quarter time, preparing for the dramatic final quarter.**

context of the game, must have seemed like a safe margin. But Fitzroy came again and attacked relentlessly in the dying minutes. Les Millis goaled on the run to bring the game well and truly to life. The difference was back to five points. One straight kick would do it: the Roys had two golden opportunities but could only bring up minor scores. Then the great Percy Trotter passed to Fitzroy skipper Gerald Brosnan, who marked just 30 yards from goal, directly in front, with three points the difference and only seconds remaining.

Brosnan – one of the sweetest and most accurate left-foot kicks in the competition – stood over the ball knowing that, in all probability, the premiership would hang on this kick. His kick. It was the kind of goal he would have kicked nine times out of ten, but luckily for Collingwood this was the tenth. The ball headed straight for the goals, but died as it neared the line and veered narrowly wide. Bill Proudfoot was standing beneath the posts and said later he had seen the lace of the football brush against the post. It was that close.

Lardie Tulloch's premiership cap presented to him after the back-to-back flags. George Angus turned his premiership medal into a personal locket.

In the tumult that followed Brosnan's miss, the bell rang. The 1903 premiership had been decided on the very last kick of the season, and it belonged to Collingwood. Players slumped to the turf exhausted, though some of the Magpies found enough energy to dance a celebratory jig. Brosnan was shattered. His teammate, Jim Sharp (who would later play for, and become president of, Collingwood) collapsed from exhaustion and did not regain consciousness for half an hour.

It had been a long road for the Magpie players. Since losing to Fitzroy in Sydney they had gone on a 15-match winning run. But three of the last four of those wins had been by a combined margin of just eight points. The overwhelming feeling at the end of the season seemed to be one of relief. Imagine what little enthusiasm the players must have felt when they learned they would have to play a post-season charity match to aid the Bendigo Hospital. The match, almost inevitably, was against Fitzroy.

Beyond dispute, Collingwood's application of strategy over the previous two seasons had changed football. 'As the game is now played, individual excellence unbacked by perfect system has no chance of achieving success,' *The Age* reported during the year, crediting Collingwood with that change. Markwell, in *The Australasian*, said the Pies victory would be welcomed by football lovers because the team had played 'the most artistic and systematic football' of the past two seasons.

The Australasian

Markwell, on Collingwood's third premiership:

Collingwood's narrow win... left them undisputed premiers for the year, and they have to be congratulated none the less warmly for their having scraped through with so little to spare. All things considered, theirs has been a particularly meritorious season. Their third premiership, in a somewhat brief course, and their second in successive seasons, deserves more than mere formal celebrations.'

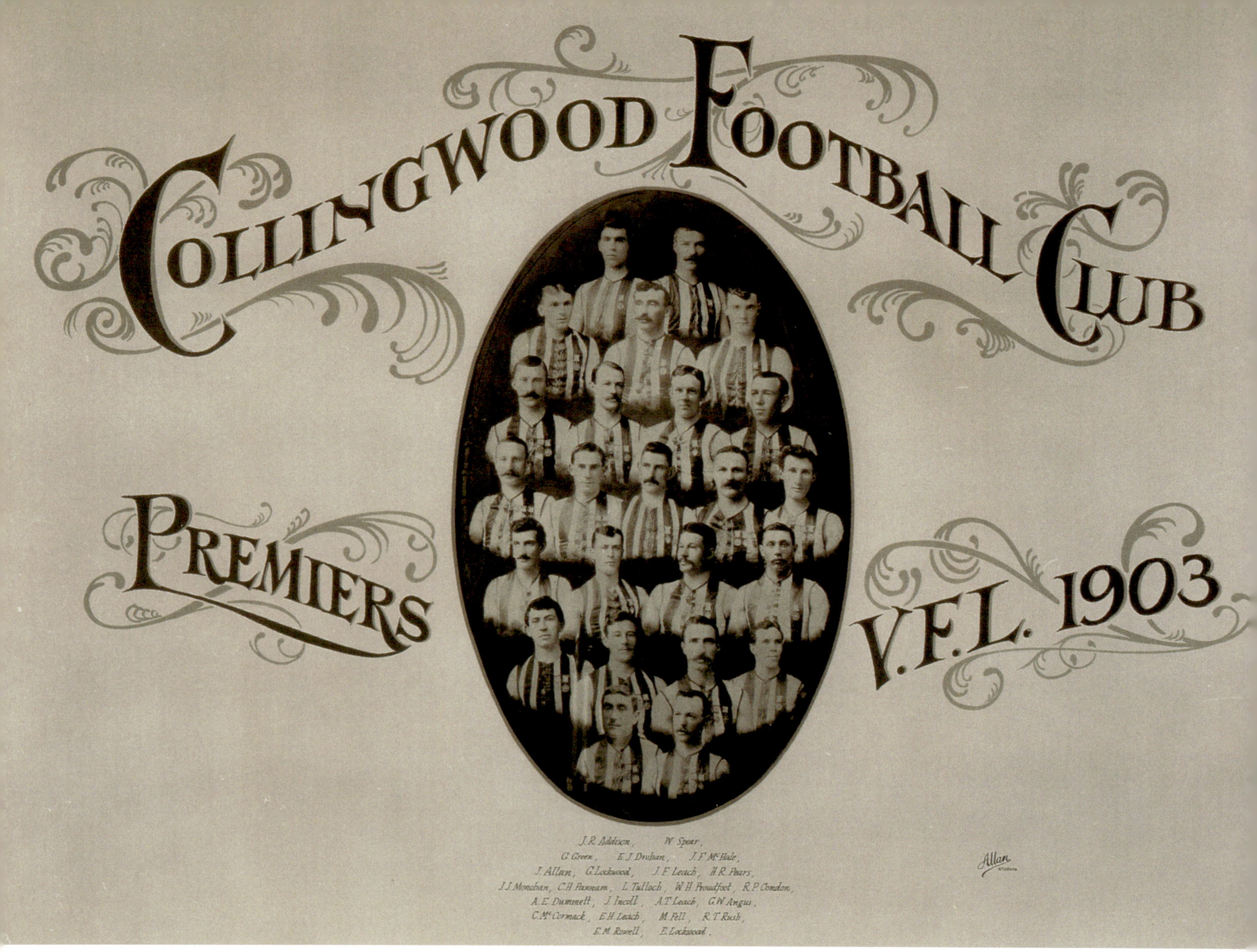
Collingwood Football Club
Premiers
V.F.L. 1903
J.R. Addison, W. Spear,
G. Green, E.J. Drohan, J.F. McHale,
J. Allan, G. Lockwood, J.F. Leach, H.R. Pears,
J.J. Monohan, C.H. Pannam, L. Tulloch, W.H. Proudfoot, R.P. Condon,
A.E. Dummett, J. Incoll, A.T. Leach, G.W. Angus,
C. McCormack, E.H. Leach, M. Pell, R.T. Rush,
E.M. Rowell, E. Lockwood.
Allan

Well Done,
COLLINGWOOD
PREMIERS
1896 & 1902
1903

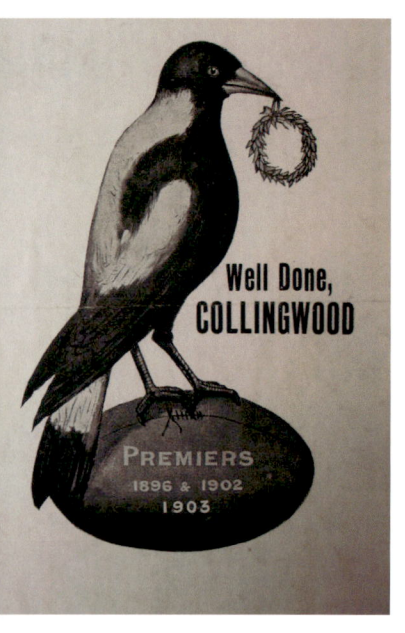

But the rest of the competition was catching up, and the late season results proved it. This was a team nearing the end of its premiership window. Proudfoot had been playing for twelve seasons, Monohan and Pannam eleven. Captain Lardie Tulloch retired a year later to take up umpiring. Two of the key exponents of 'the system' were also lost to the club: Fred Leach had already retired, and within a few years would be dead of typhoid fever, while Ted Rowell returned to Western Australia in 1904. Con McCormack, who had filled in so well for Leach, went with him. Condon stayed on but, as with his older teammates, his output gradually diminished.

As ever, new stars were emerging to take the place of the fading champions. But only three members from this year's list would be around for the club's next flag. This was a team in transition. For the first time in its history, Collingwood was going to have to rebuild.

CON McCORMACK
GRAND FINAL HERO

When Fred Leach finally retired for good midway through 1903, Collingwood had to find a new man to play in the centre. That the team hardly missed a beat without the brilliant Leach owes much to the quality of the man who replaced him, Con McCormack.

McCormack had joined the Pies in 1902 as a highly regarded youngster from Northcote. His first season was outstanding, and though he played mainly in defence it was clear he had the pace and ball skills to play a more central role.

The opportunity to do so came in 1903 when Leach opted out of football. McCormack stepped into the centre position and made it his own with a string of outstanding performances that saw him named among the best centremen of the season. He capped off a breakthrough season with a near best-on-ground display in the grand final.

Remarkably, that was Con McCormack's last game for Collingwood. He crossed to the money-rich Goldfields of WA in 1904 and never returned to the VFL, much to the regret of all at Victoria Park.

PLAYERS

Player	Games	Goals
Jim Addison	3	2
John Allan	2	1
George Angus	18	2
Bill Ayling	2	0
Jim Blair	1	0
Tom Carmody	1	0
Dick Condon	19	18
Eddie Drohan	17	3
Alf Dummett	15	0
Johnny Dunn	3	0
Matthew Fell	19	1
George Green	13	10
Jack Incoll	16	10
Arthur Leach	18	10
Fred Leach	6	0
Ted Leach	10	8
George Lockwood	11	0
Teddy Lockwood	19	35
Con McCormack	13	0
Jock McHale	14	0
Jim McKean	1	0
Jack Monohan	19	0
Charlie Pannam Snr	19	2
Henry Pears	18	12
Bill Proudfoot	6	0
Ted Rowell	17	30
Bob Rush	18	0
Billy Spears	6	2
Lardie Tulloch	17	8
Percy Wilmot	1	1

Club Awards
Gold Albert presented to Ted Rowell on his leaving for WA.
Training awards to John Allan, Dick Condon, Eddie Drohan, Alf Dummett, Matt Fell, Arthur Leach, Jack Monohan, Con McCormack, Jim McHale, Charlie Pannam, Bob Rush, Billy Spears
Leading goalkicker – Ted Lockwood (35)

1903 SEASON

ROUND 1 May 2 Princes Park
Carlton 9.4.58 v Collingwood **5.7.37**
Rowell 2, Condon, T Lockwood, Spears

ROUND 2 May 9 Victoria Park
Collingwood 13.14.92 v South Melbourne **3.6.24**
Condon 2, T Lockwood 2, Rowell 2, Tulloch 2, Green, T Leach, Pannam, Pears, Spears

ROUND 3 May 16 Victoria Park
Collingwood 16.17.113 v St Kilda **5.3.33**
Rowell 5, T Lockwood 4, A Leach 3, Green 2, Condon, Wilmot

ROUND 4 May 23 SCG
Collingwood **6.9.45** v **Fitzroy 7.20.62**
Rowell 2, Tulloch, T Lockwood, Incoll, Condon

ROUND 5 May 30 Victoria Park
Collingwood 10.17.77 v Melbourne **7.4.46**
Rowell 5, T Lockwood 3, T Leach, Tulloch

ROUND 6 June 6 Corio Oval
Geelong **8.3.51** v **Collingwood 12.12.84**
Green 3, Condon 2, Rowell 2, Allan, Drohan, Incoll, A Leach, Pears

ROUND 7 June 8 Victoria Park
Collingwood 4.9.33 v Essendon **2.13.25**
Incoll 2, T Lockwood, Rowell

ROUND 8 June 13 Victoria Park
Collingwood 12.9.81 v Carlton **10.7.67**
T Lockwood 5, Rowell 2, Condon, Green, Incoll, T Leach, Pears

ROUND 9 June 20 Lake Oval
South Melbourne **4.11.35** v **Collingwood 6.6.42**
Pears 3, Condon, Green, A Leach

ROUND 10 July 4 Junction Oval
St Kilda **2.4.16** v **Collingwood 5.11.41**
T Lockwood 2, Condon, Incoll, A Leach

ROUND 11 July 11 Victoria Park
Collingwood 8.8.56 v Fitzroy **5.6.36**
Rowell 3, Green 2, T Leach, T Lockwood, Tulloch

ROUND 12 July 18 MCG
Melbourne **4.8.32** v **Collingwood 11.8.74**
T Lockwood 4, Condon 3, Pears 2, T Leach, Tulloch

ROUND 13 July 25 Victoria Park
Collingwood 6.15.51 v Geelong **5.7.37**
Angus, Condon, Drohan, T Leach, T Lockwood, Pears

ROUND 14 August 8 East Melbourne Cricket Ground
Essendon **7.4.46** v **Collingwood 11.7.73**
T Lockwood 2, Pears 2, Rowell 2, Condon, A Leach, T Leach, Pannam, Tulloch

ROUND 15 August 15 Victoria Park
Collingwood 3.12.30 v St Kilda **2.6.18**
Incoll, T Lockwood, Rowell

ROUND 16 August 22 Princes Park
Carlton **5.11.41** v **Collingwood 6.7.43**
T Lockwood 3, Incoll, T Leach, Tulloch

ROUND 17 August 29 Victoria Park
Collingwood 13.13.91 v Melbourne **5.10.40**
A Leach 3, Rowell 3, Condon 2, T Lockwood 2, Drohan, Fell, Pears

1903 FINALS

LADDER

Team	W	L	D	For	Agst	%	Pts
Collingwood	15	2	0	1063	667	159.4	60
Fitzroy	14	3	0	985	574	171.6	56
Carlton	11	6	0	865	636	136.0	44
Geelong	9	8	0	981	813	120.7	36
St Kilda	7	9	1	635	831	76.4	30
Essendon	6	10	1	691	879	78.6	26
Melbourne	3	14	0	593	925	64.1	12
South Melb	2	15	0	595	1083	54.9	8

SEMI FINAL September 5 — Brunswick St Oval

Collingwood 4.3.27 v Carlton **3.5.23**

Incoll 2, Angus, T Lockwood

GRAND FINAL September 12 — MCG

Collingwood	2.3	3.4	3.6	4.7	(31)
Fitzroy	2.2	2.5	2.8	3.11	(29)

Goals: Addison 2, Condon, T. Lockwood
Best: McCormack, Pannam, Fell, Monohan, Proudfoot, Rowell
Umpire: Gibson
Crowd: 32,263

Grand Final Team
B: G. Lockwood, W. Proudfoot, A. Dummett
HB: M. Fell, J. Monohan, R. Rush
C: C. Pannam, C. McCormack, E. Drohan
HF: E. Lockwood, E. Rowell, L. Tulloch (c)
F: A.T. Leach, J. Addison, H. Pears
R: J. Incoll, G. Angus, R. Condon

CHAPTER FOUR

1910

Floreat Pica

'It was a sight that took one's breath away, so extraordinarily fast did incident crowd upon incident. Opposing players dashed on the ball utterly regardless of the risks they were taking.'

The Mightiest Magpies

Football has never seen a more controversial season than 1910. There were scandals and sensations from before the first bounce until weeks after the grand final. Bribery, corruption, violence, special League investigations, career-ending suspensions – the year had it all. By the time the premiership race had been run, and won, the stench surrounding football was so great that the game itself was fighting for survival.

The biggest problem in football in 1910 was the rise of illegal gambling on matches. This in turn led to players being bribed to play poorly, a disturbing trend that had football fans starting to lose faith in the integrity of the sport. Every poor performance from a player or a team was viewed suspiciously.

There were also increasing concerns about violence in football, both on and off the field. The 1910 season was the roughest and dirtiest yet seen, with a string of violent incidents, including several matches that were described as 'disgraceful' and one as 'murderous'. One vicious blow, in a particularly spiteful game, saw Carlton's George Topping rubbed out for two years. Things weren't much better in the stands: crowds at several matches turned into angry mobs and invaded the field, chased after players or threatened umpires. The Victorian Premier, Sir John Murray, even called in plain clothes police to be at matches after hearing disturbing reports of the level of foul language being used. Many observers feared for the future of the sport, and *The Australasian* spoke for many when it noted that 'the game is in great danger of being brought down by viciousness and blackguardism'. All this made for a generally unsavoury feeling that bubbled along and served as a backdrop to an increasingly controversial season.

Things weren't any calmer at Collingwood, because the team endured a horrible mid-season slump and once again found itself powerless to stop its new bogey

IS THE GAME WORTH THE SCANDAL?
GONE OUT WITH A STINK.

team – Carlton. In the years since Collingwood's last premiership, the Blues had become *the* power in football. They had broken all records by winning flags in three successive years, 1906–08, and had only lost the 1909 decider to South Melbourne by two points. Collingwood had lost 11 of their previous 12 meetings with Carlton, and just couldn't find a way past them. So it must have seemed like the worst possible start to the season when Collingwood learned it would meet the previous year's grand finalists in the first two rounds.

Still, the Magpies fancied their chances against Carlton in the opening round. The Blues had endured a tumultuous off-season, with high profile coach Jack Worrall being dumped during a players' rebellion at the end of 1909. Then, on the eve of the 1910 season, four star players crossed to North Melbourne in the VFA as the fall-out over Worrall's sacking continued. So it was a weakened and supposedly riven Carlton side that Collingwood faced at Princes Park – but it was still far too good for the Pies. The Blues led at every change and ran out comfortable winners by 28 points.

It was a disheartening start. But Magpie spirits lifted two weeks later (the second round was delayed for a week to mark the death of King George V) when the Pies proved far too strong for the reigning premiers at Victoria Park. The Southerners were widely expected to win, but they seemed to take Collingwood lightly from the start, and made their task more difficult with some atrocious kicking for goal. South had 17 scoring shots to 10 at three-quarter time, yet the home side led by three points. And the Magpies made South pay with an

Fans gather around the Victoria Park gates as they line up for the game against South Melbourne.

The Australasian

On Collingwood's magnificent final quarter against South Melbourne:

There was no gainsaying the superiority of Collingwood in every department of play... as with sharp rush after sharp rush, the Woodsmen overwhelmed South's defence and piled goal upon goal, the excitement amongst local supporters grew delirious. There had been left no room for doubt as to the excellence and vast superiority of their concluding exhibition. They had palpably outlasted their visitors, whom they had beaten in pace to the ball and artistic handling right through the quarter.

astonishing final term in which they kicked 7.5 to 1.3, eventually scooting away to an emphatic 41-point win. Dick Lee kicked three for the term, Tommy Baxter kicked two and set up several others, and rover Percy Wilson completed a best-on-ground effort with his fourth goal. The home fans were nervously hopeful at the last change, but became louder and louder as the Magpies bombarded the goals. The frustrated visitors began swinging punches in the final term as the game slipped away, but Collingwood players retained their focus and kept kicking goals. By the time the result was beyond doubt, one newspaper reported that the crowd had 'swelled to rapture'.

That win should have set the Magpies on their way, but instead, after a regulation win over St Kilda, they went down by two points at Essendon. It was a sign of things to come. Four successive wins followed, but none was convincing – all were against teams that would eventually finish outside the top four, and even the lowly University pushed them to within four points. The team was playing without confidence and, even worse, with few signs of the system and teamwork that had been so evident against South.

But if a handful of unconvincing wins against mediocre opposition was cause for concern, that was nothing compared with what came next. In Round 9, Geelong was too strong on its own ground, pulling away in the last quarter to win by 22 points. The next week, the players were embarrassed in front of their own fans at Victoria Park, when Carlton held them to a meagre tally of 2.10 and cruised to a 29-point victory. Then, opposed again to South

Right: Collingwood's thumping first round victory over South provided perfect fodder for cartoonists.
Opposite: The crowd at Vic Park against Carlton.

PLAYER OF THE YEAR
Jock McHale

Jock McHale spent so long as Collingwood coach – a record 714 games across 38 years – that it's easy to forget how good he was as a player.

Initially a half-back flanker, McHale had moved into the centre by 1910 and was, in the eyes of many pressmen, the best midfielder of the season. He was a tireless worker who would run hard from start to finish: he hated losing and would run himself into the ground in his efforts to lift his team.

McHale wasn't the most skilled centreman in the VFL, but if his play lacked a little in polish he made up for it with great cunning, and an innate ability to read the game well ahead of his rivals. He was reasonably fast, supremely fit and ultra-competitive.

McHale was a star in the 1910 finals, being named as the Pies' best player in the first two finals, and among the best in the grand final. He had missed out on playing in a flag in his first season, 1903, but made sure he got his premiership medal seven years later.

Melbourne, the Pies were humiliated by 62 points – a losing margin that would remain their biggest against South until 1987.

That loss sent the Pies tumbling to sixth spot on the ladder, and plunged their season into crisis. The team was absolutely woeful across each of those three games, making lots of unforced errors and generally playing like a unit that didn't deserve to be playing finals, let alone harbouring legitimate premiership aspirations. A supposedly easy game against bottom club St Kilda followed, but even that nearly turned into a nightmare when the Saints led early and were still within two points at the last change, before Collingwood steadied to win by 10 points.

The only thing in the club's favour was that three of those four games had been played away from home, sparing the misfiring players the full wrath of their fans at Victoria Park. When the team next played at home, against Essendon, some of those fans vented their spleens at club secretary Ern Copeland at half-time, abusing him aggressively as he walked through the pavilion. The disgruntled fans circulated a petition calling on Copeland and the committee to quit, claiming the club was stagnating and that the players were not being looked after. The club later described the incident as 'a disgraceful and totally unwarranted demonstration'. Copeland was badly shaken, and even contemplated quitting after the match, before being talked around by the players and committee members.

The incident infuriated the players, who had a deep respect for Copeland, and appreciated all that he had done for the club in

rescuing it from financial peril back in the 1890s. So they arranged a special dinner in his honour at Dennington's City Hotel in Johnston Street, where they publicly lauded both Copeland and the rest of the committee. The players said they regarded the committeemen as 'unchallenged monuments of honesty' and were proud to be associated with them. They said they were incensed and ashamed at what had happened, had full confidence in Copeland and the committee and blamed the incident on 'a few malcontents and non-entities . . . and their hirelings and satellites'.

The dinner was unprecedented in football to that time, and – remarkably – proved to be a turning point in the season. The players banded together, and that night promised to turn their season around and prove the knockers wrong. The club's annual report later described the premiership as an achievement that had 'most effectively avenged the insult to their secretary'.

The Copeland incident signalled the start of a late-season surge from the Pies. They won the last six games of the year, though again only one of those was against a finalist, and also found time for a tour of Victoria's Western District. They came from behind against Essendon, and had to fight unexpectedly hard against Melbourne and Fitzroy: only the Round 16 defeat of Richmond could be considered in any way authoritative. But other results

Action from Collingwood's 58-point semi-final drubbing of Essendon.

fell their way, and the Magpies finished in second place – two games and 38 per cent behind the Blues.

Collingwood's ladder position flattered its performances through much of the season, and many doubted whether the Pies were legitimate premiership contenders. But some of those doubts were blown away when the Magpies demolished Essendon in the first semi-final. The Pies jumped away to a great start, consolidated that start with fine defensive work in the quarter and then put the game beyond reach with a nine-goal second half. The final margin was a massive 58 points, with Dick Lee kicking six goals and Paddy Gilchrist four. This was an important victory in more ways than one: it was Collingwood's first in any final since the grand final of 1903.

Carlton and South Melbourne met in the second semi-final, but the football world was rocked when, just an hour before the game was due to start, the Blues withdrew three star players – Doug Gillespie, 'Bongo' Lang and Doug Fraser – from their side. No official reason was immediately given, but it soon became common knowledge that all three had been offered bribes to 'play dead' in the game. The crowd suspected South of being behind the bribes (though it turned out later they weren't) and supported the Blues, subjecting South players to a mixture of boos and silence. The Southerners resented the crowd reaction and the game quickly became nasty, but Carlton couldn't settle in front of goal and went down by 12 points after kicking 6.17.

The challenge system gave Carlton, as minor premiers, another chance, meaning Collingwood would now play South, with the winner to face the Blues in a grand final. The football world was consumed with talk of bribery, and the game itself at times seemed secondary. The crowd was again noticeably anti-South, but this time

PLAYER OF THE YEAR

Dick Lee

Dick Lee was not only the most dangerous forward in the game in 1910 – he was also just about the complete player.

Lee won the competition goalkicking in each of his first four full seasons, including 1910. But he did so with a style of play that was different from most full-forwards of the era, enjoying a 'roving commission' that allowed him to venture far from goal. At times he almost played like an on-baller, drifting into position near the goals when he anticipated a forward thrust. At others he stayed within 40 yards of goal, where his famous leap, strong hands and precision kicking brought him many goals.

In 1910 he not only kicked an equal-record 58 goals and played for Victoria, but some scribes also named him as the best player in the competition. His spectacular marking had also made him a crowd favourite – and that made him marketable. In 1910 he became one of the first individual footballers to lend his name to a product endorsement – in this case Empire Cocoa, which he found to be 'invigorating from an athletic point of view'.

But Dick Lee didn't need Empire Cocoa or anything else: he was simply the most brilliant footballer of his day.

Above: Collingwood and South Melbourne players are locked in a race for the ball in the preliminary final.
Below: The mighty Ted Rowell breaks clear from defence and looks up field for a teammate.

the South players directed their feelings of injustice towards the ball, rather than the man. Indeed it was the Magpies who seemed overanxious, and they made far more errors than their counterparts in the first three quarters. The Pies led by five points at the first, second and third changes, though South had probably enjoyed the better of the play. Every score to this point had been won through sheer hard work, but the Pies suddenly produced a dazzling burst of three goals in five minutes that tore the game apart. Paddy Gilchrist kicked two, Lee the other and Collingwood dashed to a 23-point lead. South had time to snatch back two late goals, but the bell rang with the Pies 11 points up.

Collingwood would now have to face Carlton, having managed only one win over them in their last 13 encounters – and that by a single point. There

1910: Floreat Pica

was yet more drama on the night before the big game, when the League announced its findings into the semi-final bribery allegations. Carlton's own enquiry had already exonerated Gillespie, but Lang and Fraser were each suspended for five years. It set the scene for one of the most infamous grand finals in VFL/AFL history.

There were portents of what was to come when Les 'Flapper' Hughes was flattened before the ball had even been bounced. Hughes' teammate Richard Daykin retaliated, but for the rest of the first half, players from both sides forgot about the rough stuff and instead put on a display of fast, tough and sometimes wonderful football. 'Every man on the field hurled himself with reckless valour into the fray,' wrote *The Australasian*. 'It was a sight that took one's breath away, so extraordinarily fast did incident crowd upon incident. Opposing players dashed on the ball utterly regardless of the risks they were taking.' The Pies were brilliant in the first quarter, their attacking approach to the game delivering four goals to one, with Carlton's only goal coming after an unlucky slip from Ted Rowell as he was coming out of defence.

The Pies led by 19 points at quarter-time, but spent the whole second quarter oddly intent on defence: even Dick Lee, who had kicked two goals in the first quarter, was sent into the back line. The Pies weren't helped by serious injuries to two of their better players, ruckman Dave Ryan and defender Joe Scaddan. Even so, it was a strange strategy for a team that had so dominated the first term, and one bemused VFL official described it as 'a winning side

Left: Nobody seems too sure where the ball is during the grand final.
Right: Joe Scaddan is carted from the field by trainers.

PLAYER OF THE YEAR

Dave Ryan

Dave Ryan crossed to Collingwood from Geelong in 1907, but it wasn't the kind of transfer that made huge headlines. Ryan had only played two games with the Pivotonians, and hadn't done enough in either of them to warrant much attention.

But something clicked for the big man when he came to Victoria Park, and he soon became an automatic selection in the team as a highly capable follower/forward.

His best season was undoubtedly 1910, when he played every game and kicked a very handy 18 goals – the second most by any Magpie. The *Australasian* summed up his play nicely when it described him as being 'head and shoulders above the field'. The paper wrote, 'His ruck work was sure, cool and quick; his marking was clean and his kicking a lesson in utility.'

Ryan's contribution on grand final day was curtailed by injury, after he severely damaged his elbow in the second quarter. He courageously stayed on the field, though he could do little more than stand in the forward line and hope the ball would fall into his good arm. But that didn't matter – Dave Ryan had already done enough throughout the year to earn his premiership medal.

playing a losing game'. The approach would have backfired badly had Carlton kicked straight: instead, the Blues managed only 1.4, and still trailed by 15 points at the main break.

The quality of play fell away badly after half-time, and the second half quickly became a scrappy affair dotted with 'sly knocks and frayed tempers'. The Magpies were never really threatened on the scoreboard, and as a result all the attention fell on a series of final quarter incidents that one newspaper described as 'the most disgraceful scene ever witnessed in a Melbourne football final'.

The problems started when Carlton's Jack Baquie and Collingwood's Tom Baxter tangled after a marking contest. Baquie elbowed Baxter, who in turn hit Baquie. They then fell to the ground, fighting, and players came from everywhere to join in. Collingwood's Jack 'Soldier' Shorten ran from the other end of the ground and belted Baquie with a mighty punch to the face, before himself being felled by a fierce blow to the ribs and stomach from Percy Sheehan. Baquie got to his feet, knocked Flapper Hughes senseless and then collapsed again. Several spectators jumped the fence, and police started making their way to the warring players. It was absolute mayhem, and only abated when umpire Jack Elder bounced the ball to restart play.

The rest of the game was marked with further displays of violence and bad temper, and most people couldn't wait for it to end. Elder later said the fighting was the worst he'd ever seen on a football field. The episode was universally condemned, with *The Age* just one of many newspapers saying it had left football 'considerably degraded'.

Kickero in *The Herald* said he was relieved the season was over, 'lest the reputation of the game should be further besmirched'. The two undercurrents that had dominated the season – bribery and violence – had come together in a perfect storm during the finals, and the season finished with the game in disgrace.

The unsavoury end to the season overshadowed Collingwood's premiership celebrations, and also its post-season trip to South Australia to play SANFL premiers Port Adelaide. So, too, did the subsequent League hearing into the grand final melee. Shorten and Sheehan were each suspended for a year-and-a-half, and Baxter and Baquie for a season. Baxter's suspension was lifted later, however, when teammate Richard Daykin wrote to the VFL claiming it was he who had been involved in the fight with Baquie. So Baxter got off, and Daykin himself escaped suspension because of his noble action in coming forward.

It was a suitably remarkable end to a remarkable year, one which had delivered a Collingwood flag that had not seemed remotely possible mid-season, when the team lost three in a row and the fans were in uproar. In addition to the flag, the club also provided a positive footnote to the season, when it accepted treasurer Bob Rush's suggestion for a new club motto. That motto, based on Eton College's, was *Floreat Pica* – loosely translated as 'May the Magpies Prosper'. It was a well-chosen motto, for, while football itself had not prospered in 1910, the Magpies certainly had.

> **The Australasian**
>
> **On the grand final's last quarter brawl:**
>
> It was a disgraceful occurrence. The episode was certainly the worst of its kind that has ever occurred in connection with senior football in or about Melbourne. Everyone who had the reputation of Australian football at heart was disgusted with the very unbecoming exhibition, and the opinion was freely expressed that the police should take proceedings against the offenders.

GEORGE ANGUS
GRAND FINAL HERO

The redoubtable George Angus went into the 1910 season at the ripe old age of 35, knowing he didn't have long left in the game. But at a time when he could have been forgiven for slowing down a little, he instead produced some of the best football of his career. He was not only captain of the team but coach as well, and courageously returned from a broken rib mid-season to guide the team to a flag.

Angus was brilliant amidst the mayhem of grand final day. The club's annual report said he had 'never appeared to better advantage than in the final game'. Sport newspaper said he 'absolutely excelled himself'. 'Never at a loss what to do with the ball and always cool, Angus played well to his forwards, his driving drop kicks sending the ball well up every time.'

So outstanding was his play that day that the Ladies of Collingwood presented him with a silver coffee service for his 'gallant efforts'. It was a great performance from a great Collingwood leader.

PLAYERS

Player	Games	Goals
George Angus	14	4
Tom Baxter	21	15
Wal Burleigh	1	0
Sam Campbell	1	0
Roy Crisp	1	0
Richard Daykin	16	5
Andy Duff	2	0
Alf Dummett	1	0
Artie Freeman	1	0
Percy Gibb	20	2
Paddy Gilchrist	9	11
Charlie Hackett	9	0
Ned Harper	1	0
Bill Heatley	16	4
Marshall Herbert	13	8
Les Hughes	16	10
Jim Jackson	5	1
Horrie Jones	10	0
Dick Lee	21	58
Ernie Lumsden	2	0
Bertie McDougall	1	0
Jock McHale	21	3
Duncan McIvor	4	0
Charlie Norris	11	4
Dave O'Donoghue	8	0
Norm Oliver	18	1
Ted Rowell	16	0
Dave Ryan	21	18
Jim Sadler	16	0
Joe Scaddan	21	0
Jack Shorten	21	0
Bob Strachan	2	3
Dick Vernon	18	3
Percy Wilson	20	11

Club Awards
Training awards presented to 19 players. Gold medals for training awarded to Percy Wilson and Marsh Herbert.
Kit bag awarded to J McHale for 'Fine Play'
Silver Flower Epergne awarded to Dave Ryan for his 'fine work as a follower'
Silver coffee service presented to George Angus by the Ladies of Collingwood for 'his gallant efforts in the Final game'
Leading goalkicker – Dick Lee (58)

1910 SEASON

ROUND 1 April 30 Princes Park
Carlton 9.9.63 v Collingwood **5.5.35**
Goals: Lee 3, McHale, Ryan

ROUND 2 May 14 Victoria Park
Collingwood 13.9.87 v South Melbourne **5.16.46**
Goals: Wilson 4, Baxter 3, Lee 3, Daykin, Herbert, Ryan

ROUND 3 May 21 Victoria Park
Collingwood 13.13.91 v St Kilda **2.6.18**
Goals: Lee 6, Baxter 2, Ryan 2, Herbert, Hughes, Vernon

ROUND 4 May 28 East Melbourne Cricket Ground
Essendon 6.7.43 v Collingwood **4.17.41**
Goals: Lee 2, Baxter, Wilson

ROUND 5 June 4 Victoria Park
Collingwood 10.16.76 v Melbourne **4.4.28**
Goals: Lee 3, Ryan 2, Baxter, Heatley, Hughes, Jackson, Wilson

ROUND 6 June 6 Brunswick St Oval
Fitzroy **7.9.51** v **Collingwood 11.14.80**
Goals: Lee 3, Ryan 3, Wilson 2, Baxter, Heatley, McHale

ROUND 7 June 11 Punt Rd Oval
Richmond **5.7.37** v **Collingwood 6.9.45**
Goals: Lee 4, Herbert 2

ROUND 8 June 18 Victoria Park
Collingwood 6.10.46 v University **6.6.42**
Goals: Herbert 3, Baxter, Hughes, Wilson

ROUND 9 June 25 Corio Oval
Geelong 10.9.69 v Collingwood **6.11.47**
Goals: Lee 3, Daykin, Herbert, Ryan

ROUND 10 July 2 Victoria Park
Collingwood **2.10.22** v **Carlton 6.15.51**
Goals: Heatley, Lee

ROUND 11 July 9 Lake Oval
South Melbourne 13.17.95 v Collingwood **4.9.33**
Goals: Lee 2, Daykin, Ryan

ROUND 12 July 16 Junction Oval
St Kilda **6.8.44** v **Collingwood 7.12.54**
Goals: Lee 2, Ryan 2, Hughes, Norris, Wilson

ROUND 13 July 23 Victoria Park
Collingwood 5.13.43 v Essendon **2.9.21**
Goals: Lee 2, Gilchrist, Hughes, Ryan

ROUND 14 July 30 MCG
Melbourne **7.6.48** v **Collingwood 9.12.66**
Goals: Hughes 3, Lee 2, Baxter, Gilchrist, Heatley, Norris

ROUND 15 August 6 Victoria Park
Collingwood 7.12.54 v Fitzroy **6.6.42**
Goals: Ryan 3, Lee 2, Norris, Vernon

ROUND 16 August 20 Victoria Park
Collingwood 8.13.61 v Richmond **5.4.34**
Goals: Lee 3, Gilchrist 2, Hughes, Norris, Oliver

ROUND 17 August 27 East Melbourne Cricket Ground
University **9.5.59** v **Collingwood 10.15.75**
Goals: Baxter 3, Strachan 3, Lee 2, Daykin, Gibb

ROUND 18 September 3 Victoria Park
Collingwood 4.13.37 v Geelong **2.9.21**
Goals: Baxter 2, Lee 2

1910 FINALS

LADDER

Team	W	L	D	For	Agst	%	Pts
Carlton	15	3	0	1167	729	160.1	60
Collingwood	13	5	0	993	812	122.3	52
South Melb	12	6	0	1080	884	122.2	48
Essendon	12	6	0	1113	963	115.6	48
Geelong	10	7	1	1008	952	105.9	42
University	10	8	0	994	979	101.5	40
Richmond	7	10	1	937	913	102.6	30
Fitzroy	5	13	0	952	1048	90.8	20
Melbourne	4	14	0	802	1347	59.5	16
St Kilda	1	17	0	692	1111	62.3	4

SEMI FINAL September 10   MCG

Collingwood 14.11.95 v Essendon **5.7.37**

Goals: Lee 6, Gilchrist 4, Hughes, McHale, Ryan, Wilson

PRELIM FINAL September 24   MCG

Collingwood 8.7.55 v South Melbourne **6.8.44**

Goals: Angus 3, Lee 3, Gilchrist 2

GRAND FINAL October 1   MCG

Collingwood	4.3	5.3	8.5	9.7	(61)
Carlton	1.2	2.6	4.9	6.11	(47)

Goals: Lee 4, Angus, Daykin, Gibb, Gilchrist, Vernon
Best: Lee, Angus, McHale, McIvor, Rowell, Scaddan, Shorten
Umpire: Elder
Crowd: 42,577 at the MCG

Grand Final Team
B: J. Sadler, E. Rowell, C. Norris
HB: J. Scaddan, J. Shorten, D. McIvor
C: P. Gibb, J. McHale, N. Oliver
HF: G. Angus (c), L. Hughes, R. Vernon
F: P. Gilchrist, R. Lee, P. Wilson
R: D. Ryan, R. Daykin, T. Baxter

CHAPTER FIVE
1917
Sacrifice and success

'The thanks of all football lovers are due to
Fitzroy and Collingwood for the glorious exhibition
of all that was best and brightest in the national pastime.'

A patriotic carnival held at Victoria Park drew a large crowd and raised around 500 pounds.

It might not always feel like it, but there *are* times when football isn't the most important thing in the world. And with World War 1 still raging, the VFL's 1917 season was one of those times.

Football was struggling for support at all levels as the new season approached. Memberships had plummeted, Collingwood's having fallen from just under 4000 in 1915 to 735 in 1916. Attendances, too, had fallen away dramatically. Only four clubs had taken part in the competition in 1916, leading to the farcical situation where Fitzroy finished on the bottom of the ladder but still played in the finals – and won the premiership. Many vocal critics believed that major sports like football should be suspended for the duration of the war.

But officials at the Collingwood Football Club held the view that football was a welcome weekly diversion from the war, helping to keep up the spirits of those at home. While acknowledging that costs had to be kept to a minimum to maximise profits, and that those profits should be channelled into the war effort, they strongly resisted all attempts to halt the competition until the war ended.

For a time it looked as if Collingwood was fighting a losing battle: two months before the scheduled start of the 1917 season, only the Magpies and Richmond were confirmed starters. Fortunately, Carlton, Fitzroy, Geelong and South Melbourne all relented, and the season not only went ahead, but did so with two more teams than in 1916, giving the competition more credibility. Each team would play the other three times, meaning a 15-round home-and-away season, plus finals.

Collingwood's previous commitment to patriotic efforts had been patchy, but not so in 1917. The club made a real effort to pare back expenditure in order to generate larger profits for the war effort. Payments to players were suspended, and weekly expenses (for things like travel and equipment) were limited to a total of five pounds for the whole team. Five players – Harry Curtis, 'Torchy' Laxton, Matt Cody, Pen Reynolds and Maurice Sheehy – refused to take even expenses, playing for nothing. The club spent time and money helping the local council with a number of fundraising appeals, including a carnival at Victoria Park that raised around 500 pounds for the Returned Soldiers' Repatriation Fund (the day's entertainment included a past-players' match against Fitzroy old-timers). Army recruiting officers were invited to speak at the annual meeting in March, and received 'a splendid hearing'.

The League had decided to stem some of the criticisms football was receiving by allowing recruiting officers to speak to crowds at games in the opening round. Strangely, they received mainly hostile receptions, with one at Fitzroy being assaulted. At Victoria Park the officers gave up and left after the crowd responded badly. The fans weren't unpatriotic: as Collingwood thought, they just wanted to forget about the war for two hours and focus on their favourite footy team instead.

Despite the welcome distraction on offer, crowds started off small for the first round of matches, which saw a draw between the previous year's grand finalists, Fitzroy and Carlton. Collingwood started with a win over Richmond at Victoria Park, and felt they would be strong contenders for the flag. The Pies still retained a core of players from the 1910 premiership year, including the wonderful

PLAYER OF THE YEAR
Charlie Brown

Charlie Brown might have hailed from Balmain in Sydney, but he took to VFL football as if he was a native Victorian.

Brown was a powerful, strongly-built man who joined the Collingwood Football Club in 1916. He played every game that year, and missed only one in 1917 as he quickly made one of the key defensive posts his own.

Most often that was at centre half-back, where his prodigious leap and strong marking came to the fore. When Harry Saunders, the goal-kicking hero of an early game in 1917, moved to full-back, he and Brown formed a terrific defensive combination that lasted several years.

Brown was not an eye-catching player, but he was rarely beaten in one-on-one contests, and he played his role so well that one journalist in 1917 was moved to remark, 'Brown, in his second year, is developing into a star, with superb marking and judgement and perfect ball-handling'.

Charlie Brown was one of those quiet achievers that every footy club loves to have. He might not have grabbed too many headlines, but his teammates and coaches knew how important he was to the side.

PLAYER OF THE YEAR — Percy Wilson

Percy Wilson's finest moment in the black-and-white of Collingwood was a long time coming. The brilliant rover played his first games for the club back in 1909, and he'd been an outstanding servant ever since.

Wilson made up for his lack of inches with a combination of courage, speed, toughness and skill, and he became one of the top handful of players in the team. He rarely put in a bad game.

But in 1917 he really hit his straps as a footballer. Wilson was appointed captain early in the season to replace Jock McHale, and at the same time moved into the centre. Both moves proved to be masterstrokes, and newspaper reports said he 'beat everything on the football map that season, and was generally judged the best man in the League'.

He also led the team to the premiership, having been among the best in all three of Collingwood's final games and, in the eyes of many critics, was the best player on the ground in the grand final triumph over Fitzroy. It was the perfect end to a perfect season.

rover Percy Wilson, giant ruckman Les 'Flapper' Hughes, 'Snowy' Lumsden, Jim Sadler and Dick Lee, still the most dangerous forward in the game. The team was led by the seemingly indestructible captain-coach Jock McHale, who entered the season having not missed a game as a player since 1906! His run of 191 successive matches finally ended in Round 3 of the season, when he missed the 16-point win over Fitzroy. A few weeks later he was forced to the sidelines for a further six weeks, as age finally started to catch up with his 35-year-old body.

The Pies won four of their first five games, losing only to an impressive Carlton, and were well placed on the ladder. Their next month of matches contained enough thrills and spills to fill an entire season.

First up was the Round 6 encounter with Richmond at Punt Road, where a goalless first quarter and some atrocious kicking cost Collingwood dearly. The Tigers led by a goal at the main break, but, with Percy Wilson starring in the middle, the Pies turned things around to lead by the same margin at the last change. They held onto that lead until the dying minutes of the game, when a long goal from Richmond's Ted Keggin tied the scores. The Pies were left ruing their woeful return of 6.14, a tally that included several posters.

The next week, Collingwood avenged its early-season loss to Carlton with a 37-point thrashing of the Blues in a game marked by a number of spiteful incidents, and a five-goal haul from Snowy Lumsden. This was followed by a memorable duel with Fitzroy at Victoria Park that provided one of the most thrilling finishes of the season. The contest was tight and tough throughout, with some observers criticising the 'unpleasant' atmosphere that surrounded the game and which led to a number of players becoming involved in heated exchanges. At times the game threatened to degenerate into 'outright fighting', especially after Collingwood's brilliant rover Torchy Laxton was knocked out in the first 10 minutes and had to leave the field. The Maroons led by two points at the first change and Collingwood by three points at both the main and last breaks. Fitzroy charged early in the final term and led by 11 points with just a few minutes to play. It had been a fierce final term, and *The Argus* noted that several players 'seemed disposed to run amok'. Both sides were exhausted, but the Pies made a late rally, drawing to within three points with just a minute left. Then Alex Mutch marked and found Harry Saunders with a clever pass, about 35 metres from goal.

This was only Saunders' seventh game for the club, and he had never before had to take a kick under such pressure. There were only seconds left, and he must have known the result of the match would likely hang on his kick. Young Harry held his nerve, kicked truly and the Victoria Park crowd erupted in wild cheering. Local newspapers described him as 'the hero of the hour' and praised his 'admirable coolness' under extreme pressure. Saunders would go on to enjoy a distinguished career at Collingwood – ironically, at full-back.

The Magpies had a setback the following week when they unexpectedly lost to South after being on the receiving end of a stunning last-quarter burst of five goals in as many minutes. Even so, the Pies retained top spot, a standing they would hold until the end of the season, despite a second loss to Carlton in appalling conditions in Round 12.

The club was hit by a wave of injuries as they prepared for the third-last game of the season against Fitzroy. Half a dozen of the team's best were out of action, and two club officials (both former players) declared themselves ready to play if needed. Jock McHale returned to the team – but not as captain. McHale had been chosen by the players to be skipper (he was already coach) at the start of the year, with 1916's captain Dan Minogue having gone to the front. When McHale missed a swag of games after Round 6, Percy Wilson was installed as captain. At the same time, to help give him better control over the game and the players, Wilson moved into the centre position, where he immediately started playing some of his best football for the club. Wilson wanted McHale to reclaim the captaincy when he returned, but McHale had been so impressed with Wilson's form during his absence that he declined. Under the circumstances, with such a depleted side, the thumping win over Fitzroy that day was a huge triumph.

Opposite: **Experienced players Jim Sadler, Les Hughes and Jock McHale were again in the line-up for 1917.**
Below: **Harry Saunders, the last-gasp goalkicking hero against Fitzroy.**
Following page: **Dick Lee was back to his high-flying best in 1917, and brought up the 500th goal of his career late in the season.**

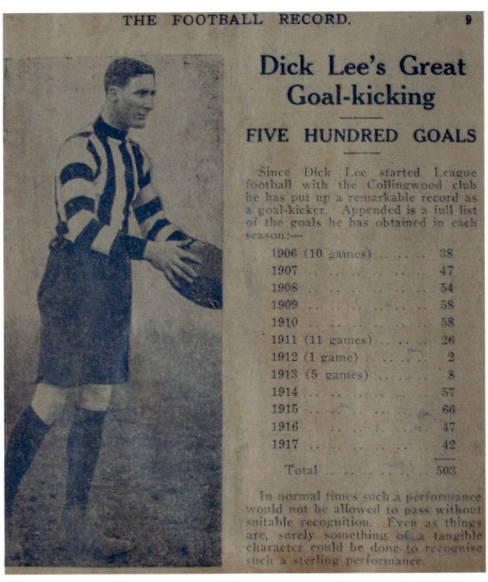

PLAYER OF THE YEAR

Dick Lee

The team's assault on the flag received a killer blow when champion forward Dick Lee was injured in the second-last game of the season against South Melbourne. Just a couple of weeks before, Lee had become the first player in VFL history to bring up a career tally of 500 goals, and he was on his way to his fourth successive VFL goalkicking title. But he'd struggled with injuries after the 1910 flag, missing the best part of three seasons with a major knee injury that eventually required football's first known cartilage operation. Lee had returned to the field full-time in 1914 and immediately reclaimed his place at the top of the goalkicking tree. But against South Melbourne, having just brought up his fiftieth goal for the season, he damaged his knee again, putting his finals campaign in jeopardy. All of Collingwood waited anxiously to see if he would recover in time.

There was another casualty in the final round, albeit a less serious one, when the team travelled to Geelong with top spot already secured. Les Hughes, the team's genial ruckman, missed the train with his teammates, potentially leaving the team one man short. So club president Jim Sharp offered to fill in. Sharp had been an outstanding player in his day, first with Fitzroy and later with Collingwood. But he was now 35, and hadn't played since 1912. His clubmates had serious doubts about whether he could last the distance but they need not have worried. Stamina didn't really come into it – Sharp injured his knee in the first few minutes and had to be carried from the field.

The injury to Dick Lee's knee was still the major talking point as the finals began. He was absent from the first final against South Melbourne, but the team didn't miss a beat, powering to a 10-goal win that included an amazing eight-goal third quarter that was then the biggest single-quarter tally in a final. Beanpole forward (and future club president) Harry Curtis stepped up in Lee's absence, his notoriously unreliable kicking straightening up for the day and

Throughout a long and glorious career, Dick Lee became famous for his amazing leap, freakish high-marking skills and prolific goal-kicking. But there was another side to his game that rarely received the same attention – his courage.

Lee had shown plenty of that quality in twice coming back from serious leg injuries that hit him early in his career. He showed more again in 1917 – just to get on the ground and help the Pies to a flag.

Lee enjoyed yet another terrific season in 1917, kicking 54 goals and topping the VFL goalkicking for the fourth successive year, and the eighth time overall. However, the knee he injured late in the year should have ended his season (it would trouble him throughout 1918 and force him to miss most of that season).

Instead, Lee was determined to play in the grand final, even though he was far from fit. He came back into the team, kicked four goals and still managed to soar for several wonderful high marks. It was a gutsy performance – and one of immense skill – that played a major role in Collingwood winning the game, and the premiership.

> **The Australasian**
>
> **On the thrilling final against Fitzroy:**
>
> It is many a day since such a magnificent contest has taken place and … the honours of the game decidedly belonged to Collingwood, who, with a man short, and a brilliant man at that, played certainly the more skilful part.

Alex Mutch, Percy Wilson and George Anderson were all important players in the finals – especially stand-in skipper Wilson.

producing four goals, all in the third quarter blitz. Torchy Laxton also managed four as the Pies became unbackable favourites for the flag.

Their opponents in the second final, Fitzroy, had taken comfort from the nail-biting match between the two sides back in Round 8. They believed if they could get close to the Woods at Victoria Park, then they could repeat the dose on neutral territory. And they were right. The result was one of the greatest finals matches the VFL had seen.

The Pies were again without Dick Lee, and again lost the influential Laxton inside the first 10 minutes after he received an accidental kick on the ankle, leaving them a man short for much of the game. Collingwood started brilliantly, kicking the first two goals of the game, but Fitzroy capitalised on the extra man and hit back to trail by only three points at quarter-time. That's where the margin remained at the long break after a fiercely fought hour of football. Fitzroy had missed a golden opportunity to lead when star forward Thomas Heaney, having had his shorts almost torn off while marking near goal, opted to run off to get new shorts rather than take his shot. The umpire, following the rules of the time, correctly decided to bounce the ball, and Fitzroy's golden opportunity was lost.

The Maroons grabbed the lead early in the third quarter, but Collingwood fought back to first level the scores, then again claim the lead. It was pulsating, end-to-end football, though scoring remained low, and Fitzroy took a one-point lead into the final quarter. That term turned out to be a brilliant one, with Fitzroy breaking away to lead by as much as nine points before the Pies reeled them in and drew level with seven minutes left. Both sides missed a string of chances before two quick goals to the Roys sealed the game, a late major from Pen Reynolds serving only to narrow the final margin to

six points. Harry Curtis had again stepped up with five goals, but it wasn't enough. Jack Worrall, in *The Australasian*, loved the game: 'It was a great match and a great finish, and the thanks of all football lovers are due to Fitzroy and Collingwood for the glorious exhibition of all that was best and brightest in the national pastime.'

The result meant that, once again, a grand final would be needed. The Pies and Roys would meet for the fifth time in the season, this time to decide the premiership. Two of those five matches had been absolute classics, and hopes were high that the sides could produce a repeat for grand final day. But Fitzroy was an unpredictable, inconsistent side, and their performance in the decider was a pale shadow of that from the final.

Collingwood dominated from start to finish. Coach McHale was convinced that it was his players' complacency that had cost them the previous final against Fitzroy, and he was determined it would not happen again. He set out with a plan for his team to unsettle the talented Maroons by playing especially hard, tough, uncompromising football – a strategy that was helped by the MCG being sodden after days of rain. The football that ensued wasn't pretty – in fact, it was decidedly scrappy. The Pies should have been out of sight at half-time, but a woeful return of 3.8 meant there was only a two-goal difference. A military band marched around the ground during the interval, with recruiting officers once again appealing for help. But, as *The Argus* reported, 'Apart from the very large contingent who were already in khaki, there was not a single man among the 28,000 who wanted any other game than football.'

The margin stretched to 28 points by the last change, and the Roys never looked like making a game of it. Collingwood finished with 9.20, and it was only that inaccuracy that prevented the 35-point margin blowing out to a full-scale shellacking. Dick Lee, back in the side despite still being troubled by his knee, kicked four wonderful goals, while Harry Curtis rounded off a stellar finals campaign with another bag of three. Replacement skipper Percy Wilson was best-on-ground, and he was well supported by Charlie Pannam Jnr, George Anderson and Tom Drummond.

Celebrations were, naturally, more understated than usual, and thoughts soon returned to the war. The Collingwood players had been given a reminder of events overseas on the eve of the grand final, when they received a good luck charm – a German shell that had been fashioned into a horseshoe – sent to them from the front by their former teammate, Malcolm 'Doc' Seddon. The inscription on the horseshoe read, 'France to C.F.C. Good luck from Doc. 1917' Reminders were there in other ways, too. As part of its determination to

Top: **Doc Seddon (seated, left) in his army gear.**
Bottom: **The good-luck horseshoe Seddon sent to his teammates from the front.**

maximise profits for the war effort, the club decided against spending money on premiership medallions, and instead relied on donations (mostly from John Wren) to make the mementos possible.

There were grounds for optimism amid the subdued celebrations. More than 28,000 had turned out for the grand final, a major improvement on the previous year, and crowds had been growing steadily throughout the season. Interest had been reignited in the competition, and fans were coming back to the game. Two more clubs would return to take part in 1918. Football had come through its biggest challenge to date, with Collingwood leading the way. Just as it should have been.

HARRY CURTIS
GRAND FINAL HERO

Collingwood fans were understandably worried when Dick Lee missed the club's first two finals matches in 1917. Who would step up and kick the goals in the great forward's absence?

The answer, as it turned out, was the tall, skinny, centre half-forward **Harry Curtis**. Lee and Curtis had formed a dangerous attacking combination all year, but it was with Lee absent that Curtis made not just the grand final, but the entire finals series, his own.

Despite a reputation for goal-kicking that could at best be described as 'unreliable', Curtis hit a purple patch in the 1917 finals. He bagged four against South in the first final, five against Fitzroy in the memorable contest the next week, and finished off with a further three in the grand final, when Lee was back in the team. That made it 12 goals in September – not bad for a bloke who'd kicked only 12 goals in the *entire* home-and-away season.

Curtis played more than 100 games for the club and would go on to act as president for many years. Despite all that service, it's arguable that his greatest contribution came in those three games, when he did so much to bring the 1917 flag back to Victoria Park.

PLAYERS

#	Player	Games	Goals
1	George Anderson	18	0
2	Charlie Brown	17	0
6	Matt Cody	2	1
4	Bert Colechin	12	0
?	Harrie Cross	1	1
3	Harry Curtis	17	24
7	Gus Dobrigh	14	10
8	Tom Drummond	14	0
9	Jack Green snr	10	0
10	Les Hughes	16	12
11	Horrie Jose	3	1
14	Charlie Laxton	16	11
12	Charlie Lee	15	3
13	Dick Lee	15	54
26	Ernie Lumsden	12	12
16	Sam Mackechnie	7	0
18	Con McCarthy	8	0
17	Jock McHale	9	2
27	Alec Mutch	12	4
19	Charlie Pannam jnr	16	1
20	Pen Reynolds	18	5
21	Jim Sadler	7	1
23	Harry Saunders	15	5
21	Jim Sharp	1	0
23	Maurie Sheehy	15	5
24	Percy Wilson	18	3
25	Tom Wraith	16	13

Club Awards
Suit of clothes presented to Pen Reynolds for regular attendance at training.
Gold medal presented to Charlie Pannam for regular attendance at training.
Other training awards to Jock McHale, Dick Lee, Maurice Sheehy, Percy Wilson, Tom Wraith.
Leading goalkicker – Dick Lee (54)

1917 SEASON

ROUND 1 May 12 Victoria Park
Collingwood 11.11.77 v Richmond 4.4.28
Goals: D Lee 4, Hughes 3, Cody, Curtis, Jose, Wraith

ROUND 2 May 19 Princes Park
Carlton 13.7.85 v Collingwood 8.6.54
Goals: D Lee 3, Curtis, Laxton, C Lee, Wilson, Wraith

ROUND 3 May 26 Brunswick St Oval
Fitzroy 8.14.62 v **Collingwood** 11.12.78
Goals: D Lee 4, Dobrigh 2, Saunders 2, Hughes, C Lee, Wraith

ROUND 4 June 2 Victoria Park
Collingwood 8.18.66 v South Melbourne 6.9.45
Goals: D Lee 3, Curtis, Dobrigh, Hughes, Laxton, Reynolds

ROUND 5 June 9 Corio Oval
Geelong 6.7.43 v **Collingwood** 8.9.57
Goals: D Lee 4, Curtis, McHale, Saunders, Wraith

ROUND 6 June 16 Punt Rd Oval
Richmond 7.8.50 v Collingwood 6.14.50
Goals: D Lee 3, Curtis, Dobrigh, Laxton

ROUND 7 June 23 Victoria Park
Collingwood 13.14.92 v Carlton 8.7.55
Goals: Lumsden 5, D Lee 4, Hughes 2, Mutch, Saunders

ROUND 8 June 30 Victoria Park
Collingwood 11.11.77 v Fitzroy 10.14.74
Goals: D Lee 4, Lumsden 2, Hughes, Reynolds, Saunders, Sheehy, Wilson

ROUND 9 July 7 Lake Oval
South Melbourne 13.12.90 v Collingwood 10.13.73
Goals: D Lee 3, Curtis 2, Hughes, Mutch, Reynolds, Wilson, Wraith

ROUND 10 July 14 Victoria Park
Collingwood 10.19.79 v Geelong 2.11.23
Goals: D Lee 4, Curtis 3, Lumsden, Sadler, Sheehy

ROUND 11 July 21 Victoria Park
Collingwood 11.19.85 v Richmond 7.7.49
Goals: D Lee 6, Wraith 3, Dobrigh, Lumsden

ROUND 12 July 28 Princes Park
Carlton 4.13.37 v Collingwood 3.8.26
Goals: D Lee, C Lee, Sheehy

ROUND 13 August 11 Brunswick St Oval
Fitzroy 7.3.45 v **Collingwood** 14.17.101
Goals: D Lee 5, Wraith 3, Curtis 2, Cross, Laxton, Reynolds, Sheehy

ROUND 14 August 18 Victoria Park
Collingwood 6.16.52 v South Melbourne 2.9.21
Goals: D Lee 2, Dobrigh, Laxton, Pannam, Sheehy

ROUND 15 August 25 Corio Oval
Geelong 8.17.65 v Collingwood 9.9.63
Goals: Dobrigh 2, Laxton 2, Lumsden 2, Mutch 2, McHale

1917 FINALS

LADDER

Team	W	L	D	For	Agst	%	Pts
Collingwood	10	4	1	1030	772	133.4	42
Carlton	9	5	1	843	724	116.4	38
South Melb	9	6	0	911	772	118.0	36
Fitzroy	6	8	1	832	963	86.4	26
Geelong	6	9	0	735	927	79.3	24
Richmond	3	11	1	761	954	79.8	14

SEMI FINAL September 8 — MCG
Collingwood 13.17.95 v South Melbourne **3.17.35**
Goals: Curtis 4, Laxton 4, Hughes 2, Dobrigh, Lumsden, Wraith

PRELIM FINAL September 15 — MCG
Collingwood **7.10.52** v Fitzroy **8.10.58**
Goals: Curtis 5, Reynolds, Wraith

GRAND FINAL September 22 — MCG

Collingwood	2.6	3.8	6.14	9.20	(74)
Fitzroy	1.0	2.2	3.4	5.9	(39)

Goals: Lee 4, Curtis 3, Dobrigh, Hughes
Best: Wilson, Anderson, Curtis, Lee, Drummond, Pannam, Dobrigh
Umpire: Norden
Crowd: 25,512 at the MCG

Grand Final Team
B: J. McHale, H. Saunders, A. Mutch
HB: G. Anderson, C. Brown, J.W. Green
C: T. Drummond, P. Wilson (c), C.E. Pannam
HF: G. Dobrigh, H. Curtis, C. Lee
F: C. McCarthy, R. Lee, E. Lumsden
R: L. Hughes, P. Reynolds, C. Laxton

CHAPTER SIX

1919

Order restored

'While they never spared themselves or their opponents, it was still the triumph of skill over strength.'

Doc Seddon (left) and Percy Rowe – war heroes and best mates. Tragically, Rowe was killed in World War 1.

As Australians slowly came to grips with life after the war that was supposed to end all wars, and as the repatriation of hundreds of thousands of soldiers was underway, Melburnians were looking forward to the 1919 football season more than ever before. The Melbourne Football Club had become the last to return to the VFL fold, and, with the competition finally back at full strength, everyone knew there would be greater interest in the game, bigger crowds and more excitement. Footy was back.

At Collingwood, there was an odd mixture of anticipation, sadness and resolve. The anticipation was centred not just on the season to come, but also on the expected return of war heroes Malcolm 'Doc' Seddon and former skipper Dan Minogue. There was sadness for former player Percy Rowe, who never made it back from the war, and also for coach Jock McHale, whose six-year-old son, James Francis, died from pneumonia just before the start of the season. That cast a pall over the whole club, and had a significant effect on McHale's early-season involvement.

The resolve came from the Magpies' determination to atone for what had been a heartbreaking grand final loss the previous year. They had gone into the 1918 Grand Final as underdogs against a South Melbourne team that had lost only one regular season game, but the Pies led at every change. At the start of the last quarter they were two goals up. Then South staged a comeback and, in the dying seconds, a late goal from Chris Laird snatched the premiership from the Magpies' grasp.

Collingwood and South players fly for a mark during the opening match of the 1919 season at the Lake Oval.

It was a bitter pill to swallow, and the Pies used their disappointment to steel themselves for a big assault on the 1919 title. Naturally enough, South Melbourne loomed as the side to beat in the race for the flag, and Collingwood got an early crack at them when they were drawn to play each other in the opening round at the Lake Oval. The bulk of the Magpies line-up was the same as it had been through 1917 and 1918, with Ernie Wilson, a rugged 18-year-old from South Yarra, making his debut. Con McCarthy, a fine follower and respected leader, had taken over as captain from Percy Wilson, who remained as the team's first rover.

The teams played out a close first half before Collingwood opened up a three-goal break in the third term. The game seemed to be safe when Ernie Wilson and Tom Wraith combined for another goal early in the final quarter, but South came storming home, dominating the rest of the game. Memories of the 1918 Grand Final quickly came back to haunt Magpie fans but this time the Southerners' radar was off target and they finished with a miserable 6.13, allowing the Pies a 13-point win despite having fewer scoring shots.

That was an important win for Collingwood, but just a week later they stumbled against St Kilda, of all clubs, at Victoria Park, of all locations. McHale couldn't tell if it was complacency or exhaustion, or perhaps a mix of both. What made the win even more incredible was that a couple of St Kilda's better players were ill and did not play.

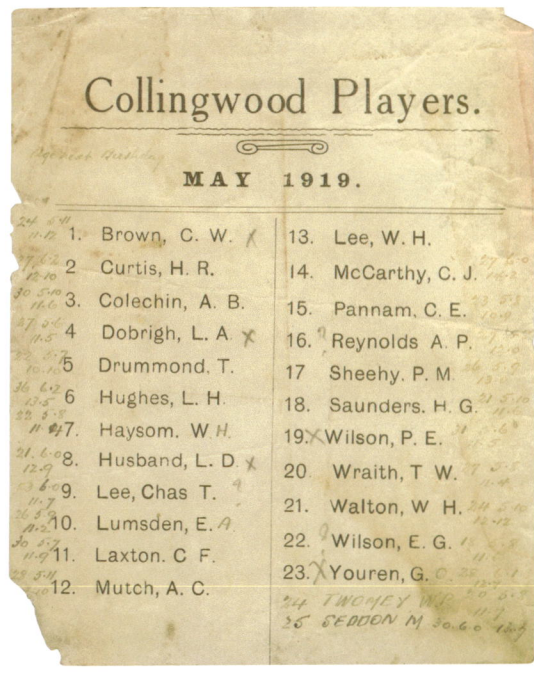

PLAYER OF THE YEAR
Tom Drummond

For a couple of magical seasons, the Collingwood centre line of Tom Drummond, Charlie Pannam and Bill Twomey Snr was one of the most scintillating the game had seen.

All three players were lightning fast, highly skilled and always likely to produce bursts of brilliance. Pannam and Drummond had been there for the 1917 flag, and were joined by Twomey in 1918 to complete a thrilling centre combination.

Tom Drummond was perhaps the most hard-working of the three, and he certainly had something the others lacked – extraordinary abilities overhead. He was an outstanding mark for his size and possessed a great leap. He also was a fine ball-handler and an all-round clever player who knew how to make the most of the spaces on the wing.

Drummond would go on to play for Victoria and also to captain the club in 1922. But his work in the 1919 season was some of the best he produced for Collingwood when, alongside Twomey and Pannam, he ran riot. Week after week he won plenty of kicks and created numerous opportunities for his forwards, and he rarely played a poor game. He didn't star in the finals, but he'd done more than enough throughout the year to justify his standing.

Collingwood had the assistance of the wind in the first and third quarters, but still could only stumble their way to a paltry 1.9 by the last change. The Saints led by 28 points going into the final quarter, and would finish with the wind behind them. There seemed to be no hope for the home side. But the ironic cheers that greeted Les Hughes' early goal were followed by enthusiastic ones when Harry Curtis added two in quick succession in the middle of the term. Then Bill Twomey made a thrilling run to within sight of goal and passed to Gus Dobrigh, who goaled to narrow the gap to just two points.

By this stage, according to newspapers, 'some 12,000 people were wrought up to the highest pitch of excitement by a match full of pace, keenness and sensation, for the verdict might have been reversed in the last kick of the day'. Dobrigh was the target again when the ball went forward one last time. He managed to mark just as the bell rang, leaving him on the boundary line, about 20 yards out. But victory was not meant to be – his kick missed, and St Kilda was left to rejoice in their first win at the ground since the start of the VFL in 1897. It would be another 43 years until their next success at Victoria Park.

Richmond was unbeaten when it met Collingwood in Round 4. They had never legitimately played finals football before, having just made up the numbers when four teams played off in 1916, but now there was a new dawning at Punt Rd. They gave a good

account of themselves, even getting to within seven points halfway through the last term, before the Magpies steadied to win by 20 points. Richmond had shown itself to be a real contender but, as *The Argus* concluded at the time, 'the great advantage to Collingwood is that it has no drones'.

It was one of three successive wins for Collingwood ahead of its meeting with old rivals Carlton in Round 7. There was deeper significance to this clash at Princes Park. Doc Seddon was making his comeback in black and white after returning to Australia from active service. Seddon had arrived back from Europe in late May, and just weeks later ran out with his teammates again. His previous game had been in the 1915 Grand Final against Carlton. He had played that game with his best mate, Percy Rowe, who went by the name of Paddy Rowan for his football and boxing pursuits. Rowe had been killed in action in 1916.

Seddon had sent a horseshoe fashioned from a German shell to his teammates before the 1917 Grand Final to spur them on. Now he could provide an even more tangible inspiration in their chase for the next flag. There was to be no fairytale return for him, however, as the Blues won by 11 points – but only after they'd held off a late Collingwood charge that included Seddon's first goal in four years. It was an emotional moment both for Seddon and his teammates.

More of this was anticipated with the return from service of one of the club's former captains, Dan Minogue. After his farewell match in 1916, Minogue had been carried from the field by adoring fans and the whole club could not wait for his comeback to the team. There were even plans afoot to honour him with an official 'welcome home' function. But those ideas were dropped immediately when Minogue sensationally revealed that he wanted to transfer to Richmond. Collingwood opposed the move, of course, which meant he had to stand out of football for 1919. But that didn't deter Minogue, who would join Richmond in 1920.

Above: **Doc Seddon (26) punches the ball away during his first match back from the front.**
Below: **Dan Minogue turned his back on the Pies.**
Opposite: **Dick Lee gathers the ball in the game against Carlton.**

The Argus

On the frenetic Round 9 finish against Fitzroy:

[Umpire] Elder, who was well up the field, ran down to give the all clear signal, but the goal umpire was apparently rattled by the excitement and the players crowding around him ... for on his decision the result rested. [He] kept repeating to Elder 'It was below the knee', while the field umpire kept his cool and again said 'You must give your decision.' The goal umpire finally remarked: 'Well, I must give it a goal' and hoisted the two flags.

Below: **Dick Lee (left) flies for a mark in the semi-final against Carlton, with Harry Curtis (front) having badly misjudged the flight.**
Opposite: **Bert Colechin (3) and Alex Mutch (12) defend valiantly against Carlton.**

At Collingwood, those who had idolised their former skipper felt angry, let down and betrayed. Nobody could understand what had happened. Minogue's reasons were never fully explained, though years later he wrote that he had been upset over Collingwood's treatment of former player Jim Sadler, a close friend, and felt he had to leave on principle. Another factor likely to be at play was that Jock McHale was firmly entrenched as Collingwood coach, and Minogue knew he'd have to go elsewhere if he held coaching aspirations (which he did, joining Richmond as captain-coach and later coaching four other VFL clubs). Whatever the reason, Minogue's defection fuelled the emerging rivalry between inner-city neighbours Collingwood and Richmond.

Minogue's desertion was hard to take, but his absence did not seem to impede the Magpies' strong form. Still, a few hurdles emerged every now and then to test the club. One of them came against Fitzroy in Round 9. Collingwood appeared to be coasting to yet another win when it led by five goals at the last change. But the Maroons staged a remarkable comeback, storming home with a burst of goals that stunned Collingwood. There was less than a goal in it in the dying stages when a desperate struggle ensued right in front of their goal. The ball came off Tom Heaney's shin and went through the goals for Fitzroy. After much discussion between the field and goal umpires, the goal was eventually given and Fitzroy had won by two points. *The Argus* reported that Collingwood, on learning the facts, 'took their defeat like sportsmen'. The Victoria Park crowd was not as forgiving.

As frustrating as the result was, it shook the Magpies into action, and they embarked on an eight-game winning streak that included a 23-point win over reigning premiers South Melbourne; a hard-fought 13-point win over Richmond; a massive 109-point victory over Melbourne (which is still Collingwood's greatest winning margin over them); and a 67-point flogging of Carlton. Dick Lee was in stellar form, snaring 20 goals in just three matches. The last round win over Fitzroy cost the Maroons a finals berth, allowing Richmond to make the last stage. It also cemented top spot for Collingwood, after South had been defeated by Geelong down at Corio Oval. It was the first time all season that the Magpies had been on top of the ladder.

Collingwood had reason to be confident going into its semi-final clash with Carlton, following their big win over the Blues just four weeks earlier. Such was their confidence that smart forward Tom Wraith arranged to get married on the morning of the game, and a number of his teammates attended. It seemed

Player of the Year
Con McCarthy

The Collingwood players knew what they were doing when they chose Con McCarthy to take over from Percy Wilson as captain for the 1919 season.

McCarthy was a resolute, selfless, tough team man, and his work in the ruck had won him many admirers among his teammates. But he lifted his game to another level once he was skipper, and was a major influence in the club winning the premiership.

He completed a season of high-quality, consistent performances with a stand-out showing in the grand final. He sacrificed his own game that day, staying on the ball the whole time and doing most of the hard work to break up Richmond's ruck division, allowing the taller but less physical 'Flapper' Hughes to control the ruckwork. He left the ground completely spent, but knowing he'd done a huge amount to bring another flag to Victoria Park.

Unusually for a man renowned for his leadership qualities, McCarthy asked to be relieved of the Magpie captaincy after just one season, saying he didn't feel comfortable with it. But he'd already done enough in that one season to leave his mark on Collingwood history forever.

---

to be the perfect preparation, as the Pies delivered a stunning first term in which they piled on 4.7 to 0.2. That set the tone and gave them an early ascendancy they never relinquished. They were never seriously challenged and led by more than seven goals at the last change, before a late burst of scoring by Carlton made the result look more respectable. As *The Argus* described it: 'Collingwood jumped out to the lead in the first furlong, had the race won at the home turn and it was only long after the distance was passed that Carlton put in its late run.' Dick Lee was brilliant, with four of his team's nine goals in the 18-point win, including his fiftieth for the year. He also took a screamer in the first quarter that had the big crowd roaring. He was well supported by captain Con McCarthy, Bill Twomey, Alex Mutch, Les Hughes and Bert Colechin. The only downside was that champion rover and former skipper Percy Wilson broke his arm in the third quarter, putting paid to the rest of his season.

The win left Collingwood to meet Richmond for the premiership. The 'Wasps', as Richmond was also known because of its black and yellow jumpers, would have to beat the Magpies twice in successive weeks to win their first VFL premiership and no one gave them much hope of doing it. In fact, the Pies were so confident of success in their first crack at Richmond that they had already booked an end-of-season trip to the Gippsland Lakes beginning the

The Argus

On the build-up to the big game:

For the past week excitement has been at fever pitch. The affairs of Commonwealth and State have been forgotten. Mr Hughes (Prime Minister) has been pushed off the map; the supermen of today are Con McCarthy, captain of the 'Woods, and Percy Maybury, who leads the Tigers. The whole metropolis is possessed, and talks and argues nothing but the prospects of the rival teams.

Fans grabbed every possible vantage point – even clambering on to the roof of the grandstand – to see the grand final.

following Saturday. But *The Herald* sagely noted that 'there is such a condition as over confidence', and the newspaper was right: Collingwood played like a team already on holidays. Richmond led from the outset and, when the Pies' anticipated comeback never eventuated, ran out winners by 29 points. As one of the Collingwood players said after the game, 'They made hacks of us.' A grand final would be needed, and Collingwood had to postpone its trip.

The build-up to the contest was huge, as the whole town once again embraced football. Pre-match, much of the focus was on the tactics of both sides. Part of Richmond's success in the first final came from the way it used big man Dave Moffatt to negate the influence of ruckman Les Hughes. McHale was not about to let it happen again, and worked out a counter-strategy. He asked McCarthy to come between Moffatt and Hughes at almost every opportunity, effectively giving the Collingwood player the extra space he needed. It was, as *The Australasian* concluded, 'the most telling move of the match'. Hughes would be one of the most effective players on the field.

More than 45,000 fans, including plenty of men in khaki, saw the match – the biggest grand final crowd since 1913 – and more than a few of them were perched on the grandstand roof. Richmond got the first goal in a bruising opening. The Magpies kept attacking, and scored their first goal soon after, taking a three-point lead to the first change of ends. But while the first term was full of defensive actions, the floodgates opened in the second. Seven goals

were scored, four of them for Collingwood, to keep their noses in front by four points at the long break. However there were concerns amongst Collingwood fans when the team ran back onto the oval after half-time – their star forward Lee was limping. Those concerns were exacerbated when a goal early in the third quarter gave the Tigers the lead.

But it would be their only goal for the term, as the Magpies stemmed the tide with three of their own. One of them came from Lee, who had recovered enough to play on. The margin was out to 16 points at the last change, and the match looked to be within Collingwood's keeping. But McHale wasn't taking any chances, as Richmond still had the assistance of a slight breeze in the final half hour. Instead of shutting the game down and playing defensive football, the Collingwood coach asked for the complete opposite from his charges. He wanted them to keep pushing, to keep playing attacking football and to keep putting Richmond under pressure.

This bold strategy was rewarded when 'Snowy' Lumsden helped Doc Seddon to his second goal of the game early in the last term, before adding one of his own soon afterwards. Any hopes of a miracle comeback evaporated when 'Torchy' Laxton kicked Collingwood's last goal of the game, and by the bell the margin had crept out to 25 points. 'The Tigers of the Saturday before were all caged, the Magpies flying high and fast and staying right out to the finish,' wrote *The Argus*. 'Decisively as Richmond on the merits won the first game,

PLAYER OF THE YEAR
Les Hughes

Les Hughes turned 35 just before the start of the 1919 season, so he could have been forgiven if his performances had started to show signs of decline. Instead, by the end of the year, *The Football Record* declared that 1919 had been one of Hughes' best-ever seasons. 'As a follower Hughes has no superior in the league,' the *Record* wrote.

That was typical of Hughes, a player who was used to defying expectations, and who ended up playing until he was 38.

Les Hughes was unusually tall for the time – around 6 foot 2 (188 centimetres) – and strongly built. He looked ungainly and raw when he first appeared, and many thought he wouldn't make it. But make it he did, with his trademarks being strong marking and wonderfully accurate tap-outs from the ruck. In the latter area he was almost without peer in the competition, and he made life easy for his rovers over many years.

Hughes was magnificent in 1919. He even kicked a remarkable six goals in one game. His great form was rewarded not only with another premiership but also with interstate selection, and captaincy of a VFL representative side against Ballarat. Not bad for an old bloke!

just as meritoriously Collingwood won this time. While they never spared themselves or their opponents, it was still the triumph of skill over strength.'

The 'peace premiership' was Collingwood's. To make things even better, Collingwood Districts, the club's unofficial seconds side, also won their flag, with Ernie 'Tich' Utting kicking 97 goals. It had been a tough season, physically and mentally, but the Magpies had triumphed. McHale had closed out a season where he lost a child with a superb coaching performance in the grand final. And Collingwood had served a lesson to Dan Minogue that the club was greater than any individual, even a beloved former captain. Minogue would be back to haunt the Magpies as Richmond's captain-coach, but that could wait. For now it was time to celebrate. Football had resumed its place in Melbourne's sporting and social landscape, and Collingwood had returned to the top of the VFL. The war was over, and the natural order was being restored.

A fabric band and logo used on players' hats as part of their official club outfits of blazers, ties and hats.

BILL TWOMEY
GRAND FINAL HERO

Bill Twomey Snr is perhaps best remembered as the father of three sons – Bill Jnr, Pat and Mick – who all played for Collingwood in the 1950s. But the Twomey patriarch was himself an outstanding footballer who briefly lit up the VFL competition.

Twomey debuted midway through 1918 and quickly won a reputation as one of the most exciting wingmen in the competition. He was super-fast, highly skilled and a thrilling player to watch.

In just his second season he enjoyed a magnificent finals campaign. He was very good against Carlton, and probably the team's best player in both finals against Richmond. The *Argus* summed up his campaign this way: 'Twomey played a dashing game, and has proved to be one of the bright particular stars in the three finals, the one player of all others who has most frequently brought the ball from the centre to scoring range.'

Twomey enjoyed two more excellent seasons at Victoria Park before leaving to pursue a running career – he would go on to win the Stawell Gift in 1924. He packed a lot into a teasing 54-game career, and the 1919 flag was undoubtedly the highlight.

PLAYERS

#	Player	Games	Goals
1	Charlie Brown	15	1
4	Bert Colechin	16	0
2	Harry Curtis	16	25
4	Gus Dobrigh	7	4
5	Tom Drummond	16	0
7	Wally Haysom	16	0
6	Les Hughes	19	18
27	Horrie Jose	2	0
11	Charlie Laxton	13	5
9	Charlie Lee	7	1
13	Dick Lee	15	56
10	Ernie Lumsden	18	14
14	Con McCarthy	16	3
12	Alec Mutch	16	0
15	Charlie Pannam Jnr	18	4
16	Pen Reynolds	11	0
18	Harry Saunders	18	2
26	Mal Seddon	13	10
17	Maurie Sheehy	17	2
24	Bill Twomey Snr	16	4
23	Ern Utting	1	2
21	Bill Walton	15	8
19	Ernie Wilson	10	3
19	Percy Wilson	14	5
20	Tom Wraith	14	30
23	George Youren	3	1

Club Awards
One guinea awarded to Dick Lee for his goalkicking
Suit of clothes awarded to Charlie Lee for regular attendance at training.
Other training awards presented to Bert Colechin, Tom Drummond, Les Hughes, Wally Haysom, Ernie Lumsden, Con McCarthy, Alex Mutch, Charlie Pannam, Pen Reynolds, Harry Saunders, Maurice Sheehy, Ernie Wilson, Tom Wraith
Pipes presented to each member of the premiership team.
Rose Bowl presented to Mr Balfour to mark 23 years as doorman.
Leading goalkicker – Dick Lee (56)

1919 SEASON

ROUND 1 May 3 — Lake Oval
South Melbourne **6.13.49** v **Collingwood 9.8.62**
Goals: Curtis 2, B Walton 2, Wraith 2, Laxton, Lumsden, P Wilson

ROUND 2 May 10 — Victoria Park
Collingwood **5.15.45** v **St Kilda 5.18.48**
Goals: Curtis 2, Dobrigh, Hughes, Wraith

ROUND 3 May 17 — Corio Oval
Geelong **5.2.32** v **Collingwood 5.19.49**
Goals: Hughes, Lumsden, Sheehy, Wraith, Youren

ROUND 4 May 24 — Punt Rd Oval
Richmond **8.6.54** v **Collingwood 11.8.74**
Goals: Saunders 2, Utting 2, B Walton 2, Curtis, Dobrigh, Hughes, Lumsden, Pannam

ROUND 6 June 7 — Victoria Park
Collingwood 16.20.116 v Melbourne **8.7.55**
Goals: Hughes 6, Dobrigh 2, D Lee 2, B Walton 2, McCarthy, Sheehy, Twomey, Wraith

ROUND 7 June 14 — Princes Park
Carlton 9.16.70 v Collingwood **8.11.59**
Goals: D Lee 3, C Lee, Pannam, Seddon, P Wilson, Wraith

ROUND 8 June 21 — East Melbourne Cricket Ground
Essendon **6.8.44** v **Collingwood 10.10.70**
Goals: D Lee 4, Twomey 2, Wraith 2, Lumsden, Seddon

ROUND 9 June 28 — Victoria Park
Collingwood **9.14.68** v **Fitzroy 10.11.71**
Goals: Curtis 4, D Lee 2, Laxton, McCarthy, Sheehy

ROUND 10 July 12 — Victoria Park
Collingwood 8.11.59 v South Melbourne **3.18.36**
Goals: D Lee 4, Curtis 2, Hughes, E Wilson

ROUND 11 July 19 — Junction Oval
St Kilda **5.9.39** v **Collingwood 13.13.91**
Goals: D Lee 6, Curtis 3, Lumsden 2, McCarthy, Wraith

ROUND 12 July 26 — Victoria Park
Collingwood 12.11.83 v Geelong **4.7.31**
Goals: Lumsden 3, Hughes 2, Pannam 2, Wraith 2, Curtis, D Lee, Seddon

ROUND 13 August 9 — Victoria Park
Collingwood 11.12.78 v Richmond **9.11.65**
Goals: D Lee 7, Curtis 2, Hughes, Seddon

ROUND 15 August 23 — MCG
Melbourne **5.6.36** v **Collingwood 20.25.145**
Goals: D Lee 7, Wraith 6, Curtis 3, E Wilson 2, Seddon, P Wilson

ROUND 16 August 30 — Victoria Park
Collingwood 17.11.113 v Carlton **5.16.46**
Goals: D Lee 6, Curtis 4, Wraith 4, Lumsden 2, Hughes

ROUND 17 September 6 — Victoria Park
Collingwood 9.13.67 v Essendon **5.14.44**
Goals: D Lee 3, Wraith 3, Hughes 2, Laxton

ROUND 18 September 13 — Brunswick St Oval
Fitzroy **6.10.46** v **Collingwood 9.10.64**
Goals: D Lee 2, P Wilson 2, Wraith 2, Brown, Hughes, Lumsden

1919 FINALS

LADDER

Team	W	L	D	For	Agst	%	Pts
Collingwood	13	3	0	1243	766	162.3	52
South Melb	12	4	0	1111	700	158.7	48
Carlton	10	6	0	1150	901	127.6	40
Richmond	10	6	0	1083	916	118.2	40
Fitzroy	9	6	1	1074	857	125.3	38
Essendon	7	9	0	924	977	94.6	28
St Kilda	7	9	0	772	1093	70.6	28
Geelong	3	12	1	794	1082	73.4	14
Melbourne	0	16	0	647	1506	43.0	0

SEMI FINAL September 27 MCG
Collingwood 9.10.64 v Carlton 6.10.46
Goals: D Lee 4, Seddon 2, Wraith 2, Walton

PRELIM FINAL October 4 MCG
Collingwood 6.9.45 v **Richmond 10.14.74**
Goals: D Lee 2, Wraith 2, Laxton, Lumsden

GRAND FINAL October 11 MCG

Collingwood	1.5	5.5	8.8	11.12	**(78)**
Richmond	1.2	4.7	5.10	7.11	(53)

Goals: Lee 3, Seddon 2, Curtis, Hughes, Laxton, Lumsden, Twomey, Walton
Best: McCarthy, Twomey, Hughes, Colechin, Curtis, Pannam
Umpire: Elder
Attendance: 45,413 at the MCG

Grand Final Team
B: W. Haysom, H. Saunders, M. Sheehy
HB: A. Mutch, W. Walton, A. Colechin
C: T. Drummond, C.E. Pannam, W.P. Twomey
HF: E. Wilson, H. Curtis, M. Seddon
F: P. Reynolds, R. Lee, E. Lumsden
R: L. Hughes, C. McCarthy (c), C. Laxton

Subiaco Oval
Perth W.A. 1921

WAREHAM HUGHSON MUIR DIBBS MILBURN

CHAPTER SEVEN

1927

Whatever it takes

'Never have the Magpie players been as keyed up by the intention to win a premiership as they have been all season.'

Jock McHale provides some handy hints to his players – including soon-to-be-ex captain Charlie Tyson – during the 1927 pre-season.

If somebody ever produces a manual on what teams need to win premierships it's a fair bet that 'club stability' would be high on the list of must-have items. The last thing any serious premiership assault needs is internal club turmoil. And a team *definitely* doesn't want to be dumping its captain in controversial circumstances on the eve of the season. But that's just what Collingwood did in 1927, as it threw the premiership handbook out the window.

The club has known few more tumultuous pre-seasons, and it was born out of a barren and frustrating period. Since the last flag in 1919 there had been four losing grand finals in 1920, 1922, 1925 and 1926, but no more premierships. In 1923 and '24 the club missed the finals in successive years for the first time. And the particularly meek capitulation in the 1926 decider to Melbourne – by a then-record margin of 57 points, after the team had been red-hot premiership favourites midway through the season – burned with many Magpies throughout the summer.

So anger and resentment were simmering when members and officials gathered at the Collingwood Town Hall on a balmy evening in March for the club's annual meeting. A crowd of angry supporters demanded to know what the committee was doing to arrest the slump and, when they weren't satisfied with the answers, some tore up their membership tickets in rage. President Harry Curtis, a former player, struggled to keep a hostile gathering in check. Long-time *Herald* journalist, Kickero, said he had never seen such angst at the club. He said he'd never seen Collingwood supporters as upset after a loss as they had been after the 1926 Grand Final, and that many 'had not recovered from the shock'.

Something had to give . . . or perhaps some*one*. There had been speculation after the annual meeting that there could be casualties. Captain Charlie Tyson led the senior team in a series of internal practice matches, and played well in those games, leading many to conclude that the status quo would be maintained. But in what was one of the most controversial and contentious decisions in the club's history, the committee opted to sack Tyson as captain and, even more remarkably, as a player. The club also axed Jim Shanahan, Reynolds Webb and Laurie Murphy, casting aside more than 300 games of experience. And all this just days before the start of the season. The committee's decision came as a huge shock – not least to Tyson. He said he was at a loss to explain it, and felt he had been playing and training well. His public comments were mostly measured, but he believed a certain section of the committee – headed by Curtis – had had him 'in the gun' for some time. He wondered whether a players' meeting he'd organised the previous December to discuss the possibility of a bonus payment had been behind his dumping.

Others had more sinister explanations. The timing of the sacking and the fact that the former captain had been spotted driving a new Fiat led some to speculate that Tyson had received money for 'playing dead' in the previous year's grand final. Tyson had a poor game that day, but he was hardly alone. He was also criticised for two positional changes he made at the start of the second half, which backfired and cost the team dearly. The whispering campaign became more audible as the season wore on and finally became intolerable for Tyson, who felt his name and reputation were being besmirched. Almost three months after his departure from Victoria Park he felt compelled by the injustice to write to the *Herald*, emphatically denying the allegations and threatening legal action if the 'untrue and ungenerous statements' continued.

For decades the theory that a Collingwood captain had 'played dead' in a grand final became an accepted part of football folklore. It wasn't until nearly 60 years later that the first detailed examination of the facts, by Richard Stremski in *Kill For Collingwood*, came down heavily on Tyson's side. The harsh reality was that Tyson had outlived his usefulness at the club. Some club

Two administrators who would figure prominently through the season, president Harry Curtis (left) and secretary George Connor.

The makers of this supporters' badge were obviously optimistic.

Charlie Tyson, left, was replaced as captain by Syd Coventry (right) on the eve of the season.
Opposite: The architects of Collingwood's resurgence in the late 1920s, Syd Coventry and Jock McHale.

officials believed he was too much of a 'gentleman' to be the inspirational captain the club required. There was also the view that, at 29, he had passed his prime, something reinforced by club statements that he had been overtaken by faster, younger alternatives. The fact that the sacking came seven months after the grand final loss proves there must have been some resistance at committee level: if not, he would surely have been dumped much earlier. Even so, the sacking of a respected and popular captain on the eve of the season created headlines and conjecture that no one wanted.

Clearly, the committee thought they had a better captain in the wings. That man was Syd Coventry, one of the premier big men in the competition. He was hard but almost always fair, a man who was inspirational in on-field deeds and who led by example off the field. He cut the perfect frame as a footballer, standing at about 5' 11" and 13 st 8 lb (180 cm and 86 kg), and he was utterly fearless. He was, above all, a quintessential team player who was completely committed to the Collingwood cause. And he was a born leader.

Despite the frustrating results of the preceding years, Coventry inherited a team on the rise. His brother, Gordon, had started at Collingwood in 1920 and was just beginning to show signs of becoming a gun full-forward. Albert Collier, Harry Collier, Frank Murphy, Billy Libbis and Jack Beveridge had all joined in the previous two years, and the seconds team had won the premiership in 1925. To this promising crop were added a former Carlton player in Harold Rumney and another youngster in Norm MacLeod.

Rumney was a last-minute inclusion for the Round 1 game against Geelong at Victoria Park (by season's end he had played 17 matches and won a stylish new hat as best first-year player), but all eyes that day were on Syd Coventry.

On Syd Coventry as captain:

To the Collingwood Football Club, Syd Coventry... is an ideal mixture of Napoleon and Nelson with a dash of Caesar and Alexander the Great. He is their beau ideal. Syd Coventry commands respect because of his even temper in a game where heat is easily generated; his general sportsmanship and his fine rearguard courage. Syd plays everywhere. Back, centre, forward or moving around with the ruck, he is always something like a logarithm to solve by the enemy – always a cool brain with icy resolutions in the warmth of the fray.

Above: Champion full-forward Gordon Coventry in action against Geelong.
Below: The rugged Ernie Wilson was an inspiration in the first game of the season.

As expected, he rose to the occasion in a manner befitting a true leader. 'Never have I seen a man display such indomitable spirit as did Syd Coventry . . . he pulled down the ball almost every time he went up for it and seemed to be in the air every other minute,' wrote 'Jumbo' Sharland in *The Sporting Globe*. Coventry's dominance in Collingwood's 23-point win over Geelong that day silenced many of the critics of Tyson's sacking. Meanwhile, across town, Charlie Tyson ran out for his new club, North Melbourne, and played a blinder.

Two other players, Gordon 'Nuts' Coventry and Ernie Wilson, were also prominent in that first game. Syd's brother dominated from the first quarter of the new season, kicking four goals in the first half-hour and finishing with eight. It was a taste of things to come. Wilson's contribution was even more inspiring. He dislocated his shoulder early in the match, but returned to the field with his limp arm hanging by his side. He took part in several passages of play, and even managed to pick up the ball in his good hand and kick a behind, prompting a huge cheer. Wilson's courage was held up to his teammates as an example they must follow for the rest of the year.

If the players derived any satisfaction from that first win of 1927, they were brought back to earth when they fronted for training the following week. On the bulletin board in the training room, club secretary George Connor had posted a picture of Melbourne unfurling its 1926 Premiership pennant on the

MCG from the previous Saturday. Scrawled across the picture in Connor's handwriting was a message: 'The flag that we could not win in 1926 . . . what about the one we can win in 1927? Players – it is now left up to you.' The message from the secretary was simple but to the point. The administration felt the players owed the club and its fans a premiership. Nothing else would do.

Those ambitions looked a bit optimistic after Richmond came from behind to upset the Pies at Victoria Park in Round 3. A week later, however, the players showed they had taken to heart Ernie Wilson's opening game heroics with a win full of courage and character against South Melbourne at the Lake Oval. After a brutal first half, the Magpies appeared to be in serious trouble at the main interval. They led by just two points at the break, and Syd Coventry had been knocked out in a head-on collision and 'carried off insensible'. He regained consciousness in the rooms at half-time and stunned teammates by insisting on returning to the field. He then starred in the third term, inspiring his team during a five-goal burst that won the game for the Pies. Half-back Joe Poulter showed similar spirit, remaining on the ground despite serious injuries to his ribs and leg, and managing to kick a goal despite scarcely being able to stand up.

Ruckman Percy Rowe's helps to carry Syd Coventry off against South Melbourne (above), while Harry Rumney leaps high, but unsuccessfully, in the same game.

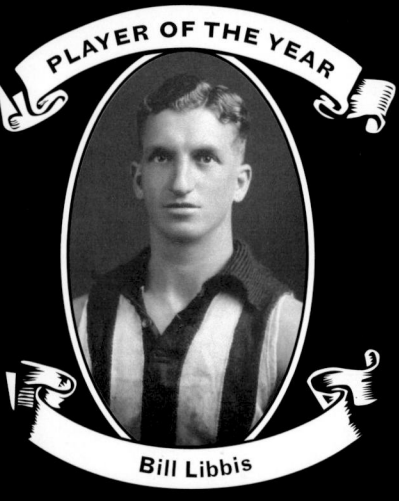

PLAYER OF THE YEAR — Bill Libbis

Billy Libbis is one of those footballers who should be more famous than he is. Had he not played in a team with the Coventrys and Colliers, that surely would be the case.

For it was Libbis, not the far better known Harry Collier, who was the team's number one rover during their four successive premierships. A brilliant, fast and skilful player, he was widely regarded as one of the best players in the competition.

In 1927, as Harry was making a name for himself, Libbis had a terrifically consistent season. He rarely put in a bad game and finished third in the Copeland, teaming especially well with Syd Coventry in the ruck.

Libbis missed only a couple of games through the Machine Team's reign, and maintained throughout the high standards he set in 1927. As Harry Collier himself said many years later: 'Somehow I ended up with the name but Billy Libbis . . . well, he was the player.'

The Pies had plenty of heart, but they were also capable of playing brilliant football. Five successive wins – and a couple of 11-goal hauls from the increasingly prolific Gordon Coventry – impressed the critics. One said that football fans 'could not but be astounded and delighted with the magnificent football of Collingwood', while another commented on the Pies' machine-like attack. 'What tremendous havoc Collingwood is capable of when they get a side on the run.'

But the growing sense of confidence was shattered soon after by another loss at Victoria Park, this one an unexpected setback in Round 9 at the hands of Carlton – or more correctly, the hands of Carlton centre half-back Alex Duncan. The Magpies were beaten that day by what one observer described as 'the greatest individual effort in the history of the game in Victoria', with Duncan repelling countless Collingwood forward moves and bringing down an incredible 33 marks. The match has been known ever since as 'Duncan's match'. His performance was so dominant that the Magpie players saluted him after the game, and even the famously parochial Collingwood fans applauded him from the field.

Connor's messages on the bulletin board in the training room were by now providing a constant update on the season's progress. He advised the players to 'keep fit by being regular with meals', and told them that they 'should not indulge in eating, drinking, or in smoking, and if they go jazzing, the early part of the week was the time for it'. Friday night, he said, was to be 'a night of rest'.

The Carlton loss aside, the team was playing good, consistent football. Such was the competition for spots in the Magpie team that even good form was not enough to secure positions. Hector Ross was named among Collingwood's best players in the narrow win against Melbourne in Round 11, but had to make way for the returning Harold Rumney the next week. Ross never played senior football with the club again.

That win against Melbourne was important for coach Jock McHale, and a huge confidence boost for the players. The coach, clearly with the events of 1926 still fresh in his mind, candidly told one newspaper: 'To tell you the truth, I am most afraid of Melbourne. Should the Red Legs get into the four, they will cause no end of trouble on the Melbourne ground. I greatly fear the pace of their men, and the lightning manner in which they attack.'

The return match against Geelong at Corio Oval attracted plenty of interest, as both teams went into the match on equal points at the top of the ladder, along with Richmond. It turned out to be a 'Super Saturday', with the Tigers playing the fourth-placed Melbourne on the same day. Several special trains ran to Geelong that afternoon to cater for the large number of black and white fans travelling to see their team. Those fans went home happy after seeing the Pies lead all day to win by 16 points, but the game itself was scrappy and disappointing. Richmond, meanwhile, proved far too good for Melbourne at Punt Road, leaving the Magpies and Tigers clear in the top two positions.

That added even more spice to the contest two weeks later when the Pies visited Punt Road to take on the Tigers, because whichever team won was almost certain to finish in top spot, giving it the right to challenge should it lose either of its finals. Unlike the Geelong contest, this one didn't disappoint.

The Pies began brilliantly, despite kicking into a swirling wind, and Syd Coventry goaled inside the first minute. But Richmond slowly gained the ascendancy and ended the first term 15 points to the good. When it came Collingwood's turn to kick with the wind, they produced a blitzkrieg of attacking football. The Tigers seemed powerless to halt their opponents' progress as the Magpies, teaming together superbly, peppered their goals and kept the home team scoreless. Only some wayward kicking – the Woods added 4.8 for the term – kept the margin to a respectable 17 points at half-time.

Collingwood paid for its profligacy in the third quarter as Richmond kicked into gear, adding two goals inside two minutes. Suddenly the difference was

The feisty and fearsome George Clayden leaves a trail of Carlton players in his wake in Round 9 at Victoria Park.

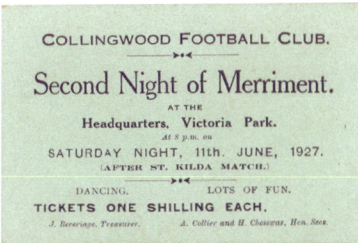

PLAYER OF THE YEAR
Syd Coventry

It's hard to imagine a player coming into a season under more pressure than Syd Coventry in 1927. Filling the shoes of a popular and capable captain who was dumped just days before the season started can't have been easy.

But you'd never have known it from the way Syd responded. He was easily Collingwood's best and most consistent player of the season, and was a worthy winner of the first-ever Copeland Trophy. He showed outstanding leadership throughout, but also played such brilliant football in the ruck and defence that he also won the Brownlow Medal. And to cap off a stunning season he was best-on-ground in the grand final.

Kickero, from *The Herald*, rated Coventry as the number one player in the competition, describing him as 'a player of dogged determination, fearless, fair, good tempered and capable in the highest degree, whether following or in the last line of defence'. The *Argus* agreed, tagging him 'the hero of the season'. 'He dominated . . . completely with his wonderful play. At times [he] rose to phenomenal heights and he was the main factor in winning the Premiership.'

just five points, and the massive Punt Road crowd was roaring. Billy Libbis settled the visitors with an invaluable goal into the wind, but the relief was short-lived as the Tigers grabbed two more late goals to lead by two points at the last change. The Magpies were still favourites, coming home with the wind, and things seemed to be going to script when Harry Rumney goaled to reclaim the lead inside the first minute. But the Tigers obviously hadn't read that script, because Jack Huggard kicked a quick reply to put the home team two points up again. The see-sawing battle had the crowd in full voice, but the Woods grabbed a decisive break with back-to-back goals from Rumney, following a brilliant run out of defence by 'Bottles' Chesswas, and Harry Collier. Then George Clayden and Chesswas added late goals to seal a hugely important win – made even more impressive by the fact that Gordon Coventry had been held goalless for the only time in the season.

Having accounted for their three main rivals in a month, Syd Coventry was feeling understandably contented. 'How does the old song go – "It's fine to be the leaders in the band",' he said. 'That's how it is for me just now, as the Magpies are the leaders and that's what we hope to be from now right up to the day when football shuts up shop this season.'

After a ruthless demolition job on South Melbourne, Collingwood players headed to Western Australia during the interstate carnival break for another of the club's team-bonding trips. The Collingwood administration had helped fund the holiday through a number of novel activities, including an athletics carnival at Victoria Park featuring attractions such as 'a lecturette on wrestling' by world champion light-heavyweight wrestler Sam Clapham. Club treasurer and VFL delegate Bob Rush made an extraordinary appeal to the League *not* to choose Collingwood players in the Victorian team, arguing that a depleted Magpie team would be the cause of 'great disappointment' in Perth. But the League ignored Rush's request and the Coventry brothers were selected for Victoria, while their teammates boarded a train and headed west.

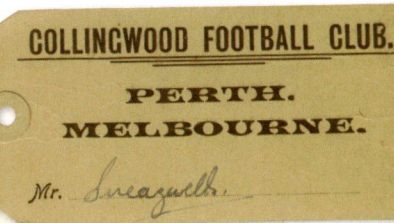

Opposite: **Bill Sneazwell takes a tumble against St Kilda.**
Below: **For many players, the trip to Western Australia in August was a career highlight.**

The band of players and officials, along with some prominent supporters, left Melbourne on the Monday after the South Melbourne game with 'the delight of schoolboys on their annual holidays'. They took the train across the Nullarbor, and were welcomed on Friday morning at Perth Railway Station by a large crowd. They spent the next week enjoying a range of dinners and social excursions. They also played two games against combined Western Australian teams (for one win and one loss), before boarding a steamship for the journey home.

Many of the players, most of whom had rarely ventured out of Melbourne, later described the holiday as one of the highlights of their career, and they retained friendships made on it for the rest of their lives. Even the notoriously hard-to-please Jock McHale branded the trip the best he'd been on.

The club always believed that the bonds formed by players and officials during that fortnight were a key factor in the successes that were to come. But the early signs after the team's return were not encouraging.

Respected sporting correspondent Jack Worrall, of *The Australasian*, had warned before the players left that mid-season trips could work against clubs as much as they could benefit them. There were risks, he felt, in long periods of train and boat travel and socialising. His warnings seemed prescient when the Magpies played Fitzroy a few days after getting home. This was a game Collingwood was expected to win, but the Pies were blown away by nine goals to three in the second half as the players tired badly. Most of them had put on a little weight during the break: one was said to have returned a stone heavier! One of the players later candidly admitted he was so tired he'd 'have given a quid for a sleep at three quarter-time'.

Not surprisingly, Connor's bulletin board messages were savage. When the weary players fronted training the week after the Fitzroy game they were greeted by this assessment. 'Do you realise the seriousness of that defeat? Are you going to allow history of the past two seasons to be repeated by failure at the critical time? Loss of the 1927 premiership would be the greatest blow which could be given the club and a repetition of Saturday's performance means premiership suicide. Buck up. Pull yourselves together.'

With only two weeks until the finals, some at the club questioned whether the players would regain their spark in time. Those concerns became serious at half-time of the penultimate game of the season against Essendon. Collingwood went to the long break without having kicked a single goal, its meagre tally of 0.4 telling a sorry tale. It wasn't much better at the last break, trailing 1.8 to 4.6 on a wildly windy day. Luckily the Pies managed to hold Essendon scoreless in the last term and scraped their way to a one-point victory, thanks to a late behind kicked by wingman Charlie Milburn after he had spectacularly managed to evade three opponents.

Below: **The mighty Coventrys of Collingwood, as depicted in** Table Talk **magazine.**
Opposite: **Bill Libbis in action against Geelong in the semifinal, while Jiggy Harris gets some running repairs from the trainer in the same game.**

That was the lucky break the team needed. A relatively comfortable win over North the next week, despite a second-quarter scare, enabled the Pies to finish in top spot. They would take on third-placed Geelong in the second semi-final, while second-placed Richmond would face Carlton, who had finished fourth. But finals preparations were momentarily overshadowed when the VFL announced that Syd Coventry had become the fourth man to win the League's highest individual honour, the Brownlow Medal. 'Bravo Syd', the bulletin board said that week. 'You're a credit to the club. Heartiest congratulations from your club mates.' To complete a rare family double, Syd's brother Gordon had topped the VFL goalkicking with 88 goals – and still the finals to come.

Richmond won their semi against Carlton, by just a goal. Collingwood started as slight underdogs against Geelong the following week, with critics concerned about the Magpies' post-Western Australia form and convinced the Cats had the pace to trouble the ladder leaders. Instead it was the Pies who delivered a 66-point demolition job

1927: Whatever it takes

that made the supposedly speedier Geelong look slow, fumbling and distinctly second rate.

It was a bleak day, windy and freezing cold, with plenty of showers. But the Magpies' blistering performance was enough to warm the hearts of all their fans. They piled on five goals from 11 scoring shots in a scintillating first term, then held Geelong to just two behinds while adding four goals into the wind in the second. At half-time it was 9.10 to 1.2, and a quarter later an even more emphatic 13.15 to 2.4. Geelong, said one reporter 'were annihilated, being eclipsed at every point from start to finish'. Gordon Coventry kicked a lazy seven goals to take his tally to 95 in what was overall a stunning team performance.

It was hardly surprising, then, that brother Syd exuded confidence after the match, saying he 'did not have a moment's anxiety about the result' and predicting his boys would beat Richmond the following week. Under the challenge-based finals system still in operation, Richmond had to defeat Collingwood on successive Saturdays to win the flag. 'I fancy there'll be no need for a grand final this year', Syd predicted.

On the eve of the final against Richmond the heavens opened with such force that, for a time, the match faced the serious possibility of being postponed. By Saturday morning the VFA preliminary final had been called off. It rained

The Australasian

Jack Worrall on the semi-final win over Geelong:

Collingwood excelled in all phases of play in all parts of the field. Its men know the game better, were decidedly faster and cleverer in manipulation, had better judgement, passed with greater skill and certainty, excelled in the air and in kicking and... were decidedly stronger in muscular power, in addition to scouting out with an intuition that was absolutely lacking in Geelong ranks.

How the cartoonist Ward, from *Table Talk*, saw the Collingwood players.

Below: The hardy crowd braved appalling conditions to watch the 1927 Grand Final. **Opposite:** Players fumble and struggle for the ball on the waterlogged MCG.

solidly – and torrentially – from Friday all through Saturday. The MCG was completely waterlogged, with one wing under water. A journalist commented that it was 'more suitable for an aquatic carnival than for football'. To make things worse the wind was bitterly cold. It was one of the worst days imaginable to be playing football.

But Collingwood remained determined to win. 'Never have the Magpie players been as keyed up by the intention to win a Premiership as they have been all season,' wrote Kickero, in *The Herald*. And they weren't going to let freezing cold and incessant rain get in the way. Coach McHale told his men to keep things simple: marks were to be taken on the chest, not in the hands, while the ball was to be kicked off the ground wherever possible.

Richmond won the toss and kicked with the wind (or 'with the tide', as one wag in the crowd put it), hoping to get a couple of quick goals on the board before the ball got too heavy. But after a few minutes the game degenerated into what looked like a mud-coated arm wrestle as players slipped, slid and sloshed their way around the sodden turf. The match was spiteful and fists flew surreptitiously as huge packs developed. It was clear from the beginning that this game was likely to be decided not so much by system or skill but by strength, toughness and stamina – all areas where Collingwood fancied it had a decided advantage, thanks to the work of veteran trainer Wal Lee and his colleagues.

Neither side scored a goal in the opening quarter. The rain pelted down even harder in the second, and after Collingwood had forced the ball forward with

a succession of soccer kicks, Gordon Coventry marked and finally kicked the game's first goal. Richmond players made the mistake of trying to pick up the ball and Collingwood hit them hard. They also made the error of defending to the Magpies' attacking flank, and the Pies made them pay late in the term when Nuts snapped a second goal just before half-time to take his season tally to 97 and give the Magpies a half-time lead of 14 points.

Thousands of fans headed home at half-time to escape the foul conditions. The players had hot showers, massages with warm oil and changed their shorts. Many donned anything warm they could find, meaning some reappeared wearing coloured sweaters under their club jumpers. Richmond began the third term with a fierce attack on the football, and the man, and three Magpie stars were knocked down in the opening minutes. But it was all just bluster, because neither team could find a way to score goals in the mud and slush, and Collingwood maintained its lead at the last change. Richmond finally scored a goal early in the last quarter but never looked like bridging the gap, while the Pies' resolute defence – like the rain – showed no signs of weakening. When the bell rang, to the great relief of the fans who'd remained, the scoreboard showed 2.13 to 1.7.

That was Collingwood's lowest score in a match since 1910, but nobody cared: it was still enough to bring home the flag that mattered so much. The sodden supporters at the MCG were delirious, rushing onto the ground and unsuccessfully trying to hoist Syd Coventry and others onto their shoulders. Some even planted kisses on their favourite players. A local Scottish band 'serenaded' the Magpies back to

PLAYER OF THE YEAR
Gordon Coventry

The VFL's magical 100-goal barrier remained frustratingly out of reach at the end of 1927 – but only due to Melbourne's notoriously fickle weather.

If the rain that deluged the MCG on and before grand final day had held off for another couple of days, then Gordon Coventry would surely have broken the 100-goal milestone in this year. As it was, the two goals he did kick in the decider were worth their weight in gold, because they brought Collingwood a flag. But they weren't quite enough to reach the ton, and Nuts finished on an agonisingly close tally of 97.

Coventry was close to unstoppable in 1927. Two bags of 11, two others of eight and a semi-final haul of seven against Geelong signalled the arrival of a player who had been promising great things for several years. And as we now know, the best was still to come.

their dressing rooms, where there was a mad rush to congratulate the players on their wonderful achievement. There were 21 (yes, 21) speeches in the rooms, and the crush was so great to get to the dressing room door that many leading supporters and some officials were unable to get in.

McHale spoke glowingly about his team, forecasting that it had such a good blend of youth and experience that there was a good chance of another tilt at the premiership the following year. The coach said he considered this to be one of the best teams to have ever represented the club. Syd Coventry had starred yet again on grand final day, and he'd been well supported by the unheralded Bob Makeham, 'Jiggy' Harris and Percy Rowe, as well as stars like Harry Collier, Frank Murphy, Billy Libbis and Jack Beveridge.

Amongst all the delight, there was also relief – and vindication. The small band of officials, including Curtis, Connor, McHale and other committee members who had decided to replace Tyson with Syd Coventry six months earlier, could finally breathe more easily. Their actions, however ruthless, however cruel, had been justified. Collingwood had the flag it so desperately wanted. McHale had already noted that he thought the club would again be in premiership contention in 12 months time. That would prove to be a mighty understatement.

ERNIE WILSON
GRAND FINAL HERO

The 1927 Grand Final was a day for hard, tough players playing hard, tough footy. And that's the way Ernie 'Sugar' Wilson liked it.

The sole survivor of Collingwood's 1919 flag side, Wilson was a tiny ball of muscle with big shoulders, exceptionally strong legs and a willingness to dash fearlessly off half-back. He loved nothing more than being in a scrap, and regularly annoyed opposition fans with his hard-at-it approach. But Magpie fans loved him for the whole-hearted way he played.

On grand final day, Wilson was part of a magnificent defensive unit that continually held Richmond at bay in the shocking conditions. He turned back many Tiger attacks, working well with Syd Coventry, Charlie Dibbs and Albert Collier, and launched just as many the other way with aggressive runs out of defence.

True to form, he also finished the game bleeding from a deep cut above his eye. And that's just the way Sugar would have liked it.

PLAYERS

#	Player	Games	Goals
5	George Beasley	6	2
2	Jack Beveridge	20	3
10	Harry Chesswas	16	5
11	George Clayden	12	2
4	Albert Collier	19	2
5	Harry Collier	20	36
7	Gordon Coventry	20	97
8	Syd Coventry	20	3
12	Charlie Dibbs	19	0
11	John Harris	20	13
29	Les Hughson	1	1
13	Albert Lauder	1	0
14	Billy Libbis	20	15
16	Norm MacLeod	3	0
15	Bob Makeham	20	3
16	Charlie Milburn	16	1
18	Clarrie Morelli	7	1
19	Bob Muir	3	0
20	Frank Murphy	20	20
18	Joe Poulter	18	11
28	Hector Ross	2	0
22	Percy Rowe	17	6
23	Trevor Rowlands	2	0
24	Harold Rumney	17	19
27	Bill Sneazwell	10	0
26	Leo Wescott	20	0
24	Ernie Wilson	11	0

Club Awards
Copeland trophy – Syd Coventry
Runner-up – Harry Collier
Third – Bill Libbis
Most consistent play – Harry Collier (travel bag)
Best player – Syd Coventry (a hat)
Best first season player – Harry Rumney (a hat)
Wal Lee Trophy for regular attendance at training – Jiggy Harris
Training prize – Leo Wescott
Other training awards – 17 players
Austral Cup (donated by the Austral Theatre) – Jiggy Harris
Leading goalkicker – Gordon Coventry (97)

1927 SEASON

ROUND 1 April 30 Victoria Park
Collingwood 16.11.107 v Geelong **12.12.84**
Goals: G Coventry 8, H Collier 4, Rumney 2, Libbis, Murphy

ROUND 2 May 7 Glenferrie Oval
Hawthorn **7.9.51** v **Collingwood 11.11.77**
Goals: G Coventry 4, H Collier 2, Poulter 2, Rumney 2, Harris

ROUND 3 May 14 Victoria Park
Collingwood **6.13.49** v **Richmond 7.13.55**
Goals: G Coventry 4, H Collier, Rowe

ROUND 4 May 21 Lake Oval
South Melbourne **9.13.67** v **Collingwood 16.10.106**
Goals: G Coventry 4, H Collier 3, Beasley 2, Murphy 2, Rumney 2, Harris, Libbis, Poulter

ROUND 5 May 28 Victoria Park
Collingwood 18.15.123 v Fitzroy **9.5.59**
Goals: G Coventry 11, Harris 3, Libbis 2, Rowe, Rumney

ROUND 6 June 4 Windy Hill
Essendon **7.7.49** v **Collingwood 7.14.56**
Goals: Rumney 3, H Collier 2, G Coventry 2

ROUND 7 June 11 Victoria Park
Collingwood 25.19.169 v St Kilda **7.15.57**
Goals: G Coventry 11, Rumney 4, H Collier 3, Harris 3, Murphy 3, Rowe

ROUND 8 June 18 Whitten Oval
Footscray **4.12.36** v **Collingwood 7.16.58**
Goals: G Coventry 4, H Collier 2, Rumney

ROUND 9 June 25 Victoria Park
Collingwood **13.5.83** v **Carlton 14.11.95**
Goals: G Coventry 4, H Collier 3, Beveridge 2, Murphy 2, S Coventry, Rowe

ROUND 10 July 2 Victoria Park
Collingwood 8.11.59 v North Melbourne **3.11.29**
Goals: G Coventry 3, A Collier, H Collier, Libbis, Morelli, Murphy

ROUND 11 July 9 MCG
Melbourne **10.12.72** v **Collingwood 11.13.79**
Goals: G Coventry 5, Libbis 3, Chesswas, H Collier, Makeham

ROUND 12 July 16 Corio Oval
Geelong **7.7.49** v **Collingwood 9.11.65**
Goals: G Coventry 4, H Collier, Libbis, Milburn, Murphy, Poulter

ROUND 13 July 23 Victoria Park
Collingwood 18.13.121 v Hawthorn **6.11.47**
Goals: G Coventry 8, Muphry 2, Poulter 2, Beveridge, A Collier, S Coventry, Harris, Hughson, Rowe

ROUND 14 July 30 Punt Rd Oval
Richmond **9.7.61** v **Collingwood 12.12.84**
Goals: Chesswas 2, Clayden 2, Harris 2, Rumney 2, H Collier, S Coventry, Libbis, Murphy

ROUND 15 August 6 Victoria Park
Collingwood 18.14.122 v South Melbourne **6.7.43**
Goals: G Coventry 6, Libbis 3, Poulter 3, H Collier 2, Chesswas, Harris, Murph, Rumney

ROUND 16 August 27 Brunswick St Oval
Fitzroy **14.11.95** v Collingwood **13.10.88**
Goals: G Coventry 4, Murphy 3, H Collier 2, Libbis, Makeham, Poulter, Rumney

ROUND 17 September 3 Victoria Park
Collingwood 3.13.31 v Essendon **4.6.30**
Goals: H Collier, G Coventry, Murphy

ROUND 18 September 10 Arden St Oval
North Melbourne **7.14.56** v **Collingwood 11.16.82**
Goals: G Coventry 5, H Collier 3, Chesswas, Makeham, Poulter

1927 FINALS

LADDER

Team	Won	Lost	Draw	For	Agst	%	Pts
Collingwood	15	3	0	1559	1035	150.6	60
Richmond	14	4	0	1483	1102	134.6	56
Geelong	14	4	0	1594	1208	132.0	56
Carlton	13	5	0	1434	1178	121.7	52
Melbourne	12	6	0	1548	1169	132.4	48
South Melb	9	9	0	1373	1431	95.9	36
St Kilda	8	10	0	1178	1564	75.3	32
Essendon	6	11	1	1198	1237	96.8	26
Fitzroy	6	11	1	1335	1558	85.7	26
Footscray	6	12	0	1131	1325	85.4	24
North Melb	3	15	0	1085	1476	73.5	12
Hawthorn	1	17	0	1087	1722	63.1	4

SEMI FINAL September 24   MCG

Collingwood 16.18.114 v Geelong **7.6.48**

Goals: G Coventry 7, H Collier 4, Murphy 2, Harris, Libbis, Rowe

GRAND FINAL October 1   MCG

Collingwood	0.1	2.6	2.9	2.13	(25)
Richmond	0.4	0.4	0.7	1.7	(13)

Goals: G. Coventry 2
Best: S Coventry, Makeham, Murphy, Wilson, Beveridge, Rowe, H Collier
Umpire: McMurray senior
Crowd: 34,551

Grand Final Team
B: L. Wescott, C. Dibbs, J. Poulter
HB: E. Wilson, G. Clayden, A. Collier
C: H. Chesswas, J. Beveridge, C. Milburn
HF: F. Murphy, R. Makeham, J. Harris
F: H. Rumney, G. Coventry, H. Collier
R: S. Coventry (c), P. Rowe, W. Libbis

CHAPTER EIGHT
1928
Band of brothers

'Can Richmond stand up to the strain and fight back like our fellows when they get behind? I do not think so. Collingwood will be premiers all right.'

The Mightiest Magpies

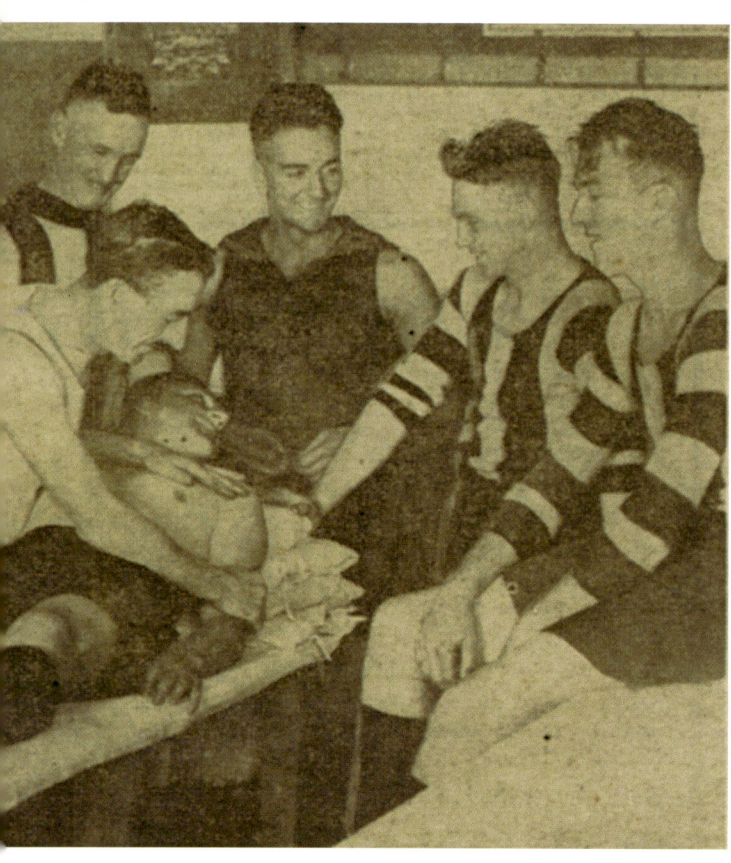

Trainer A Longden goes to work on Harry Lauder while Jock McHale, George Beasley, Harry Collier and Les Hughson look on.

The contrast could not have been more stark. A year before, the club's annual meeting had been marked by angry confrontations, heated exchanges and disgruntled members tearing up their seasons tickets in protest. But in March 1928 the mood is buoyant, and those same fans are now cheering their heroes. They see VFL president Dr W. McClelland present the club with its 1927 pennant and the players with their premiership medals. There is a mad crush inside the Collingwood Town Hall when the players appear on stage. An elderly man is almost knocked over by the wave of worshippers rushing to get close to the champions. Another clambers on to the stage to shake hands with Syd and Gordon Coventry, then almost breaks his neck trying to get back down. It is chaos. But the Magpies are champions, and everyone is happy.

The mood does not stay that way for long, though, as the club endures a troubled 1928 season. There is a threatened players' strike, contentious pay cuts in the worsening economic situation, allegations of bribery against players, a slur on the club's name over a shock loss, an injury list that leaves the team undermanned and a late-season form slump. These would have crippled the premiership defence of a less resilient club. But not Collingwood.

Only two members of the 1927 Premiership team were missing, with speedy wingman Charlie Milburn and reliable defender Leo Wescott both having accepted country coaching offers too good to refuse. Coach McHale had already identified Norm MacLeod, who'd played three games in 1927, as a replacement for Milburn, while another youngster from the seconds, Percy Bowyer, was slated to take over from Wescott. Another important addition to the list was Len Murphy, the younger brother of the club's talented centre half-forward, Frank. Williamstown refused to clear Murphy and the VFA disqualified him when he resolved to play for Collingwood anyway. But the ban was incidental, and did not stop the big, raw-boned 18-year-old from crossing to Victoria Park.

Bowyer, MacLeod and Murphy were all named in the senior side for the Round 1 game against Geelong at Corio Oval – a piece of fixturing that angered Magpie officials, who felt they shouldn't have to wait until the second round to once again hoist a premiership flag at Victoria Park. McHale tried to blow away any early-season cobwebs by making the players walk from the train to the ground, but it didn't seem to work as the Pies couldn't kick a goal in the first quarter of the season and trailed by 17 points at half-time after an hour of exciting, free-flowing football. The third term saw a stirring fightback from the Pies, with Jiggy Harris starring on a wing and Gordon Coventry a constant threat in the goal square. They led by four points at the last change.

The final quarter was a beauty. Geelong peppered the goals early but could manage only a string of behinds, including a poster, before Tom Fitzmaurice goaled to put them in front. Gordon Coventry reclaimed a one-point lead for the Pies after taking a strong mark in a big pack of players, then Warren hit back for the home team. Both teams then added behinds before Harris broke away and hit Coventry on the chest with a stab pass to set up the fourth lead change for the term. There was desperate defence from both sides with the Woods leading by just a point, before a late goal from – who else? – Coventry sealed the result. It had been a pulsating final quarter, and journalists described it as one of the best opening round matches seen in years. Percy Rowe (ribs) and George Beasley (knee) suffered serious injuries, a portent of the year to come.

Twenty-five thousand fans turned out at Victoria Park the following week for the unfurling of the premiership flag before the match against Fitzroy. Fans milled around the ground long before the start of the game, desperate to gain admittance. The club sold a record 1300 memberships on that day alone – no mean feat, given that so many Magpie fans were already beginning to feel the first bites of the Depression. The players put on a good show, cruising to a comfortable win on the back of nine goals from Gordon Coventry. Brother Syd gave an ominous warning after the match to the chasing pack: 'I think we are going to be harder to beat for the premiership this season. Perhaps the sight of that 1927 pennant fluttering in the breeze did the job, for the boys went to work with a thoroughness and cohesion that Fitzroy could not counter.'

The Mightiest Magpies

Right: **Harry Collier goals on the run against Fitzroy on the day the 1927 premiership flag was unfurled.**
Below: **Young fan Peter Martin shows his true colours.**

Richmond had no such problems, though, and upset the Magpies the very next week, using both fair means and foul to triumph by two points in a rugged battle. Collingwood had a chance to wrench back the game at the death when Frank Murphy had a late shot from close in, but he could only manage a point. McHale and the committee were furious that the team had lost after leading at every change, and they were also incensed by what they felt was the unfair attention Gordon Coventry had received from his opponents.

A few weeks later, Collingwood faced Carlton in a crunch game at Princes Park. The two teams were sharing second place on the ladder, and there was a big build-up to the contest. The Pies went in without the injured Syd Coventry, missing his first match since becoming captain, and his teammates only just snuck home in yet another nail-biting finish – their third in the first seven games. The Magpies blitzed early with a six-goal first quarter that featured some brilliant passages of play, but somehow found themselves behind at half-time after Carlton hit back in the second. A scintillating six-goal third quarter gave the Pies a seemingly safe 29-point cushion at the last change. But Carlton attacked hard in the last quarter, and closed to within less than a goal with two minutes to go. Had Harry Davie been able to hold on to a low, stooping mark in the final seconds, the Blues would probably have emerged with the points.

Syd returned to the side for the next round, which was played just two days later on King's Birthday Monday. The VFL had scheduled full rounds of matches for both Saturday and Monday. That was enough to stretch the resources even of clubs with fit and healthy lists, let alone Collingwood, which was experiencing a horror run of injuries. George Beasley's knee injury essentially ended his VFL career, while Percy Rowe's ribs were causing him problems. Harold Rumney had damaged an ankle, Len Murphy and Syd Coventry shoulders and many others were carrying niggling injuries into matches. Even secretary George Connor succumbed to the injury curse, dislocating his shoulder when caught in a crush of fans on the train to Geelong.

The King's Birthday schedule meant all clubs played three games in eight days, so there were some tired players on both sides by the time the Pies took on the unbeaten Melbourne in the battle for top spot. On the day that Charles Kingsford Smith and Charles Ulm steered the *Southern Cross* into Brisbane

When a newspaper revealed Syd Coventry's nasty case of boils, he was approached by the manufacturers of a tonic designed to assist athletes suffering from boils and 'nerves'. A little later the Magpie skipper featured in a quaint advertisement spruiking its benefits.

Below: **Timekeepers Manning and Keating looking after the match day bell at Victoria Park.** Bottom: **Collingwood's trusty team of trainers, headed by veteran Wal Lee (front).**

after becoming the first airmen to cross the Pacific Ocean, the two teams put on a show befitting their lofty ladder positions. It was a fast, high quality, see-sawing contest, and Collingwood's defence had to hold on grimly in the last quarter for a two-goal win. Bob Makeham (5 goals) and Billy Libbis (4) starred.

Collingwood was now top of the ladder at the half-way point of the season, and should have been preparing its assault on September and a second straight premiership. Instead the players found themselves confronting their biggest challenge of the year – and it came from within.

Just hours before the Round 12 game against Geelong at Victoria Park, the team learned that the committee had decided to cut players' wages from three pounds per game to two pounds and 10 shillings. The club felt the looming Depression justified the decision. Most of the players did not: they just felt angry and betrayed. There was still a game to play, however, and the players took to the field with emotions running high. They lost to Geelong by 11 points, but the loss could not be blamed solely on the reaction to the proposed pay cuts; Rowe and Wilson were injured and out of the game before the end of the first quarter, and two more players were lame before game's end. In the circumstances, it was a brave effort.

On the Tuesday night after the Geelong game the players met behind closed doors to discuss what action they would take to fight the club's proposals. The fiery meeting saw Ernie Wilson, the longest-serving player at the club, put

forward a motion that they refuse to play for the reduced amount. The motion gained plenty of support, perhaps a bit surprising given the nature of this group of Collingwood men. Some of the younger players, or those who had outside jobs, were less worried by the prospect of cuts, but the team's senior players, most of whom were family men, were far more aggrieved. For much of the meeting, it appeared the players would go on strike.

Then Syd Coventry stepped in. He'd earlier said he would support the majority decision, but as the meeting moved closer to strike action, he could not help but intervene. He understood his teammates' frustrations, but he also knew the likely ramifications of strike action. The team spirit and mateship that were such an important part of the Machine would be threatened, the players' good names would be tarnished and the club itself would be damaged. Such was the respect for Coventry that his arguments convinced the players to cop the pay cuts – however unpalatable they might have been.

It was around this time that the Collingwood Council decided to commit to a new grandstand for Victoria Park. The Council took advantage of 1200 pounds in government grants from programs set aside to promote capital works carried out by the unemployed, and borrowed a further 8000 pounds to complete the project funding. The grandstand would be built by many unemployed locals and was scheduled to be ready for the opening of the 1929 season.

Remarkably, the pay wars had no apparent on-field repercussions. The team carried on, lighter in the pocket, but seemingly more determined than ever to win another flag. The week after their stop-work meeting, they produced a performance of rare courage and team spirit to demolish Fitzroy, despite once again suffering injuries and finishing with only 16 men on the field for the second game in a row. The *Sporting Globe* said the Magpies had 'upheld their tradition for doggedness and courage in the face of adversity'. Collingwood's plight in this match prompted many to call for the introduction of a reserve player in the VFL.

The break for the interstate match came when Collingwood needed it most. Bowyer, Wilson, Rowe, Frank Murphy, Muir and MacLeod were all injured, as were Syd Coventry and Albert Collier, who could not be considered for Victorian selection against Western Australia. Instead it was Charlie Dibbs, Harry Collier and Gordon Coventry who pulled on the Big V. But Collier and Coventry were

PLAYER OF THE YEAR

Charlie Dibbs

Charlie Dibbs was one of the quiet achievers of the Collingwood teams of the 1920s and 1930s.

He played more than 200 games across 12 seasons and held down the crucial full-back post in six grand final sides – five of which produced Collingwood premierships. He was a no-frills, no-fuss player who played it close, tight and disciplined, making life hell for opposition full-forwards. He preferred to punch rather than mark, and was a safety-first cornerstone of the defence. He was also a magnificent kick, his long, raking drop kicks frequently turning defence into attack.

In 1928, Dibbs was at his best. He was one of only a handful of players to take the field in every game, and he did not put in a poor showing all season. He was rewarded with his first Victorian jumper, and also a special award for 'excellent services rendered to the club'.

But one of the best things about Charlie Dibbs was his consistency – there was not much gap between his best and worst. So while 1928 might have been his best season, he kept giving Collingwood great service until his final game in the black and white, in the 1935 grand final.

Syd Coventry (right) was confident heading into the 1928 finals.

also injured on state duty, the big full-forward copping a knock to the ear that would plague him for the rest of the year.

The players who weren't pulling on Victorian jumpers used the break to recover and recuperate, while the club took the opportunity to repay some favours from 1927, hosting the East Fremantle club with a car trip and picnic down to Mornington. When the VFL competition resumed, the refreshed Magpies had fewer players in the medical room and more back in training.

Collingwood's confidence was growing, so much so that Syd Coventry penned a candid article in *The Sporting Globe*, extolling the virtues of the team and forecasting another premiership. He said he had been confident of the 1927 flag right throughout that season, and was even more confident that the club would triumph again in 1928, because he felt the 1928 Pies were a 50 per cent better team than the 1927 model. Coventry held a strong belief that the team was everything in football, and hated singling out specific players for attention. But he named no fewer than 18 of his teammates in this article, and claimed he feared no side in the competition. 'I have a wholesome respect for Melbourne on their own ground . . . but cannot see them beating us this season. Richmond promises to be dangerous. I think they will be our most serious rival. Yet can Richmond stand up to the strain and fight back like our fellows when they get behind? I do not think so. Collingwood will be premiers all right.'

It was an extraordinary display of bravado from Collingwood's skipper, and it's hard to imagine any club allowing it in today's football. But his confidence seemed justified: five successive wins had guaranteed Collingwood top spot – and the double chance – leading into the final-round clash with Carlton at Victoria Park. With the Magpies safe as minor premiers, and the Blues needing to win to grab fourth spot, there were plenty of fans doubting whether the Pies would have the motivation to go in as hard as usual. Some took it further, and rumours swirled throughout the football world that the Pies would 'lie down' and be easily beaten. Major newspapers reported the scuttlebutt, saying that no match for years had been subject to such 'rumour and talk'. The *Sporting Globe* noted that everyone at Collingwood 'strongly resented these insinuations.'

The Collingwood camp might have resented the insinuations, but the players did nothing to prove them wrong. Instead, Carlton led from the start against a lethargic Magpie outfit, and the home side were booed off when they eventually left the field, having lost by 20 points. The excuse from the rooms after the game was that the team had 'grown stale'. Others were less charitable. There were allegations that two Collingwood players were paid 50 pounds to perform poorly that afternoon. The allegations were never proved, but Syd Coventry admitted later he had been offered a similar bribe and had instantly knocked it back. Coventry joked that he might as well have taken it because his form had been so poor. Money *had* been offered in the Carlton rooms, where club officials offered their players an extra three pounds each as an incentive to win and make the finals. The chance to secure a finals berth, the promise of double pay and an unmotivated Collingwood all combined to cause the upset result.

Remarkably, some critics – including Carlton skipper Horrie Clover – were quick to write off Collingwood in the wake of that last-round performance. They must have been ready to eat their words at three-quarter-time of the second semi against Melbourne two weeks later, when the resurgent Pies led by a seemingly unassailable 32 points, having played some outstanding

The SPORTING GLOBE

'Jumbo' Sharland on the Carlton game in the final round:

Had a stranger from another state casually visited the Collingwood ground on Saturday, he would have been entitled to the opinion that Collingwood were not taking the game seriously. In no other game this season have they played with such apparent indifference and lack of devil . . . in the 18 there were only a handful of men putting any devil into their work. If Collingwood were not worrying last Saturday, and were saving themselves for the finals, it will do the game no good. My faith in the integrity of Collingwood football was severely shaken last Saturday.

Above: **Genial giant Bob Makeham snaps a goal in the drawn semi-final against Melbourne.**

Opposite: **Harry Collier is heading for a fall during the drawn semi-final against Melbourne, while Gordon Coventry moves in.**

football. But somehow, against the tide of the match, Melbourne staged one of the most remarkable comebacks in finals history. In a finish never to be forgotten, the Red Legs stormed home with the wind and booted 5.2 to nil to level the scores in the dying moments. They'd closed to within a goal with more than 10 minutes to go, and the Magpie defence repelled wave after wave of Melbourne attacks in that time, before finally conceding a goal close to the end.

It was the VFL's first finals draw, and the players didn't know how to react. Jock McHale, though, was ropeable: he felt it was almost inexcusable that his team had squandered such a lead – especially in a final. The replay was much more hard-fought in the opening stages and the margin was always tight. This time the Magpies managed to just sneak past the resolute Red Legs, winning by four points after a stunning last quarter that produced 11 goals from both sides, but they were hardly convincing. Melbourne almost stole the game again in the final seconds and the poor form of so many key Magpies made the club look tired and stale.

Collingwood was most worried by the form of Gordon Coventry, who was in the middle of a major slump. Coventry had enjoyed another fine season, kicking 78 goals for the year heading into the finals. But the sharpshooter had not kicked more than two goals in a game since Round 15. He appeared slow and his usual accuracy had deserted him.

But Coventry hadn't just lost form. It turned out that the knock to the back of the ear he had received in the state game had temporarily affected his balance and made him sluggish to the point where he felt he could hardly move at times. Incredibly, he kept the ailment from everyone other than his doctor, and did not reveal his secret until he and Syd took part in a rare, dual interview with the *Sporting Globe* in 1938. Syd said: 'Well, I'm blessed. That's the first time I've heard that story. He had me worried stiff, he was playing so badly. I couldn't make him out.' Gordon said he was afraid he'd have been dropped from the side if he told the club – or Syd – about the injury. 'A man at Collingwood in those days had to be really crook before

PLAYER OF THE YEAR
Frank Murphy

Frank Murphy first played for Collingwood in 1925 and enjoyed what Gordon Coventry once described as one of the best debut seasons he had ever seen.

Although he was a regular from that point, Murphy wasn't able to take his game to the next level until 1928. By then his confidence on the field had grown and he became more assertive in his play, a vital ingredient for a centre half-forward. Murphy made huge strides in 1928 and never looked back.

Frank Murphy was a quiet, unassuming man, but he had a profound influence upon the team. He was a talented, highly skilled player whose signature was his football brain – he read the game beautifully, ran to the right places and led intelligently. When he got to the ball, he had good hands that allowed him to take a swag of marks, and he used the ball well on both sides of his body. Gordon Coventry was in no doubt about his importance.

'He was a champion,' Coventry wrote once. 'For ten years he played in front of me, and could take credit for hundreds of the goals I scored.'

PLAYER OF THE YEAR — Harry Collier

In just his second season of VFL football, Harry Collier had finished runner-up in Collingwood's best and fairest voting, and also won an award for most consistent player. In his third season he went one better, becoming only the second player to win the Copeland Trophy.

Collier did so on the back of an outstanding season of high quality, often brilliant football. He was again voted the team's most consistent player and was chosen to represent Victoria for the first of many occasions.

Harry was not especially fast for a rover but he was strong, elusive, a superb ball-handler and an excellent kick with either foot. He was dangerous around goals, and nipped in for 26 majors in 1928, third best for the season.

But Harry brought much more to the team than talent. He was an inspirational and fearless player who threw himself into the fray with total disregard for his own well-being, frequently lifting his teammates with his courage and will to win.

When Bob Rose was in his pomp in the 1950s, supporters used to liken his style of play to that of Harry Collier. There can be no higher praise.

---

he reported a crack,' Gordon said. 'While I was out there they had to look after me, bung ear or no bung ear.'

Both Collingwood and Coventry looked as if they were limping into the final against Richmond. Confidence was flagging, the forwards were sorely out of form and their defenders under siege. Many experts felt Richmond would be too swift in the midfield and too strong in the air. To make matters even more difficult, the opponents had enjoyed the luxury of three weeks off, given the semi-final draw. Richmond was strongly favoured to prevail, with many expecting them to run the Woodsmen off their feet. There were even concerns within the club that the team might be a bit worn out after such a turbulent season.

With that in mind, McHale gave his exhausted players a light workout on the track on the Thursday night before the final, then brought them together in the dressing rooms for a unique think-tank session, years ahead of its time. The team sat down to work out plans for the final.

The players and coaches dissected the Richmond team player by player, line by line. The deficiencies of their opponents were laid out in stark detail. Chief among them was the fact that Richmond seemed almost too confident of winning the premiership. 'Richmond was brimming with confidence,' Syd Coventry said. 'That is a great thing for a side, but it seemed to us that they were just a little too sure of their own ability to dominate the whole field.'

The Pies also suspected a mental fragility in the Tiger camp. So they decided they would try to 'suck in' their opponents through continual goading. As the skipper said: 'Richmond have some fine players, but some of them are very easily annoyed and thrown out of their natural stride, even by jokes made at their expense on the field.' So the Magpies made a conscious decision that they would sledge Richmond players throughout the game, with a view to getting a rise out of their opponents. Steve Waugh would have called it 'mental disintegration'. Collingwood knew this would likely provoke a physical response from the Tigers, but they were determined that, no matter what happened, their own focus would be solely on the ball.

There was, however, more to the Magpie strategy than mere sledging. The meeting had made it a team rule that players would punch the ball unless they were absolutely certain they could mark it. This would shake Richmond's supposed ascendancy in the air, and the team's small men were told to be aware of this and scout the packs at all times. The Pies also decided to regularly change their followers in the first half, rotating a range of big men on the ball for a few minutes at a time, in the hope of confusing the Tigers and keeping their own men fresh.

The Magpie tactics might not have seemed too revolutionary, but within minutes of the game getting underway it became clear that they were working. All over the field, Collingwood players took it up to their Richmond opponents, harassing them both physically and verbally. The Tigers duly took the bait, and both Harry Collier and George Clayden were flattened early in the game (Clayden's assailant received an eight-week suspension for the incident). Sly punches flew and there were plenty of nasty incidents. But through it all, Collingwood kept playing the ball and creating opportunities. Around the ground, the 'punch at all times' mantra denied Richmond's big men the opportunity to dominate in the air, and the frequent rotations of Collingwood's tall timber had their Tiger counterparts struggling to keep up. Just as the Magpies had hoped, Richmond looked confused by the tactics and was unable to counter them. As the *Herald* explained: 'The success of Collingwood's preconceived plan [was] so cleverly camouflaged that at times Richmond aided in its own defeat without being conscious at all.'

Collingwood's plans to intimidate their opponents were personified that day by Percy Rowe, who had spent a month on the sidelines due to injury. He

Above: **The men who brought home the 1928 pennant, pictured on the ground before the game.**
Below: **How the teams lined up.**

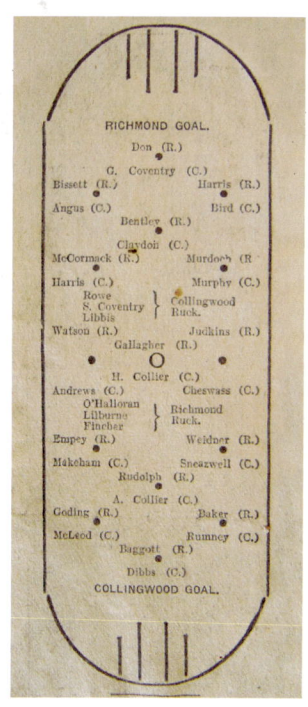

returned to the team in the forward pocket with the sole purpose of providing the out-of-sorts Gordon Coventry with some extra protection. As they took their positions at the start of the game, Rowe told Coventry he would help him to kick 'a bagful', and promised that the Richmond defenders would not know what had hit them when he'd finished with them. Rowe was true to his word. He blocked, bumped and harassed the Tiger defenders to the point of distraction. He psyched them out both physically and verbally and simply refused to let them anywhere near the champion full-forward, getting bruised and battered all over.

The first of Coventry's bagful came just before quarter-time, helping to set up a 13-point lead at the first break. Collingwood had dominated much of the term, keeping Richmond goalless, and probably should have been further in front. The game had been tight and tough, with plenty of bruising clashes, but the Pies split it wide open in the second quarter with a paralysing burst of four goals in 10 minutes. The Coventry-Rowe combination was dominating, with the full-forward booting four of his team's five goals for the term and helping to open up a 21-point half-time lead. The game wasn't a great spectacle, but Collingwood fans didn't care: their team was playing its best football in weeks.

While Richmond managed to reduce the deficit to 16 points by the last change, they never really looked a serious threat to the Magpies, and goals to Gordon Coventry and Bob Makeham early in the last quarter sealed the win. With the result secured, Collingwood turned on the style and played the best

Above: **Percy Rowe was one of the stars of Collingwood's grand final win. He spent much of the game alongside Gordon Coventry, as illustrated in the picture below.**
Opposite: **Gordon Coventry in full flight, again being protected by Percy Rowe, and kicking one of his record-breaking nine goals in the grand final.**

football of the match, clearing away to win by 33 points. *The Australasian*'s Jack Worrall said the Pies 'enthralled the crowd with as glorious a display of football as has been seen for many a day'. 'The black and white players were so fresh, so eager, so brimful of life and dash, so spectacular in every branch of play that they were wildly cheered from every part of the ground,' he wrote. Coventry finished with nine of Collingwood's 13 goals, the best tally by any player in a premiership play-off match. It would be another 61 years before Geelong's mercurial Gary Ablett Snr, would match it.

Magpie fans were exultant when the game finished, and they invaded the ground to pat their heroes on the back. Fittingly, Syd Coventry was the centre of attention, though the captain was said to be 'the quietest spoken and calmest of them all . . . only his smiling eyes and lips told of his delight.' Syd was especially proud of his brother Gordon, and the work of Percy Rowe, who he said was 'worth his weight in gold'. Secretary Connor was so taken by Gordon's performance that he presented him with an 1820 sovereign.

The win was a great boost to the people of Collingwood. The Great Depression was already biting, but for now, at least, supporters could forget about their troubles and enjoy another premiership. The team itself did not exactly go over the top in its celebrations. A number of the younger players called in for a milkshake at Don Taylor's milk bar near the Collingwood Town Hall before they headed off for a night at the Austral Theatre to watch one of the latest shows. 'Few of us were drinkers in those days,' recalled Bruce Andrew, a youngster elevated from the seconds after the Geelong loss when McHale decided the team needed more speed. 'I could count the chaps who had a beer in that 1928 team on one hand. But we had a good night.'

The Australasian

Jack Worrall on a great team effort:

What makes Collingwood a dreaded and masterly band when in playing condition and on the warpath is that it is so well disciplined and balanced that it can be depended upon in any set of circumstances... and as is invariably the case in industrial districts, the combination is not only a band of footballers, but practically a band of brothers, who assist each other in whatever crisis may arise, and who fight for the honour of their district and club with a whole-souled devotion that compels admiration and respect.

McMurtrie Boots tried to cash in on Collingwood's premiership victory, while the club also produced its own souvenirs, like this matchbox holder.

The club's celebrations culminated with a trip to Mornington a few weeks later. There, the season that had produced hurdle after hurdle provided one final one. For a time it appeared as if the career of 20-year-old Bruce Andrew, the team's best first-year player, would be tragically cut short after he jumped into the water, hit a shallow sandbank and fractured his neck. Doctors initially feared Andrew would be crippled for life. They wrapped him in plaster from the waist up and left that on for 12 weeks. Andrew spent months recovering in hospital but, incredibly, was there when the flag was unfurled in Round 1 of 1929.

Nothing, it seemed, could stop the Collingwood Machine.

PERCY ROWE — GRAND FINAL HERO

The 1928 grand final was Percy Rowe's 96th and final game with the Collingwood Football Club. He could not have picked a better game, or a better way, to leave League football.

Rowe was loved, admired and respected by his teammates. A hulk of a man, regarded as one of the toughest and most selfless players in the VFL, he was always prepared to do the hard work and cop the knocks in ruck contests. He was renowned as a protector of young players, and at times acted as a one-man buffer zone for some of his higher-profile teammates.

The most famous example of that came in the 1928 grand final, when Rowe played bodyguard to Gordon Coventry. Rowe's contribution that day was as important as in any other match he played in the black and white, and Syd Coventry was convinced it was a major factor in Collingwood's win. 'Percy saved Gordon from any interference in going for marks, and to a man who relies so much on his marking ability, it meant the difference between the nine goals he [Gordon] got and the two or three he might have got without protection.'

No wonder many people in Collingwood referred to the 1928 flag for many years as 'Rowe's Premiership'.

PLAYERS

#	Player	Games	Goals
27	Bruce Andrew	9	0
26	Les Angus	9	1
27	Reg Baker	1	0
2	George Beasley	1	1
1	Jack Beveridge	18	4
28	Tommy Bird	7	5
3	Percy Bowyer	14	0
9	Harry Chesswas	18	2
6	George Clayden	19	17
4	Albert Collier	21	2
5	Harry Collier	21	26
7	Gordon Coventry	20	89
8	Syd Coventry	19	2
10	Charlie Dibbs	21	0
12	John Harris	20	16
29	Cyril Kent	1	0
14	Albert Lauder	3	0
13	Billy Libbis	21	28
16	Norm MacLeod	15	0
19	Bob Makeham	20	17
30	Bob Muir	5	1
18	Frank Murphy	21	19
17	Len Murphy	19	7
20	Joe Poulter	2	0
21	Percy Rowe	14	5
22	Harold Rumney	17	4
23	Bill Sneazwell	6	0
24	Les Thomas	2	0
25	Ernie Wilson	14	0

Club Awards
Copeland Trophy – Harry Collier
Austral Cup – Albert Collier
Most consistent player – Harry Collier
Excellent services rendered to the club – Syd Coventry (5 pounds)
Excellent services rendered to the club – Charlie Dibbs (3 pounds)
Leading goalkicker – Gordon Coventry (89)
Hats presented to Bruce Andrew and Harry Collier
Travel bag – Harry Rumney
Training awards – 17 players

1928 SEASON

ROUND 1 April 21 Corio Oval
Geelong **8.12.60** v **Collingwood 9.12.66**
Goals: G Coventry 6, Beasley, H Collier, Rumney

ROUND 2 April 28 Victoria Park
Collingwood 14.18.102 v Fitzroy **9.13.67**
Goals: G Coventry 9, Libbis 3, Harris, L Murphy

ROUND 3 May 5 Punt Rd Oval
Richmond 5.14.44 v Collingwood **5.12.42**
Goals: G Coventry 4, Libbis

ROUND 4 May 12 Victoria Park
Collingwood 15.22.112 v Hawthorn **5.9.39**
Goals: G Coventry 5, Harris 5, Makeham 2, Angus, H Collier, L Murphy

ROUND 5 May 19 Junction Oval
St Kilda **11.8.74** v **Collingwood 15.12.102**
Goals: G Coventry 9, H Collier 2, S Coventry, Harris, Libbis, Rumney

ROUND 6 May 26 Victoria Park
Collingwood 12.12.84 v North Melbourne **6.9.45**
Goals: G Coventry 6, Clayden 2, F Murphy 2, H Collier, Libbis

ROUND 7 June 2 Princes Park
Carlton **12.12.84** v **Collingwood 13.9.87**
Goals: G Coventry 4, Bird 3, Harris 2, H Collier, Libbis, F Murphy, L Murphy

ROUND 8 June 4 Lake Oval
South Melbourne **9.14.68** v **Collingwood 13.7.85**
Goals: G Coventry 5, Libbis 2, Makeham 2, F Murphy 2, Chesswas, H Collier

ROUND 9 June 9 Victoria Park
Collingwood 13.14.92 v Melbourne **11.14.80**
Goals: Makeham 5, Libbis 4, H Collier 3, G Coventry

ROUND 10 June 23 Whitten Oval
Footscray **9.10.64** v **Collingwood 11.12.78**
Goals: G Coventry 3, H Collier 2, Rowe 2, Clayden, Libbis, Makeham, Rumney

ROUND 11 June 30 Victoria Park
Collingwood 12.13.85 v Essendon **8.9.57**
Goals: G Coventry 6, Beveridge, Chesswas, H Collier, Harris, Libbis, Makeham

ROUND 12 July 7 Victoria Park
Collingwood **9.13.67** v **Geelong 12.6.78**
Goals: G Coventry 3, Clayden 2, F Murphy 2, Beveridge, A Collier

ROUND 13 July 14 Brunswick St Oval
Fitzroy **7.12.54** v **Collingwood 14.15.99**
Goals: G Coventry 4, Libbis 4, Clayden 2, F Murphy 2, Beveridge, S Coventry

ROUND 14 July 28 Victoria Park
Collingwood 11.15.81 v Richmond **10.13.73**
Goals: Clayden 4, G Coventry 3, F Murphy 2, Libbis, Rumney

ROUND 15 August 4 Glenferrie Oval
Hawthorn **9.9.63** v **Collingwood 17.18.120**
Goals: G Coventry 8, Libbis 3, F Murphy 2, H Collier, Harris, L Murphy, Rowe

ROUND 16 August 11 Victoria Park
Collingwood 15.16.106 v St Kilda **6.14.50**
Goals: G Coventry 5, Clayden 3, Bird 2, F Murphy 2, Rowe 2, Libbis

ROUND 17 August 18 Arden St Oval
North Melbourne **8.9.57** v **Collingwood 8.17.65**
Goals: Clayden 3, H Collier 2, Harris, Muir, F Murphy

ROUND 18 September 1 Victoria Park
Collingwood **8.19.67** v **Carlton 12.15.87**
Goals: H Collier 2, G Coventry 2, Harris 2, F Murphy, L Murphy

1928 FINALS

LADDER

Team	W	L	D	For	Agst	%	Pts
Collingwood	15	3	0	1540	1144	134.6	60
Richmond	14	4	0	1640	1228	133.6	56
Melbourne	14	4	0	1507	1233	122.2	56
Carlton	11	7	0	1598	1316	121.4	44
Essendon	11	7	0	1441	1275	113.0	44
St Kilda	11	7	0	1499	1470	102.0	44
Footscray	9	9	0	1465	1340	109.3	36
Fitzroy	7	11	0	1480	1675	88.4	28
Geelong	6	12	0	1336	1343	99.5	24
South Melb	5	13	0	1461	1709	85.5	20
North Melb	5	13	0	1058	1563	67.7	20
Hawthorn	0	18	0	1171	1900	61.6	0

SEMI FINAL   September 15   MCG
Collingwood **9.8.62** v Melbourne **9.8.62**

Goals: Makeham 3, G Coventry 2, F Murphy 2, H Collier, Libbis

SEMI FINAL REPLAY   September 22   MCG
Collingwood **10.8.68** v Melbourne **9.10.64**

Goals: Libbis 3, H Collier 2, Makeham 2, Beveridge, A Collier, Harris

GRAND FINAL   September 29   MCG

Collingwood	2.4	7.8	9.11	13.18	(96)
Richmond	0.3	4.5	7.7	9.9	(63)

Goals: G. Coventry 9, L. Murphy 2, Harris, Makeham
Best: A. Collier, H. Collier, G. Coventry, Rowe, S. Coventry, F. Murphy, Rumney, Libbis
Umpire: McMurray senior
Crowd: 50,026 at the MCG

Grand Final team
B: H. Rumney, C. Dibbs, A. Lauder
HB: A. Collier, G. Clayden, R. Makeham
C: N. McLeod, J. Beveridge, B. Andrew
HF: J.D. Harris, F. Murphy, H. Chesswas
F: P. Rowe, G. Coventry, H. Collier
R: S. Coventry (c), Len Murphy, W. Libbis

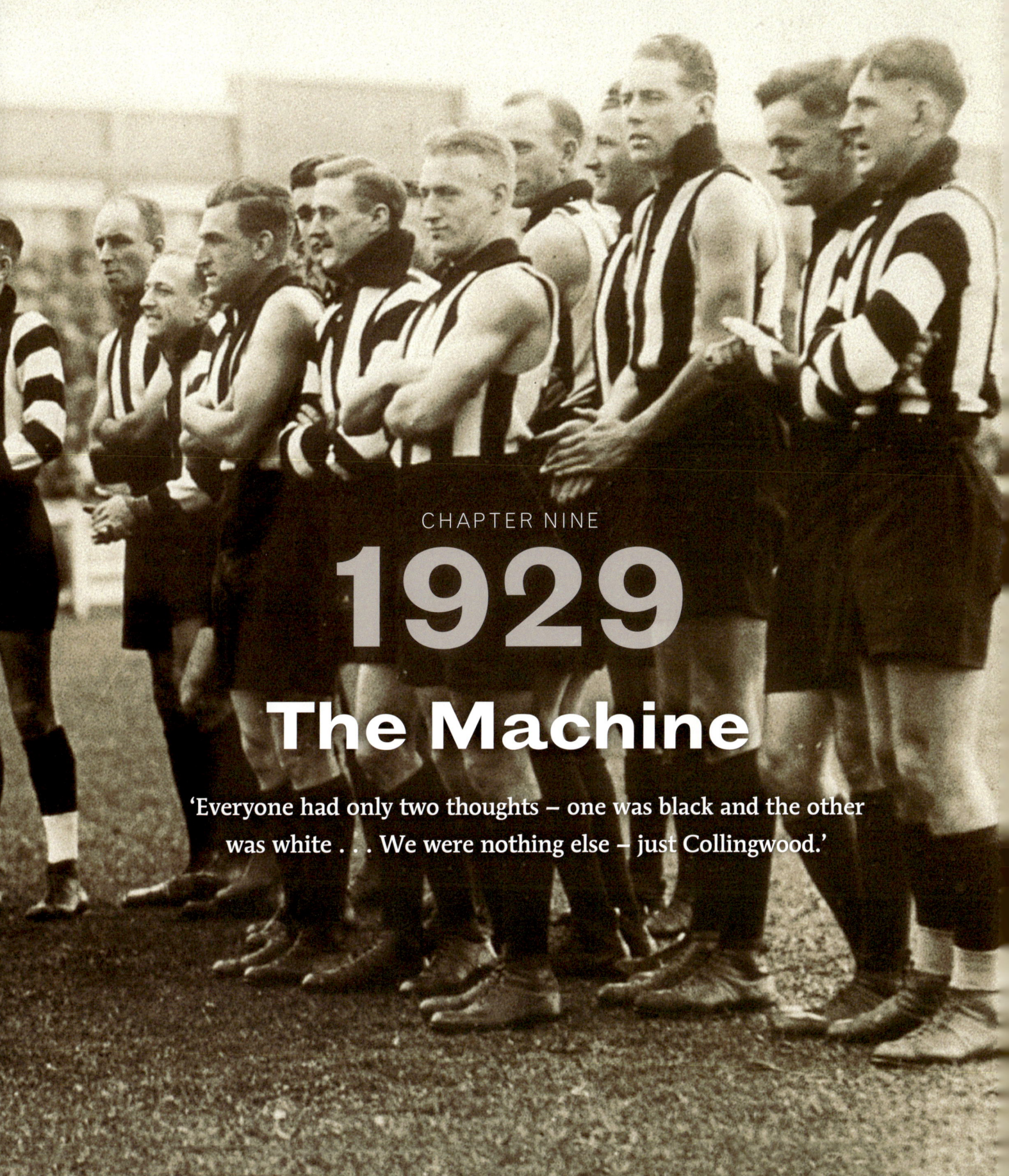

CHAPTER NINE

1929

The Machine

'Everyone had only two thoughts – one was black and the other was white . . . We were nothing else – just Collingwood.'

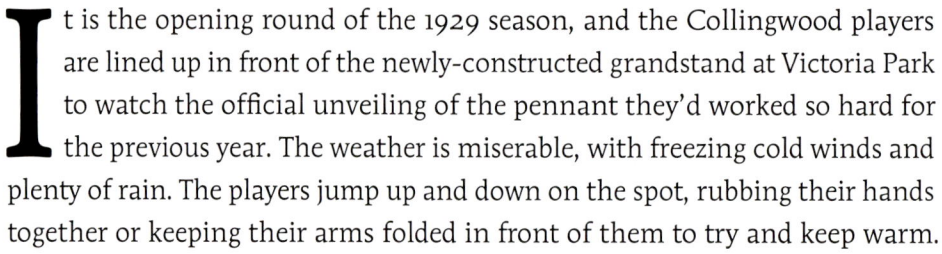

It is the opening round of the 1929 season, and the Collingwood players are lined up in front of the newly-constructed grandstand at Victoria Park to watch the official unveiling of the pennant they'd worked so hard for the previous year. The weather is miserable, with freezing cold winds and plenty of rain. The players jump up and down on the spot, rubbing their hands together or keeping their arms folded in front of them to try and keep warm.

Even by Victoria Park standards, this is a big occasion. In addition to the flag unfurling, and a re-match against last year's finalists, Richmond, the new grandstand is being officially opened. This grandstand had been built mainly by local, unemployed labourers, giving it even greater significance for a club that is so much a part of its community. Bickering between the cricket and football clubs means the grandstand doesn't have a name yet, but it will soon be called the Ryder Stand, after the man known as 'the King of Collingwood', test cricketer Jack Ryder.

No wonder, then, that a huge crowd has braved the elements and packed out Victoria Park. Such is the anticipation that the club exhausted its full supply of 1500 membership tickets long before the first bounce. The fans lucky enough to secure a seat in the new stand have the perfect vantage point as the mayor of Collingwood, Councillor A. J. Dunkin, officially opens the new feature. A few minutes later the ground explodes with cheering when the secretary's wife, Mrs Connor, unfurls the premiership pennant.

Sixteen of the 18 Magpies who had triumphed in the final game of 1928 are there, including Bruce Andrew, who has miraculously recovered from his broken neck. The players break and jog to their positions, no doubt glad just to be moving again in the biting cold. The *Australasian* would later marvel at the fact that a handful of them 'played in bare arms' on such a day. The pressure on this group of players is enormous. They are not just bearing the usual burdens that fall on the reigning premiers, nor those that accompany a team carrying the hopes of a suburb falling deep into the Great Depression. Just weeks before, club president Harry Curtis had set this group *extra* challenges.

Action from the opening round game against Richmond.

He wanted them to emulate the famed deeds of Carlton's 1906–08 teams by winning a hat-trick of pennants. And he challenged them not only to bring home a flag, but also to win everything they could and break as many records as possible along the way. This had to be a season beyond compare.

That sort of pressure can crush even the strongest sporting teams. But not this one. Despite greasy conditions, a ground dotted with miniature lakes, a heavy ball and a strong westerly breeze, the Magpies' response to the challenges of their president is swift and bold: they go out and bang through 13 straight goals without a single miss. The first behind does not come until Harold 'Bottles' Chesswas sprays a ball through the points early in the final quarter. The fans had turned out this day to celebrate the achievements of last year's team, but already find themselves giddy with excitement watching a stunning display of skill and ruthless efficiency from the 1929 model. As they file out of Vic Park at the end of the day, those fans are asking themselves: has the team that won the last two flags somehow got even better?

That opening round performance was a sign of things to come. Throughout the season this team did whatever was asked of it – and more. Whatever

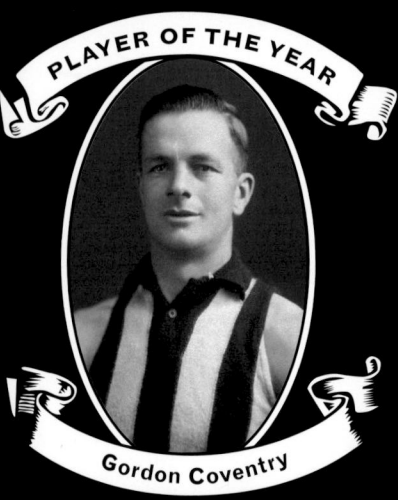

PLAYER OF THE YEAR
Gordon Coventry

Gordon Coventry had come close to becoming the first player to kick 100 goals in a VFL season back in 1927, but in 1929 he didn't just break through that milestone – he obliterated it.

His weekly tallies read: 6, 6, 11, 2, 6, 8, 4, 3, 8, 7, 7, 7, 16, 4, 4, 7, 10, 2, 4, 2. That added up to an extraordinary 124 goals for the season.

Coventry stood just on 6 foot (183 cm) and weighed about 13 stone (83 kilos) with huge shoulders, a big rump and massive hands. He was a master at out-positioning defenders, who often couldn't get to the ball around his enormous frame. He was one of the first players to develop the skill of marking the ball with his hands well in front of him. With his backside stuck out and his arms extended he was an extremely tough opponent to counter.

Coventry was also a strong pack mark, and had a vice-like grip that rarely dropped the ball. He didn't venture too far from goal, but could kick long when he needed to, and usually accurately.

In all, it was a package that defenders found hard to counter at the best of times. And in 1929 it was impossible.

challenges were set for it were achieved. The players set out on a quest to create as many team and individual records as they could in what ultimately would be considered the most successful home-and-away season in VFL–AFL history. They would do so with a clinical efficiency and consistent brilliance that would cement the legend of the 'Machine Team' and further entrench Collingwood as *the* club in terms of support, popularity and achievement.

By the end of the home-and-away season, almost all of Curtis's pre-season objectives had been ticked off. Collingwood won all 18 of its home-and-away games in 1929 (with an average winning margin of 43 points), something no other VFL–AFL team has ever been able to achieve. The Magpies became the first team in competition history to kick more than 2000 points in a season. With the final two matches of 1928 included, they became the first team to win 20 consecutive matches, a record that would last 24 years. Gordon Coventry chipped in with a swag of personal records in a staggering season that brought the VFL's first century of goals, the most goals in a match (16) and the most goals in a season (124). The club also boasted the Brownlow Medallist in Albert Collier, and the best player in the seconds competition, Bob Ross. Rival clubs could only look on with a mix of awe and jealousy.

Those achievements were even more impressive given that the team lost two of its most important players before the start of the season. Percy Rowe, the giant who was the hero of the 1928 final, had been appointed coach of Northcote in the VFA. Rowe had coaxed the club's popular vice-captain, inspirational defender Ernie Wilson, to join him. McHale had tried to retain Wilson for one last season, but to no avail. Footscray had approached Syd Coventry with a lucrative offer that would have quadrupled his wages, but there was never a chance the Magpies would let their champion player leave.

Coach Jock McHale did not have to look too far afield when reinforcing his squad, with hundreds of youngsters desperate to get an opportunity. As Harold Rumney, one of the team's leading lights, said: 'Winning a spot in the Magpies' side was a bit like winning the lottery.' The new recruits included Horrie Edmonds, a young neighbour of the Coventrys from Diamond Creek; Charlie Ahern, a strong Northcote lad who didn't mind a stoush on or off the field; George Gibbs, a talented young footballer and boxer from Fitzroy; and Bob Ross, a small player who had roved against Harry Collier

1929: The Machine

in school matches. All would experience wild – and vastly different – rides through the year.

Collingwood's opening fortnight produced a solid win over Richmond and a 53-point thrashing of Hawthorn. But it was the Round 3 mauling of South Melbourne that gave a better indication of the team's intentions. They totally crushed South, having 21 more scoring shots than their opponents and winning by a massive 96 points. Gordon Coventry helped himself to 11 goals, and brother Syd was so impressed he told the media that 'the team seemed to work like a machine'.

There was something else significant about that win – or, more correctly, about the players who delivered it. The 18 players who ran out against South on 11 May were exactly the same group who took the field for the next five weeks. Six weeks without *any* changes to the team was unheard of in VFL history, and it's never been repeated. Today, the Machine Team moniker is used as a general term to describe the 1927–30 premiership teams. But if there is one classic line-up that best embodies the Machine, then it would be the one that ran out together six weeks in a row:

B: Wescott, Dibbs, Makeham
HB: Lauder, A Collier, Rumney
C: Chesswas, Beveridge, MacLeod
HF: F Murphy, L Murphy, Harris
F: Gibbs, G Coventry, H Collier
R: S Coventry, Clayden, Libbis

It was a scarily good team. Bruce Andrew and Percy Bowyer were missing through injury, but otherwise it was hard to find fault with it. *The Argus* described the team as 'splendid specimens of Australian manhood'. The Colliers and Coventrys were, of course, four of the greatest Magpies of all time. But their support acts were outstanding players in their own right. Billy Libbis, Jack Beveridge, Harry Rumney, Charlie Dibbs and Len and Frank Murphy were all Victorian representatives who would have been top-five players at any other club. Beyond that, the 'good ordinary' types such as Clayden, Wescott, Makeham and Harris were far better than their counterparts at other clubs. It was a magnificently talented bunch, but also one that teamed together superbly and played *for* each other, with no hint of individualism. Like the Magpies of 2010, this was a team where every player knew his role and played it to perfection. There was no weak link.

You had to feel sorry for some of the players outside that core group. First-year player Bob Ross, for example, was listed as the team's emergency every week for those six weeks, but found it impossible to displace the likes

Right: Harry Lauder battles Geelong's Lloyd Hagger for the ball during the Magpies' six-goal win.
Below: Perennial bench-warmer Bob Ross.

The SPORTING GLOBE

Jumbo Sharland on Collingwood's Round 8 battle:

The tenacity of the Collingwood players in holding on when St Kilda were a couple of goals ahead in the third quarter was responsible to a large extent for their victory. Most teams would have gone to pieces when behind in such adverse conditions, but not so Collingwood.

of established stars Libbis and Harry Collier. He ultimately won the seconds competition's best-and-fairest award but could manage only four senior games in 1929, when he almost certainly would have been the rover at most other VFL clubs.

That six-week period brought victories over South Melbourne (96 points), Geelong (36), Fitzroy (56), North Melbourne (51), Melbourne (24) and St Kilda (4 points). It was after the North game that Kickero, in *The Herald*, reported the club had set itself to go through the year undefeated. The win over St Kilda two weeks later, in Round 8, was the only time all year the Pies won by less than two goals – and it was a narrow escape.

This was one of the games where it looked beforehand as if the Pies could be tested. The St Kilda team was strong (it would finish the season in fourth spot), the game was being played at the Saints' home ground, conditions were bleak and the ground was caked with mud. Almost 30,000 people turned out to watch what one reporter described as a 'gloriously sustained struggle on a horrible day'. St Kilda led by five points at half-time, and stretched that lead to a couple of goals during the third quarter. The Pies were up against it at this stage, but some tenacious defence, led by Albert Collier, enabled them to first stem the tide, then fight back to lead by a point going into the last quarter.

The Saints reclaimed the lead in the last quarter and were still leading late in the game. Then, as the clock ticked past 22 minutes, Gordon Coventry, who had been well held for most of the day, gathered a loose ball near goal. St Kilda full-back Ernie Loveless delivered a fearsome bump just as Coventry got his kick away. Coventry said later the bump 'shook [him] to his foundations', but as he fell to the ground the ball made contact with the side of his left boot and trickled through for the match-winning goal. The self-effacing Coventry was the first to acknowledge the good fortune that had accompanied the kick, telling a reporter afterwards: 'It was one of the flukes of the game.'

1929 / The Machine

That was as close as any team would come to the Pies throughout the home-and-away season. Such was Collingwood's dominance that one bored supporter came up with the idea of running a sweep on which team would be the first to knock them off. But when he tried to sell tickets at a training session at Victoria Park, he found no takers. Increasingly, football lovers and the media began to realise that here was a team with the potential to go through a season without losing a single game. It soon became the talking point of the year, and sparked a vigorous debate in the sports pages of *The Herald* between those who believed the Magpies were 'lucky' and those who believed the club deserved full credit.

As Collingwood's unbeaten run continued, there were some external critics who believed their sustained success was not good for the game. Even Syd Coventry admitted later that he had thought the standard of VFL football may have degenerated, because 'we were beating everybody'. Some experienced football writers claimed that Collingwood's domination had killed interest in the competition, and believed the team's obvious superiority was not in the game's best interests. One newspaper headline expressed the views of many when it said: 'No Victorian team is capable of beating Collingwood.' Another, more mischievous, headline in *The Australasian* read: 'Collingwood defeated'. Only on closer inspection did it reveal that the Collingwood Rifle Club, not the Collingwood Football Club, had suffered a loss.

Other clubs might have begun to feel the pressure of an extended run without a loss, but Collingwood seemed to revel in the attention. The players had taken on the challenge as some kind of collective responsibility.

---

22   THE SUN NEWS-PICTORIAL, MONDAY, MAY 20, 1929

Collingwood Alone at the Head of the League

GEELONG WAS BEATEN BY A STRONGER SIDE

Essendon Had Narrow Escape at Hawthorn and Carlton Only Won on the Bell

PLAYER SUSTAINS BROKEN LEG

(By Gerald Brosnan)

COLLINGWOOD'S defeat of Geelong, and close finishes in the matches at Hawthorn and South Melbourne were features of the fourth round of League premiership games on Saturday.

ESSENDON had only five points to spare against Hawthorn when the final bell rang, and Carlton just managed to struggle home against South Melbourne by a bare goal, kicked in the last two

ST. KILDA'S FINE WIN

Too Good In The Air For Fitzroy

LUDLOW BRILLIANT

| St. Kilda | 16-21—117 |
| Fitzroy | 12-8— 80 |

SUPREMACY in the air, greater pace, and a sterling defence, won the day for St. Kilda against Fitzroy. It was a thrilling game from start to finish, and the Maroons, who played really good football, were not disgraced, in spite

TIGERS DID NOT IMPRESS

Footscray Forwards Fail In Poor Game

| Richmond | 14-19—103 |
| Footscray | 11-19— 85 |

IN a poor exhibition at Richmond the Tigers were fortunate to run out winners by such a margin from Footscray. The game was devoid of system or individual sparkle, and at times Richmond supporters must have wondered if theirs was the same team which defeated Carlton so brilliantly a fortnight previously.

MAGPIES' RUCK TOO STRONG

Geelong's Forward Work Faulty

EVEN IN CENTRE

| Collingwood | 12-13—85 |
| Geelong | 6-13—49 |

A MARKED superiority in the ruck together with cleaner handling, and better position play,

PLAYER OF THE YEAR

Albert Collier

Albert Collier was a prodigiously talented, strongly built youngster who made his VFL debut for Collingwood in 1925 aged just 15 – at full-forward.

The next year, with Gordon Coventry having secured his hold on the full-forward spot, Albert – the younger of the Collier brothers – was moved to centre half-back. And it was there that he made a name for himself, quickly becoming one of the best defenders in the competition. So rapid was his rise that at the time of his breakout season in 1929, when he won the Brownlow Medal, the Copeland Trophy and Victorian selection, he was still just 20 years old.

Colllier was brilliant that season – strong in the air, fast across the ground, and fearsome in the packs, where his take-no-prisoners approach made opponents tread warily. Despite his age, Collier was already a leader within the team and provided a real presence on the ground. His teammates loved him.

The umpires get a lot of things wrong, but in 1929, as with Syd Coventry in 1927, their voting for the Brownlow Medal was spot on.

And this was one of the 1929 team's greatest strengths: besides the undoubted individual brilliance of many of the players, there was also a remarkably strong team spirit throughout the group. When Albert Collier, who was proving to be an exceptional young leader on and off the field, found out that Bob Ross was receiving only one complimentary ticket for each match when he was an emergency (senior players received two), he marched his embarrassed teammate into the secretary's office and demanded parity. Collier insisted that everyone was treated equally – and Ross got his extra ticket.

This team ethos extended socially to the dance nights that were put on by the players' social committee and held in the club's new training room. After home games the players would clear out the training room, then go to the nearby Railway Hotel for a meal, and return about 8 o'clock for a night of dancing. Good mates Bruce Andrew and Percy Bowyer helped organise the functions, which soon became so popular that they had to be moved to the Collingwood Town Hall to meet the growing demand. 'The place was always so packed that we'd have to close the room,' Bowyer recalled years later. 'We always had a great night.'

The games ticked by, and the Machine rolled on. Challengers came and challengers fell. A tight contest was expected in Round 10, against a Carlton side that had lost only one game and was sitting in second place. They were dispatched by a comfortable 29 points, prompting some black and white fans to goad their opposing fans by chanting: 'Is this the team that was going to beat us?' *The Herald* said afterwards that this Collingwood team ranked among the best

1929: The Machine

Left: George Clayden shows his aerial strength in the Round 10 match against Carlton.
Opposite: Newspaper headlines throughout the season told the story of Collingwood's superiority.

the game had ever seen. 'There was an understanding between them that was thrilling, making it a combination so decidedly superior to Carlton that it caused surprise, even to its enthusiasts who regard Collingwood as invincible.'

The next week it was Essendon, who jumped out of the blocks with a five-goal opening term and actually had the temerity to be in front at half-time before crumbling in the face of Collingwood's relentless pressure to go down by 19 points. Then it was Richmond, at Richmond – surely a combination to provide the stern test so many neutral observers craved? The Tigers themselves couldn't have felt too confident, for they announced a 'camouflage team' on Thursday night with a number of players named out of position. When the team lined up as usual, not as named, they drew strong criticism from the media for the attempted ruse – especially for misleading the public and causing so many users of the *Football Record* to have to make changes themselves. For a while it looked like the deception might have worked, as the Pies led by just a goal after three quarters. But the Machine switched into overdrive in the final quarter, kicking a staggering 7.7 to finish with 17 more scoring shots and a lazy seven-goal victory.

149

The Mightiest Magpies

Gordon Coventry was regularly double-teamed by the opposition but it didn't stop him setting a new record for goals in a season.

Hawthorn was never expected to provide a serious test, and Gordon Coventry took the opportunity to deliver yet another element of president Curtis's pre-season wish list when he booted an individual record of 16 goals before a deliriously happy Victoria Park crowd. He bagged four goals in the first five minutes and an astounding eight in the first quarter, to set him up to break the decade-old record of 14 kicked by South Melbourne's Harold Robertson. 'Nuts' broke the old mark in the last quarter and was cheered off the ground by friends and foes alike. Even the umpire shook Coventry's hand.

Four goals in each of the next two weeks took Coventry's season tally to 99 ahead of the Round 16 game against Fitzroy. The miserable weather in the 1927 final had cost him VFL football's first century of goals, but nothing would deny him the honour this time around. Just 11 minutes in, he took a neat pass from Harry Collier and punted truly. The crowd broke into hearty and sustained applause, and several Fitzroy opponents shook his hand. Oddly, Coventry's milestone was not massive news in the media. There were a few stories in the newspapers, but it was generally a low-key affair, something which would have suited the unassuming Coventry down to the ground.

The Pies beat Fitzroy by 56 points that day, as their seemingly inexorable march towards an unbeaten season continued. North were crushed by 77 points. The major challengers had all been stared down, and the only hurdle that remained was an away game to Melbourne in the final round. There was no hint of the staleness that had hit the team the year before, nor were there any signs of either over-confidence or 'choking' when the record was within sight. Instead the team wrote itself into the history books with an emphatic 56-point victory. It was the first and only time a team has gone through a home-and-away season undefeated, and seemingly the perfect preparation for the finals.

The lead-up to the finals got even better for Collingwood when the League announced that 20-year-old Albert Collier had become the youngest player to win the Brownlow Medal. Just as with Syd Coventry's victory two years earlier, there was universal agreement that the umpires had got it right. And there was a nice confluence when Bob Ross, the man Collier had helped out earlier in the year, was named as best player in the seconds competition.

For non-Magpie fans, it was hard to get excited about the finals. Indeed, September had all the hallmarks of being a huge anticlimax for everyone outside Victoria Park. Many observers were afraid the finals would turn out to be a fizzer. Kickero, of *The Herald*, summed up the feelings of many when he wrote that 'the public agreed that the premiership was won two months ago, and there was not a team which could stop Collingwood's run of success'.

Richmond's wily coach, Frank 'Checker' Hughes, didn't share those views. The Tigers had finished third for the season and would face up to Collingwood in one semi-final, while second-placed Carlton would meet St Kilda in the other. Richmond were massive underdogs but, sick of playing second fiddle to the Pies for so long, Hughes urged his players to hit the Magpies with a physical barrage. Collingwood, as minor premiers, had the right of challenge, which meant Richmond would have to beat Collingwood twice to claim the flag. Hughes knew that, to do so, his players would have to shake up the Magpies physically.

It was clear from the first bounce of the semi-final that the Tigers were going to follow Hughes's instructions to the letter. Syd Coventry and George Clayden were flattened within the first five minutes – both at the hands of the normally fair Basil McCormack, who was subsequently given an eight-week ban for the Clayden blow. Soon after the captain was felled, the Magpies' other follower, George Gibbs, had the chance to even the score. But he hesitated, McCormack ran out of range and the opportunity was lost. That split-second hesitation would cost Gibbs a spot in the grand final side.

Those early incidents set the scene for a game played in what *The Australasian* called 'a reprehensible spirit'. Fists and elbows flew with abandon as the Tigers hit the over-confident Magpies with everything they had. In between they attacked the ball with equal gusto, and played some good football into the bargain. The shocked crowd watched in disbelief as the rank outsiders stormed to a 41-point half-time lead. Everyone expected a Collingwood fightback in

> **The Australasian**
>
> **Jack Worrall on Collingwood's consistency:**
>
> Collingwood keeps up the same standard week in and week out, and though it has been at its top since April, it shows no sign of staleness. Collingwood played as it always does with rare grit and skill, and the precision with which the various component parts fitted in made one the more admire the excellent organization which can produce such a machine. I cannot see how any team is going to beat Collingwood under equal conditions.

Even Harry Collier (left) and Gordon Coventry (on the ground) couldn't stop Richmond running away with the semi-final win in a shock result.

The Herald
On the effect of Collingwood's only loss:

Several [females] left the ground sobbing and dabbing their eyes with their handkerchiefs. The male escort of one sobbing sister clumsily tried to console her by saying 'Never mind, Richmond would have won against a combined team on their show today'. The woman turned on him like a tiger cat and, as she stamped her foot on the footpath, shrieked 'we didn't come here to see Richmond play, but to see Collingwood win'.

the second half but it never eventuated. The final margin, 62 points, was just as stunning as the result.

The *Herald* claimed it was 'the most extraordinary upset in the history of football' and nobody disagreed. Under a headline that read 'The Machine Wrecked', the paper said: 'Eighteen spanners were thrown into the works, and the Machine was smashed to smithereens . . . it was one of their worst performances on record. They may never play as badly again.'

Even 60 years later, Magpies who played that day could scarcely believe they lost the game – and with it the chance to go through an entire season undefeated. The result was just as crushing for the club's fans. McHale copped some of the blame. Some felt he hadn't responded well enough to Richmond's roughhouse tactics. Others, like former Carlton coach Jack Worrall, felt he'd pushed the players too hard on the track. McHale's view was that the result simply came from the fact that 'we had many players off their form'.

The coach ordered his players to attend the final between Richmond and Carlton at the MCG the following week. He hoped for a tough clash and that is exactly what he got, with the Tigers coming from behind to win by a goal after a taxing, tense struggle. Whether inspired by Worrall's criticism or not, McHale eased up on training in grand final week. Syd Coventry later commented on how McHale 'would not let us handle a ball'. 'We did nothing at all,' the skipper said.

McHale knew Richmond would hit his men with similar tactics in the grand final to those they'd employed in the semi. So he and the selection committee decided that changes had to be made. First to go was Gibbs, who had played well in his 17 games that year but who now paid dearly for his failure to take the opportunity to deck McCormack in the semi. McHale sought the advice of district coach Hugh Thomas on which of his players would be best able to provide Syd Coventry with some protection. Thomas instantly nominated Charlie Ahern. The rugged 24-year-old, who had played only two games, would go into the grand final with the specific brief to protect the captain.

There were other casualties. 'Jiggy' Harris and Norm MacLeod, who had both played in every game that season, were also dropped to make way for Percy Bowyer and Len Murphy. Gibbs and MacLeod were disappointed, but dealt with the decision. Harris was furious. Excepting a couple of games on the club's end-of-season trip to Tasmania, he never played for Collingwood again, and transferred to Hawthorn the following season.

Collingwood had reacted savagely at the selection table, especially given how few unforced changes had been made throughout the year. There were some who began to wonder if the Pies were panicking, or at least starting to feel the pressure. To make matters worse, the club received eleven handwritten letters threatening the lives of most of the team's stars (the letters were intercepted and kept from the intended victims until after the grand final). But if there was pressure, McHale seemed to be happy to soak it up. In a pre-match press conference he pointedly reinforced that his players would be playing the ball, thereby throwing the focus back on Richmond's expected aggressive approach. 'Collingwood want to win the Premiership by fair means only,' he said. The club then also broke with tradition by hosting a dinner for the players at the ground after the last training session. McHale spoke that night, warning his players about the 'pitfalls of egotism' and reinforcing all that had got the team this far.

Players Snowy Barr, Rupert Perrett, Frank Murphy, Don Harris, Doc Seddon (background), Charlie Dibbs, Harry Collier, Leo Wescott, Harry Rumney and Jack Ross hang on Jock McHale's every word.

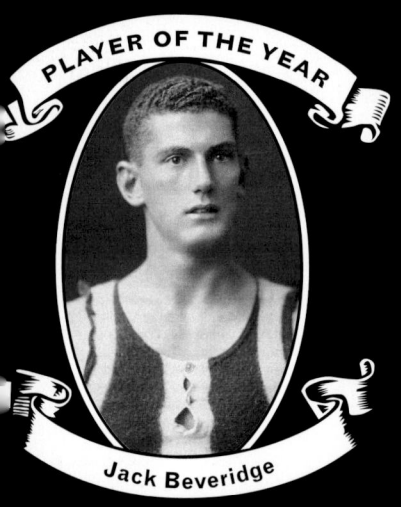

PLAYER OF THE YEAR

Jack Beveridge

Jack Beveridge was a class act from start to finish. A centreman of rare poise and polish, he looked at home in senior football from his very first game in 1926, when he won rave reviews as an 18-year-old for an exceptional debut performance against Fitzroy.

He maintained the same level through most of his 148-game career. Beveridge had great skill, wonderful balance and a casual elegance about his play – he rarely looked hassled and always seemed to have plenty of time. He used the ball beautifully, whether foot-passing to his forwards or handballing to teammates in the middle of the ground.

He was also remarkably consistent, rarely putting in bad games, let alone below-par seasons. But 1929 was a particularly good one for him: he won Victorian selection for the first time and was among the team's best in most of its big games.

It was really only the presence of so many other champions around him that stopped Jack Beveridge getting the attention his talents warranted. In any other team, he would surely have been a star.

The anticipation of a close contest brought out 63,336 on a day that dawned overcast but cleared to a bright afternoon. Fans began to arrive at the ground early, and queued in their thousands. Even the famous old trees around the Melbourne Cricket Ground proved perfect vantage points for dozens of men and boys. The Magpies approached the game knowing that their best would be good enough to win. They also knew they'd be facing a fierce physical assault from the Tigers. But this time they were ready for it. And from early in the game it was obvious that there would be no repeat of the semi-final upset. Instead, the Pies blew the game apart with a brilliant opening term.

One reporter described the feeling in the crowd as 'vociferous and even bloodthirsty'. The on-field action was not much different, as the two teams fought fiercely, and frequently outside the spirit of the game. Richmond kicked the first goal inside the first few minutes, then wasted several other opportunities as they had the best of the early going. The Pies soon made them pay, and Harry Collier kicked Collingwood's first from a dubious mark. Then Horrie 'Tubby' Edmonds took centre stage in the biggest game of his life. Stationed alongside Gordon Coventry in the forward pocket, the smart forward grabbed a brilliant goal after he backed cleverly out of a crush with the ball and steered it through. But Allan Geddes responded for Richmond and, after seven minutes, it was two goals apiece in what was becoming a thrilling contest.

Then came the burst that won the flag, as the Machine kicked into overdrive. Charlie Ahern was given a free kick after a heavy clash with Stan Ryan, and his long punt kick landed with Frank Murphy, who kicked a brilliant long goal. Three behinds followed, including a poster from Libbis, as Collingwood bombarded the Richmond defence. Gordon Coventry eventually got clear for his first, and Edmonds added two more in a stunning opening term. His third late in the quarter was Collingwood's sixth, giving the Pies a sizeable 27-point quarter-time lead.

Richmond made no headway with the breeze in the second quarter, but they did manage to knock Bob Makeham senseless. Edmonds continued to be prominent, as did the rugged Ahern, who was being battered from pillar to post as he valiantly worked to shield Syd Coventry from the worst of Richmond's physical assaults. The lead stayed around the same level as scoring slowed and both teams went goal for goal. Two quarters of football shaved only two points off Collingwood's lead and, though there were a few anxious moments in the last quarter when Richmond kicked the first goal, a quick response from Libbis put the result beyond doubt. Gordon Coventry finished the game off with his 124th goal for the season. The Machine was firing on all cylinders.

The final margin was 29 points – almost exactly what it had been after that blistering opening quarter. And this despite a lopsided 61-34 free kick count in Richmond's favour. The victory owed much to Collingwood's rock-solid defence, where Albert Collier, Leo Wescott and Charlie Dibbs were magnificent, the brilliant roving of Bill Libbis, and the work of Syd Coventry, George Clayden and the brave Ahern in the ruck. Gordon Coventry was held to just two goals, his equal lowest tally for the year, but Tubby Edmonds stepped in to fill the breech with a match-winning five-goal haul. There has long been debate about whether Gordon deliberately played as a 'decoy' in this game, allowing Edmonds to slip in for his handful of goals, or whether Edmonds just used his football brain and canny reading of the play to be in the right place at the right time. Either way, Tubby had five goals and the Pies had another flag.

Top: George Clayden flies for a mark in the last line of defence as Charlie Dibbs (11) and Albert Collier (5) lend support.
Above: Grand final hero Tubby Edmonds.
Opposite: Captains Syd Coventry and Dooley Lilburne toss the coin with the 'Queen of Football', Kate Harrison.

The Collingwood players danced with joy when the final bell rang, and many of them were hoisted onto the shoulders of supporters and carried from the field. Syd Coventry was one of those, chaired off by some of the club's trainers, and that image has become one of the most recognised in football history. There were chaotic scenes in the rooms as hundreds of fans clamoured to see their heroes, and the players had to fight through the cheering throng. The captain reportedly wore the broadest grin of anyone in the rooms after the game, and in his after-match speech made a special point of congratulating Ahern and thanking him for his courageous performance. McHale spoke of his pride in his players, the 'team spirit' within the group and also said he had no doubt that Syd was the finest captain the club had ever produced. There was even a touch of theatrics in the rooms as secretary George Connor got up to speak. He removed his jacket to reveal a placard on his waistcoat that read: 'Collingwood – the hat-trick – Premiers 1927–28–29'. Connor said he had been so confident of the team's success that he had stuck the placard on his back when he left home that morning.

The next day there were wild celebrations at the Collingwood Town Hall. The Wall Street stockmarket crash that signalled the 'official' start of the Great Depression was only a few weeks away, and once again the team had given its supporters happiness in a time of hardship. The players were presented with a cheque for 200 pounds and new blazers and ties for their end-of-season trip to Tasmania. The trip was just reward for a team that had done everything its president had asked of it. By the end of the season they were being lauded as perhaps the greatest VFL team thus far. By the end of the century they were

Snapshots from the players' trip to Tasmania after their all-conquering 1929 season. **Opposite: Syd Coventry** is chaired off by trainers and support staff, with Len Murphy on the left.

admitted to the Australian Sports Commission's Hall of Fame as one of the greatest teams in the history of Australian sport.

For those on the inside, it was all about commitment to the Collingwood cause. As Bruce Andrew would recall many years later: 'Everyone had only two thoughts – one was black and the other was white. We were a very strong unit, made up of 25 committed players, a great coach, a full committee and everyone associated with the club was just Collingwood. We were nothing else – just Collingwood. We believed it in our own hearts, and played our football accordingly. Every player backed up his mates whenever he took the field. That's why we were called the Machine Team.'

CHARLIE AHERN — GRAND FINAL HERO

The 1929 Grand Final was only Charlie Ahern's third game of football. It was also his last.

Ahern was a tough character, and his toughness was never needed more than in this game. He had few fears and didn't mind using his fists when called upon, and he found some willing opponents in yellow and black. Early on he was twice badly fouled by Richmond in incidents that were criticised by journalists. He soldiered on manfully throughout the game, protecting his captain at every turn and taking a battering in the process.

It was later revealed that Ahern had broken his arm during the game, but he played on without complaint. The break couldn't even stop him playing the piano at the post-match celebrations! After the game he was lauded by teammates, including Syd Coventry, for his gutsy and selfless contribution.

But Ahern would get little opportunity to revel in his moment of footballing glory. He became sick soon after the grand final, and within a few months was listed as 'seriously ill'. He never played another minute of football, and was dead within 18 months from a combination of bowel cancer and 'exhaustion'. He was just 25.

PLAYERS

#	Player	Games	Goals
2	Charlie Ahern	3	0
1	Bruce Andrew	4	5
4	Jack Beveridge	19	1
13	Leo Bird	1	0
3	Percy Bowyer	10	2
9	Harry Chesswas	19	4
10	George Clayden	20	8
5	Albert Collier	18	0
6	Harry Collier	20	27
7	Gordon Coventry	20	124
8	Syd Coventry	20	4
11	Charlie Dibbs	19	0
12	Horrie Edmonds	9	19
14	George Gibbs	16	13
15	John Harris	19	9
16	Albert Lauder	15	0
17	Billy Libbis	19	24
22	Norm MacLeod	19	0
18	Bob Makeham	17	10
21	Bob Muir	2	0
19	Frank Murphy	13	18
20	Len Murphy	16	24
23	Bob Ross	4	3
24	Harold Rumney	20	3
25	Ken Veevers	1	0
26	Leo Wescott	17	0

Club Awards

Copeland Trophy – Albert Collier
Austral Cup – Gordon Coventry
President's Trophy – Syd Coventry
50 pounds awarded to Gordon Coventry from John Wren for kicking 16 goals in one game
Training awards to 20 players
Hats to George Gibbs and Albert Collier
Leading goalkicker – Gordon Coventry (124)

1929 SEASON

ROUND 1 April 27 Victoria Park
Collingwood 15.2.92 v Richmond **11.9.75**
Goals: G Coventry 6, H Collier 3, F Murphy 3, Andrew, Bowyer, Harris

ROUND 2 May 4 Glenferrie Oval
Hawthorn **11.7.73** v **Collingwood 18.18.126**
Goals: G Coventry 6, Libbis 4, Andrew 2, F Murphy 2, L Murphy 2, Chesswas, Harris

ROUND 3 May 11 Victoria Park
Collingwood 19.20.134 v South Melbourne **4.14.38**
Goals: G Coventry 11, H Collier 3, Libbis 3, Clayden 2

ROUND 4 May 18 Corio Oval
Geelong **6.13.49** v **Collingwood 12.13.85**
Goals: L Murphy 3, H Collier 2, G Coventry 2, F Murphy 2, Libbis, Makeham, Rumney

ROUND 5 May 25 Victoria Park
Collingwood 16.19.115 v Fitzroy **8.11.59**
Goals: G Coventry 6, Libbis 3, L Murphy 3, H Collier, Harris, F Murphy, Rumney

ROUND 6 June 1 Arden St Oval
North Melbourne **11.15.81** v **Collingwood 20.12.132**
Goals: G Coventry 8, Gibbs 5, L Murphy 4, Libbis, Makeham, F Murphy

ROUND 7 June 15 Victoria Park
Collingwood 12.11.83 v Melbourne **9.5.59**
Goals: G Coventry 4, Gibbs 2, L Murphy 2, H Collier, Libbis, Makeham, F Murphy

ROUND 8 June 22 Junction Oval
St Kilda **7.8.50** v **Collingwood 7.12.54**
Goals: G Coventry 3, F Murphy 2, Harris, Makeham

ROUND 9 June 29 Victoria Park
Collingwood 20.19.139 v Footscray **14.10.94**
Goals: G Coventry 8, H Collier 3, Gibbs 3, Harris 2, Libbis, Makeham, F Murphy, L Murphy

ROUND 10 July 6 Victoria Park
Collingwood 15.15.105 v Carlton **11.10.76**
Goals: G Coventry 7, H Collier 2, L Murphy 2, Clayden, Libbis, Ross, Rumney

ROUND 11 July 13 Windy Hill
Essendon **11.7.73** v **Collingwood 13.14.92**
Goals: G Coventry 7, Andrew 2, H Collier 2, Harris, Ross

ROUND 12 July 20 Punt Rd Oval
Richmond **11.9.75** v **Collingwood 16.21.117**
Goals: G Coventry 7, L Murphy 4, Edmonds 3, H Collier, Harris

ROUND 13 July 27 Victoria Park
Collingwood 22.10.142 v Hawthorn **7.14.56**
Goals: G Coventry 16, S Coventry 2, H Collier 2, Edmonds 2

ROUND 14 August 3 Lake Oval
South Melbourne **6.7.43** v **Collingwood 10.10.70**
Goals: G Coventry 4, Clayden, Edmonds, Gibbs, Harris, Makeham, Ross

ROUND 15 August 10 Victoria Park
Collingwood 13.9.87 v Geelong **8.12.60**
Goals: G Coventry 4, Clayden 2, H Collier 2, Edmonds 2, Gibbs, Makeham, L Murphy

ROUND 16 August 17 Brunswick St Oval
Fitzroy **8.7.55** v **Collingwood 16.15.111**
Goals: G Coventry 7, Edmonds 3, S Coventry 2, Beveridge, Clayden, Gibbs, Makeham

ROUND 17 August 24 Victoria Park
Collingwood 21.12.138 v North Melbourne **8.13.61**
Goals: G Coventry 10, H Collier 3, Libbis 3, L Murphy 2, Bowyer, Edmonds, F Murphy

ROUND 18 August 31 MCG
Melbourne **5.10.40** v **Collingwood 14.12.96**
Goals: Chesswas 3, G Coventry 2, Edmonds 2, Libbis 2, Makeham 2, F Murphy 2, H Collier

1929 FINALS

LADDER

Team	Won	Lost	Draw	For	Agst	%	Pts
Collingwood	18	0	0	1918	1117	171.7	72
Carlton	15	3	0	1589	1161	136.9	60
Richmond	12	5	1	1703	1399	121.7	50
St Kilda	12	6	0	1493	1146	130.3	48
Melbourne	11	6	1	1228	1164	105.5	46
Essendon	9	8	1	1349	1405	96.0	38
Geelong	8	10	0	1175	1082	108.6	32
South Melb	7	11	0	1338	1578	84.8	28
Footscray	6	11	1	1268	1464	86.6	26
Hawthorn	4	14	0	1170	1522	76.9	16
Fitzroy	3	15	0	1340	1827	73.3	12
North Melb	1	17	0	1070	1776	60.2	4

SEMI FINAL September 14   MCG

Collingwood **8.13.61** v Richmond **18.15.123**

Goals: G Coventry 4, Libbis 3, Clayden

GRAND FINAL   September 28   MCG

Collingwood	6.3	7.6	9.6	11.13	(79)
Richmond	2.0	3.3	5.5	7.8	(50)

Goals: Edmonds 5, G. Coventry 2, H. Collier, Libbis, F. Murphy, L. Murphy
Best: Libbis, S Coventry, Ahern, Edmonds, Clayden, Dibbs, Libbis, Wescott
Umpire: Scott
Crowd: 63,336 at the MCG

Grand Final Team
B: L. Wescott, C. Dibbs, G. Clayden
HB: A. Lauder, A. Collier, H. Rumney
C: H. Chesswas, J. Beveridge, P. Bowyer
HF: F. Murphy, Len Murphy, R. Makeham
F: H. Edmonds, G. Coventry, H. Collier
R: S. Coventry (c), C. Ahern, W. Libbis

CHAPTER TEN
1930

Mission accomplished

'They were the Bradmans of football.'

Everything came so easily for Collingwood in 1929. Records tumbled, opponents fell with little more than a whimper, injuries were few and far between and the team played consistently brilliant football. None of the key players lost form, there were no off-field dramas, and everything went according to plan. With the sole exception of the shock semi-final loss, it was as perfect a season as a football team could put together. So it's no wonder that many Magpie fans thought their team would only need to turn up to guarantee a fourth successive flag in 1930.

But football doesn't work that way. Opposing teams catch up. Your own team falls back a notch, maybe through ageing, or complacency, or both. Staleness can set in. You get hit with injuries, or key players lose form. A scandal hits your club. The things that came easily just 12 months ago suddenly become a struggle.

That, in essence, is the story of Collingwood's 1930 season. The team that had taken all before it in 1929, which made winning look easy, had to fight for its successes. The Pies lost successive matches for the first and only time in the Machine's four-year reign. They still finished on top, but only on percentage. Where there had been thumping triumphs in 1929 there were now narrow escapes. The players became the masters of the come-from-behind victory – and they left their most dramatic comeback until the last hour of the season.

The global picture had darkened considerably in the six months after Collingwood's near-perfect season ended. The Wall Street stockmarket crash in October of 1929 signalled the start of the worldwide Great Depression. In Australia, industrial, working-class suburbs such as Collingwood had already been feeling the impact of the worsening economic situation. But after the October crash, the misery and gloom hit every industry and every home across the country, in one way or another. The national unemployment rate jumped to staggering levels, from around 12 per cent when Collingwood won the flag in 1929 to more than 20 per cent at the end of the 1930 season. In the inner suburbs the suffering was even more intense: more than 31 per cent of the male population in Collingwood was out of work.

For many, sport provided the only light. Ironically, the 1930 sporting landscape was rich, the antithesis of the financial one, and the sporting heroes of the Depression would become iconic figures. Think Don Bradman, who made 1930 (and beyond) his own with a string of record-breaking performances, including a then world's best score of 334 against England. And Phar Lap, who would not only win the 1930 Melbourne Cup but also achieve the extraordinary feat of winning on all four days of the Flemington Carnival.

This was a time when people needed heroes. And to many people in Victoria, especially those in Collingwood, the Machine Team provided the biggest heroes of all – ones who lived locally, who you could see and touch just by turning up to training. Most of the suburb's 38,000 residents followed the fortunes of their team with an abiding passion, and their own moods rose and fell with the weekly results. As one Collingwood social historian acknowledged: 'If Collingwood were beaten there'd be no *Sporting Globes* sold in the shops . . . people wouldn't eat their tea . . . they [the fans] took defeat badly.'

Harry Lauder puts a smile on the face of local Magpie fans after a training session at Victoria park.

Luckily, defeat wasn't a common occurrence for the Collingwood Football Club between 1927 and 1930. And that's the way its fans wanted it to stay. The community was intensely proud of the achievements of its team, and expected that success to continue in 1930. Repeated successes had caused many Collingwood supporters to regard their team as invincible – a view also shared by many neutral observers.

It was easy to understand their confidence. Very little had changed on the playing front between 1929 and 1930. The only significant departures were the underrated Leo Wescott, who accepted an offer to coach Longford in Tasmania, and 'Jiggy' Harris, who crossed to Hawthorn in a fit of pique after being dumped for the last game. Charlie Ahern, one of the unlikely heroes of the 1929 premiership, was the other casualty. Ahern had become sick in the off-season, and by the start of 1930 the newly-married 24-year-old was seriously ill with what turned out to be bowel cancer. The club staged a benefit night at the Collingwood Town Hall in May, which raised 63 pounds. But Charlie Ahern had played his last game, and would be dead in little over a year.

As always, new faces were coming through. Jack Regan would only manage three games in his debut season, but would go on to be regarded as 'the prince of full-backs'. There was also Fred Froude, a youngster from the Collingwood districts side, and Bill Aldag, a tall, solid recruit who had played with Brunswick and Footscray. But in all, this was very much a steady-as-she-goes Collingwood line-up.

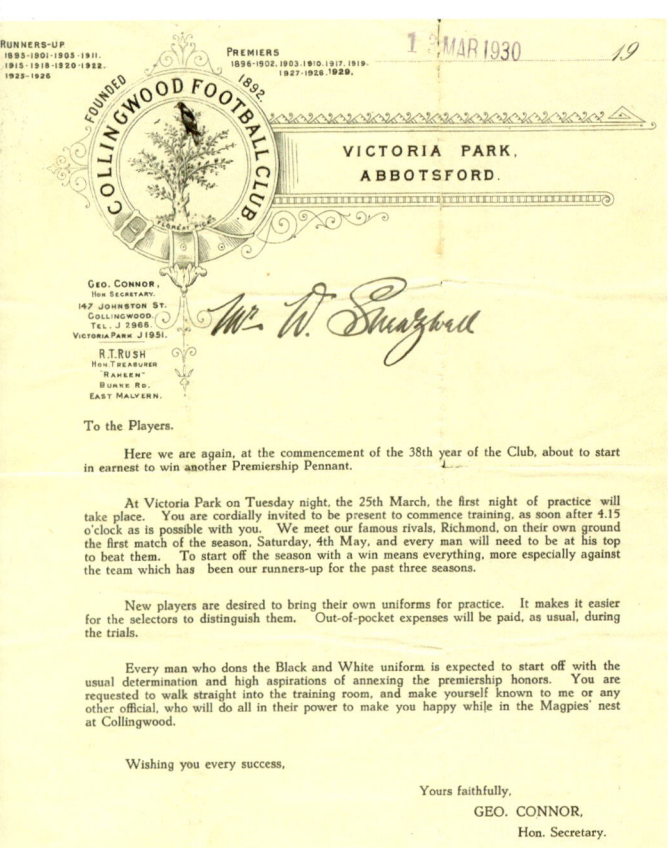

Below: **A letter to Bill Sneazwell providing details of early season training arrangements.** Opposite: **Collingwood's bench early in 1929, including George Gibbs in his dressing gown.**

Syd Coventry was again in charge – but only just. He had once again flirted with crossing to Footscray, and was one of 11 applicants for the vacant job of playing coach at the Western Oval. Coventry was duly appointed by the Footscray committee, and was set to be paid 10 pounds a week, six more than he was getting at Victoria Park. But Collingwood was not about to sit idly by and lose its captain. The Magpies protested to the VFL and were successful in stopping the move, the League agreeing that it was 'not in the best interests of the game to allow a player to switch clubs without the blessing of his original club'. That was the way of things in those times – even star players often sought moves to better-paying positions, and nobody seemed to begrudge them doing so. If the moves were refused, players mostly stayed where they were and life went on as before.

So Coventry, to the great relief of everyone at Victoria Park, led the team out as usual in the first round of the season, against old foes Richmond at Punt Road. The arrival of the season seemed to be accompanied by an even greater sense of anticipation than usual, because many fans were looking for a distraction from the Depression. So it proved for the opening match at Richmond, where more than 30,000 turned up to watch the two teams do battle again. 'What a magnet is this game of football', wrote Jack Worrall in *The Australasian*.

Collingwood chose to start the season with an experienced team, fielding no new players. But there was one major change – the introduction of a 19th man, who could come on to replace a player at any point in the game. The innovation had been a long time coming, and the Pies had suffered many times without it, being forced to play one or two men short when hit by injuries. Bruce Andrew, who had missed the 1929 Grand Final, was Collingwood's first 19th man, but spent the entire game on the bench. That was to be a familiar pattern. The Magpies used six different 19th men in the first six weeks, but rarely did they get game time. The men in the starting XVIII were hardly going to give up their spot unless they were seriously hurt, and coaches hadn't yet learned much about the art of tactical substitutions. This led to the introduction of an important football artefact, the dressing gown. As the Collingwood reserves spent almost all their time sitting watching the game from the boundary line, one trainer decided to keep them warm by giving them a thick woollen dressing gown in the club's colours. The dressing gown was first used in Round 4 and would soon become the customary garb for those on the reserves bench across the VFL.

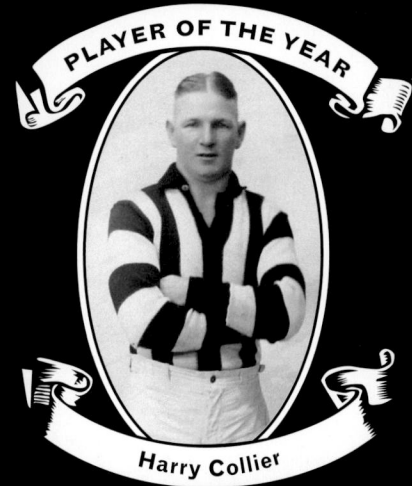

PLAYER OF THE YEAR

Harry Collier

There might have been some confusion over whether or not he'd won the Brownlow, but there was no doubting Harry Collier's importance to Collingwood in 1930.

The feisty, tough rover with an eye for goals enjoyed his best ever season as the Pies ran to their fourth successive flag. He'd been good when winning the Copeland in 1928, but he took his game to new heights in 1930, winning not just a second Copeland but also the Brownlow (belatedly), the club's most consistent player award and, yet again, selection for Victoria.

One of the highlights of Harry's play through 1930 (and also the previous year) was his great teamwork with Gordon Coventry. Collier fed Coventry with passes that led to many of the full-forward's goals, and the two developed an uncanny understanding that baffled those trying to quell the side's goal-scoring power.

Collier was also a great clubman, and he came to embody the team spirit for which the Machine became famous. Even with Syd Coventry still around, he looked for all the world like a future captain.

The Round 1 match against Richmond was close, and in many ways set the scene for the season. The Tigers led by 11 points at half-time and would have been much further in front had it not been for a horribly wayward second-quarter return of 3.9. The Pies hit back with the breeze in the third and held a narrow lead at the last change, but the only goal for much of the final quarter came from the Tigers, who led by five points with just four minutes remaining. Then George Clayden, who previously had been 'floundering about like a walrus' was sent into the ruck and changed the game. The Magpies made a sensational recovery, kicking three goals in the last few minutes to win by 14 points.

Once again, the Collingwood faithful had to wait until Round 2 to see their premiership flag unfurled. Hawthorn wasn't expected to provide much opposition, but they proved to be a far tougher proposition under Jiggy Harris's leadership. Indeed, the Magpies had to fight hard to stave off what would have been a shock defeat. Hawthorn led by two points at three-quarter-time and, when they also grabbed the first goal of the final term, home fans began to fear the worst. But Collingwood hit back through Harry Collier and Gordon Coventry in a nail-biting, see-sawing quarter of football that saw the home side add four goals and the visitors three. The Pies still led by a solitary point

Wingman Bruce Andrew is given some quarter-time attention by trainer Harry Williams.

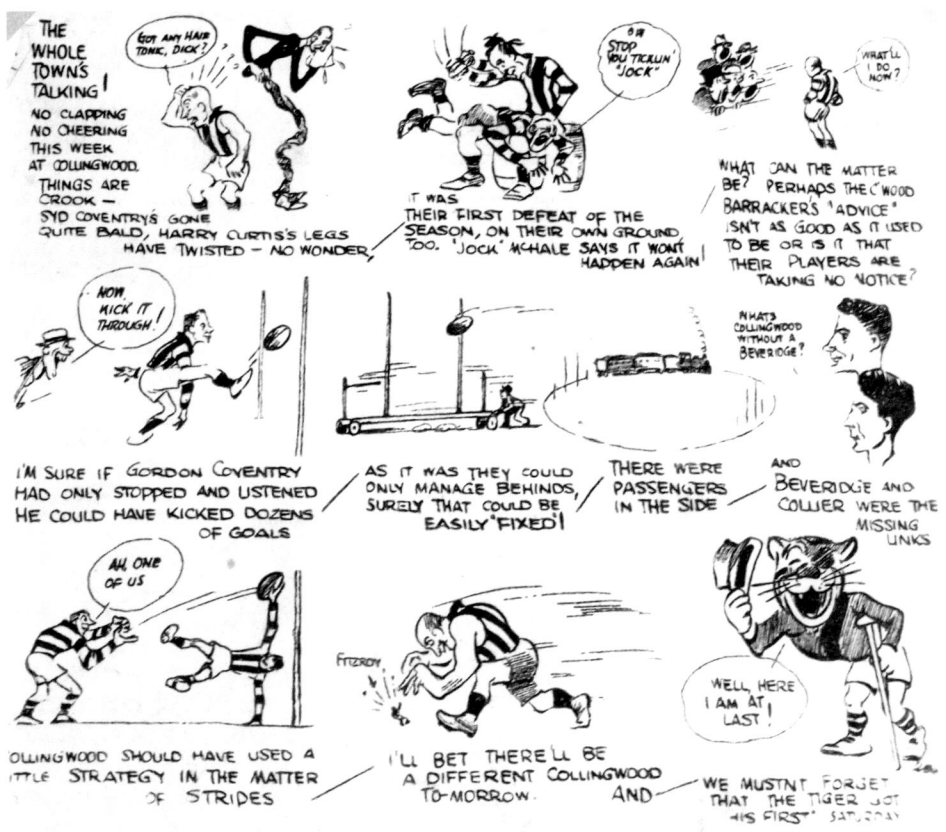

> **The Australasian**
>
> **On Collingwood's form slump:**
>
> There have been unmistakable signs that the Magpies have felt the strain of many years' exertion... and while the practice of hanging on to the same men year in and year out paid in results by maintaining the combination at full strength, there must come a relapse in the course of time. The team needs new blood. There was conclusive evidence that several men in the colours are not up to premiership standard. One defeat does not necessarily mean Collingwood is out of the running, but there is still plenty of time to strengthen forces and forge to the front.

as time-on started and once again needed some heroics from Clayden, whose goal deep in the final term sealed the result and avoided any embarrassment.

That made it two games, for two narrow, seat-of-the-pants wins. It was hardly convincing. Some neutral observers thought Collingwood displayed all the hallmarks of a team that needed fresh blood. Jack Worrall, in *The Australasian*, was not convinced the triple premiers were as potent or desperate as they had been. He felt that too many Magpies had played a lot of football, for a lot of success, and that this would inevitably mean a 'slowing-down' of the team.

Successive losses in Round 4 to Geelong and Round 5 to Fitzroy – the only time this happened in the 1927-30 era – heightened the feeling that Collingwood's reign might be coming to an end. The club suddenly looked vulnerable, especially against faster, younger opponents such as Geelong, and the challengers were coming.

Some were taken by surprise at Collingwood's sudden fallibility. 'It was scarcely believable that almost the same body of men who won the premiership three years in succession was so overmatched on the day,' wrote Worrall after the loss to Geelong. But he felt the loss could be a blessing in disguise for the Pies, and would certainly be good for football as a whole.

PLAYER OF THE YEAR — Gordon Coventry

It says much for the standards Gordon Coventry set over his career that his 118-goal haul in 1930 raised barely a whimper in the press.

Never mind that so far he was the only man to have kicked 100 goals in a season, and had now done it twice in successive years. Never mind that his nearest competitors finished 35 and 60 goals adrift in those two years. No, Coventry was just expected to kick bag after bag of goals, and many observers only really noticed on the rare occasions he failed to deliver.

But even those most accustomed to Coventry's regular goal-scoring feats had to sit up and take notice of his single 17-goal haul during 1930. It was a phenomenal performance. The record stood for 17 years, and it remains the equal second-greatest individual haul on record.

Not bad for a bloke playing his eleventh season of senior football. Gordon Coventry started his career slowly, but he definitely made up for lost time in the late 1920s.

The reaction to the Fitzroy loss was more negative, and the grumblings about Collingwood's ageing team and the need for new blood grew louder. But there were still some loyalists who refused to lose faith. One such fan was seen delivering a 'sermon' to a crowd of onlookers in Johnston Street on the Saturday night after the loss to the Maroons. 'They say we are holding on too long to old players,' he told the crowd. 'Rubbish! Ten months ago the premiership was won by almost the same team we have now. If the club would give clearances someone would be killed in the rush of other clubs to get the so-called "too old" players. Our fellows are not too old. What they want is a sound shaking up.'

That 'shaking up' seemed to come from the back-to-back losses. After the Fitzroy loss the Pies turned on a solid month of football with victories over North Melbourne (57 points), Melbourne (18 points), St Kilda (51 points) and Footscray (80 points). Half a dozen new players were tried, including Regan, who made his debut against St Kilda when Charlie Dibbs took the week off to get married (Regan promptly had 10 kicked on him by Bill Mohr). Doubters were quick to point out that three of those teams were considered little more than cannon fodder, but the win over Melbourne, in particular, provided hope that the Magpies could still be premiership contenders. Syd Coventry said afterwards: 'I fancy we'll go on winning to the end. I hope it will be so, for I've set my mind on Collingwood winning the pennant again. If so, it will be the fourth time running – a record held by no team, and one which will last a long time.'

That Melbourne win came in controversial circumstances when 'Snowy' Barr, one of the Magpie rookies, kicked two late goals to help seal the game, then flattened Billy Tymms with an elbow to the back of the head. The incident led to Barr being rubbed out for eight weeks. It also caused some nasty scenes post-match when angry Melbourne fans attacked the Collingwood players as they were leaving the field. One Collingwood player was knocked down during the melee and, as other players came in to support him, a young woman was inadvertently caught in the mayhem. She was knocked over and had her glasses broken, and later blamed a Collingwood player for the incident. Police were called in but the incident was smoothed over when the Collingwood committee 'expressed their dismay' to the woman and promised to pay for new glasses.

1930: Mission accomplished

The committee at this stage had bigger things on its mind. Club secretary George Connor had been a fixture at the club for almost 30 years, first as a singer and entertainer at the club's annual meetings before World War 1 and later as a committeeman and benefactor. But he'd been forced to resign in embarrassing circumstances on the eve of the season when a number of financial irregularities were traced back to his desk. The club somehow managed to keep the story out of the papers, and had been busy sorting through the 160 applications they'd received for Connor's job. By the middle of the year they had appointed Frank Wraith, who had filled a similar role with Brunswick in the VFA. Wraith proved to be a wise choice, steering the club in the right direction again and staying in the role for 20 years.

Despite their mini-resurgence, Collingwood came into the Round 10 game with Carlton in the unfamiliar position of underdogs. The Blues were on top of the table and looking increasingly like the team to beat for the flag. That standing was only enhanced when they emerged with the spoils after an astonishing game of football that still ranks as one of the best of all time.

The Blues were a point in front at quarter time after an open, entertaining stanza in which each team kicked three goals. Collingwood had by far the better of the next two quarters and seemed in a comfortable position at three-quarter-time with a 17-point lead. Gordon Coventry extended that to 23 points early in the last term and the game looked safe. But Carlton drove the 40,000 fans at Princes Park into a frenzy as they turned the game on its head with a four-goal barrage to grab a narrow advantage. That sparked the Magpies into life again, and they responded with a couple of majors of their own, putting them 11 points up at the 19-minute mark. As time-on neared, the Blues crept to within two points following a goal and a succession of behinds, only for Gordon Coventry to grab his fourth and, seemingly, seal it. But the quarter dragged on and on, and Carlton kept pressing as the Collingwood defence fought off wave after wave of attacks. Eventually, after 31 minutes, Allen scrambled one through off the ground and the margin was back to two points. A minute later 'Soapy' Vallence soared for a huge mark and goaled again to put the Blues in front. There was still time for more Magpie counter-attacks, and there were two ball-ups in the Collingwood goalsquare as players threw themselves desperately at the ball. 'Tubby' Edmonds managed a hurried snap shot after the second ball-up but the bell rang as the ball slid across the goalfront. Carlton was home.

Carlton had kicked 7.6 in the final term, the Magpies 4.3. Players, coaches and fans were all spent, and the media struggled to find the superlatives needed to describe the game. Collingwood's only consolation was that even

Jock McHale talks with Frank Wraith.

The Argus

On the finish of the Carlton–Collingwood game:

Everyone caught the infection of the terrific excitement, and the great crowd rocked and swayed as the players, flushed and desperate, fought like demons. When Carlton finally succeeded and gained a four-point lead the excitement was indescribable. Both sides threw every ounce into the wild battle, and the players were at collapsing point when a thrilling roar of triumph signaled Carlton's win and the termination of a magnificent struggle.

Above: **Gordon Coventry in action against Fitzroy.**
Above right: **Coventry is congratulated by trainers and teammates after kicking his 100th goal.**
Below: **The ball with which Coventry kicked his 100th goal.**

former Carlton coach Jack Worrall felt they'd been given a raw deal by the umpire. 'It is an unpleasant duty to find fault with an umpire, though it was remarkable how Scott punished the faults of the Collingwood players, while apparently not seeing the errors of the Blues.'

The Collingwood players were shattered by the loss – their third of the season and one which left them two games behind the Blues. But they reignited their season two weeks later with a thumping win over Fitzroy, highlighted by Gordon Coventry breaking his own goalkicking record. This time the tally was a phenomenal 17 goals, many coming from Harry Collier, who seemed to know instinctively where Coventry would be and delivered a string of perfect passes to his target. The performance prompted another financially rewarding dressing-room visit from the benefactor of the Collingwood forwards, John Wren.

After the loss to Carlton, the Pies quietly went about rebuilding their season. They won six games in a row, several by big margins and all with a minimum of fuss. The Blues still had a two-game break, but when they unexpectedly lost to Melbourne in Round 15, the door opened for Collingwood. If the Pies could beat Carlton at Victoria Park in Round 17 then both teams would be level on points and the battle for top spot would come down to percentage, where the black-and-whites held a slight edge. The benefits of finishing on top ensured this would be no ordinary home-and-away clash. It was, in effect, a mini-final.

Harry Collier got the home team off to the best possible start, goaling inside the first minute, but it was tight and tense for the rest of the first half. The Pies led by nine points at the long break, but early goals to the Blues in the third quarter saw them claw back the advantage. That sparked a Magpie onslaught, with five goals coming in the rest of the term. Though the memories of Round 10 ensured that no Collingwood fan felt truly safe until the end, the team held on to a comfortable lead for the rest of the game, eventually prevailing by 23 points. The day was made even sweeter for Magpie fans when Gordon Coventry brought up his second successive ton. The win convinced even the biggest doubters that the Pies were once again the team to beat, with Syd Coventry saying, 'I think we'll get the fourth successive premiership – it's a record on which we have set our determination.'

Collingwood firstly needed to win against Essendon in the final round, then make sure that its winning margin wasn't significantly less than Carlton's over Footscray. The Pies won by 43 points, the Blues by 56 and Collingwood held on to top spot by 2.7 per cent. All was in readiness for the club's shot at history.

The Magpies had become used to receiving good news from the VFL in the first week of the finals after the votes for the Brownlow Medal had been counted. And sure enough, Harry Collier was announced as one of three winners, having tied for the award with Footscray's Allan Hopkins and Richmond's Stan

Long-kicking full-back Charlie Dibbs clears against Essendon in the last home-and-away game of the season.

H. COLLIER (Collingwood)

Judkins. Collier should have won the award outright, as one vote had been recorded as 'Collier' without differentiating between Harry and his brother Albert. The umpire who cast the vote apparently said later that he meant 'the little rover fella', meaning Harry, but the vote was discounted anyway.

The League was unsure how to deal with a tied result, despite several meetings, and initially decided that no winner should be declared. Then, on the eve of the finals, a Richmond delegate claimed that the winner should be the player who had the largest percentage of votes to games played. Coincidentally (or not) that ruling, which was accepted by the VFL, saw Richmond's player declared the winner, as Judkins had missed a number of games after being dropped. Collingwood was furious with the ruling, as was Collier. They felt an injustice had been done. It wasn't until almost 60 years later that Collier received a retrospective medal, thanks to his own persistence and the club's lobbying of the VFL.

The brouhaha over the Brownlow added extra spice – as if any were needed – to the Magpies' first final, which was yet another September meeting with Richmond. Once again, the Tigers set out to spoil the Pies' party, and their seven-goal second quarter gave them a commanding 22-point lead at the long break. They also added the first major of the second half, and the game seemed as good as over. But Collingwood staged yet another thrilling comeback, kicking eight unanswered goals in a scintillating third quarter to reverse the half-time margin. Fittingly, Harry Collier had a hand in six of those eight goals. But Richmond wasn't finished, and produced its own fightback in the final quarter, clawing to within three points when the bell rang.

Tubby Edmonds heads for the turf in the semi-final against Richmond, as Bruce Andrew runs past.

Harry Lauder prepares to pounce on the ball, while two Tigers prepare to pounce on him.

The importance of claiming top spot from Carlton had been demonstrated in the first week of the finals, when the Blues lost to Geelong and found their season over. That meant the Magpies would meet Geelong in the final: a Collingwood win would deliver the premiership, while a Geelong win would necessitate a rematch between the two. In the lead-up to the game, Collingwood president Harry Curtis was forced to deny rumours sweeping Melbourne that the Magpies would 'throw' the final, thus providing the VFL and the clubs with an extra match from which to gain revenue. Curtis said the rumours were 'moonshine' and protested that a proud club such as Collingwood would never pass up the chance of securing four flags in a row. His protestations looked hollow within 30 minutes of the game starting, however, as a faster, fresher Geelong made the Magpies look second rate. The Cats opened up a 27-point lead at half-time, and this time there would be no comeback. A grand final would be needed.

Grand final week was not kind to the Magpies. George Gibbs, one of the unlucky players dropped for the 1929 decider, had only just been restored to the team for the first final against Geelong, and was likely to play in the grand final. But he broke his wrist when he came off his motorcycle while at work, robbing him of a second premiership opportunity. Of more concern was the fact that Jock McHale was seriously ill with the flu and had been advised by his doctor to stay away from the club. McHale sent instructions for the players to have an easy week on the track, and held several bedside meetings with the selectors to plan strategies. But he wouldn't be at the club all week,

The Collingwood team that took out the 1930 premiership, photographed on the ground before the start of the grand final.

and was also ruled out of the game itself. This was a huge blow. How would the Magpies operate without their famous coach? His half-time words had inspired countless fightbacks, yet he would be missing at the 1930 playoff.

The grand final was played in fine weather, yet another factor that was generally felt to be in the speedier Geelong's favour. With Gibbs injured, the Magpies recalled first-year player Bill Aldag for his third senior game, just as they had done with Charlie Ahern the year before. Aldag was brought in to add extra bulk and a strong physical presence, and the Pies made no secret of their plans to adopt a more vigorous approach to throw Geelong off its game.

But the plans didn't work. The Magpies tried to ruffle Geelong with what one observer described as 'vim and ruggedness'. They also tried to slow the game down, hoping that would make it harder for the Cats to break into open space. Collingwood led by a few points at quarter-time, but Geelong blew the game open in the second. They were just too quick, and too skilful, and led by 21 points at the long break. As the bell rang for half-time, Geelong skipper Arthur Coghlan said to Syd Coventry, 'Well I think we've got you licked now.' Coventry responded, 'Don't be too certain of that Arthur – the game's not nearly over yet.'

This was when McHale's absence was most sorely felt. If ever the team needed one of his stirring half-time addresses, it was now. Somebody had to fill the breech. So up stepped club treasurer and former premiership player Bob Rush to try to inspire the players. Rush, whose passion for everything black and white equalled McHale's, implored the players to lift their games. He told them that McHale would be listening in on the radio and would know the players who were letting him, and the club, down. Victory was, he said, the only thing that could heal their coach. The odds were overwhelming, but Rush pleaded with the Machine Team to click into gear one last time. He told them the record they craved was only an hour away. Years later, Harry Collier, Bruce Andrew and Percy Bowyer all recalled Rush's speech as one of the most inspirational they had ever heard. The roar of the players as they left the rooms showed it had hit the right note.

Collingwood responded by producing an astonishing display of brilliant, attacking football. The team dropped its ultra-vigorous approach and returned to the system and pace that had made it so successful. Within half an hour they had kicked 8.6 to 0.1 to transform the 21-point deficit into a 32-point lead. The first goal of the third quarter came from the Coventrys combined, with Gordon finishing some brilliant work from Syd. Then big Bob Makeham overshadowed Reg Hickey and moved with the agility of a rover to smartly snap another. Harry Collier slashed the difference back to one point when he snapped a beauty soon after. The crowd went wild as the Collingwood charge showed no signs of abating. Froude and Edmonds helped Coventry to Collingwood's seventh goal, giving the Pies the lead. Then Beveridge and Makeham added two more. The goals just kept coming – and there was nothing the Cats could do to stem the flow.

The *Sun* described the club's third term as 'one of the finest performances ever seen in football . . . It was an object lesson to every team in rising to the occasion

PLAYER OF THE YEAR
Harry Rumney

Harry Rumney holds a special place in Collingwood's awards history: in the first nine years of the Copeland Trophy, he was the only player other than the Coventrys and Colliers to win the honour.

That achievement came in 1931, but Rumney's 1930 season was nearly as good. He represented Victoria in the carnival side in Adelaide and won the state team's most consistent player award. He also won the Austral Trophy that season, an award voted by supporters and theatre patrons for the best Collingwood player of the year.

Rumney was a versatile running machine as a footballer, his charging runs out of defence earning him the nickname 'Dasher'. He was strong, fearless and could roost the ball a mile. Rumney spent most of his career in the back pocket or on the half-back flank, but he was also versatile enough to be moved up the ground when required, and kicked some important goals in his career.

He was a much loved figure around the club, and became such an important part of the Machine that fans were even prepared to overlook the fact that he'd got his start in League football with Carlton. That's high praise indeed.

after being apparently beaten, and by sheer grit and magnificent teamwork, sweeping down every obstacle in the way of finals success.' This withering third quarter should not have come as a surprise: in third terms during the 1930 season Collingwood kicked 89.69 (603) to 42.51 (303). In the finals their dominance of the term was even more emphatic, the club kicking 20.10 to its opponents' 2.3.

The final term was a bit of an anti-climax, with each side kicking three goals and the Magpies clinching their fourth successive flag by a resounding 30 points. The Machine Team had created more history – a fourth successive premiership. When the final bell sounded, Syd Coventry and his teammates were mobbed by trainers and fans. The crowd around the Collingwood dressing room was massive. There was a huge crush both inside and outside, and the

1930: Mission accomplished

Geelong skipper Coghlan had great trouble getting in to offer his congratulations. Syd Coventry's words were short but sweet: 'We were up against the greatest odds a team could face at half-time, and I thank the boys for the way they rose to the occasion. It was a wonderful effort from the whole team.'

The Magpies celebrated heartily after that 1930 Premiership, and so too did the fans. Each of the players from grand final day was given five pounds by a grateful supporter. There were dances and dinners and presentations. And yet another savvy company cashed in, with energy tonic Forbes' Phosferrine running ads claiming that their product was the secret behind the Magpies' success.

The 1930 premiership provided a fitting end to a four-year reign that left an indelible mark on the game. The Machine still remains the only team in VFL–AFL history to win four consecutive premierships. In those four glorious years the Magpies possessed some of the greatest players the game has known, yet no man was considered more important than any other. Forget the fact that Syd Coventry, Albert Collier and Harry Collier won Brownlow Medals in that period, or that Gordon Coventry won the VFL goalkicking in all four seasons: this was all about the team.

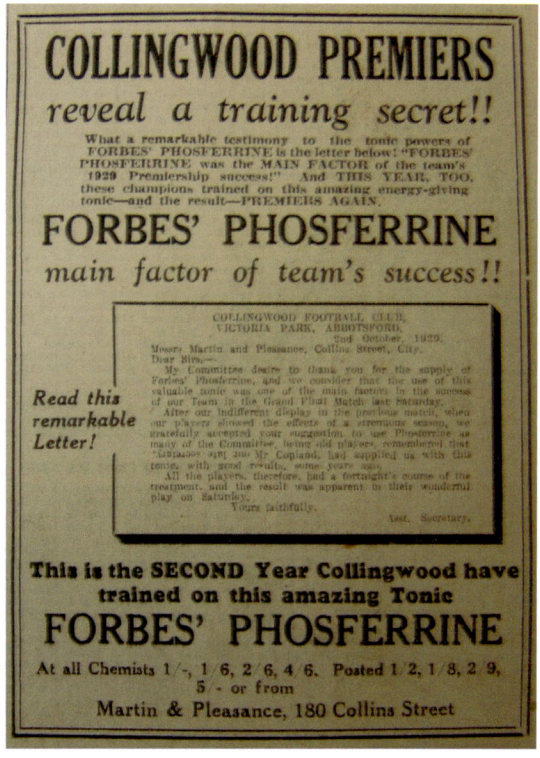

It was also about the club, and the community. By the time the fourth flag was won, the suburb was suffering badly from the effects of the Great Depression and so were many of the club's supporters. They had taken great pride, and happiness, from the Magpies' performances over the past four years and some were even bold enough to start thinking about a fifth flag. But the Machine had reached the end of its prime working life. The signs had been there for much of 1930, but Jock McHale and Syd Coventry had managed to eke out one final flag from the group before the inevitable decline hit.

Winning four successive flags was considered a mighty feat at the time. But a true appreciation of the achievement has really only been possible as the years have passed. None of the other great teams that followed the Machine have been able to match – let alone eclipse – that four-in-a-row run. Not Melbourne in the 1950s, Hawthorn in the 1980s or the Lions and Geelong in the 2000s. And that's without considering the other elements, such as Brownlow Medals, goalkicking titles and undefeated seasons. More than 80 years later, the Machine still stands alone as the greatest team VFL–AFL football has seen. They were, as one journalist wrote at the time, 'the Bradmans of football'.

BOB MAKEHAM
GRAND FINAL HERO

Collingwood has known few more reluctant grand final heroes than Bob Makeham. The tall, balding, genial farmer from Woodleigh in country Victoria was no fan of city life, and tolerated it only long enough to train Thursday nights and play on Saturdays.

He put up with it because he loved football, and he loved Collingwood. He was one of the quiet achievers of the Machine, playing in 78 of the 82 matches across four years, and in all four flags. He was versatile, playing in defence, attack and sometimes in the ruck.

Makeham had a happy knack of playing well in big games, and was among the team's best in the 1927, '28 and '29 deciders. But it was his contribution in the 1930 Grand Final that was his finest hour. He dominated the game throughout, and was especially prominent in the team's third quarter charge, kicking two goals.

The club presented special caps to just two players after the 1930 Grand Final. One was to the captain, Syd Coventry. The other was to the man who the committee had voted as the team's best player in the game, Bob Makeham. That says it all.

PLAYERS

#	Player	Games	Goals
30	Bill Aldag	3	0
1	Bruce Andrew	11	0
2	Elvin Barr	7	3
5	Jack Beveridge	12	4
3	Leo Bird	15	10
4	Percy Bowyer	18	0
10	Harry Chesswas	18	5
11	George Clayden	21	10
6	Albert Collier	19	0
7	Harry Collier	21	39
8	Gordon Coventry	21	118
9	Syd Coventry	21	2
12	Charlie Dibbs	19	0
13	Horrie Edmonds	18	39
29	Bert Everett	4	0
28	Fred Froude	7	7
14	Jack George	3	0
15	George Gibbs	11	3
17	Frank Kelly	12	0
18	Albert Lauder	13	0
19	Billy Libbis	20	23
23	Norm MacLeod	16	0
20	Bob Makeham	21	11
21	Frank Murphy	19	20
22	Len Murphy	20	17
27	Jack Regan	4	0
25	Bob Ross	5	6
26	Harold Rumney	20	0

Club Awards
Copeland Trophy – Harry Collier
Most consistent – Harry Collier
Austral Cup – Harry Rumney
Best player in Grand Final – Bob Makeham
Wal Lee Trophy for regular attendance at training – E Barr
Leading goalkicker – Gordon Coventry (118)

1930 SEASON

ROUND 1 May 3 Punt Rd Oval

Richmond **7.18.60** v **Collingwood 10.14.74**

Goals: G Coventry 3, Edmonds 2, Gibbs 2, Beveridge, Libbis, L Murphy

ROUND 2 May 10 Victoria Park

Collingwood 11.12.78 v Hawthorn **10.10.70**

Goals: G Coventry 5, Clayden 4, H Collier, Ross

ROUND 3 May 17 Lake Oval

South Melbourne **12.12.84** v **Collingwood 16.19.115**

Goals: G Coventry 7, Bird 4, Ross 3, H Collier, Libbis

ROUND 4 May 24 Victoria Park

Collingwood **10.12.72** v **Geelong 12.18.90**

Goals: Clayden 2, G Coventry 2, L Murphy 2, Bird, H Collier, F Murphy, Ross

ROUND 5 May 31 Brunswick St Oval

Fitzroy 10.11.71 v Collingwood **9.12.66**

Goals: G Coventry 4, Edmonds 2, Froude 2, F Murphy

ROUND 6 June 7 Victoria Park

Collingwood 15.24.114 v North Melbourne **8.9.57**

Goals: G Coventry 6, Edmonds 3, Libbis 2, H Collier, Froude, Makeham, F Murphy

ROUND 7 June 14 MCG

Melbourne **11.13.79** v **Collingwood 14.13.97**

Goals: G Coventry 3, Barr 2, Collier 2, Edmonds 2, Froude 2, Libbis, F Murphy, L Murphy

ROUND 8 June 21 Victoria Park

Collingwood 22.11.143 v St Kilda **14.8.92**

Goals: Edmonds 7, G Coventry 5, H Collier 3, L Murphy 3, Makeham 2, F Murphy 2

ROUND 9 June 28 Whitten Oval

Footscray **5.14.44** v **Collingwood 19.10.124**

Goals: G Coventry 9, H Collier 3, F Murphy 2, L Murphy 2, Chesswas, Clayden, Edmonds

ROUND 10 July 5 Princes Park

Carlton 16.20.116 v Collingwood **16.16.112**

Goals: G Coventry 4, Chesswas 3, Libbis 3, Edmonds 2, F Murphy 2, H Collier, L Murphy

ROUND 11 July 12 Victoria Park

Collingwood 14.14.98 v Essendon **9.14.68**

Goals: G Coventry 7, H Collier 3, Edmonds 2, Libbis, L Murphy

ROUND 12 July 19 Victoria Park

Collingwood 25.17.167 v Fitzroy **13.16.94**

Goals: G Coventry 17, Libbis 3, Edmonds 2, Chesswas, Clayden, H Collier

ROUND 13 July 26 Arden St Oval

North Melbourne **4.15.39** v **Collingwood 18.13.121**

Goals: G Coventry 7, Edmonds 6, Beveridge, S Coventry, Makeham, F Murphy, Ross

ROUND 14 August 16 Victoria Park

Collingwood 15.14.104 v Melbourne **8.9.57**

Goals: G Coventry 5, H Collier 5, Edmonds 2, Beveridge, Bird, Makeham

ROUND 15 August 23 Junction Oval

St Kilda **14.7.91** v **Collingwood 17.13.115**

Goals: G Coventry 6, H Collier 3, Libbis 3, L Murphy 2, Bird, Clayden, Edmonds

ROUND 16 August 30 Victoria Park

Collingwood 16.20.116 v Footscray **10.17.77**

Goals: G Coventry 6, H Collier 4, Bird 2, Edmonds 2, Libbis, F Murphy

ROUND 17 September 6 Victoria Park

Collingwood 16.10.106 v Carlton **12.11.83**

Goals: G Coventry 6, H Collier 3, F Murphy 2, L Murphy 2, Clayden, Edmonds, Froude

ROUND 18 September 13 Windy Hill

Essendon **10.6.66** v **Collingwood 17.7.109**

Goals: H Collier 3, G Coventry 3, Libbis 3, Edmonds 2, Makeham 2, F Murphy 2, S Coventry, F Murphy

1930 FINALS

LADDER

Team	W	L	D	For	Agst	%	Pts
Collingwood	15	3	0	1931	1338	144.3	60
Carlton	15	3	0	1747	1234	141.6	60
Richmond	11	7	0	1450	1163	124.7	44
Geelong	11	7	0	1495	1259	118.7	44
Melbourne	11	7	0	1509	1441	104.7	44
Essendon	10	8	0	1495	1417	105.5	40
South Melb	9	9	0	1553	1553	100.0	36
St Kilda	8	10	0	1454	1435	101.3	32
Fitzroy	7	11	0	1411	1581	89.2	28
Hawthorn	6	12	0	1205	1558	77.3	24
Footscray	4	14	0	1164	1535	75.8	16
North Melb	1	17	0	969	1869	51.8	4

SEMI FINAL September 27 MCG
Collingwood 14.10.94 v Richmond 14.7.91

Goals: Libbis 4, H Collier 3, G Coventry 3, Barr, Edmonds, Makeham, F Murphy

PRELIMINARY FINAL October 4 MCG
Collingwood 9.11.65 v **Geelong 12.19.91**

Goals: G Coventry 3, F Murphy 3, Bird, Gibbs, Makeham

GRAND FINAL October 11 MCG

Collingwood	3.2	3.7	11.13	14.16	(100)
Geelong	2.5	6.10	6.11	9.16	(70)

Goals: G. Coventry 7, Makeham 2, Beveridge, H. Collier, Edmonds, Froude, L. Murphy
Best: Makeham, G. Coventry, F Murphy, Andrew, Clayden, H. Collier, S Coventry, Chesswas
Umpire: Scott
Crowd: 45,022 at the MCG

Grand Final Team
B: A. Lauder, C. Dibbs, P. Bowyer
HB: H. Rumney, A. Collier, G. Clayden
C: B. Andrew, J. Beveridge, H. Chesswas
HF: R. Makeham, F. Murphy, W. Aldag
F: H. Edmonds, G. Coventry, H. Collier
R: S. Coventry, Len Murphy, W. Libbis
Reserve: F. Froude

CHAPTER ELEVEN

1935

Rebuilding the Machine

'Individual brilliance was no match for Collingwood's teamwork and the spirit of its players, who play first, last and always for their club.'

There was an unfamiliar feeling around Victoria Park as the 1935 season neared. For the first time in 13 years, the club was facing a year without Syd Coventry in the line-up. Collingwood had lost great players before, of course, and the club had always moved on seamlessly. But Syd Coventry was different. He was not just a great player, he was also a great leader, and he deserved much of the credit for piloting the team to its record-breaking four successive flags in 1927–30.

There was always going to be some decline after that miraculous run; the club won only one finals match from 1931–34, and missed the finals altogether in 1933. The Magpies were still strong enough to account for the League's lesser lights, but increasingly had trouble with the power sides of the time – Geelong, Richmond, South Melbourne and Carlton. Coming into 1935, the Pies had dropped six of their previous seven meetings with Geelong, and their previous four with South. Now they had to find their way back to the top without the man widely considered to be the club's greatest ever captain.

Syd had retired at the end of 1934 and started coaching suburban club Alphington. But early in the season, Footscray – the club that twice had come close to snaring his services in the 1920s – appointed him as coach. Collingwood this time agreed to clear Coventry, but only on the proviso that he would not play. The Magpies were taking no chances, even though he was thirty-six. Many critics believed that Coventry's service had earned him the right to a clearance without restrictions but Collingwood stood firm. Syd wrote an article for *The Sporting Globe* in which he emphasised he had not deserted his old club, and also stressed that he felt his playing days were over. It was a slightly messy way to end a glorious playing career.

Many thought Collingwood would crumble without Syd Coventry at the helm. Coach Jock McHale told *The Sporting Globe* that 'quite a wail went up from the pessimists . . . Those cheerful folk even showered us with letters . . . gloating or lamenting (according to their own sympathies) that the proud Magpies would be humbled in the dust – or mud.' The pessimism was compounded when star half-forward Frank Murphy and classy centreman Jack Beveridge, both stalwarts of the Machine era, crossed to Subiaco and West Perth respectively. The club also lost goalkicking utility Norm Le Brun in unusual circumstances, when the 27-year-old was dumped after demanding payment for a proposed exhibition match against Richmond that was to be played under lights at Olympic Park. He was snapped up by Carlton (his fourth VFL club), but then had salt rubbed into his wounds when the VFL abandoned plans for the match anyway, after a previous night game met with a lukewarm reception.

Fortunately for Collingwood, Harry Collier, and his younger brother Albert, formed the perfect duo to lead the club as it looked to rebuild the Machine. Besides the Colliers, several other Machine loyalists still survived, including Charlie Dibbs, Len Murphy, Harry Rumney, Percy Bowyer and, most importantly of all, Gordon Coventry. Jack Regan was now a fully-fledged star, and newcomers Phonse Kyne, Marcus Whelan and Alby Pannam all looked likely types. The Pies confidently looked forward to the prospect of finals, but they knew that, to go further, they needed to start beating the big teams again.

Collingwood's savvy selectors, including Jock McHale (front left), chairman of selectors Doc Seddon (next to Jock) and former player Bruce Andrew (front row, far right) run their eyes over prospective recruits at a practice match.
Opposite: **Harry Collier, left, and Albert Collier.**

Above: Heroes of the first two rounds, Lou Riley and Alan Ryan.
Right: Gordon Coventry leaps for a mark against Fitzroy at the Brunswick Street Oval.

They had the chance to do so on the very first day of the season, when the brilliant, highly-paid stars of South Melbourne's famed 'Foreign Legion' visited Victoria Park. This was a team put together by chain store king Archie Crofts, bringing together players from Tasmania, Western Australia, South Australia and some Victorians, usually lured by Crofts' money. There was so much anticipation surrounding the clash that the clubs even named their sides for the game a day early. And what a game it turned out to be.

In perfect sunny conditions before a big crowd of 30,000, Collingwood blitzed from the start and made a statement by charging to a four-goal lead, with Gordon Coventry proving too strong for Ron Hillis at one end, and Jack Regan having the better of Bob Pratt at the other. 'Collingwood showed South how class football should be played,' wrote one reporter. But South hit back through the second and third terms, with the great Laurie Nash in fine form, and trailed by only seven points at the final change. The *Sporting Globe* described the last half hour as 'football deluxe', and it looked for all the world as if South were home when they raced to a 10-point lead. But Kyne goaled against the run of play, then added a behind as time-on began. Regan, who was best-on-ground, saved several more attempts from South, and, with time running out, Vin Doherty passed to Lou Riley, who coolly steered home the winning goal as the bell rang.

First-round wins are always important, and this one had added significance for Collingwood as it broke South's ascendancy over them. Even so, it was the third successive game between the two sides that had been decided on the last kick of the day, so both camps knew there was not much between them – and that they would most likely be meeting again in September.

After the nail-biting opening to the season, Magpie fans might have been hoping for easier pickings in Round 2 against Fitzroy. Instead they got an even more thrilling encounter, in which Collingwood's Alan 'Ginger' Ryan became an unlikely hero. A journeyman whose hopes as a full-back had been destroyed 12 months earlier by a Bob Pratt blitz, Ginger now found a place in attack. In the frantic dying seconds of a tight contest highlighted by a 12-goal final term, Ryan was sent reeling out of a pack by Fitzroy's Wally Gray and given a free kick as the bell rang, with the Pies trailing by a goal. The crowd invaded the ground as Ryan prepared to take his kick, and police had to clear a pathway for him. Then, as Ryan ran in for his kick, a police horse galloped across almost directly in front of him. With the trooper's trusty steed just feet away, Ginger sent a perfectly timed drop kick through the middle to level the scores. 'The horse reared magnificently on its hind legs as the ball sailed right between the posts from 40 yards out,' reported one newspaper.

The greatest full-back of them all, Jack Regan, in yet another of his classic aerial duels with South's Bob Pratt.

Luckily for Collingwood fans, things got a little easier over the next six weeks. There were big wins over Essendon, North Melbourne and Footscray, and comfortable victories over Melbourne, St Kilda and Geelong. The game against Footscray was an emotional one, with Syd Coventry returning to Victoria Park in charge of the Doggies. The result was clear from a long way out, thanks mainly to brother Gordon's nine-goal haul, and the Collingwood members, safe in the knowledge that the game was in the bag, gave Syd a loud round of applause as he walked off the field following his three-quarter-time address. The victory over Geelong away from home was less emotional but more significant: it was the team's first win at Geelong since 1929, and meant the Magpies had accounted for both of its recent bogey teams.

The Argus

On the union threats to the St Kilda-Collingwood game:

If the dispute between the Trades Hall and the St. Kilda Cricket Club be not settled before Saturday a football match may be declared 'black', with consequences almost too momentous to contemplate. When the Trades Hall goes into action it conceals up its sleeve a 'black' ace; but the question is: would the Trades Hall be wise in playing this card when the stakes are a fixture between St. Kilda and Collingwood? What are trades union principles compared with a football match? Many things have been sacrificed on the altar of sport; and it is not improbable that principles will be offered up also. In the history of trade unionism many things have been declared 'black'. It will be interesting to discover what is the colour of a football.

Opposite: **Harry Rumney** took over the captaincy duties during the visit to New South Wales and Queensland. Here he tosses the coin in the game against South Melbourne in Newcastle.

The only drama during this time was off-field, in the lead-up to the game at St Kilda, when the Liquor Trades Union threatened to declare the ground 'black' in a dispute with the St Kilda Cricket Club over the club's use of non-union labour in its bar. Several Collingwood players who were members of the LTU said they could not play at a 'black' ground. The Collingwood committee backed its players, asked the VFL to move the game, and said it would have to forfeit if it wasn't shifted. In true industrial relations tradition, the dispute was settled the day before the match.

Collingwood came to the half-way point of the season in good shape, unbeaten and with its players in excellent form. The forward line was proving especially potent, with Gordon Coventry grabbing his usual big tallies, including nine against Footscray and seven against Geelong. He was well supported by a dangerous band of small forwards including Vin Doherty, who'd kicked seven against Footscray, Alby Pannam, who had two seven-goal hauls to his name, and Lou Riley, with two five-goal bags.

But all that forward power counted for little on a miserable day at Princes Park in Round 9, when fourth-placed Carlton inflicted the Magpies' first defeat, by 29 points. It was a day to forget for the Magpies, and also for umpire Bill Blackburn, who was famously bitten by a dog he tried to remove from the field in the opening term, then was hit by a gastric attack at half-time.

It took a lot to stop Harry Collier but he missed that game with flu – later in the year he would receive an award for missing only one training session in 10 years. He made a welcome return the next week against reigning premiers Richmond. The fifth-placed Tigers desperately needed to win this match, and the atmosphere at Punt Road was electric, especially when the Tigers roared home in the final quarter, chasing down a 22-point deficit and snatching the lead late in the term. But with only seconds to go, and the ground in near-darkness, Jack 'Cracker' Knight soccered through his fifth goal of the day to give the Magpies a two-point win – their third nail-biter of the season. Remarkably straight kicking in the Punt Road mud – 13.4 – enabled the Pies to snatch the victory.

Two weeks later came the match everyone had been waiting for, Collingwood's return clash with South Melbourne. The Bloods had not lost a match since the opening day, and they sat

half a game clear of the Pies at the top of the ladder. Both sides had brilliant forward lines, great defenders and top-class midfields, and fans and critics alike were expecting the kind of blockbuster the two sides had dished up in Round 1. Instead they got a damp squib of a game, one that quickly turned into a nightmare for the Pies, who were hopelessly outclassed from start to finish, going down by 53 points. Bob Pratt kicked a lazy 10, and would have had more had he not missed with all five of his final quarter shots.

The humbled Pies slipped to third on the ladder, and things looked bleak again the following week when they found themselves 19 points behind a Haydn Bunton-inspired Fitzroy at three-quarter time. But Collingwood dug deep, and, as he had done so often, Gordon Coventry kicked a couple of quick goals to help right the ship as he and his teammates produced a 10-minute rally that sank the Maroons.

Collingwood's late resurgence couldn't mask the fact that the side had fumbled, miskicked and lacked in all its usual systems. The split round break could not have come at a better time, and the Magpies packed their bags for a trio of exhibition games in New South Wales and Queensland – against, of all teams, South Melbourne. The trip was a promotional success, and the matches in Brisbane, Newcastle and Sydney drew good crowds. Collingwood won two and lost one, but the players and officials felt they had learned a lot from having played South four times in a month. On their return home there was confidence in the air at Victoria Park.

PLAYER OF THE YEAR

Vin Doherty

The Collingwood team of 1935 was full of big names, such as the Colliers, Jack Regan, Phonse Kyne, Marcus Whelan, Gordon Coventry, Alby Pannam and many more. So it speaks volumes that the man who finished third in the Copeland Trophy that year was the un-hyped Vin Doherty.

Doherty had joined the club in 1934 from the Carlton Breweries side, and in just his second season established himself as one of the most dangerous half-forwards in the competition. He kicked 30 goals for the year and, together with Pannam and Lou Riley, formed a dangerous trio of small forwards that made life hell for opposition defences.

Doherty was fast, clever and a wonderfully accurate kick for goal, even on the run from tight angles. He was outstanding around the packs, set up plenty of chances for his teammates, and was renowned for his smart use of handball. So good was his early form in 1935 that some critics were tagging him as a potential Brownlow Medal winner.

Vin Doherty never quite reached those heights, but he managed nearly 100 games for the club, and played a key role in the back-to-back flags of 1935–36.

PLAYER OF THE YEAR
Len Murphy

From the time he first came into the team in 1928, Len Murphy had been tagged as one of the team's tough guys. The younger brother of polished centre half-forward Frank, Len was tall, strapping, strong and not afraid to throw his weight around. He could be a bit of a wild man, and made his smaller teammates walk taller.

But Len could also play football. As his career continued, his game improved, and he became a valuable follower, an excellent tap ruckman and a big man who could fill roles either forward or back. This improvement saw Murphy finish third in the Copeland in 1934, and runner-up behind Albert Collier in 1935.

The *Football Record* praised his 'coolness in a crisis' and also noted that 'his fine physique enables him to stand up easily to the forceful style of play in vogue today'. Both those qualities made him a valuable player in the finals, but he was injured early in the preliminary final and missed the premiership. He would also miss the 1936 flag, though suspension, but fortunately he already had three premiership medals from the Machine era.

High-scoring wins over Essendon and Geelong followed, and, though still not in their best form, the Pies were on course to hold the all-important second place on the ladder as they went into the game against Melbourne. They were lacking a few players through injury, but weren't expected to be seriously challenged. Even when the Magpies led by only a goal late in the game, *The Argus* reported that they did not look worried – was it 'arrogance or deep inner confidence that they could always prevail in a tight finish?' the paper pondered. Either way, the Woods were caught out, and Ron Baggot's fourth goal just before the siren ensured the points were shared – the team's second draw in a heart-stopping season.

The surprise result made the Magpies' hold on the double chance tenuous, as they were only half a game ahead of Carlton. Unconvincing wins over Footscray and St Kilda in the last two games of the season preserved the Pies' second-place standing, but did nothing to silence the many doubters who were questioning their ability to trouble South. Those doubts grew even stronger after a disappointing second semi-final. The first half was tight and even, with South being strangled by Collingwood's disciplined spoiling in the air and ability to close down space. Both gun full-forwards were tightly marked, but Pratt still brought up his 100th goal for the season. South held a six-point lead at half-time and banged on six goals to four in an entertaining third quarter and eventually ran out comfortable 21-point winners.

Collingwood would now have to meet Richmond in the preliminary final, and Tiger skipper Perc Bentley made no secret of his disdain for the Magpies' semi-final showing: 'On today's form I don't think the Tigers will have much difficulty in winning the right to play South off for the third successive year,' he said. If the Pies needed any extra motivation, they had found it.

Collingwood's big men had been thrashed against South, and selectors brought back veteran Len Murphy from injury to face the Tigers, who boasted one of the strongest ruck divisions in the League. But the Magpies' plans to strengthen their big man stocks began to unravel before the game even started, when the strapping Keith Fraser withdrew from the side with appendix trouble. The bonus of Murphy returning was now cancelled out, for he had to take Fraser's spot at centre half-back. Worse still, Murphy was forced off the ground at quarter time with a painful shoulder injury.

Harry Collier pressures Richmond's Danny Guinane in the preliminary final (left), while Gordon Coventry leaps high for a classic mark in the same game (below).

By today's standards, the pre-match warm-ups were less than conventional. *The Argus* reported that Richmond supporters in the team's dressing-room sang 'inspiring choruses to pianoforte accompaniment'. In the Collingwood room the players' final war cry came in verse:

'Tradition is your keyword, and tradition never dies
And win or lose, you'll always put the game before the prize
Sustain that fighting spirit, lads; uphold the old club's name,
And honour those immortal words, Play up and play the game.'

Collingwood started the game well and led at the first change, but it was heroic defence in the second quarter that kept their premiership hopes alive. The Tigers threw everything at them in the second term, and even though the Magpies went to the long break three points down, it could have been much, much more. The *Sporting Globe* wrote: 'Probably not another team in the League would have been able to overcome such a disadvantage as the loss of Fraser and Murphy, but Regan, Rumney and Dibbs were playing inspired football in defence and repeatedly outwitted their heavier and taller opponents.' The great Tiger full-forward Jack Titus admitted after the game that he'd thought all his Christmases had come at once when Regan was moved to centre half-back after Murphy was injured. Instead, the wily veteran Charlie Dibbs took over at full-back and kept Titus to a solitary goal for the day.

Alby Pannam, back in the team after being dropped in the wake of the Melbourne match, quickly regained the lead for the Magpies with a goal after half-time, and the Tigers never recovered. Phonse Kyne was having a big influence at centre half-forward, and when he landed his second goal just before three quarter time it stretched the lead to 16 points. Marcus Whelan dominated, the Tigers made plenty of errors under pressure and the Pies were too quick all over the ground. When Pannam, whose inclusion had been a masterstroke, goaled cleverly from a free on the boundary, Richmond's resistance was broken, and Collingwood went on to complete a 28-point victory. Jack Titus summed it up when he said, 'It was a day for small nippy men and the Collingwood midgets ran the heavier Richmond side off its legs.'

It was a stirring and memorable finals victory. But Collingwood emerged from the game with plenty of headaches. Fraser's appendix problem looked certain to rule him out of the grand final, X-rays showed that Murphy had fractured his shoulder and would definitely not play, while Jack Knight left the ground in the closing stages with a twisted ankle and a jarred shoulder. On top of that Bervin Woods had been reported on a striking charge. By contrast, the Monday papers reported that South would be at full strength – even star centreman Herb Matthews would return from injury.

Everything pointed to a comfortable South Melbourne win. The Bloods themselves seemed to believe it, and Austin Robertson told a reporter before the game that 'You can't name the odds on South Melbourne'. Collingwood skipper Harry Collier felt there wasn't much between the sides, but South had one big advantage – Bob Pratt. On his way home from training on Thursday night, Collier thought to himself that South's full-forward would be the difference. If they didn't have Pratt, he thought, we would win.

Opposite: The crowd is crammed into the MCG to watch the grand final.
Top: Lou Riley grabs a mark under fierce pressure.
Middle: Albert Collier waits for the ball, then pressures his South opponent.
Bottom: Keith Fraser tries to wrestle the ball away from two South players.

What Collier couldn't have known was that, just hours earlier, Pratt had been struck by a truck loaded with bricks as he got off a tram in High Street, Armadale. Pratt ended up sprawled on the side of the road semi-conscious, with a sprained right ankle, a lacerated right leg, an injured left foot and a bruised thumb. South initially named him in their side and sent him for 'diathermy treatment' on Friday night but it was all to no avail – the game's most dangerous forward would miss the grand final. The heartbroken driver, himself a South Melbourne supporter, visited Pratt that night and gave him a pack of cigarettes by way of apology.

It was the biggest grand final sensation for years. Think how it would have felt if Nick Riewoldt had been run over on the eve of the 2010 grand final. And however much Collingwood players and officials felt for Pratt, they knew they had been gifted a gilt-edged opportunity to snatch another premiership.

Many fans were still in shock on grand final day. Nobody could quite believe that such a freak accident had befallen one of the game's superstars, two days before the biggest game of the year. But the show had to go on, so the two teams prepared to face each other for the *seventh* time in 1935. Bervin Woods had got off his striking charge and Keith Fraser recovered from his appendix, but Murphy and Knight were both non-starters.

Initially, South looked like it would cope just fine without Pratt. They played brilliant football in the opening term, dominating the play and peppering the goals – a return of 3.6 was scant reward for their superiority. *The Sporting Globe* reported it had been a rugged opening, 'replete with hard knocks, doubtful and otherwise, and all were on tiptoe, not knowing when the next outbreak would occur'.

South went into the second quarter with a 15-point lead and once more dominated the early exchanges, but still couldn't put the score on the board. The game became more crowded and tempers frayed, with several players swinging punches at each other. South looked frustrated by their

The Herald

On Collingwood's victory over South:

The Magpies were a far more versatile team, adapting themselves to all emergencies, winning in the heavy clashes and taking the straight route to goal wherever possible. South foolishly tried to show Collingwood a few points about hard bumping, but they came off second best and declined into a ragged and uncertain team.

Jack Ross cops one over his ear for good measure, from South's Terry Brain. Veteran Charlie Dibbs waits for the ball to spill clear.

inability to turn domination into a big lead, and the Pies gradually found their feet and turned the game around. Gordon Coventry kicked three quick goals as Collingwood moved into overdrive, adding five goals to one in a thrilling period of play. The Pies went in 10 points to the good, and the lead was still just 12 points at the last change, after a pulsating third quarter in which Collingwood's magnificent defence held firm again and again.

Both sides suffered serious injuries in the final quarter: Dibbs was badly concussed, and South lost captain–coach Jack Bissett with a fractured skull. South again had chances but again wasted them, kicking 1.6 for the term. The Pies resisted South's push, then Harry Collier goaled from a free kick to ease the pressure and push the lead out to 19 points. The Southerners had fought gamely, but this was a bridge too far, and Collingwood played out time in cruise control for a 20-point win.

To their credit, South Melbourne players and officials did not blame their loss on Pratt's absence. But it's surely no coincidence that their final tally of 7.16 was their lowest of the season. Collingwood treasurer Bob Rush told the Bloods after the match that they were 'one of the best sides that ever missed a premiership'. Ivor Warne-Smith acknowledged the brilliance of South's stars, but pointed out that 'individual brilliance was no match for Collingwood's teamwork and the spirit of its players, who play first, last and always for their club'. The Colliers were magnificent, Kyne was a match winner at centre half-forward and Regan, Rumney, Fraser, Dibbs and Froude were outstanding in defence.

There were the usual chaotic scenes on the ground and in the rooms after the final bell sounded. A local Collingwood councillor made himself popular when he announced he'd give each player five pounds. The celebrations back at Victoria Park were downright riotous, even by Collingwood standards. Late at night the players wheeled a piano into the middle of the ground, and groups of players, officials and supporters belted out tunes of the day until the wee hours. The next day, Harry Collier, Harry Rumney and their wives were returning home when the captain drove his car into the front fence of the house where Archbishop Mannix lived. The car was still driveable, so Harry reversed out and made their getaway – but left the car's bumper bar wedged in the fence. Rumney and Collier were both forced to apologise to the Archbishop.

PLAYER OF THE YEAR
Albert Collier

Early in 1935, former Melbourne captain Ivor Warne-Smith wrote a newspaper article in which he said that, to be a top side, Collingwood needed 'an inspiring player who can . . . take charge of the game and dominate his own and the opposing team'. He identified Albert Collier as one who could maybe fill that role. How right he was.

Collier had played in Tasmania in 1931–32, but when he returned to Collingwood his on-field role changed. The free-running, dashing centre half-back became a hard-working defender/ruckman who did much of the team's hard yakka and protected its smaller players. In this role he became one of the most valuable players in the competition.

Most of his teammates idolised him in the same way they had Syd Coventry. So he was a natural to fill a leadership role when Syd left, and he responded in brilliant fashion in 1935, winning his second successive Copeland Trophy and being selected vice-captain for Victoria (and chosen as best player against Western Australia). He was also voted the best player in the finals series.

Syd Coventry's departure left a huge hole. But Albert Collier, and his brother Harry, made sure the club didn't miss a beat.

The Mightiest Magpies

During the celebrations, president Harry Curtis had told the crowd that this was 'the greatest premiership the club has won'. Even allowing for some post-premiership euphoria, you could understand where Curtis was coming from. The club had endured doubters all season, not just over their capacity to overcome South at the end, but right back at the start, when so many had predicted Collingwood's demise after Syd Coventry's departure.

It was to these doubters that Jock McHale directed his comments in the wake of the flag: 'Think of it. A great player and captain and one of the outstanding footballers of his time retires and despite this severe loss, the team . . . jumps from fourth to first. There's a lesson in that – the lesson that a football team functions as a complete machine. Its success depends on the co-operation of the whole 18 players on the field and the soundness and vision of its administrators. Those who had predicted Collingwood's sudden downfall . . . forgot those things.'

COLLINGWOOD PREMIERS FOOTBALL CLUB 1935

BACK ROW (L to R): L. Riley, P. Fricker, R. Gibson, K. Fraser, A. Fyfe, J. Knight, G. Kanngieser.
3rd ROW: M. Whelan, F. Froud, J. Power, A. Kyne, G. Carter, M. Boyall, R. Todd, B. Woods, J. Ross.
2nd ROW: P. Bowyer, L. Murphy, H. Rumney, A. Collier (V. Capt.), H. Collier (Capt.), G. Coventry, J. Regan, C. Dibbs.
FRONT ROW: J. Carmody, V. Doherty, L. Morgan, K. Stackpole, A. Pannam.

PHONSE KYNE — GRAND FINAL HERO

There would be plenty of fans who would probably nominate Mr C.L. Peters – the driver of the truck that flattened Bob Pratt – as the real hero of Collingwood's win in the 1935 Grand Final. But in terms of on-field exploits, it's hard to go past Phonse Kyne. It takes something special to hold down centre half-forward in a premiership team in just your second year of senior football, but that's what Kyne managed to achieve in 1935.

The strongly built Kyne was terrific throughout the season, but he lifted his game to new heights on grand final day and was proclaimed by many scribes as a match-winner. He took marks, kicked a couple of important goals, brought his small forwards into the game with clever taps and shepherding, and generally provided a strong presence up forward. 'Kyne was simply magnificent,' said one report.

Kyne's grand final performance was no fluke. He'd also been among the team's best in the first two finals, and was voted the third best player through the finals series. It was a sign of the great career to come.

PLAYERS

#	Player	Games	Goals
1	Harold Albiston	1	0
3	Tommy Boag	1	0
4	Percy Bowyer	19	9
1	Marcus Boyall	1	0
5	Jack Carmody	19	4
6	George Carter	9	9
7	Albert Collier	18	3
8	Harry Collier	20	19
9	Gordon Coventry	21	88
10	Charlie Dibbs	20	0
11	Vin Doherty	17	30
14	Keith Fraser	17	1
12	Pat Fricker	4	1
13	Fred Froude	19	0
2	Alec Fyfe	4	0
15	Reg Gibson	6	0
16	Eddie Gray	1	0
16	George Kanngieser	1	0
15	Jack Knight	14	12
17	Phonse Kyne	18	24
18	Leo Morgan	16	1
19	Len Murphy	19	5
15	Alby Pannam	15	46
3	Jack Power	3	0
25	Jack Regan	18	0
23	Lou Riley	19	38
24	Jack Ross	16	3
22	Harold Rumney	16	0
26	Alan Ryan	4	2
27	Keith Stackpole	3	1
35	Ron Todd	4	6
28	Marcus Whelan	16	2
29	Bervin Woods	20	2

Club Awards

Copeland Trophy – Albert Collier
Runner-up – Len Murphy
Third – Vin Doherty
Best player in finals series – A Collier
Second – Marcus Whelan
Third – Phonse Kyne
F J Firman Trophy – Albert Collier (a match trophy)
Treadways trophy – Marcus Whelan (match trophy)
L McCasker Trophy – Phonse Kyne (match trophy)
Best First Year Player – Bervin Woods
Wal Lee trophy for training prize – Jack Carmody
Training prizes to 17 players
Leading goalkicker – Gordon Coventry (88)

1935 SEASON

ROUND 1 April 27 Victoria Park
Collingwood 15.18.108 v South Melbourne **15.16.106**
Goals: Riley 5, Coventry 3, Kyne 3, Bowyer, H Collier, Doherty, Whelan

ROUND 2 May 6 Brunswick St Oval
Fitzroy **14.9.93** v Collingwood **14.9.93**
Goals: Coventry 4, Riley 3, Doherty 2, Kyne 2, Ryan 2, Bowyer

ROUND 3 May 11 Victoria Park
Collingwood 21.17.143 v Essendon **12.11.83**
Goals: Pannam 7, Riley 5, Doherty 4, Coventry 2, Bowyer, H Collier, Woods

ROUND 4 May 18 Corio Oval
Geelong **14.17.101** v **Collingwood 17.13.115**
Goals: Coventry 7, Pannam 3, Doherty 2, Riley 2, Bowyer, A Collier, Kyne

ROUND 5 May 25 MCG
Melbourne **9.15.69** v **Collingwood 13.20.98**
Goals: Coventry 4, Carter 3, Riley 3, H Collier 2, Doherty

ROUND 6 June 1 Victoria Park
Collingwood 23.11.149 v Footscray **14.14.98**
Goals: Coventry 9, Doherty 7, Kyne 2, Pannam 2, Riley 2, Murphy

ROUND 7 June 8 Junction Oval
St Kilda **16.15.111** v **Collingwood 19.16.130**
Goals: Pannam 7, Coventry 5, H Collier 3, Doherty 2, Carter, Kyne

ROUND 8 June 15 Victoria Park
Collingwood 16.30.126 v North Melbourne **6.10.46**
Goals: Pannam 4, H Collier 3, Carter 2, Coventry 2, Ross 2, Kyne, Murphy, Riley

ROUND 9 June 22 Princes Park
Carlton 13.9.87 v Collingwood **8.10.58**
Goals: Pannam 4, G Coventry 2, Doherty, Riley

ROUND 10 June 29 Punt Rd Oval
Richmond **11.14.80** v **Collingwood 13.4.82**
Goals: Knight 5, Carmody 3, Doherty 2, Coventry, Kyne, Pannam

ROUND 11 July 6 Victoria Park
Collingwood 17.20.122 v Hawthorn **12.3.75**
Goals: Coventry 4, Doherty 4, Pannam 3, Riley 2, H Collier, Kyne, Murphy, Woods

ROUND 12 July 13 Lake Oval
South Melbourne 18.16.124 v Collingwood **10.11.71**
Goals: Pannam 4, Coventry 3, Kyne 2, Doherty

ROUND 13 July 20 Victoria Park
Collingwood 14.21.105 v Fitzroy **12.10.82**
Goals: Riley 4, Carter 3, Coventry 3, Knight 2, Pannam 2

ROUND 15 August 10 Victoria Park
Collingwood 22.13.145 v Geelong **16.15.111**
Goals: Coventry 9, Riley 4, Bowyer 3, Doherty 2, H Collier, Fraser, Murphy, Whelan

ROUND 14 August 17 Windy Hill
Essendon **16.10.106** v **Collingwood 16.17.113**
Goals: Coventry 8, Pannam 3, Riley 3, Kyne 2

ROUND 16 August 24 Victoria Park
Collingwood **11.13.79** v Melbourne **10.19.79**
Goals: Coventry 3, H Collier 2, Knight 2, Kyne 2, Carmody, Morgan

ROUND 17 August 31 Whitten Oval
Footscray **6.17.53** v **Collingwood 12.14.86**
Goals: Coventry 5, Riley 2, Todd 2, Fricker, Kyne, Ross

ROUND 18 September 7 Victoria Park
Collingwood 9.18.72 v St Kilda **7.15.57**
Goals: Coventry 3, H Collier, Doherty, Knight, Murphy, Pannam, Todd

1935 FINALS

LADDER

Team	W	L	D	For	Agst	%	Pts
South Melb	16	2	0	1940	1410	137.6	64
Collingwood	14	2	2	1895	1561	121.4	60
Carlton	14	3	1	1958	1383	141.6	58
Richmond	12	6	0	1572	1339	117.4	48
St Kilda	11	7	0	1708	1545	110.6	44
Melbourne	8	9	1	1601	1582	101.2	34
Fitzroy	8	9	1	1488	1649	90.2	34
Essendon	7	11	0	1526	1703	89.6	28
Geelong	6	11	1	1683	1747	96.3	26
Hawthorn	5	13	0	1460	1805	80.9	20
Footscray	2	14	2	1272	1731	73.5	12
North Melb	1	17	0	1208	1856	65.1	4

SEMI FINAL September 21 MCG

Collingwood **11.17.83** v South Melbourne **15.14.104**

Goals: Coventry 3, Todd 3, H Collier 2, A Collier, Knight, Kyne

PRELIM FINAL September 28 MCG

Collingwood **14.10.94** v Richmond **9.12.66**

Goals: Coventry 4, Pannam 3, Bowyer 2, Kyne 2, H Collier, Knight, Riley

GRAND FINAL October 5 MCG

Collingwood	1.3	6.6	8.10	11.12	(78)
South Melbourne	3.6	4.8	6.10	7.16	(58)

Goals: Collingwood: G. Coventry 4, Kyne 2, Pannam 2, H. Collier, A. Collier, Stackpole
Best: Collingwood: H. Collier, A. Collier, Kyne, Regan, Froude, Rumney, Whelan
Umpire: Scott
Crowd: 54,154 at the MCG

Grand Final Team
B: J. Ross, C. Dibbs, H. Rumney
HB: B. Woods, J. Regan, F. Froude
C: J. Carmody, M. Whelan, L. Morgan
HF: L. Riley, A. Kyne, V. Doherty
F: K. Fraser, G. Coventry, A. Pannam
R: A. Collier, P. Bowyer, H. Collier (c)
Reserve: K. Stackpole

CHAPTER TWELVE

1936

Validation

'If you really wish to know which team will win the premiership this year, pin your faith to the side which retains to a greater degree the old world, manly standards . . . Collingwood has less hot air in the dressing room than any other club.'

The Mightiest Magpies

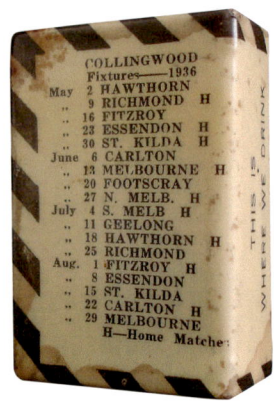

Below: **The keys to the new clubrooms at Victoria Park, officially opened on the day the 1935 flag was unfurled.** Opposite: **Captain Harry Collier prepares to pounce on a loose ball, while Fred Froude (rear) and Keith Fraser (right) provide support.**

In the court of public opinion, Collingwood had been lucky to win the 1935 premiership. Many people thought that it would have been South celebrating, but for Bob Pratt coming off worst after tangling with a truck two days before the grand final. Most Collingwood fans didn't care, of course: they had a flag fluttering from the flagpole at Victoria Park, and nothing else mattered. But it mattered to the players, and the coaches. So 1936 became something of a mission for the Magpies, as they set out to prove they were worthy premiers not just for 1936, but also for 1935. And this time the football gods were *not* on their side: if the Pies were to win the flag, they would have to do so despite a string of misfortunes – including losing one of the game's biggest names to one of the most controversial suspensions in the history of football.

This determination to retrospectively prove themselves even seemed to extend to decisions about the playing list. The reigning premiers were the only team not to introduce a new recruit in the opening round of the season, and Ivanhoe youngster Ron Dowling was the only player added to the senior list. Two old favourites, however, were gone. Defensive stalwarts Charlie Dibbs and Harry Rumney said goodbye to Victoria Park, Dibbs to captain-coach Geelong and Rumney to coach Northcote in the VFA.

The mid 1930s have come to be regarded as the game's golden age, and the opening day of the 1936 season saw the game in its full pomp. The *Age* proudly pointed out that the 115,000 spectators who turned out for Round 1 constituted more than 10 per cent of the population of Melbourne and suburbs. The Magpies easily accounted for Hawthorn at Glenferrie, but all eyes were already on the unfurling of the flag in Round 2 against Richmond.

In 1929, Collingwood unveiled its pennant from the previous season against Richmond, opened its new grandstand and promptly went out and kicked 13 goals straight. Seven years later, against the same opponent, the club celebrated another premiership and also opened new club facilities, this time palatial new clubrooms and administrative areas. Then, to complete the parallels, the Pies went out and kicked nine straight goals, and a staggering 14.1 in the first half.

The Tigers were simply blown away. Jack Regan and Phonse Kyne marked everything in sight, and small men Vin Doherty, Charlie Pannam and skipper Harry Collier tore Richmond apart. But the real star was Gordon Coventry, by now into his seventeenth season, who kicked 8.1 and was far too strong for Richmond's Joe Murdoch. Incredibly, after a 14.1 first half, the Magpies went out and kicked eight straight behinds in the third quarter but it didn't matter. The Pies cruised to a six-goal win, easing up.

Collingwood's brilliant forward work was again on display the following week at Fitzroy – the team had 14 goals on the board by half-time. This time, however, there was no letting up and the Pies won by 80 points, with Coventry bagging another eight and Pannam seven. Big wins over Essendon and St Kilda followed, setting up a vital Round 6 clash with Carlton.

The Argus

Percy Taylor on Collingwood's Round 1 win over Richmond:

Collingwood played like a team possessed. All the finer points of the game were exploited by the players, who were adept at position work, excellent in the air and deadly accurate in front of goal. Against this machine, Richmond was hopeless.

PLAYER OF THE YEAR
Jack Regan

Jack Regan was the greatest full-back in Collingwood's history, and he was never in better form than in 1936. That was the year he won his only Copeland Trophy, finished fifth in the Brownlow and again won selection for Victoria.

Regan started his career as a forward but moved to the other end of the ground in the early 1930s and never looked back. He was without peer in the last line of defence. He was quick, skilled and graceful, and preferred to back his judgement and outmark opposing forwards rather than punching or spoiling. This approach was a revelation for a full-back in the 1930s, and made him as exciting to watch as the glamour full-forwards he was minding.

Regan's attacking approach led to a series of memorable one-on-one duels with the gun full-forwards of his day, especially South's Bob Pratt. In the games that mattered most in 1936 he kept Pratt to a solitary goal in the semi-final and just three in the grand final.

They were typical Regan performances – not focused solely on negativity, but defensively effective nonetheless. It was the way Regan played football, and the crowds who watched him in the 1930s loved him for it.

The Blues had lost just one game and were already looking like certain finalists. More than 45,000 fans crammed into Princes Park, setting a new home-and-away record. Fortunes see-sawed throughout a tense, sometimes brilliant, match played in questionable spirit, with many ugly clashes. The Magpies jumped out of the blocks, kicking the first three goals of the game, but the Blues hit back and finished the first quarter in front, and from then until late in the game there was never more than a few points in it. Carlton led by a point at the last change after frittering away chances in the third quarter and, with the parochial home crowd roaring, extended that to eight points early in the final term. Then Kyne grabbed a great goal out of a pack tussle, sparking a burst that saw two more added in quick succession. The Pies led by 11 points with 10 minutes left and looked home, but Carlton charged again, goaling to narrow the gap to five points. The Blues had three great chances to grab the lead in the final, desperate minutes but all three shots missed, including one from Harry Vallence that drew gasps from the crowd when it hit the post. The Pies defended grimly, then took the ball to the other end and added a couple of late behinds to win by a goal. 'There is no doubting the ability of Collingwood in fighting out a finish,' wrote Percy Taylor in *The Argus*. 'It never gives up, and never loses its poise in a crisis.'

The rapidly emerging Melbourne gave Collingwood a huge scare at Victoria Park in the next game. Only more phenomenally straight kicking (8.0 at three quarter time) kept the Magpies close enough to charge home over the top of the visitors with a 6.5 to 0.3 final term. Regulation wins over Footscray and North followed, setting up a top-of-the-ladder clash with South Melbourne at Victoria Park. This would be the two sides' only home-and-away meeting for the year, and there was much riding on it. The Swans were coming off their first loss of the season – to Richmond at Punt Road – while the undefeated Pies were a game clear at the head of the ladder. But Collingwood would have to take on their great rivals without one of their most important players. Vice-captain Albert Collier, a mighty force within the game, had been rubbed out for six matches for clobbering North's Jack Smith.

To make matters worse, while the Pies had lost a star, South had gained one. 'Mocha' Johnson – the ex-Carlton skipper and a ferocious combatant in Carlton–Collingwood clashes over the years – had been cleared to South during the week. Johnson had become embroiled in a dispute with Carlton that ended with the committee saying it would clear him. He called what he thought was a bluff by suggesting the unthinkable – that they could clear him to Collingwood – and the Blues promptly signed the papers. The only trouble was that Johnson hadn't even spoken to Collingwood! When he did so, Collingwood secretary Frank Wraith told him he'd 'have to prove himself' in the reserves before getting senior selection. That was hard to stomach for a 29-year-old player with over 100 games and Victorian representative honours beside his name, so Johnson went to South instead.

The highly-anticipated Collingwood–South game had to be postponed for a week when heavy rainfall led the VFL to postpone the entire round. The ground at Victoria Park was in shocking condition, but had recovered by the time the teams ran out the following week. Collingwood started as favourites, despite missing Albert Collier, and with doubts surrounding Gordon Coventry, who had dropped a hammer on his foot during the week. But favouritism counted for nothing when South opened with a six-goal-to-two first quarter, then held out against a final quarter comeback to leave with an 11-point

PLAYER OF THE YEAR
Phonse Kyne

Phonse Kyne achieved such fame as a Collingwood coach – especially as the man who led the Pies to the 1958 triumph – that his record as a player is often forgotten.

His career started in 1934 and stretched until 1950, by which time he'd totalled nearly 250 games and a similar number of goals. In 1936, aged just 20, he was good enough to hold down the centre half-forward spot in a premiership team, and finish third in the club's best and fairest voting. He also won his first Victorian guernsey.

He was among the team's best few players in the grand final, and kicked three goals in the semi-final. He'd shown in 1935 that he was a big game player, and his performances in 1936 confirmed it.

Kyne went from strength to strength in the years that followed. In the 1940s, as a ruckman, he would become the first player (and still only one of four) to win three Copelands in a row. But despite his brilliance, the club's next two premierships would be won not while Kyne was playing, but with him as the team's coach.

The Mightiest Magpies

Previous page: **Jack Regan soars from behind for a characteristically graceful spoil against Richmond at Punt Road.** Below: **Gordon Coventry tangles with three Tiger opponents – the incident that sparked one of the most controversial suspensions in football.**

victory. Almost inevitably, Mocha Johnson kicked four goals, including the final one that sealed the win.

Collingwood still sat atop the ladder after the loss, though only by percentage from South and Richmond. But a shock loss to seventh-placed Geelong upset the club's plans, and placed huge pressure on the Round 13 game with Richmond at Punt Road. That pressure was exacerbated during an acrimonious lead-in when Collingwood threatened to refuse to play at Punt Road in a dispute over whether Richmond had the right to charge entry fees to their ground. The club backed down only after a heated League delegates meeting the night before the game.

The *Sporting Globe*'s P.J.Millard noted the tension in the Collingwood rooms before the game: 'Entering the Collingwood room, one experienced something of a chill. A tense grim atmosphere here. No jokes, no levity and definitely "no smoking". Trainers went about their tasks with profound solemnity. In pensive silence Captain Harry Collier laced his boots. It was hard to imagine more serious looking players. Iron appeared to have entered their very souls.'

But any drama before the game was nothing compared with what happened afterwards. The Pies won by 16 points, but nobody was talking about the result. Instead, the focus was on a wild brawl that had erupted in the third quarter. It was described as 'one of the worst football incidents of the year', saw four players reported and eventually led to one of the most controversial suspensions in the history of football.

1936: Validation

Left: Coventry's lengthy suspension provoked outrage among the public and in the newspapers.
Below: Alby Pannam proved himself a dangerous forward and brilliant goalkicker in 1936.

Mild-mannered Gordon Coventry had played in the match with a crop of painful boils on the back of his neck, and Richmond's full-back, Joe Murdoch, had targeted the area throughout the game. Eventually it all got too much, even for Coventry, and he hit Murdoch, who retaliated with gusto, sparking the brawl. It was the first time Coventry had been reported in a 17-year-career during which most opponents could scarcely remember him raising his voice, let alone his fists. It was a huge news story, sharing top billing in Monday's papers with Adolf Hitler opening the 1936 Olympics.

At the Tuesday night hearing, Coventry opted to plead concussion, rather than provocation. But his defence didn't work, and the tribunal found he was the aggressor in the incident. Even so, everyone thought his 280-odd games without blemish would guarantee him a reprimand, or a light sentence. Instead the tribunal rubbed him out for the rest of the season – eight weeks in all. Murdoch copped four games, on account of having been provoked, and Coventry's teammate Harry Jones was given six weeks for his involvement in two separate incidents.

Coventry's was an extraordinarily harsh suspension, and it sparked a public furore. A crowd had gathered outside League HQ and they responded angrily when told the news, as did those in picture theatres in and around Collingwood when the result was projected onto their screens. Commentators rushed to defend Coventry and deride the suspension as unfair, but it was all

209

The Mightiest Magpies

REGAN (Collingwood) SOARS. An incident in the Melbourne-Collingwood match showing J. Regan, Collingwood's goal-keeper, flying high for a mark. No. 4 is Smith, of Melbourne, and others in the picture are Crowe (C'wood) and Reiffel (No. 2), of Melbourne.

Right: Another classic Jack Regan mark.
Opposite page: Harry Collier and South skipper Jack Bissett with the Governor, Baron Huntingfield, before the grand final.

The SPORTING GLOBE

Ivor Warne-Smith on whether footballers in the 1930s were as tough as their predecessors:

The very old players tell us that they are not, and that footballers now are following the modern trend of youth and are becoming effeminate. Today the men have hot baths and hot showers. In the good old days it was cold water, or perhaps no water at all. The ancients too, point with scorn at all the electric treatment given for bruises. There is too much hot air around the players these days. The boys of today nurse minor abrasions too lovingly and too long... If you really wish to know which team will win the premiership this year, pin your faith to the side which retains to a greater degree the old world, manly standards. Looking around the teams in the finals I find that Collingwood has less hot air in the dressing room than any other club.

to no avail: the tribunal finding stood, and Coventry's season was over. The dismayed champion retired a few days later, apologising to Collingwood fans for 'forgetting my good manners'. Fortunately he would change his mind, leaving the game on much better terms in 1937.

Of more immediate concern to Collingwood, however, was the depletion of their playing ranks. Albert Collier was still suspended, as was Fred Froude, Jack Ross was injured and Phonse Kyne and Jack Regan were on state duty. Then star centreman Marcus Whelan got tonsillitis. But that didn't stop the gutsy Pies winning their next game, against Fitzroy, or the two that followed, to secure a top-two finish. A one-point loss to Carlton in the penultimate round of the season saw Collingwood slip to second, but a semi-final against South Melbourne was already locked in.

Collingwood was by now much closer to full-strength, though Coventry's absence still seemed likely to be decisive. There was great expectation ahead of the semi-final, but the game was a disappointing spectacle. Both teams kicked poorly for goal (the scores stood at 1.7 to 1.6 at quarter time) and made numerous errors under the finals pressure. As usual, South produced bursts of sporadic brilliance, but Collingwood was more solid and steady throughout the day. The Pies looked like they had broken the game wide open with a five-goal second quarter, but South hit back with six goals to none in the third quarter to lead by 13 points at the last change. Goals to Vin Doherty and 'Cracker' Knight, after a great mark, tied the scores early in a nail-biting final term. Both sides strove desperately, but unsuccessfully, to fashion a winning break. 'Neither side could gain any appreciable advantage at that stage, and there were any amount of thrilling duels between the clever attackers and the dashing defenders,' wrote *The Age*.

Then Phonse Kyne grabbed a goal, and Alby Pannam got another from a brilliant snap over his shoulder, and the Pies looked safe. Instead, South came again and laid siege to the Magpies' goal. Wave after wave of attacks ensued, and first Laurie Nash, then Bob Pratt, goaled to give South the lead by a point. When Collingwood missed at the other end, scores were level again with just minutes to play. Kyne took a great mark at centre half-forward to reclaim the lead, then Keith Fraser's leap on the goal-line denied Nash a goal at the other end. The Pies snared a couple of valuable behinds that took the margin beyond a goal, then sealed a spot in the grand final with a late goal from Keith Stackpole.

Oddly, Collingwood's win didn't make them favourites. South had been plagued with injuries throughout the year, and many of its returning players were short of a gallop. There was a general feeling that the semi-final loss would tune up South perfectly. The Pies were worried about injuries to Jack Carmody, Harry Collier and Jack Regan, but all three ended up playing. Instead it was the tribunal – again – that caused the selection headaches when Len Murphy was suspended for eight weeks for belting South star Brighton Diggins and leaving him with a broken jaw.

With Murphy and Coventry suspended, Collingwood brought back Ron Todd to play at full-forward, shifting Jack Knight to the forward pocket/resting ruck role. The Pies also sprang a surprise when they named the apparently under-sized Jack Ross as centre half back to mind the brilliant Laurie Nash. It would prove to be one of Jock McHale's most masterly moves.

PLAYER OF THE YEAR

Marcus Whelan

The Collingwood teams of 1935–36 had plenty of class – players like Alby Pannam, Jack Regan, Vin Doherty, Ron Todd and Harry Collier saw to that. But for sheer classic brilliance, none could eclipse centreman Marcus Whelan.

Everything about Whelan's football was carried out with poise and an unhurried precision that made him a delight to watch. Like Jack Beveridge before him, he had great skills, great composure and always seemed to have plenty of time to decide what to do with the football. He also had a great football brain, so the decisions he made were usually the right ones.

The other thing that set Whelan apart from many of his contemporaries was his marking. He was a superb mark for his size, and regularly outpointed taller opponents. So good were his aerial skills that he was able to spend the last years of his career holding down the full-back position.

He finished second in the Copeland in 1936, and would go on to win it a few years later when he also won the Brownlow Medal. Class from start to finish – that was Marcus Whelan.

1936: Validation

The game opened at a ferocious pace and Collingwood were on the board inside the first minute, when Cracker Knight goaled. Todd added a second soon afterwards and the Pies were away. It set the scene for a brilliant first half that was marred only by inaccuracy. South hit back after the Pies' early onslaught and trailed by only two points at quarter time, then grabbed two goals at the beginning of the second term to lead by nine points. But that's when the Magpies put their foot to the floor, producing an astonishing burst of football that should have killed the game. They had 14 shots on goal in the second quarter, but a frustrating return of 4.10 meant the half-time lead was only 21 points. Todd was unstoppable at full-forward, leading and marking superbly but kicking 'like the nerviest novice'. Alongside him, Alby Pannam was a constant menace.

Collingwood's terrible kicking – 7.16 at half-time – had left the door open. And after another goal to Todd early in the third quarter it became all South Melbourne. Only some resolute defending from Regan, Ross and Fraser kept the Magpies in front at the last change, by just seven points. That lead narrowed to a single point within minutes of the resumption, and the Swans seemingly had all the momentum. But Pannam created a goal out of nothing with a brilliant snap, then pounced again just minutes later after Harry Collier caused a crucial turnover with a bone-crunching tackle on a South defender. 'For the next 10 minutes South Melbourne strove magnificently to bridge the gap,' wrote *The Sporting Globe*. 'The crowd rocked and roared as South tore down toward goal. Two great marks by Pratt were followed by two behinds and South's fighting finish was not meeting with any luck.' Two more points followed as South peppered the goals, but a canny pass from Albert Collier to Phonse Kyne gave the centre half-forward the chance to seal the game, and he coolly steered it through. Collingwood by 11 points at the final siren.

The SPORTING GLOBE

Ivor Warne-Smith on Collingwood's grand final performance:

Collingwood's play was very nearly perfect. The anticipation of its place was remarkable and its speed against an admittedly fast team was staggering. Splendid co-operation between the players was always in evidence. It did not matter how its men were hemmed in, they always found someone to whom they could handball or kick. For sheer brilliance, Collingwood's exhibition in the first half has rarely been excelled. In only one phase of the game was there a breakdown and that was at kicking for goal. Despite this Collingwood was by far the better team and every player fitted perfectly into his position.

**Opposite page: Action scenes from the 1936 Grand Final, as seen in *The Leader* newspaper.
Far left: Ron Todd's kicking was wayward but he still played brilliantly.
Left: Todd and skipper Harry Collier celebrate Collingwood's premiership win.**

COLLINGWOOD FOOTBALL CLUB
PREMIERS. 1936.

The Magpies had been superb, with Pannam having 32 kicks and booting five goals and Ross completely blanketing Nash. If Ron Todd (4.10 from 16 shots) had found his range the game would have been over by half-time. Harry Collier led the side well, Albert Collier was an inspiration in the ruck, Marcus Whelan superb in the middle, Jack Carmody dangerous on the wing and Fraser ran himself to a standstill.

Hundreds of jubilant fans forced their way into the rooms after the match, creating a massive, joyous crush. Harry and Albert Collier's mum threw a party in Northcote that night, in honour not just of the premiership but also Harry's 29th birthday, which he'd reached the Thursday before the grand final. This was Collingwood's eleventh premiership in 40 seasons of the VFL, and its sixth in the last ten. As everyone who had been a part of this era of sustained success acknowledged, it had been a hell of a ride.

ALBY PANNAM
GRAND FINAL HERO

Grand final performances don't come much better from a small forward than gathering more than 30 possessions and kicking five goals out of a team total of 11. That's what Alby Pannam racked up in the 1936 decider, in a commanding display of brilliance that did much to bring the premiership pennant back to Victoria Park.

Pannam had already enjoyed a wonderful season, having kicked 40 goals before the grand final, mainly from a half-forward flank or forward pocket. He worked in beautifully with key forwards like Gordon Coventry (until suspended), Phonse Kyne and Ron Todd, and his trickery, evasiveness and skills made him a nightmare for opponents to mind.

Pannam was at his best in the grand final. He kicked three goals in the first half, when his teammates were spraying the ball everywhere. Then, when the game looked like slipping from Collingwood's grasp early in the last quarter, he manufactured two goals out of nothing.

In between he got plenty of the football and set up chances for other players, too, but it was his goals that had the biggest impact. Alby Pannam kicked plenty in his career, but rarely have his goals been more important than on grand final day 1936.

PLAYERS

#	Player	Games	Goals
3	Percy Bowyer	20	6
24	Marcus Boyall	3	1
4	Jack Carmody	18	2
5	George Carter	7	8
2	Albert Collier	14	1
1	Harry Collier	20	24
6	Gordon Coventry	13	60
34	Jim Crowe	13	0
7	Vin Doherty	20	33
23	Ron Dowling	10	6
9	Keith Fraser	18	1
25	Pat Fricker	8	1
8	Fred Froude	16	0
10	Reg Gibson	2	1
28	Harry Jones	2	1
12	Jack Knight	15	18
12	Phonse Kyne	19	36
35	Ron McCann	1	0
13	Leo Morgan	12	3
14	Len Murphy	18	4
21	Alby Pannam	19	45
16	Jack Regan	19	0
17	Lou Riley	6	4
18	Jack Ross	18	0
33	Alan Ryan	5	0
19	Keith Stackpole	15	12
20	Ron Todd	12	18
21	Marcus Whelan	19	4
22	Bervin Woods	18	1

Club Awards

Copeland Trophy – Jack Regan

Second – Marcus Whelan

Third – Phonse Kyne

Best First Year Player – Ron Dowling

Austral Cup – Fred Froude

Wal Lee Trophy for training – Ron Todd

Leading goalkicker – Gordon Coventry (60)

1936 SEASON

ROUND 1 May 2 Glenferrie Oval

Hawthorn **12.11.83** v **Collingwood 15.14.104**

Goals: Kyne 5, Doherty 4, Coventry 3, Pannam 2, Todd

ROUND 2 May 9 Victoria Park

Collingwood 16.12.108 v Richmond **10.12.72**

Goals: Coventry 8, H Collier 3, Knight 2, Doherty, Kyne, Pannam

ROUND 3 May 16 Brunswick St Oval

Fitzroy **12.12.84** v **Collingwood 25.14.164**

Goals: Coventry 8, Pannam 7, H Collier 3, Stackpole 3, Whelan, Murphy, Morgan, Doherty

ROUND 4 May 23 Victoria Park

Collingwood 20.17.137 v Essendon **13.10.88**

Goals: Coventry 6, Kyne 4, H Collier 3, Doherty 3, Dowling 2, Carter, Pannam

ROUND 5 May 30 Victoria Park

Collingwood 16.17.113 v St Kilda **9.14.68**

Goals: Coventry 6, Doherty 5, Kyne 2, H Collier, Morgan, Riley

ROUND 6 June 6 Princes Park

Carlton **11.16.82** v **Collingwood 12.16.88**

Goals: Pannam 3, Coventry 2, Doherty 2, Knight 2, Bowyer, Kyne, Riley

ROUND 7 June 13 Victoria Park

Collingwood 14.5.89 v Melbourne **9.13.67**

Goals: Coventry 4, Doherty 2, Knight 2, Kyne 2, Pannam 2, Morgan, H Collier

ROUND 8 June 20 Whitten Oval

Footscray **11.13.79** v **Collingwood 16.10.106**

Goals: Coventry 4, Doherty 4, Dowling 3, Knight 2, H Collier, Pannam, Woods

ROUND 9 June 27 Victoria Park

Collingwood 17.19.121 v North Melbourne **8.7.55**

Goals: Coventry 5, Doherty 3, Bowyer 2, H Collier 2, Dowling, Knight, Kyne, Pannam, Stackpole

ROUND 10 July 11 Victoria Park

Collingwood **12.19.91** v **South Melbourne 14.18.102**

Goals: Coventry 3, Kyne 3, Pannam 3, H Collier 2, Doherty

ROUND 11 July 18 Corio Oval

Geelong **13.15.93** v Collingwood **11.9.75**

Goals: Kyne 3, Pannam 2, Todd 2, Gibson, Fraser, Coventry, Boyall

ROUND 12 July 25 Victoria Park

Collingwood 14.18.102 v Hawthorn **6.12.48**

Goals: Coventry 5, Pannam 2, Bowyer 2, H Collier, Doherty, Fricker, Jones, Kyne

ROUND 13 August 1 Punt Rd Oval

Richmond **11.14.80** v **Collingwood 14.12.96**

Goals: Coventry 5, Carmody 2, Carter 2, H Collier 2, Pannam 2, Doherty

ROUND 14 August 8 Victoria Park

Collingwood 13.12.90 v Fitzroy **11.8.74**

Goals: Todd 5, Carter 4, Pannam 2, Riley, Stackpole

ROUND 15 August 15 Windy Hill

Essendon **8.10.58** v **Collingwood 14.16.100**

Goals: Pannam 5, Kyne 3, Stackpole 3, Carter, Todd, Whelan

ROUND 16 August 22 Junction Oval

St Kilda **11.11.77** v **Collingwood 14.13.97**

Goals: Todd 4, Stackpole 3, Kyne 3, Pannam, Doherty, H Collier, Bowyer

ROUND 17 August 29 Victoria Park

Collingwood **13.11.89** v **Carlton 13.12.90**

Goals: H Collier 3, Knight 2, Kyne 2, Pannam 2, Whelan 2, Todd, A Collier

ROUND 18 September 5 MCG

Collingwood 11.18.84 v Melbourne **9.13.67**

Goals: Knight 3, Murphy 3, Doherty 2, H Collier, Kyne, Pannam

1936 FINALS

LADDER

Team	W	L	D	For	Agst	%	Pts
South Melb	16	2	0	1806	1524	118.5	64
Collingwood	15	3	0	1854	1367	135.6	60
Carlton	12	6	0	1877	1504	124.8	48
Melbourne	12	6	0	1755	1477	118.8	48
Geelong	11	7	0	1884	1498	125.8	44
Richmond	10	8	0	1673	1550	107.9	40
St Kilda	9	9	0	1845	1919	96.1	36
Essendon	6	12	0	1565	1840	85.1	24
Hawthorn	6	12	0	1391	1720	80.9	24
Footscray	5	13	0	1462	1690	86.5	20
North Melb	4	14	0	1274	1679	75.9	16
Fitzroy	2	16	0	1367	1985	68.9	8

SEMI FINAL September 19   MCG
Collingwood 12.18.90 v South Melbourne **10.17.77**

Goals: Knight 3, Kyne 3, Pannam 2, Doherty 2, Riley, Stackpole

GRAND FINAL October 3   MCG

Collingwood	3.6	7.16	8.19	11.23	(89)
South Melbourne	3.4	5.7	8.12	10.18	(78)

Goals: Pannam 5, Todd 4, Knight, Kyne
Best: Pannam, Whelan, Kyne, Carmody, Ross, Todd, Fraser
Umpire: Blackburn
Crowd: 74,091 at the MCG

Grand Final Team
B: J. Crowe, J. Regan, B. Woods
HB: J. Ross, K. Fraser, F. Froude
C: J. Carmody, M. Whelan, L. Morgan
HF: L. Riley, A. Kyne, V. Doherty
F: J. Knight, R. Todd, A. Pannam
R: A. Collier, P. Bowyer, H. Collier (c)
Reserve: K. Stackpole

CHAPTER THIRTEEN

1953

A very Collingwood flag

'You have the great tradition of Collingwood to uphold. You are not playing for yourselves. You are playing for your wives and families. Make them proud of you. Most of all you are playing for Collingwood. Don't forget that.'

Belief. It's one of the things that can separate good sporting teams from great ones. And Collingwood didn't have it entering the 1953 season. The Magpies and their fans had hope, to be sure, having just ended what still remains the longest drought between grand final appearances in the club's history, but belief was something else again.

The stumbling block was Geelong. Like their counterparts of 2007-09, the Cats of the early 1950s were an all-conquering League powerhouse. Fast, skilful and spectacular, they had won back-to-back flags in 1951 and 1952, the second of those against a Collingwood side making its first grand final appearance since 1939. The Woods were relieved to simply be back in a grand final again after such a long absence, but must have cursed their misfortune in running up against one of the all-time great VFL teams. And as 1953 began

The Magpie dressing rooms in 1953.

there were no early signs that Geelong's era of domination was about to end: indeed, the Cats entered the season in the midst of what became the longest winning run in VFL history, one that would eventually total 23 successive wins. To make matters even worse, the Cats had demolished the Pies in both finals in 1952, with a combined margin of exactly 100 points. So it was with a sense of hope, at best, but more likely trepidation, that Collingwood prepared to entertain Geelong in their Round 3 meeting at Victoria Park.

It had already been a rocky start to the year for the Pies. There was a sensation before the season even began when the club dumped popular ruckman Harvey Stevens from its list. Stevens had played 54 games and kicked 56 goals in five seasons, but he'd played the last of those matches at the unfamiliar position of full-forward in the 1952 Grand Final. He had a poor game that day, but had plenty of company from his teammates in the 46-point loss. Stevens returned to training for 1953 a little overweight, largely because he'd been recovering from a rib injury. It was expected that his slow start would see him miss the beginning of the season, but few people thought the Pies would cut him from their final list.

But on the eve of the season, that's exactly what happened. There was widespread shock at Stevens' axing, with many believing he'd been made a scapegoat for the club's dual final failures the previous year. Footscray pounced and snapped him up almost immediately, and he repaid their faith by winning his new club's best and fairest in his first year.

The Pies also faced pre-season confusion over the future of young players Jack Finck and Kevin Coghlan, and star wingman Des Healey. Forward-turned-defender Finck had taken up a teaching position in Portland and asked for a clearance to play with local club Heywood. But Collingwood refused his clearance, forcing Finck to drive six hours each week from Portland – then the same back again – to play. Remarkably, he became one of the best full-backs in the competition. Healey was another who entertained thoughts of leaving for a better paid position in the country, but he too was refused a clearance and stayed. Coghlan, one of the smallest players of his time, had managed 31 games in four years but was released to Hawthorn, where he became a highly successful rover/forward who won the club's goalkicking three years in a row.

Still, coach Phonse Kyne was confident as the season approached. Collingwood, he said, had been unlucky with injuries in 1952 but had still made the grand final. Given a reasonable run in the medical room, he felt sure the Pies would be in contention come the end of the year. 'This will be another good year for the Magpies,' he told *The Argus*. 'We'll be right up there near the top again. I'm sure of it.'

Harvey Stevens (top) was dumped from the club pre-season, while Jack Finck (bottom) had to be talked into staying on.

Bill Twomey marks against South Melbourne during his best-on-ground performance in Round 1, when he kicked nine goals.

When the season itself got underway, the mercurial Bill Twomey bagged nine goals as the Pies proved far too strong for South Melbourne at Victoria Park. The next week, Collingwood played Fitzroy in an ANZAC Day Eve exhibition match 'under electric lights' at the Showgrounds. The match, played to raise funds for the St Vincent's Hospital Appeal, was billed as a chance for the footballing public to make their own judgements about the merits or otherwise of night football. The League did all it could to spice up the occasion, even scheduling half-time entertainment in the form a VFA versus VFL relay race, and a goalkicking competition between the great John Coleman and Williamstown ace Johnnie Walker. Despite such heady attractions, *The Sun* reported that the 22,000 crowd was 'pleased but not wildly excited' by the experiment.

The Pies won £100 that night (donated by John Wren) but paid a hefty price for winning, losing Twomey for four weeks after a fierce collision with 'Butch' Gale late in the game left him with a shoulder injury. The gifted Twomey had backed up his nine-goal haul with six against the Roys and seemed headed for a big year. Collingwood's disappointment at losing him was compounded when the team was trounced by North Melbourne by more than seven goals at Arden Street the following week.

None of this was the perfect lead-in to their eagerly-awaited rematch with Geelong – the third time the two had faced off in the Pies' last six VFL matches. Bill Twomey was still missing, along with his brother Mick, inspirational captain Lou Richards, 1952's leading goalkicker Maurice 'Mocha' Dunstan and star half-back Peter Lucas. In their place, among others, came a youngster named Tom Tarrant (no relation to Chris, as far as we can tell), plucked from virtual obscurity to fill a spot in the back pocket, another debutante in Neville Waller and youngster Kevin Flint, playing what turned out to be his fourth and last game for the club. Essendon coach Dick Reynolds, writing in *The Argus*, said the Pies needed a miracle. Hec de Lacy, in the *Sporting Globe*, put it more pithily when he predicted the Cats would 'murder' their hosts.

It might have been a depleted Magpies line-up – something the club and its fans would sadly have to get used to this season – but it was one that fought hard. The home team unsettled Geelong with a fierce attack on the footy, and an equally vigorous approach to tackling, Bob Rose twice flattening opponents in the first quarter to set the scene. But it wasn't only Collingwood's physical battering that surprised Geelong – they outpaced and outplayed their more fancied rivals as well. Incredibly, the patched-up Pies led by 28 points at half-time: the margin would have been much wider but for some horrible kicking for goal. The Woods tired badly after half-time and, even though they were still hanging on by a point at three-quarter time, most of the crowd knew Geelong would finish on top. That's what happened, with the reigning Premiers pulling away to win by 25 points.

The experts, however, liked what they had seen. Dick Reynolds said he believed a full-strength Collingwood team would have won. 'Yet a weakened Magpie side, until it ran out of steam, got away with something that will set every League coach thinking hard. A close, buffeting, niggling game can worry Geelong and throw it out of its stride.'

Umpires rush in to separate players as things get heated between Collingwood and Geelong in the Round 3 clash at Victoria Park. Neil Mann is on the far left, Arthur Gooch (14) and Jack Hamilton on the far right.

The gallant Magpies might not have won the game, but they came away *believing*, rather than merely hoping, that the Cats could be beaten – and knowing they were the team to do it. A Collingwood team missing five of its best players had completely outplayed the League's premier team for a half, and pushed them close through the rest of the game. The teams had enjoyed the same number of scoring shots, but the Pies' profligacy in front of goal (9.19 to 14.14) had cost them dearly. They'd kicked 1.11 in the second half. Bob Rose surely wouldn't kick seven behinds again. If ever there was a defeat to provide hope, this was it.

But hope didn't change the fact that the Magpies had lost two of their first three games – hardly premiership-winning form. Still, the confidence the players drew from their effort against Geelong produced immediate results, and they won the next six games on the trot. This winning run was not without its scares, however: the team overcame more poor kicking (14.19) and a late Carlton fightback to beat the Blues in Round 4, and was stuck on a miserable 4.13 at three-quarter time against Hawthorn the following week before piling on nine goals in a final term blitzkrieg.

Lou Richards was at his cheeky best against Carlton in Round 4, pushing away George Ferry and giving him some lip for good measure.

Just as it would in 2010, poor kicking for goal was proving a big problem. It was again in the team's narrow escape in Round 7 against Footscray at the Western Oval. This was always going to be a strange affair, given it was one of the few times in League history that two teams have met each other twice in the space of five days. This oddity occurred because a Lightning Premiership – a single-day, round-robin knockout competition of short matches – was played on Tuesday 2 June, in honour of and on the same day as Queen Elizabeth's Coronation. The Pies were paired against the Dogs in their first round game (which they lost 0.2 to 3.3). Four days later the teams met again – playing for keeps, this time – at the Doggies' home ground.

The visitors dominated from the start, playing brilliant, free-flowing football, and piled on five goals to Footscray's solitary behind in the opening term. By half-time the margin had been trimmed to 23 points but still the Pies looked comfortable. All that changed in the third term. Collingwood was held goalless, managing only four behinds from at least 10 direct attempts on goal as the forwards sprayed shots all over the place. The final term was even worse, as the Pies could not manage any score at all and the Bulldogs charged home. The final minutes of the game were complete madness, as the Pies clung to their diminishing lead and the Dogs closed in on what would have been a famous victory. At this point 'finesse, artistry and frills were thrown to the winds', Hugh Buggy reported in *The Argus*.

In the end, it was only three towering marks in the teeth of goal from best-on-ground Neil Mann that saved the game for the Magpies, who managed to hang on for a one-point win. And as most Collingwood fans would have predicted pre-season, former Magpie Harvey Stevens was named best player for the Dogs.

The season's defining moments were approaching. The Pies sat in second spot with seven wins after nine rounds, and in Round 10 travelled to Windy Hill to take on third-placed Essendon. Collingwood had won only once at Windy Hill since the Second World War (and that by a point) and never looked like adding to that tally. The Bombers were far too good and won by 28 points, though they were helped by yet another woeful Collingwood display – 6.16. The goalkicking yips were by now seemingly chronic. The following week against Fitzroy it was 7.19 – a deplorable effort that allowed the 'Roys to stage a magnificent comeback at Victoria Park and snatch a one-point win at the death.

Suddenly, the Pies were wobbling. The team had slid to fourth and, with a trip to South Melbourne to come, were staring down the barrel of a third successive loss for the first time since 1948. All season the club had battled three

---

The Argus

Hugh Buggy, on the tussle between Collingwood and Footscray

Risks were scorned and players just hurled themselves at the ball or into the writhing packs, while the delighted, swaying crowd roared and stamped. In the most desperate finish seen this season, the resolute young Bulldogs turned a triumphal march by Collingwood into a tense, swaying goal-mouth grapple. [Collingwood's] harried and overworked defenders... had to struggle like swimmers to keep their heads above the turbulent waves of tricolour. In those frenzied closing minutes Collingwood seemed without punch or purpose.

PLAYER OF THE YEAR

Bob Rose

Perhaps Collingwood's greatest ever player, Bob Rose enjoyed probably his best ever season in 1953.

Whether roving or up forward he was simply unstoppable. Fast, tough, supremely courageous and highly skilled, Rose had it all. His fearless and fanatical play frequently lifted his teammates and turned games in Collingwood's favour: he was the most inspirational player in the competition.

He won the Copeland Trophy for the fourth time, finished second in the Brownlow Medal behind Essendon's Bill Hutchison and was chosen in the All-Australian team. He also led the club's goalkicking with 36 goals, a tally that would have been greater but for several bouts of inaccuracy (including the grand final, where he had nine shots on goal for only three majors)

But that was the only blot on an otherwise near-perfect season. He was among the team's best in both finals and almost all its other big matches. It was only fitting that Bob Rose kicked the sealing goal to bring home the flag.

major problems – horrible inaccuracy in front of goal, a shocking run with injuries and the absence of a stable, dangerous forward set-up. The team's spirit and tenacity had carried it for much of the season, together with the brilliance of midfielders such as Bob Rose, Thorold Merrett, Des Healey, Lou and Ron Richards and Neil Mann, who was a colossus in the ruck. But would that be enough to go the whole way? There was no gun full-forward, and the biggest attacking threats, Bill Twomey and Mocha Dunstan, were mercurial and injury-prone. Critics doubted whether the Pies had what it took to win a flag.

The players had a week off after the Fitzroy loss, with a split round scheduled while interstate matches were played. They relaxed by putting on their annual Kia-Ora Sports Parade show at the Melbourne Town Hall. Every club had its own 'edition' of the show, which was compered by the legendary Doug Elliott and broadcast on radio station 3KZ. Collingwood's version included a 'mystery voice competition', songs from Mocha Dunstan and Jack Parker and a 'Footballers' Drama' starring Ron Richards, Frank Tuck and Mick Twomey, among others. Luckily, the Pies' dubious singing and acting talents were supported by other performers such as 'The Blonde Bombshell', Gloria Dawn, and Cafari, the International Illusionist.

Maybe the selectors should have drafted Cafari into the team's forward line, because he surely couldn't have done any worse kicking for goal. At three-quarter time the next week against South the tally was 10.15, and the Pies trailed by five points. Phonse Kyne had pleaded with his players after the Fitzroy loss to give an extra effort 'for the old black and white uniform', but it seemed to have done no good. A third successive loss loomed, and with it possibly the grip on a place in the four, let alone the double chance.

Then, 10 minutes into the final term, the team suddenly rediscovered its mojo and, just as importantly, the forwards found their radar. The result was a 7.2 to 0.1 final term and a win that looked much more comfortable on the scoreboard than it had been on the ground. But the Pies had the four points, and some momentum. They would not lose again for the season.

A regulation win against North Melbourne followed, and then it was down to Kardinia Park for the biggest test of all. Geelong had won 23 matches in a row, and had gone 26 without defeat (including a draw). They had broken Collingwood's record of successive

A tense goalmouth battle during the season-defining win against South Melbourne in Round 12, as Arthur Gooch flies to prevent a Swans' goal.

victories just a few weeks earlier and, though critics had started to detect signs of tiredness in their game, they were still unbackable favourites for the flag.

But this time the Woods had a secret weapon – steak and eggs. Up until now, the system on match days was for players to have their lunch when they arrived in Geelong. Pre-match lunches tended to be heavy in those pre-dietician days, too – not the sort of thing that would have been digested two hours later. So club officials introduced early lunches of steak and eggs and cups of tea *before* the players set off for Sleepy Hollow. It was a system the club followed for many years.

And this day in 1953 it – or something – did the trick. Early on it was all Geelong, and, in a reversal of fortunes from the early season game at Victoria Park, it was only the Cats wastefulness in front of goal that kept their half-time score to 5.11 and the margin to two goals. That was close enough for the Pies to strike, and the team emerged re-energised after half-time following a stirring address from Phonse Kyne. There were just two points in it at the final change,

Coach Phonse Kyne and captain Lou Richards are elated after the Magpies broke Geelong's winning run at Kardinia Park.

The Argus

Hugh Buggy, on Collingwood's defeat of flag favourites, Geelong

Collingwood on Saturday applied with ruthless efficiency a plan of masterly frustration to crush Geelong's deadly pace,' he wrote. 'That plan demanded that every Collingwood player should gallop along at his opponent's elbow – bumping, jostling and blocking. Each Magpie applied himself to the task with such tigerish energy as to dislocate smooth teaming and stud the game with frenzied individual tussles for the ball.

but captain Lou Richards admitted afterwards that 'we had run ourselves into the ground matching pace with them and were just about exhausted'. But Richards and his men dug deep and, with Bob Rose, Healey and Merrett starring in the middle, the outsiders stormed home with a four-goal last term to deliver a 20-point win that provided a huge psychological boost. 'That win was a turning point,' wrote Lou Richards later. 'We felt that if we could beat them down on their own ground we could beat them any time.'

So it was that we saw an amazing reversal of what had come to be accepted as the 1953 football pattern. Instead of the fleet-footed Geelong rampaging away to victory, they saw an exultant Collingwood flashing the ball on to the open spaces with a flagging Geelong in weary pursuit.

The optimism the players had drawn from the loss at Victoria Park earlier in the season had been vindicated, and the Pies were now right back in the hunt for second spot. But their problems hadn't disappeared overnight. The injury woes continued: star defender Jack Hamilton broke his hand against Geelong and missed the rest of the season. The team still couldn't kick straight: the Round 8 win over St Kilda was the last time the team managed more goals than behinds in a game until the finals (indeed, the team would finish the year with a lop-sided tally of 232 goals, 293 behinds, and only kicked more goals than behinds on five occasions). And the search for an effective forward structure continued.

That search saw Collingwood turn to two untried youngsters before the finals. At the start of the year, the club had named four teenagers on its senior supplementary list with instructions they were to be played in the thirds. But two of them, Murray Weideman and Keith Bromage, quickly showed they were far too good for under-19s, and even reserves, football. Weideman, 17, was given his senior debut the week after the Geelong triumph in what proved to be a routine win against Carlton. Two weeks later, Bromage became the youngest-ever VFL player (at 15 years and 287 days) when he was given his chance against Richmond after kicking 14 goals in two games in the reserves.

Bromage's debut came in what turned out to be one of Collingwood's most meritorious wins of the season. The Woods looked in dire straits at three-quarter time at Punt Road. Their score of 9.15 left them four points adrift of Richmond but, more seriously, they were running out of players. They had only 17 fit players on the field from early in the third quarter, and two of those remaining in the forward line were seriously hampered by injury. But captain Lou Richards inspired his team with three wonderful goals, including two brilliant snapshots over his shoulder, and the Magpies got home by 14 points.

Above: Murray Weideman's first kick in VFL football, a point against Carlton.
Left: Lou Richards snaps another brilliant goal during his inspirational burst against Richmond at Punt Road.

PLAYER OF THE YEAR
Neil Mann

Neil Mann stood tall in all ways at Victoria Park in 1953. The man affectionately known as 'Super' to his teammates had a big frame, big hands and a big heart – and all came to the fore in the club's premiership year.

In a team not over-blessed with big men, Mann's indefatigable spirit in the ruck was priceless. Time and again he carried the rucks almost single-handedly, running himself into the ground in pursuit of a Magpie victory. Then, when he rested either forward or back, his legendarily huge hands proved a potent weapon, saving games with marks in the last line of defence, or creating and kicking goals in attack.

He finished runner-up in the Copeland, third in the Brownlow, would have played for Victoria but for injury and was named the club's best player in the finals. But his favourite 'award' was a five-pound note given to him after the grand final by club great Albert Collier – a heartfelt expression of admiration from one champ to another that Mann never forgot.

At this point, with just one game to go in the home-and-away season, the League ladder was delicately poised, at least as far as the top four was concerned. After losing to Collingwood in Round 14, Geelong had lost to both Essendon and South Melbourne. But Essendon surprisingly went down at home to North by a point in Round 17, leaving the Bombers safe in fourth, Geelong secure on top and Collingwood and Footscray to fight it out in the final game of the year for second position – and the much coveted double chance. It was, in effect, a third semi-final.

The game was hyped as the 'match of the season', just as that with Geelong had been a few weeks earlier. A huge crowd was expected at Victoria Park, and there were hopes that the record ground crowd of 47,224 could be eclipsed. But rumours spread throughout Collingwood that the gates had been shut early, and the crowd ended up being just under 34,000. They witnessed a start that would have done justice to a final.

'It was a game that opened on that feverish, almost hysterical note so dearly loved by the Magpies,' wrote Hugh Buggy in *The Argus*. 'Buffeting in the crushes was relentless. Tackling was fierce. Elbows jabbed at ribs. Players went down in wild tangles of arms and legs. Courage and morale were sternly tested by a session of crash and tumble.'

After the initial skirmishes, however, the game quickly became all Collingwood's. The still injury-ridden Pies kept the Dogs scoreless in a devastating first quarter, and to only two goals at three-quarter time. The Dogs fought back late to go down by only 19 points in the end, but the margin flattered them and understated how well Collingwood had played. The black-and-white hordes could not have wished for a better tune-up for their second semi-final against Geelong two weeks later.

Despite the week's break, the Pies still couldn't put together a full-strength team for the semi-final, with Jack Hamilton, Pat Twomey and Mocha Dunstan among those missing through injury, and Frank Tuck suspended. Then Billy Tebble, who had been named at centre half-back, had to withdraw on the morning of the match with the flu. There was a major surprise at the selection table when Keith Batchelor, who had played most of his seven games at full-back, was named at full-forward. The even-less-experienced Terry Waites, who had debuted during the year and played mostly on a half-forward flank, was brought in at centre half-forward. Clearly, the club's forward problems remained unsolved.

Yet coach Phonse Kyne was confident – and a little bemused by Geelong's favouritism. 'Collingwood does not regard itself as "underdog" for the League semi-final against Geelong at the MCG today,' he wrote in *The Argus*. 'On our recent form we feel we should be favourites to qualify for the grand final. We have won our last seven matches and have been gradually building up to "concert pitch". Geelong, on the other hand, has been defeated in three of its last five appearances. To us, Geelong is just another side – a side we can defeat today.'

Kyne's confidence spread through the playing group. Bob Rose, pacing the rooms before the game, was heard to say, 'Get on us. We'll win today. It's in the bag.' Kyne told his players: 'You have the great tradition of Collingwood to uphold. You are not playing for yourselves. You are playing for your wives and families. Make them proud of you. Most of all you are playing for Collingwood. Don't forget that. And don't let the club down.'

The game was a beauty, with Collingwood backing its ferocity, tackling and pressure to prevent Geelong using its pace to break into the open, and tight, one-on-one defence to nullify the brilliance of the Geelong forwards. The result was some thrilling football.

The Cats recovered their poise quickest, and by midway through the second term led by 15 points, with rover Peter Pianto having kicked four of their six goals. Mick Twomey, Bill Twomey and Neil Mann were starring for the Pies, and two late goals left them only three points adrift at the long break. The third quarter, as is so often the case, was the telling one: Geelong, kicking with the breeze, absolutely

Bill Rose soars for a classical high mark during the second semi-final.

The Argus
Hugh Buggy on the second semi-final against Geelong

From the first bounce the game hit an exhilarating tempo. With a wholesome respect for the quality of Geelong's pacy, long game, the Magpies tore into it with terrific zest. They tackled hard, and applied jolting vigour in the right places with telling effect. Geelong battled with equal intensity to break into the open spaces, and this clash of aims led to much contested football. It clotted into grappling packs, and both sides in the early duels played a nervy, highly strung game.'

dominated the play but were woefully astray in front of goal, managing a disastrous 1.8 for the term. The Pies scrambled a couple of goals against the run of play and went into the last quarter only four points down.

Ron Richards put the Pies in front for the first time in the game with an early last quarter goal, but 'Nipper' Trezise regained the lead soon after for Geelong as the game hung in the balance. Then the mighty Bob Rose burst through a pack to put the Pies back in front, and shortly afterwards broke away from trainers who were treating him for cramp to slot through another. Neil Mann was swung to full-forward and began taking mark after mark – two of which resulted in goals to seal a memorable five-goal win.

The result stunned – and impressed – Collingwood's many critics. 'No band of players could have shown more grit in rising above adversity, in confounding expert opinion and in upholding the honourable traditions of a famous club,' said *The Argus*. 'Here was a side that was riddled with critical gaps in key positions because of the absence of stars. Its forward line looked nebulous. It had no dependable or experienced spearhead, and its bizarre half-forward line . . . ran counter to all the textbooks. It had a dangerous vacuum at centre half-back that had to be plugged with lesser ability. But young second-line players who had waited eagerly for their big chance seized it with both hands. There was not a weak link among them. They hurled themselves into a harsh, sapping encounter with a gay abandon that scoffed at the reputation of their formidable opponents.'

Almost inevitably, Collingwood's brilliant win came at a cost. Star half-back Peter Lucas dislocated his shoulder and wingman Jack Hickey broke his hand, forcing both out of the decider two weeks later. Pat Twomey and Jack Parker, themselves only just recovered from injuries, came back into the team for the grand final, with Twomey's selection meaning that three brothers would for the first time play together in a grand final side. Back pocket player George Hams, who had been battling a shoulder injury, was named on the bench. They would once more be up against Geelong, who had overcome Footscray in the preliminary final.

Somehow, the Cats were still favourites. Many football observers refused to believe their era had ended, or that the Pies were good enough to beat them three times in a row. All acknowledged the Magpies' heart and ferocity; few felt it would be enough. Phonse Kyne wasn't among the doubters. 'Although we are outsiders

The three Twomey brothers: Pat, Bill and Mick.

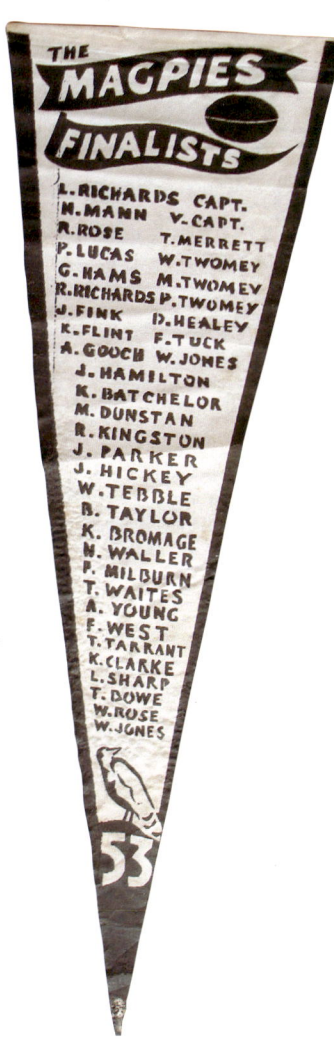

with many of the critics, I have still to be convinced they are right. I don't believe we fluked our two previous wins against Geelong this season.'

Nevertheless, there were a few nerves in the Collingwood dressing room. Bill Rose arrived at the ground to discover that he'd left his jumper at home, and had to have the sleeves hurriedly cut out of a spare one. Bill's famous brother, Bob, saw former coach, still selector, 70-year-old Jock McHale sitting on a bench, eyes fixed on the floor, 'as quiet as a mouse'. 'Jock just sat there with his head bowed as though there had been a death in the family,' Rose wrote in *The Sporting Globe* a few days later. 'It wasn't that he didn't expect a Collingwood win. He was visualising the horrible anti-climax of possible defeat.'

Lou Richards greeted every player with a quiet word upon arrival: he wanted to make sure that everyone associated with Collingwood understood the importance of this day. Seventeen years without a flag seemed like a huge drought at the time: little would anyone have predicted the longer waits that lay ahead. The embarrassment of the previous year's flogging by Geelong was

Above: The huge grand final crowd spills onto the ground, bringing many fans uncomfortably close to the action.

Opposite: Mick Twomey flies high for a speccie, as Bob Rose waits for the crumbs that didn't come.

still fresh in everyone's mind, too. Kyne alone addressed the players, emphasising yet again the importance of team ahead of individual, and stressing the weight of Collingwood history and the responsibility they carried. But even he was secretly nervous, fiddling incessantly with a good luck charm in the shape of a kangaroo's paw that had been given to him by a family friend on the eve of the game.

Outside the rooms, another story was developing. The ground was not fully reserved seating in 1953, so fans had started arriving from 4.30 on the afternoon before the game, and others joined them overnight. There were long queues from early on game day, and by the time the gates were opened at 9am, two hours ahead of schedule, 25,000 fans were waiting to get in. The situation looked like getting out of control over the next few hours as 89,060 – 510 more than the Health Department's safety limit – crammed into the ground. The gates were shut at 12.30, and hundreds of angry fans claimed their money back because they couldn't see anything. Thousands were turned away, while some who were locked out tried to scale the high concrete wall around the ground. The Collingwood players had to enter their dressing rooms via the Members stand and then the ground, because they couldn't get through the milling fans. More worryingly, the crowd crush broke a fence in front of the scoreboard, and hordes of spectators ignored police advice and jumped onto the arena. By the time the players ran onto the ground there were thousands sitting inside the boundary line.

In such a highly-charged atmosphere, even experienced players noticed the 'wall of sound' that greeted their arrival. Lou Richards led the team onto the field through what by today's standards was a skimpy banner of streamers held between two poles. 'You run down the race and the crowd around you yells,' he told *The Argus*. 'Then you brace against the streamers, they hold you for a second, then you're through, and the roar you heard on the way down doesn't count against the roar from them all as you step on to the field. Those streamers remind me of breaking through the sound barrier.'

By the time the game started the crowd was in a feverish state of anticipation, desperate to see whether Collingwood's earlier wins over Geelong had indeed been flukes. Those wins had been built on a fast and furious attack on the ball,

Above: **Bill Twomey heads for goal against Geelong.**
Opposite: **Things are tight in the heat of battle as Magpies Jack Finck, Jack Parker (18) and Lerrel Sharp desperately defend their goal.**

and an equally physical approach to the Geelong players. Lou Richards said after the game that the Collingwood players had decided to throw their Geelong opponents hard to the ground whenever they had the chance, thereby tiring them out. When the rival skippers shook hands pre-match, Geelong's Fred Flanagan wished Lou luck. 'I won't need the luck, Fred. You'll need it. Anyone who comes near us today will get their head kicked over the grandstand.'

Whether or not it's true, that sledge summed up Collingwood's approach: they were going to play the same hard, tough, uncompromising footy they'd been playing all year. Nobody doubted Geelong's brilliance, but if there was a query over the Cats it was about their ability to withstand physical pressure. The Collingwood game plan had worked well against Geelong in two-and-a-half of their past three matches, and no one at Victoria Park saw a reason to change.

Collingwood had by far the better of the early exchanges while kicking with a slight breeze but, once again, failed to make the most of their chances, kicking only 2.4 from numerous attempts. The play was fierce, with players from both sides hurling themselves into the contests. It was exactly the style of game Collingwood wanted, but they hadn't made it count on the scoreboard, and a late goal to the Cats saw them only two points down at quarter-time.

The second term bore eerie similarities to the third quarter of the second semi. Geelong, with a breeze at their backs, controlled the game but fell down woefully in front of goal, managing only 1.7 from a raft of mainly hurried shots. Collingwood, on the other hand, kicked three into the wind and took a nine-point lead into the long break. The Magpies' game plan had, as hoped, unsettled the Cats, and they felt the game was within their grasp. 'As we trooped off at half-time we all agreed we had the show,' said Bob Rose later. 'We were nine points up, had the wind in the third quarter, and that would give Geelong the score to chase at the turn for home. In the rooms we figured on four or five goals lead at three-quarter time. That was the target to make things safe.'

Two quick goals to Lou Richards and Des Healey soon after play resumed set the Pies on their way, and sparked a paralysing burst of four goals in 10 minutes. With Ron Richards starring in the unfamiliar position of wing, Healey doing likewise on the opposite wing and Bob Rose always a danger, Collingwood attacked and attacked, putting Geelong under fearsome pressure. Bill McMaster was a victim of that pressure, taken from the ground after being flattened by a bump from Pat Twomey (Twomey himself followed a little later after tearing his ankle ligaments). But the Pies were playing brilliant football by now, and even though Geelong grabbed two goals of their own, a late goal to Batchelor saw the Woods lead by 29 points at three-quarter time. Rose and his teammates had got exactly what they wanted.

Now it just remained to be seen whether the players had got their calculations correct. A 29-point margin should have been comfortable enough. But suddenly Geelong kicked into life. Bob

PLAYER OF THE YEAR

Des Healey

Collingwood officials must have been mighty pleased they resisted Des Healey's pre-season overtures in 1953 to be released to a country club, because by the end of the year he was regarded as one of the best wingmen in the game.

He capped off a stellar season that produced all-Australian selection and third place in the Copeland Trophy with a best-on-ground performance when it mattered most, in the grand final.

Healey was brilliant that day, as he was for most of the year. He had dazzling pace, superb evasive skills and exquisite ball control. He could twist, turn and baulk at top pace, and possessed a left-foot almost as lethal as that of his fellow wingman Thorold Merrett. Forwards on the end of his passes rarely had to stoop or stretch for the ball.

Healey was highly consistent and rarely put in a bad game throughout his career. That career ended in 1955 in an infamous clash with Melbourne's 'Bluey' Adams, but in 1953 he played a pivotal role in Collingwood's long-awaited flag.

The Argus

Hugh Buggy, on Collingwood's premiership win

They proved a team of plucky fighters can overcome an odd technical deficiency here and there, even under the intense pressure of a grand final. No side in the League has been so dissected, analysed, criticised, and damned with faint praise by the experts. It had little of the equipment essential to win a flag, they said. Where was its top-class full forward? It had none. Where was its stabilized half-back line? It had been wrecked completely by the loss of Frank Tuck and Peter Lucas. Where was its experienced centre half-forward? It had none. But whatever unbalance there may have been at odd spots in the field, the Magpies possessed in full measure some of the basic ingredients to success in the finals. They had courage all over the field – sheer pluck that no buffeting or bullocking could disturb.

Davis, one of their very best players, broke free and kicked two team-lifting goals. The Cats looked faster and fresher and were running all over their opponents. In a reversal of the previous two matches, it was the Magpies who now looked tired. Defender Arthur Gooch limped off. The margin was just 14 points, and the crowd was roaring madly. Midway through the term Collingwood managed a rare forward surge that ended with Bob Rose taking a pass from Ron Richards and steering through the game-steadying goal. 'As the ball sailed forward I had the horrible thought of what might happen if I missed,' Rose said later. 'As it went through somebody in a black and white guernsey waved to me and I returned him the "thumbs up" sign. It was in the bag!'

So it was. Geelong came again and managed another goal, and should have had two more when Ron Hovey missed two sitters that would have made things interesting, but in the end fell 12 points short. As had happened in the second semi, their wayward kicking (8.17) had cost them dearly. Thousands of spectators stormed the field as the siren rang and mobbed the Collingwood players: many, including the captain, ended up being chaired from the field on the shoulders of jubilant fans. They were wild, euphoric scenes.

A 17-year drought was over: the premiership was Collingwood's. That fact owed much to the brilliant work of established players such as Des Healey (23 touches), Ron Richards (27), Bob Rose (30), Neil Mann, Mick and Bill Twomey and Ron Kingston. But the team's much-maligned lesser lights had also done their bit. Full-back turned full-forward Keith Batchelor kicked four goals, while Neville Waller did well at centre half-back on Fred Flanagan. And Terry Waites' seemingly bizarre selection at centre half-forward had turned out to be a masterstroke: the Pies knew his opponent, the dangerous John Hyde, had an injured leg that the Cats tried to keep secret. So they played the smaller Waites on him with instructions to run Hyde off his legs. Waites played that role to perfection, nullifying Hyde's influence and picking up a dozen touches himself.

Percy Beames, writing in *The Age*, said Collingwood's victory would go down as one of the club's greatest premiership wins. 'More talented teams have won flags for the Magpies,' he wrote. 'But never has there been one to display finer battle calibre.' Another journalist wrote: 'The name Collingwood will be synonymous with football courage as long as the 1953 League football finals are remembered. For the second time in two weeks Collingwood, badly weakened by injuries, defeated Geelong, Premiers for the past two years and leading team throughout the season. Only Collingwood could have done it.'

Thousands of delirious Collingwood fans invade the ground after the final siren and carry their heroes from the field.

The Mightiest Magpies

Lou and Ron Richards toast the Magpies' premiership success with drinks from appropriate cups.

As always, Hugh Buggy in *The Argus* summed up the win beautifully: 'Nobody who really loves the game will begrudge the Magpies a richly deserved triumph, which was achieved the hard way,' he wrote. 'They confounded most of the experts and critics. They flouted all the rules postulated about field balance . . . [But] they had team spirit developed to the highest degree under Spartan training, a team spirit which has made Collingwood one of the most formidable forces in the League down the years. And they had discipline of a kind that has been handed on as a legacy from the great Collingwood sides of the past.'

Not surprisingly, the club celebrated long and hard. There were any number of dinners, concerts and other social events, including a slightly more adventurous one hosted by Mr Dave Lee at his Kum Ling Café in Smith Street (with food that, while delectable, would have been a 'novelty' to some, according to the club's annual report). The players also got to enjoy a week-long end-of-season trip to Tasmania, fortified by a pre-trip gift of a carton of Black & White cigarettes.

But there was sadness too. The strain of that tense last quarter proved too much for the club's most famous figure, Jock McHale, who suffered a heart attack the day after the grand final and died a week later, plunging the club into a period of mourning. A similar fate befell another near-mythical figure in John Wren, a generous club benefactor over many decades. He suffered a heart attack a few days after the grand final and died a month later, one of his last acts having been to donate £500 to the players after their premiership win (his two sons donated a similar amount). Cornered by *The Sporting Globe* after the game, the media-shy Wren had said: 'Well, just say it's a little token of appreciation of the grand job the boys did throughout the season.'

From today's perspective, the 1953 flag bears some remarkable similarities to that of 2010. Both teams were seeking to end an era of Geelong domination. Both teams were said to possess few stars and lack key forwards, leaving goalkicking responsibilities to be shared among many. Both teams were plagued by chronic inaccuracy throughout the year. Both teams took great heart from an early-season loss to their grand final opponent and turned it into a victory at the next attempt. Both had clearly defined game plans centred around applying fierce pressure to the opposition. Both had young players who stood up with surprising maturity when it counted – for Waites, Waller, Weideman and Sharp you can substitute Sidebottom, Beams, Reid, Brown, Wellingham. Both had strikingly similar second quarters in the deciding games – in 1953 Collingwood kicked 3.2 to 1.7, in 2010 it was 3.3 to 1.6. And, finally, both were premierships that ended long droughts.

A constant theme of the 1953 post-premiership reviews was that this had been a very *Collingwood* type of flag – one that was won in a typically

Lou Richards and Syd Coventry among the pallbearers carrying Jock McHale's casket at the legendary coach's funeral.

Below: The football presented to captain Lou Richards after the match.

Collingwood way. That concept was perfectly summed up by Ben Kerville in *The Sporting Globe,* when talking about how well the club had covered its run of injuries: 'Because, no matter who's in the line-up, Collingwood always are a team. They're always Collingwood. And that means something, not only in the way every man pulls his weight for the colours in keeping with the club's great tradition, but because of the impact on other sides of the never-say-die brand of football they turn on. So much is written about the "Collingwood tradition" and the "Magpie fighting spirit" that it has seemed like poppycock or wishful thinking to some. Yet there has been ample evidence these past few weeks that the traditional fight of Collingwood really is something tangible in football – not merely a myth.'

And that's as true today as it was nearly 60 years ago.

RON RICHARDS

GRAND FINAL HERO

Although he played nearly 150 games for Collingwood, Ron Richards' career was mostly that of a solid contributor rather than a star. But he had his moments in the sun – often, tellingly, in finals matches.

His finest moment of all, undoubtedly, came in September of 1953. He'd already played an outstanding game as a half-forward flanker in the second semi but was controversially moved to the wing for the grand final. The selection – a brainwave from former coach Jock McHale – raised a few eyebrows, but it proved to be a stroke of genius.

Richards played a magnificent game, racking up 27 touches, including a remarkable (for the time) 11 handballs. He set up goals for teammates, harried Geelong's pacy midfielders and seemed to be in every tight midfield pack. Along with Des Healey, he was widely considered to have been best on ground.

Ron's September efforts saw him named as the club's second best player in the finals series – a high accolade in a premiership year. And one which allowed him, briefly, to step out of older brother Lou's shadow.

PLAYERS

#	Player	Games	Goals
4	Keith Batchelor	9	8
35	Keith Bromage	2	4
30	Kevin Clarke	9	5
6	Maurie Dunstan	13	22
5	Jack Finck	19	6
13	Kevin Flint	1	0
14	Arthur Gooch	13	0
8	Jack Hamilton	13	3
7	George Hams	12	0
12	Des Healey	17	6
19	Jack Hickey	17	4
9	Ron Kingston	19	4
16 & 34	Dave Little	3	0
3	Peter Lucas	18	0
2	Neil Mann	17	8
17	Thorold Merrett	20	15
11	Pat Milburn	6	3
18	Jack Parker	13	0
1	Lou Richards	19	25
20	Ron Richards	19	13
33	Bill Rose	5	0
22	Bob Rose	19	36
29	Lerrel Sharp	5	0
28	Tom Tarrant	4	0
15	Bill Tebble	16	6
24	Frank Tuck	17	1
26	Bill Twomey Jnr	15	27
25	Mick Twomey	17	14
27	Pat Twomey	12	8
10	Terry Waites	7	1
31	Neville Waller	16	9
16	Murray Weideman	5	4
34	Fred West	3	0

Club Awards
Copeland Trophy – Bob Rose
RT Rush Trophy – Neil Mann
J J Joyce Trophy – Des Healey
Best player in finals – Neil Mann
Second best player in finals (joint) – Ron Richards and Mick Twomey
Third best player in finals (joint) – Bob Rose and Des Healey
Leading goalkicker – Bob Rose (36)
Training prizes to 14 players

1953 SEASON

ROUND 1 April 18 — Victoria Park
Collingwood 17.16.118 v South Melbourne 11.11.77
Goals: W Twomey 9, L Richards 3, R Richards 2, B Rose 2, Batchelor

ROUND 2 May 2 — Arden St Oval
North Melbourne 18.10.118 v Collingwood 11.9.75
Goals: Batchelor 2, L Richards 2, B Rose 2, Kingston, Mann, Merrett, M Twomey, R.Richards

ROUND 3 May 9 — Victoria Park
Collingwood 9.19.73 v **Geelong 14.14.98**
Goals: B Rose 3, Healey 2, Mann, Merrett, Tebble, Tuck

ROUND 4 May 16 — Princes Park
Carlton 14.11.95 v **Collingwood 14.19.103**
Goals: Finck 4, B Rose 3, Kingston 2, R Richards 2, Tebble 2, Clarke

ROUND 5 May 23 — Victoria Park
Collingwood 13.18.96 v Hawthorn 3.8.26
Goals: Hickey 2, B Rose 2, Tebble 2, Clarke, Finck, Healey, Kingston, Merrett, L Richards, R Richards

ROUND 6 May 30 — Victoria Park
Collingwood 9.8.62 v Richmond 5.9.39
Goals: W Twomey 4, B Rose 3, M Twomey 2

ROUND 7 June 6 — Whitten Oval
Footscray 7.9.51 v **Collingwood 7.10.52**
Goals: M Twomey 3, Clarke, Hickey, Mann, R Richards

ROUND 8 June 13 — Victoria Park
Collingwood 19.17.131 v St Kilda 8.8.56
Goals: W Twomey 6, Dunstan 3, Merrett 3, L Richards 3, R Richards 2, Clarke, B Rose

ROUND 9 June 20 — MCG
Melbourne 7.6.48 v **Collingwood 9.9.63**
Goals: L Richards 2, W Twomey 2, Clarke, Dunstan, Healey, P Twomey, Waites

ROUND 10 June 27 — Windy Hill
Essendon 11.14.80 v Collingwood 6.16.52
Goals: Dunstan 3, Merrett, M Twomey, P Twomey

ROUND 11 July 4 — Victoria Park
Collingwood 7.19.61 v **Fitzroy 9.8.62**
Goals: Dunstan 4, Finck, Tebble, W Twomey

ROUND 12 July 18 — Lake Oval
South Melbourne 12.9.81 v **Collingwood 17.17.119**
Goals: Dunstan 4, L Richards 3, Waller 3, Merrett 2, Milburn 2, Hamilton, W Twomey, P Twomey

ROUND 13 July 25 — Victoria Park
Collingwood 13.16.94 v North Melbourne 8.17.65
Goals: B Rose 3, Merrett 2, L Richards 2, Dunstan, Hamilton, Hickey, Milburn, M Twomey, Waller

ROUND 14 August 1 — Kardinia Park
Geelong 7.13.55 v **Collingwood 10.15.75**
Goals: Dunstan 3, B Rose 2, Hamilton, Mann, Merrett, L Richards, W Twomey

ROUND 15 August 8 — Victoria Park
Collingwood 12.15.87 v Carlton 9.16.70
Goals: B Rose 3, P Twomey 2, Waller 2, Dunstan 2, Merrett, L Richards, M Twomey

ROUND 16 August 15 — Glenferrie Oval
Hawthorn 11.6.72 v **Collingwood 12.16.88**
Goals: Weideman 3, P Twomey 2, Waller, W Twomey, B Rose, R Richards, L Richards, Merrett, Dunstan

ROUND 17 August 22 — Punt Rd Oval
Richmond 12.9.81 v **Collingwood 13.17.95**
Goals: L Richards 4, Bromage 2, R Richards 2, Mann, B Rose, M Twomey, P Twomey, Weideman

ROUND 18 August 29 — Victoria Park
Collingwood 10.14.74 v Footscray 8.7.55
Goals: B Rose 3, Bromage 2, Waller 2, Merrett, W Twomey, M Twomey

1953 FINALS

LADDER

Team	W	L	D	For	Agst	%	Pts
Geelong	15	3	0	1546	1079	143.3	60
Collingwood	14	4	0	1518	1229	123.5	56
Footscray	13	5	0	1309	959	136.5	52
Essendon	13	5	0	1529	1177	129.9	52
Carlton	10	8	0	1409	1310	107.6	40
Fitzroy	10	8	0	1208	1421	85.0	40
North Melb	9	9	0	1388	1287	107.8	36
South Melb	9	9	0	1385	1323	104.7	36
St Kilda	5	13	0	1065	1323	68.2	20
Richmond	3	14	1	1220	1501	81.3	14
Melbourne	3	14	1	1137	1420	80.1	14
Hawthorn	3	15	0	974	1421	68.5	12

SEMI FINAL September 12 MCG

Collingwood 13.12.90 v Geelong **8.12.60**

Goals: B Rose 4, Mann 3, M Twomey 2, Batchelor, L Richards, R Richards, W Twomey

GRAND FINAL September 26 MCG

Collingwood	2.4	5.6	10.10	11.11	(77)
Geelong	2.3	3.9	5.11	8.17	(65)

Goals: Batchelor 4, B Rose 3, Healey 2, L Richards, M Twomey
Best: Healey, Mann, R. Richards, L. Richards, R. Rose, Merrett
Umpire: McMurray
Crowd: 89,060 at the MCG

Grand Final Team

B: L. Sharp, J. Finck, A. Gooch
HB: J. Parker, N. Waller, R. Kingston
C: D. Healey, W. Twomey, R. Richards
HF: P. Twomey, T. Waites, T. Merrett
F: M. Twomey, K. Batchelor, L. Richards (Capt.)
FOLL: N. Mann, W. Rose, R. Rose
RES: M. Weideman, G. Hams

CHAPTER FOURTEEN

1958

Destiny

'Those Collingwood players had something more than courage and determination behind them. They were defending the League record of four successive premierships . . . and they played throughout the grand final as though their very lives depended on keeping that record.'

As George Orwell might have said if he'd written about football: all premierships are special, but some are more special than others. And when it comes to Collingwood premierships, the 1958 flag is arguably the greatest in the club's history.

Of course, it has competition. The 1990 flag holds a revered place in the hearts of Magpie fans because it ended the most infamous drought in football and killed the Colliwobbles. The 1953 and 2010 versions also ended long droughts, and each was heroic in its own way. The 1896 victory was historically significant, being the club's first, and set the club on its way to the VFL and four decades of unparalleled success. Then there's 1929, which capped off the most successful home-and-away season in VFL history, and 1930, which established a record that has never been equalled, let alone eclipsed.

But for a magical, against-the-odds, fairytale triumph, nothing compares with 1958. The Magpies of '58 were not the best side in the competition that year, not by a long shot. They were opposed to one of the all-time great VFL/AFL teams. They lost more matches during the year than any other Collingwood premiership team, and struggled into the last fortnight on the back of a late-season form slump that saw them lose four games out of six. What makes 1958 so special, however, is not just that the team somehow found a way to win in all those circumstances; it's that, by doing so, they ensured that the club held on to one of its most cherished records, the four-in-a-row of the Machine. That's what gives the 1958 flag its added romance, its sense of destiny, and elevates it above so many others. Even beyond Collingwood, this is one of the most famous, and fabled, premierships in VFL/AFL history.

To understand the significance of what the Collingwood players achieved that year, you first have to understand the force they confronted. The Melbourne team of the mid-to-late 1950s was one of the most formidable football has ever known. The Demons played in seven successive grand finals, winning five, and finished on top in six of those seasons. They were led by one of the game's greatest coaches, Norm Smith, and included one of the game's greatest players, Ron Barassi, in his prime, along with a host of other big names such as Laurie Mithen, Stuart Spencer, Brian Dixon, 'Big Bob' Johnson, Ian Ridley and many more. The Magpies seemed to have no answers to them: by the time of the grand final they'd lost nine of their previous 10 encounters, including the 1955 and 1956 grand finals, and had not beaten Melbourne in a final for 20 years. To make matters worse, Collingwood had missed the finals completely in 1957, finishing in fifth position after having a bad run with injuries.

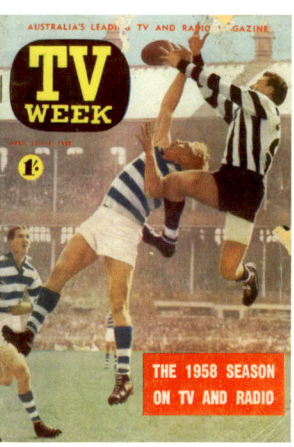

So Magpie fans went into the 1958 season with few reasons to believe that this could be their year. There were relatively few changes to the list over the off-season, with full-back Jack Hamilton the only big name to retire and most of the recruits being hopeful youngsters from whom little was expected. There was still a strong core to the line-up: Thorold Merrett and Murray Weideman were now established stars of the competition, while fellow '53 survivors Frank Tuck, Peter Lucas, Ron Kingston, Mick Twomey and Bill Twomey were all senior players nearing the end of their careers (Tuck replaced Bill Twomey as captain after the committee decided it, rather than the players, would choose the skipper). Others like wingman Ken Turner, giant ruckman Ray Gabelich and full-back Harry Sullivan had joined and made names for themselves in the years since that '53 flag. If this group was to improve on its disappointing 1957, then the improvement would have to come from within.

To its credit, the club set out with a bold approach to the season, publicly articulating a three-point plan that would guide it to the flag. The announcement of a plan sounded impressive, though the detail of that plan was less so. Point 1 was to beat Footscray at Footscray in the opening round of the season.

Ken Bennett kicks a goal in the opening game of the season, despite the close attention of Footscray's Ted Whitten.

Right: New skipper Frank Tuck flies for a mark against Footscray, while Bulldogs' debutante and future Brownlow Medallist John Schultz has no impact on the contest.
Below: Recruit Errol Hutchesson prepares for his first game.
Opposite: Ken Smale finds himself squeezed between two Hawks during the Round 2 thriller at Victoria Park. Ken Bennett is waiting for any crumbs.

That was declared a 'must'. Point 2 was to beat Melbourne in the teams' only meeting of the home-and-away season, on Queen's Birthday weekend. And Point 3 was to 'plan games carefully so they can be in a position to win the premiership'. A more vague Point 3 is hard to imagine, but at least it would be easy to judge how the club measured up to points 1 and 2.

Footscray at Footscray was a tough test, and the Dogs were clear favourites before the bounce. The Magpies gave debuts to several youngsters, including Errol Hutchesson and Barry Harrison, and stunned their hosts with a brilliant display, built around a resolute defence that restricted the home side to a paltry 4.5 for the afternoon. The scene was set for a fierce, physical contest early when Footscray debutante John Schultz was flattened and lost two teeth the first time he touched the ball. The Pies led from the start, even managing a quarter time lead despite kicking into a strong wind, and were untroubled in coasting to a nine-goal win. 'They outclassed Footscray in the air, left them standing with their handball and precision-like teamwork, and were physically stronger in the packs,' wrote Ian McDonald in *The Sporting Globe*.

So Collingwood had ticked off the first plank of its pre-season plan. And coach Phonse Kyne reiterated after the match what he felt Collingwood would need to go all the way. 'We're a team of fighters again – and we're going to stay that way,' he said. 'Anyone who doesn't give his utmost all the time is OUT.'

That warning seemed to have fallen on deaf ears at three-quarter time the following week, when the Magpies trailed Hawthorn by 24 points at Victoria Park. The Hawks had just piled on seven goals in a stunning third term, and Murray Weideman had been forced off with a knee injury. Ten minutes into the last quarter, the margin was still 23 points and the Pies looked gone. Then Hawthorn's Graham Arthur flattened young Barry Donegan, and players came from everywhere to join in a wild melee. A game that had featured plenty of spiteful clashes looked like it was now about to get out of control. Instead, Donegan regained his senses and passed to Ian Brewer, who goaled. Brewer, who was on fire, grabbed another just two minutes later and suddenly the game was alive.

The Hawks began to panic as their lead narrowed, and the revitalised Magpies found their old spark as the game became more and more frenzied in front of a roaring Vic Park crowd. Barry Harrison, in just his second game, took two towering marks near goal but missed both easy shots, bringing loud

IAN BREWER
COLLINGWOOD
Age 22, Height 6' 2", Weight 13½ st. Position — Full Forward. First League game 1956. *Remarks* — Top V.F.L. goal kicker 1958.

groans from the stands. Brendan Edwards had a chance to make the game safe for the Hawks but sprayed his running shot, before Don Howell marked and steered through a major to cut the difference to less than a goal. Then, with the clock ticking past 27 minutes, big Ray Gabelich soared for a spectacular mark in the goal square and put the Pies in front by a point.

The last couple of minutes were frenzied, as both sides threw everything at each other. The Pies forced the ball forward and, from a goalmouth scramble, Ian Brewer kicked one off the ground to seal a seven-point win. That goal capped an amazing solo display from the Collingwood full-forward: Brewer kicked 5.2 of his side's three-quarter time score of 5.6 and finished with 8.2 out of 11.9, including the sealer. By any measure, it was a big day out.

The following week was a mirror image of the Hawthorn game, with the Pies 26 points in front of Fitzroy and cruising at the last change. But Collingwood tired, the Lions charged and the game turned 180 degrees. Fitzroy closed to within five points with minutes to play, and the Magpies held on desperately in the closing stages. *The Age* reported that coach Phonse Kyne and his fellow selectors panicked, making wholesale changes throughout the last quarter trying to stem the flow, but nothing worked.. Lion Keith Wiegard looked like he'd won the game when he soccered a goal through, but the umpire paid a contentious free kick to Lerrel Sharp and the Magpies escaped. Then, with just seconds to go, Tony Ongarello grabbed what seemed to be a mark within kicking distance, only for the umpire to call for a bounce instead. The siren rang before play could resume. In the end, a 'weary and bewildered' black-and-white team managed to hang on and win. Had it not been for these controversial umpiring decisions, Collingwood would have gone down.

The Bear (Ray Gabelich), goes toe-to-toe with Fitzroy's Butch Gale during the Pies' nail-biting victory in Round 3.

That left the Pies 3–0 after three rounds, and already starting to eye off their big clash with Melbourne in Round 10. Maybe that caused the players to lose focus, because results over the next few weeks were inconsistent, to say the least. The Magpies lost to Essendon at Windy Hill in Round 4 when, in the final term, 'the ruckmen stopped to a walk, the rovers were useless, the half-back line cracked and the forwards lacked direction'. The team recovered from that damning assessment to bounce back and demolish Carlton in a spiteful game that featured brawls in the crowd as well as on the ground, and then beat Richmond before losing to North at Arden Street by three points. Big wins at home over South and St Kilda followed, but it was hard to run a form line through the Pies as they prepared for the match of the season against the Demons on Queen's Birthday weekend.

This was the game everyone in football had been waiting for. The Demons were already clear on top of the ladder, having only dropped one game, a shock loss to St Kilda by just a point. Collingwood, despite the losses and close scrapes and the continued improvement from North and Fitzroy, was still considered the team most likely to be able to stop their premiership run. In the lead-up to the game, *The Sporting Globe* predicted that the record for a home-and-away crowd of 58,543 could well be broken. That proved to be the understatement of the season, as a phenomenal 99,346 fans crammed in to the MCG to watch. It was then the third biggest crowd ever to watch a football match (behind the previous two grand finals) and it is still the biggest crowd to watch any VFL/AFL home-and-away match. The size of the crowd caught traffic and transport officials by surprise, and there was chaos on the roads, train stations and tram stops near the ground before and after the match.

Ian Brewer (above left) was an important goal kicker for the Pies right through the season, and especially in some of the early rounds. Harry Sullivan (in action during the loss against North, above) was equally important at the other end, holding down the full-back position with aplomb.

The Mightiest Magpies

Above: **The record-breaking crowd squeezed into the MCG on Queen's Birthday.**
Below: **Bill Serong snaps for goal during the thrilling contest, despite John Beckwith's attempts to spoil. Thorold Merrett (17) and Murray Weideman provide support.**

It all made for a heady pre-match atmosphere, and the game itself lived up to expectations. Both sides went at each other hammer and tongs from the first bounce, and players threw themselves into every contest with reckless abandon. The Demons established an early lead and had pushed that to four goals just before half-time. The Pies weren't playing terribly well: they were fumbling badly, teaming poorly and being beaten in most key positions. Star players like Weideman and Merrett were well down. Melbourne were dominating the rucks and the air, and their rovers were far too quick and skilful.

But then the first Magpie comeback began. Two late goals in the second quarter, and two more to begin the third, saw Collingwood lead for the first time, and against the overall balance of play. The Demons then hit back, responding with three goals to reclaim the lead and establish a comfortable

three-quarter-time margin of 20 points. The natural order seemed to have been restored. Only Collingwood's intense desire and fighting spirit, and the work of Ian Brewer up forward, kept the Pies within striking distance.

The last quarter provided astonishing drama. Melbourne kicked the first goal and led by four goals half way through. The game looked safe. Then everything changed. Perhaps the Demons relaxed a bit, or perhaps the Woods found another gear. Whatever the cause, the effect was that Collingwood came charging back at the death, with four quick goals – three from Brewer – that brought the crowd to fever pitch. The last of Brewer's match haul of six goals came with just two minutes to play when he snapped truly out of a pack: incredibly, it gave Collingwood a one-point lead. It looked as if the Pies might be about to break their Melbourne hoodoo in the most unlikely circumstances. But in a breathtaking finish, Geoff Tunbridge wobbled one through for the Demons, then Ian Ridley goaled from the square to end Collingwood's spirited resistance.

'Words cannot describe the drama of this memorable game,' wrote the *Football Record* the following week. 'It always had the crowd yelling for more as men hurled themselves into packs regardless of injury . . . in an exhibition of the grand Aussie game that was a delight, an inspiration and a never to be forgotten experience for all those privileged to see it.'

Melbourne certainly deserved to win: they'd played the better football through most of the day. But Collingwood took great heart from the loss. They hadn't played at their best, but still pushed Melbourne to the very end and actually had the game in their grasp with just two minutes left. 'There should be a consolation prize for a team like Collingwood,' wrote Barrie Bretland in *The Sun*, 'which hates to be beaten and never admits that it is.'

Many fans thought they'd seen a preview of the grand final, and wanted to fast forward to the sides' inevitable meetings in September. So there was a sense of anti-climax after the Queen's Birthday game – Melbourne were thumped by Fitzroy the next week and the Magpies made heavy weather of the rest of their season.

Initially, all seemed to be going according to plan. A solid win over Geelong at Kardinia Park was followed by an 11-point defeat of Footscray that was more comfortable than it appeared. After a two-week break for a national football carnival celebrating 100 years of football, the players again showed their famed fighting spirit with a stunning come-from-behind win against Hawthorn in Round 13.

In Round 2 they'd trailed Hawthorn by 24 points at the last change. This time around it was 25, and the team looked lacklustre and insipid after the

The Sun

On the Queen's birthday clash:

Battle of the Giants. Premiership preview. Match of the century. Name your own superlatives and probably you still will be understating the magnificence of this Melbourne-Collingwood 'dream game'. Even if only 10,000 people had seen it, it would have been one for the history books. But that all-time record 99,346 multitude was an added feature of a game that had everything. [The match was] saturated in muscle-jarring tackling, scorching pace and aerial agility seldom seen outside the Big Top. And to complete this classic contest, the two teams staged a nerve-sapping climax that would have made Alfred Hitchcock green with envy.

PLAYER OF THE YEAR

Ken Turner

If the sign of a truly great player is his ability to turn it on in the biggest games, then Ken Turner's 1958 season confirmed his standing as a Magpie champion.

By 1958 Turner was regarded as one of the game's most outstanding wingmen – a wonderfully consistent player noted for his exceptional wet weather skills and a marking ability that enabled him to regularly outpoint much taller opponents in the air.

He was magnificent throughout 1958, so much so that he finished a narrow second to Thorold Merrett in the Copeland. Lou Richards said Turner 'shows more toe than a Roman sandal and can rise as high as Mum's sponge cake'.

But it was in the finals that Turner really stepped up. He was among the best players in the badly-beaten semi-final side, proved too good for the great Laurie Dwyer in the preliminary and then grabbed 21 kicks and 11 marks in the wet on grand final day to be widely acclaimed as best player on the ground.

Those performances cemented Turner's standing in the game, and stayed as a kind of signature throughout the rest of a career that didn't end until 1965.

---

long carnival break. But Murray Weideman inspired an extraordinary turnaround, taking two big marks and kicking two goals in the opening minutes of the final quarter. Suddenly the margin was just 12 points, and the game was well and truly alive. The two teams slugged it out ferociously for the rest of the term. Ken Smale burst through a pack to cut the difference to six points, but Hawthorn responded with a goal to O'Brien. Smale took a glorious mark but hacked his kick out of bounds, before the Hawks made a crucial error, when Brendan Edwards kicked across goal in defence and Ian Brewer intercepted and goaled. Again, though, the Hawks responded with a goal off the ground. The margin was still 12 points, and the Pies just couldn't find the extra goals they needed. Then, as time-on approached, Weideman grabbed his third for the term, Ron Reeves tied the scores with another and Brewer snapped a point to put the Pies in front for the first time in the match. After John Peck missed a couple of chances for Hawthorn to again hit back, Mick Twomey finally sealed a great win with a towering mark over a big pack, from which he kicked Collingwood's seventh goal of a brilliant final quarter.

As good as that win was, it seemed to take something out of the Magpies. Fitzroy thumped them by eight goals the following week, a result that allowed the Lions to leapfrog Collingwood into second spot, and Essendon compounded the misery by storming home for an 11-point win at Victoria Park the week after. With just three weeks to go before the finals, the Pies were in third place and wobbling. Comfortable, but far from decisive, victories over also-rans Carlton and Richmond followed, but Footscray's shock thrashing of Fitzroy ensured a dramatic final round of matches.

From Collingwood's perspective, the equation was simple: it needed to beat North Melbourne at Victoria Park to be sure of finishing in second spot, and getting the double chance. Well, almost sure. Fitzroy was level with the Pies but trailed on percentage, so technically a massive Roys victory over Hawthorn could have catapulted them into second place even if Collingwood won. But if Collingwood lost, then Fitzroy only needed to win to grab second place. North Melbourne had plenty of motivation of its own, knowing that a win at Vic Park would guarantee them fourth spot. And Hawthorn, Fitzroy's opponent, was also playing for a spot in the finals, but needed Collingwood to beat North and Richmond to beat Essendon.

So all eyes at Victoria Park, Glenferrie and Punt Road were only partly trained on the games going on before them – they were equally focused on the scores filtering through from other grounds. The Collingwood–North game, on which so much depended, was a beauty. Both teams played desperate, attacking football throughout, and the game was punctuated with a series of behind-the-play incidents. Bill Twomey, fighting his way back from a knee injury, was reported over one clash, while Neville Waller was injured in another. There was nothing between the sides all day: the Pies led by a goal at the first change, North by three points at half time and the Pies by three points at the last change. With the home crowd behind them, most expected Collingwood to charge home. Instead it was North, with a four-goal final quarter, that grabbed the points and left the Magpie fans stunned and disconsolate.

All attention was now focused on the other games. Essendon had hung on over Richmond, killing any chances Hawthorn had of sneaking into the finals. It all came down to Fitzroy and Hawthorn at Glenferrie. A Fitzroy win would see them take second and drop Collingwood to third, to face a cut-throat semi against North. A Hawthorn win would keep the Pies in second by virtue of their superior percentage. The Hawks had been just in front at three-quarter time but the Lions came hard in the final quarter, clawing their way to within four points when the final bell rang. But it wasn't enough, and the Lions remained in third spot.

So the Magpies limped into a second semi-final against the might of Melbourne. They lost Bill Twomey to suspension and Keith Burns to injury from the game against North, and in a risky move named four players under injury clouds – Gabelich, Kingston, Waller and Dorman. Skipper Frank Tuck looked like being able to play again, having missed the previous two weeks with a thigh strain, but he felt it twinge again with his last kick at training on the Thursday night, and left the ground in tears. The worst thing for the Pies, though, was that they went into the game in the middle of a terrible run of form, having lost three out of their previous five games. And it soon became obvious that was going to become four out of six, as the Demons dominated from the start.

Melbourne opened with a five-goal-to-one first quarter and never looked back. The Magpies were dreadful – the side was top-heavy, and most of the big blokes were too slow. In fact, lack of pace was a problem all over the ground, and the speedier Demons left their opponents in their wake. Collingwood players always looked under pressure on the

> **The Age**
>
> **Percy Beames on Collingwood's second semi-final team selection, game plan and approach:**
>
> Crude vigour, applied by slow-moving players on the big MCG against men who have pace, courage and a set intention to ignore everything but the ball can only lead to one result – defeat.

rare occasions when they got the ball, and as a result handpasses went astray, kicks were grubbed along the ground and marks were spilled. The forwards – described in *The Age* as 'lumbering' – could manage only four goals for the game, in near-perfect conditions. The Magpies had hoped that, by going for height and strength, they'd be able to out-muscle the highly skilled Demons. But even that plan failed miserably: several of Melbourne's early goals came from free kicks, or from openings created when Collingwood players were too busy trying to soften up their opponents rather than attacking the ball.

The game was largely a foregone conclusion after quarter time, and Melbourne cruised to a 45-point victory that was even more emphatic than it appeared on the scoreboard. The Woods played only negative football and were reduced to vain attempts to rough up the Demons, and the game remained spiteful throughout. But it was an ordinary spectacle, and convinced just about everyone that the 1958 premiership flag was as good as decided. Two weeks out, and regardless of whether they'd be playing North or Collingwood, the Demons were unbackable favourites.

Many at Victoria Park shared that view. They knew they'd been terrible in the semi-final, and that changes needed to be made for the preliminary. But few anticipated the scale of those changes. Ron Kingston and Brian Dorman were injured, Neville Waller dropped and Ken Smale relegated to the bench. Kevin Rose was brought in for his first full game at half-back, Brian Gray to the wing, Brian Beers to half-forward and giant Graeme Fellowes from the bench to first ruck. But in an era where players mostly played in the positions in which they were named, it was the positional changes to the team that grabbed the headlines. There were changes to every single line in the Collingwood team as the selectors turned the line-up inside out in a desperate bid to inject more pace. John Henderson, in just his fourth game, moved to

Magpie fans cheer on their heroes during the 1958 preliminary final.

the centre, Mike Delanty from the wing to centre half-back, Thorold Merrett to first rover and Mick Twomey from defence to a forward pocket.

The Magpies were up against a North Melbourne outfit that had won at Victoria Park just three weeks earlier in a testy, rugged match. There had been plenty of rough stuff and ill-feeling in that game, and the Kangaroos knew there would be more of it in the preliminary. They'd also seen how Collingwood had approached the second semi. So they came prepared, ready to engage the Pies in a no-holds-barred stoush from start to finish.

But they were caught off-guard. The recast Collingwood team focused only on the ball and ran the Kangaroos off their legs. By quarter time the Pies had piled on 5.5 to 1.1 and a shellshocked North didn't know which way to look. Collingwood dominated from the start, but kicked five straight behinds until Kenny Bennett snapped the first goal after 14 minutes. Fellowes, Brewer, Merrett and Weideman all added majors as the Magpies piled on five goals in 12 minutes, storming to a 22-point lead at the first break.

It was thrilling football. Collingwood remained strong in the air (23 marks to nine in the first quarter) but the team looked far quicker, more resolute and more assured than it had a week earlier. Still, as some journalists pointed out, they weren't playing Melbourne.

Top: The high-flying Mick Twomey adopts a safety-first approach by smashing the ball clear against North.
Above: Murray Weideman shakes hands with North's John Brady after the final siren.

259

PLAYER OF THE YEAR
Thorold Merrett

The brilliant, highly skilled Thorold Merrett was in the middle of a career purple patch in 1958.

The diminutive Merrett had made his name as a fleet-footed wingman who had one of the deadliest left feet in the game, his low, spearing stab passes being things of particular beauty. He was fast, courageous and made life easy for his forwards.

But from the mid-1950s he spent more time as a rover, backed up with spells in the forward line, and it was in this role that he won Copeland Trophies in both 1958 and 1959. He was almost unstoppable roaming around the packs, his clever reading of the game ensuring he got plenty of the ball and his skills meaning those opportunities were rarely wasted. When resting near goal he was equally dangerous, as shown by the fact that his 30 goals in 1958 made him the club's second highest goalkicker for the year.

Early in 1960, coming off his second successive Copeland, Merrett badly broke his leg. He was just 26 and never played again. Had he remained fit, who knows what he might have achieved out of a career that, even cut short, made him a Magpie legend.

North hit back strongly with the wind in the second term but frittered away chance after chance. Collingwood could manage only a solitary goal, while the Kangaroos blazed away to finish with a staggering 1.9 – though most of those behinds came from hurried snap shots under great pressure from a committed Magpie defence. The teams went to the dressing rooms at half-time with North trailing by 19 points, despite having one more scoring shot. Having wasted so many chances, North was made to pay when Collingwood produced a brilliant third quarter, kicking 5.3 to 2.1 to lead by 39 points at the final change. The margin would have been narrower if not for some magnificent Magpie defence late in the quarter, especially from Ray Gabelich, who took four spectacular goal-saving marks in quick succession. North couldn't bridge the gap, even with the wind at their backs, and as the game degenerated into a series of ugly clashes (several players were belted in behind-the-play incidents), the Pies held out for a comfortable 20-point victory.

This was by some distance the Magpies' best performance since the Queen's Birthday clash with Melbourne. Lou Richards described it as a 'new-look Collingwood team, playing in the old Collingwood style' and likened it to the legendary Machine. The team was faster and looked far more dangerous in attack. The changes at the selection table had all worked. Delanty looked a different player at centre half-back, Fellowes added height and agility to the ruck, Henderson provided great drive from the middle and inclusions Rose, Gray and Beers all did well. Big Gabbo was outstanding in defence, and he was well supported by fellow defenders Ron Reeves and Harry Sullivan. Former Carlton captain Ken Hands, writing in *The Sporting Globe*, summed it up when he said: 'Collingwood

looked so much better today than they did in losing to the Demons last week that it makes one wonder if they have improved so much, or just how good is the Melbourne side.'

And that, in a nutshell, was the widespread perception leading into the grand final. Collingwood had played much, much better against North but even with their newly-revamped side, nobody gave the Pies a realistic chance against the Demons on grand final day. Melbourne was a 5-2 favourite, and almost all the media tipsters plumped for them. *The Age* described the Magpies as 'the greatest outsiders in a finals game for many years'. Barrie Bretland, in *The Sun*, said Collingwood simply didn't have the class to beat Melbourne and it would take a miracle to even get close. 'Wrap up that pennant and deliver it to the MCG, marked Melbourne, 1958,' he wrote. Even Lou Richards described Melbourne as the 'hottest favourites since Phar Lap' and admitted they looked 'certainties' to win the flag.

The only thing Collingwood had in its favour was the knowledge that there's no such thing as a certainty in football. That, and the emotional pull of protecting the club's four-in-a-row premiership record, and the hope that the players would be inspired to produce something extraordinary. But even the most optimistic fan knew that was only hope, not expectation.

Other than the issue of Collingwood's 1927–30 record, and the question of how much Melbourne would win by, the biggest talking points of the week surrounded three of Collingwood's most senior players. Would captain Frank Tuck get over his torn thigh muscle? Would Mick Twomey, who'd been forced off in the preliminary final with a groin injury, recover in time? And would Bill Twomey, now available again after suspension, force his way back in despite still battling the knee problems that had dogged him since Round 6?

The answers wound up being no, yes and no. Mick Twomey was a gamble, but one the selectors were prepared to take. Brother Bill, on the other hand, was one gamble too many, and the selectors opted to leave him out of the final side, bringing about a sad end to a wonderful career. Tuck's story was the real heartbreaker, though. He got through an exhaustive session on the Thursday night and was a relieved man as he chatted to coach Phonse Kyne in the middle of the ground afterwards. As he was about to head to the showers, Kyne called on him to do one more set of sprints up and down the ground. Halfway down the return leg, Tuck felt his muscle tear again – and with it went his hopes of leading the team out on the Saturday. It was a doubly cruel blow for Tuck, who had also missed out on the 1953 flag through suspension.

Frank Tuck (top), Bill Twomey (middle) and Mick Twomey (bottom) provided selection dramas in the lead-up to the grand final.

The Mightiest Magpies

The end result was no change to the Collingwood team that had so emphatically disposed of North. It was a line-up that certainly lacked Melbourne's class, but it did have something that almost nobody noticed at the time – youth. There were five teenagers in the starting 18 (Reeves, Rose, Henderson, Bennett and Beers), plus a couple of others (Harrison and Fellowes) who were just starting out in their careers. The Demons had nobody under twenty. And while that gave Melbourne a tried, trusted and experienced look, it also meant that more than a third of Collingwood's team had not been involved in too many of the defeats that had made the Demons seem almost unbeatable. Norm Smith's men held fewer fears for some of those young guys than they did for their older teammates.

There was drama on the morning of the game when *The Sun* newspaper published 'pen pictures' of the players from both sides, complete with their

The spread in *The Sun* newspaper that caused all the problems. The publishing of players' numbers prompted the VFL to force both teams to change their guernsey numbers for the biggest game of the year.

Above: **Acting captain Murray Weideman, Thorold Merrett and Mick Twomey wait to meet the governor and his party before the first bounce.**
Below: **Weideman leads his team onto the field.**

guernsey numbers. This was in direct contravention of VFL rules that stipulated only the *Football Record* was allowed to run players' guernsey numbers. Various media outlets had tested the League's patience previously, and officials were so incensed by *The Sun*'s grand final breach that they forced all players to change their jumper numbers for the day. *The Football Record* carried two player lists, one bearing the players' usual numbers and a second one with the alternatives, and mass confusion reigned in the crowd. Only Ray Gabelich got to wear his usual number, because property stewards couldn't find another jumper big enough to fit him.

The day didn't get off to the most promising start for Collingwood when the club's reserves side went down in the grand final by four points, despite a late comeback. But there was better news on the weather front, with some Magpie fans hoping the cold, wet conditions might nullify some of the Demons' advantages in pace and skill, and turn the game into an ugly scrap.

Those hopes seemed forlorn just 30 minutes later, when the teams returned to their quarter-time huddles with Melbourne already 17 points up after a five-goal opening term. The Collingwood players had emerged, led by acting captain Murray Weideman, backed by the majority of the crowd and fired up by an emotional and uplifting pre-match speech from their coach. Phonse Kyne asked his players to 'bleed for the club'. He said the players of the past, especially those who had created the 1927-30 record, would be with them in spirit, and 'feeling every bump, every mark, every kick'. He pleaded with them to do everything in their power to stop Melbourne from equalling that record, to go harder than any Collingwood players had ever gone before, no

Above: Graeme Fellowes wins a tap-out during the grand final. Kenny Bennett is in the foreground, John Henderson to the left and Ron Barassi is in the unfamiliar number 2 guernsey on the far right.
Opposite: Temperatures ran hot and there were plenty of skirmishes throughout the game.
Below: Phonse Kyne

matter how tired or sore they became. The club's history was at stake, and the 20 players in the rooms were the only ones who could protect it.

Experienced players like Thorold Merrett and Murray Weideman would later recall Kyne's speech as the most inspirational they had ever heard. The atmosphere inside the rooms afterwards was electric, and the players felt like nothing could stop them. Kyne's speech has passed into Collingwood folklore, but what is often forgotten is that it had virtually no impact on the game itself, at least initially. The first quarter was rough and rugged, but it was the Demons who jumped out of the blocks with the first three goals. Collingwood finally got on the scoreboard with goals to Beers and Merrett, but Melbourne added two late ones to end the quarter well in front.

At this stage it looked like a repeat of the second semi-final. Collingwood's 'new look' team was playing the same way the superseded model had two weeks earlier. They were too focused on negating Melbourne's stars and not enough on their own game. Melbourne just looked like they had for the past few years – too damned good.

As the players returned to their positions after the break, Weideman, the acting captain, and Barry 'Hooker' Harrison decided to ramp things up a notch. Upon the restart, Weed almost immediately crashed into several Demons, and Harrison flattened Melbourne's most important player, Ron Barassi. Harrison had tagged Barassi with limited success in the second semi, but today took his harassment to new levels. As Barassi struggled to regain his senses, his enraged teammates started looking for ways to even up with their opponents. And this is when the game turned.

Rather than continue with the rough stuff, the Magpies began to use their newly-acquired pace and system to advantage. Having sucked Melbourne in, they focused more on the ball while their Demon opponents ran around trying to deck Magpie players left, right and centre. Dick Fenton-Smith gave away a free to Thorold Merrett and crashed the ball onto his head in disgust. Laurie Mithen ran 20 yards to flatten John Henderson after he'd marked, then a few minutes later swung a wild left hook at another Magpie, sparking a melee that involved trainers as well as players. 'Ugly scenes developed as players hurled themselves into packs, throwing punches wildly,' reported *The Sporting Globe*.

There were skirmishes everywhere, but in the midst of it all, Kenny Bennett, the youngest and smallest player on the field, twice tore through packs for two goals. Then another foolish attempt at physical pressure saw Mick Twomey goal from a free kick. Nineteen minutes into the quarter and the Magpies – incredibly – were in front. Two more goals to each team saw the Pies go into the main break two points to the good.

The Collingwood players weren't used to being in front of Melbourne at half-time of any game, let alone a grand final, and most of them drew great confidence from the fact. Phonse Kyne seemed more stunned than anyone, and circulated among the players, unsure of how they'd come to be in front but urging them to continue what they'd done in the second quarter. In the Melbourne rooms, Norm Smith was imploring his own players to stay away from the fights and return their attention to the ball. Everybody at the game knew that Melbourne's best football was still way better than Collingwood's.

Any resolve Smith had instilled in his players evaporated within minutes of the restart. Demon Ian Thorogood was flattened, and so was Peter Lucas. Weideman and Mithen clashed again, then Weideman and Barassi went toe-to-toe. Weideman ran through a couple of packs of Demon players and the game returned to the way it had been in the second quarter, with wild scrimmages all

PLAYER OF THE YEAR
Ian Brewer

Ian Brewer might be just about the lowest profile player ever to have topped the League goalkicking table. But he was outstanding when it mattered, enjoying his best-ever season in Collingwood's premiership year of 1958.

His tally of 73 goals seems modest, but this was an era of defensive football, muddy, heavy grounds and highly physical defenders who had a nasty habit of clobbering those players they couldn't otherwise stop.

Brewer was highly talented, a master at using his body cleverly and a lovely kick for goal. He was difficult to match up on, because he was too agile for big defenders but too strong in the air for more mobile opponents.

In 1958 he grabbed four six-goal bags, and one eight-goal haul against Hawthorn which almost single-handedly won the game for his side. He also kicked four in the preliminary against North and two in the grand final to cap a consistent, productive season.

Brewer's career was over just three years later, and he never again quite reached the heights he scaled in 1958. But he did more than enough in 1958 alone to make him a Magpie favourite for life.

over the ground. 'Players went down like nine-pins,' according to *The Sporting Globe*. Barassi and Harrison were reported. Then Bill Serong decked Ian Ridley with a magnificent bump that broke his nose and jaw. It was like the infamous 'Bloodbath' grand final of 1945 all over again.

Much of the rough stuff was coming from Melbourne players, clearly unhappy and frustrated at being behind. 'It was a pity to see the Demons attitude to the game,' wrote *The Sporting Globe*. The play was fierce, and some Melbourne players seemed to become hesitant about putting their head over the ball in the packs. Collingwood players, on the other hand, while more than willing to take part in the physical exchanges, seemed more capable of playing footy in between the fights. And in the third quarter they capitalised on Melbourne's ill-discipline, their magnificent defence keeping Melbourne goalless for the term while the Magpie forwards piled on five goals.

Young John Henderson showed he'd recovered from Mithen's fierce bump as he smartly gathered and guided through the first of the second half, then Brewer marked and goaled to extend the lead to 14 points. Weideman and Fellowes both goaled after towering

marks, and when Brian Beers added another late in the term, Collingwood went into the last huddle for the year with a stunning 33-point lead.

It looked like a match-winning advantage. But such was the regard for Melbourne that no Magpie fan, let alone the players, thought the game was completely safe. So the team spent the last quarter focused almost entirely on defence, forcing ball-ups, kicking to the boundary at every opportunity, wasting time wherever they could. Reeves, Sullivan and Gabelich fought superbly in defence and closed down every Demon surge. Melbourne grabbed a couple of goals, while Collingwood could manage only a single behind, but it didn't matter. The siren sounded with those mighty, magnificent Magpies 18 points in front – and the four-in-a-row record safe.

Phonse Kyne and the rest of the officials on the bench leapt high into the air in jubilation. Players were carried from the field on the shoulders of teammates and support staff, and there was complete chaos in and around the rooms, as thousands of fans crammed the walkways underneath the MCG. Norm Smith battled his way through the throng to tell the Collingwood players how much he admired (and hated!) them. The fans stayed around and cheered wildly when the Magpies left for their celebration dinner, their back-slapping making it almost impossible for the players to get through. About 1000 attended the

Above: Phonse Kyne and the rest of his bench, including Peter Lucas (far left), former captain Gordon Hocking (two to the left of Kyne), and president Syd Coventry (next to Kyne) celebrate the historic victory.
Opposite: Thorold Merrett and Murray Weideman are carried off by their teammates as the celebrations start.
Below: Harry Sullivan

Left: **Coach and captain can't contain their happiness in the rooms after the game.**
Right: **Kyne and his players start toasting the victory.**

dinner that night in the Royale Ballroom at the Exhibition Buildings, where Kyne and his wife led the dancing with a foxtrot to 'Alexander's Rag Time Band'. 'I still can't realise we've won it,' he told the happy crowd. 'I thank the players, not only the 20 who played today, but also the Seconds, and men like Frank Tuck and Bill Twomey, who helped us to get to the finals.' Another 750 crammed into the clubrooms on Sunday morning and there was a further dinner on Monday night. On Tuesday, players and officials left by train for a two-week holiday in West Australia, and the celebrations resumed almost as soon as they returned, with half a dozen more functions, including a massive dinner at the Collingwood Town Hall.

Those celebrations honoured an extraordinary team performance. Much of the focus through the years has centred on what is euphemistically described as Collingwood's 'vigorous' play, and especially the roles played by Murray Weideman and Hooker Harrison in sucking in the Melbourne players. But the first ignores the fact that it was Melbourne, not the Magpies, doing most of the sniping. Collingwood players certainly bowled over plenty of opponents, but mostly through brutally hard bumps. It was the Demons who went headhunting afterwards. And it was also the Demons who, when things got really hot in the packs, found a few of their players less than willing to commit their bodies or take the physical risks needed to get the ball. Collingwood had no such problems.

The focus on Weideman and Harrison was almost inevitable, the former because of his larger-than-life personality (and involvement in so many stoushes on the day), the latter because of his role in shutting down another of the game's larger-than-life figures in Ron Barassi. But that focus ignores the contribution made by the rest of the team. Ken Turner and Thorold Merrett were magnificent in the wet, as was the diminutive Kenny Bennett. Graeme Fellowes and Ray Gabelich were outstanding in the ruck, and Gabbo, Harry Sullivan, Mike Delanty and Ron Reeves impassable in defence. Bill Serong added muscle to speed. Young players like Beers, Henderson and Rose, as well as Reeves and Bennett, all stood up when needed. Every single player did his bit to ensure that Collingwood held onto its most cherished record.

It was a staggering result, and still remains the greatest grand final upset in VFL/AFL history. Critics were unstinting in their praise. 'Their victory must go down not only as one of the most important in the illustrious history of their great club, but also as one of the best on record,' wrote former Melbourne player Percy Beames, in *The Age*. Alf Brown in *The Herald* described Collingwood's performance as 'courageous and amazing', and said they had

The Age

Percy Beames on Collingwood's success:

The deciding weapon in [Collingwood's] win was something Melbourne simply could not match on the day – the fierce desire of Collingwood's players to win Saturday's honour for their club. Those Collingwood players had something more than courage and determination behind them. They were defending the League record of four successive premierships... and they played throughout the grand final as though their very lives depended on keeping that record. Regardless of danger, they hurled themselves recklessly into packs, fiercely blocked or met any Melbourne player attempting to break away, shepherded, backed up, lifted each other with encouragement and did everything with only the thoughts of teamwork and Collingwood in mind.

The impossible dream. The players with the spoils of victory in the clubrooms at Victoria Park.

won 'because they were tougher, stronger and more fearless, and were prepared to keep going no matter what the cost'. St Kilda coach Alan Killigrew said the premiership was 'a triumph of courage and spirit – the will to win'. 'There was inspiration for everyone in the 1958 grand final. I know I will remember it when I have forgotten all the others,' he wrote in *The Truth*. 'Collingwood's win was a great thing for football.'

The club's annual report was equally effusive. 'This victory was the most remarkable and memorable premiership ever won by your club, and never has the success of the team been more popularly received. By their success the players have added greatness to their deeds and must be ranked in the same category as those great players of 1927–30 era whose records they so ably defended.'

But perhaps the final word should be left to the great Syd Coventry, the man who piloted the team to those four successive flags, and who was president of the club in 1958. 'This was the greatest performance in the history of the Collingwood Football Club,' he said.

MURRAY WEIDEMAN — GRAND FINAL HERO

Over the years, Murray Weideman's teammates have probably grown sick and tired of hearing the stories about how **Weed** and **Barry Harrison** won the '58 flag for **Collingwood** on their own.

While those stories unfairly underplay the roles of the other **18** blokes in black-and-white jumpers, there's no denying the influence Weideman, in particular, had on the game.

Collingwood's acting captain that day, Weideman truly led from the front, taking the game up to Melbourne when all seemed lost, throwing his weight around when needed and always – always – putting his body on the line when it counted, whether in protecting teammates or getting the ball himself.

The club's annual report for the year left no doubt how his role was viewed within the rooms at Victoria Park. 'In the vital grand final match Murray . . . was easily our most effective player, and his strong play and leadership contributed much to the premiership success.'

Weed went on to become an outstanding and inspirational full-time captain just a year later, and he always showed the same sort of leadership that guided the Magpies to a premiership that rainy day back in 1958.

PLAYERS

#	Player	Games	Goals
35	Keith Beckwith	1	1
20&7	Brian Beers	10	12
33&11	Ken Bennett	12	12
6&5	Ian Brewer	21	73
19	Keith Burns	1	2
2&24	Mike Delanty	19	1
30	Don Dixon	13	4
23	Barry Donegan	5	1
8	Brian Dorman	16	5
28&8	Graeme Fellowes	4	4
13	Ray Gabelich	19	3
4&22	Brian Gray	10	7
7&12	Bob Greve	19	6
32&3	Barry Harrison	20	7
21&4	John Henderson	6	1
14	Don Howell	9	2
12	Errol Hutchesson	3	2
37	Bill Jones	8	11
9	Ron Kingston	17	1
3&2	Peter Lucas	18	0
17&16	Thorold Merrett	21	30
21	Eddie Millar	2	0
12	John Powell	2	0
16&17	Ron Reeves	13	1
48&15	Kevin Rose	5	0
22&14	Bill Serong	12	4
29	Lerrel Sharp	8	0
5&6	Ken Smale	15	5
26&20	Harry Sullivan	20	0
24	Frank Tuck	14	13
11&9	Ken Turner	20	2
1	Bill Twomey	8	6
25&23	Mick Twomey	11	2
31	Neville Waller	18	2
27&1	Murray Weideman	20	24

Club Awards
Copeland Trophy – Thorold Merrett
RT Rush Trophy – Ken Turner
J J Joyce Trophy – Harry Sullivan
Best player in finals – Ken Turner
Reserves best & fairest – Kevin Rose
Thirds best & fairest – F Smith
Leading goalkicker – Ian Brewer (73)

1958 SEASON

ROUND 1 April 12 Whitten Oval

Footscray **4.5.29** v **Collingwood** **12.11.83**

Goals: Brewer 3, Bennett 2, Merrett 2, W Twomey 2, Weideman 2, Hutchesson

ROUND 2 April 19 Victoria Park

Collingwood **11.9.75** v Hawthorn **10.8.68**

Goals: Brewer 8, Gabelich, Howell, Smale

ROUND 3 April 26 Victoria Park

Collingwood **7.15.57** v Fitzroy **7.10.52**

Goals: Bennett 2, Brewer 2, Donegan, Harrison, Hutchesson

ROUND 4 May 3 Windy Hill

Essendon **13.9.87** v Collingwood **9.15.69**

Goals: Brewer 2, Greve 2, Weideman 2, Beers, Bennett, Harrison

ROUND 5 May 10 Victoria Park

Collingwood **16.10.106** v Carlton **3.15.33**

Goals: Brewer 6, Beers 3, Tuck 2, W Twomey 2, Weideman 2, Greve

ROUND 6 May 17 Punt Rd Oval

Richmond **8.8.56** v **Collingwood** **13.17.95**

Goals: Beers 3, Brewer 2, Harrison 2, Tuck 2, Bennett, Greve, Merrett, Weideman

ROUND 7 May 24 Arden St Oval

North Melbourne **9.8.62** v Collingwood **7.17.59**

Goals: Bennett 2, Merrett 2, Brewer, Howell, Weideman

ROUND 8 May 31 Victoria Park

Collingwood **20.20.140** v South Melbourne **9.12.66**

Goals: Brewer 4, Dixon 3, Merrett 3, Serong 2, Delanty, Gray, Harrison, Jones, Tuck, Turner, Waller, Weideman

ROUND 9 June 7 Victoria Park

Collingwood **12.23.95** v St Kilda **5.9.39**

Goals: Brewer 4, Merrett 2, Tuck 2, Gabelich, Gray, Jones, Kingston

ROUND 10 June 16 MCG

Melbourne **12.12.84** v Collingwood **10.13.73**

Goals: Brewer 6, Dorman, Merrett, Tuck, Weideman

ROUND 11 June 21 Kardinia Park

Geelong **9.12.66** v **Collingwood** **14.15.99**

Goals: Jones 4, Tuck 3, Beers, Brewer, Greve, Harrison, Merrett, Waller, Weideman

ROUND 12 June 28 Victoria Park

Collingwood **12.13.85** v Footscray **10.14.74**

Goals: Brewer 6, Jones 2, Greve, Merrett, Tuck, Weideman

ROUND 13 July 19 Glenferrie Oval

Hawthorn **12.14.86** v **Collingwood** **14.9.93**

Goals: Weideman 4, Brewer 3, Beers 2, Harrison, Reeves, Smale, Tuck, M Twomey

ROUND 14 July 26 Brunswick St Oval

Fitzroy **15.15.105** v Collingwood **8.9.57**

Goals: Brewer 3, Merrett 2, Dixon, Dorman, Weideman

ROUND 15 August 2 Victoria Park

Collingwood **11.9.75** v **Essendon** **12.14.86**

Goals: Brewer 3, Gray 3, Merrett 3, Jones 2

ROUND 16 August 9 Princes Park

Carlton **7.11.53** v **Collingwood** **10.12.72**

Goals: Brewer 3, Merrett 2, W Twomey 2, Jones, Smale, Weideman

ROUND 17 August 16 Victoria Park

Collingwood **16.11.107** v Richmond **13.10.88**

Goals: Brewer 6, Dorman 2, Gray 2, Merrett 2, Bennett, Henderson, Smale, Weideman

ROUND 18 August 23 Victoria Park

Collingwood **12.16.88** v **North Melbourne** **14.17.101**

Goals: Brewer 4, Burns 2, Fellowes 2, Merrett 2, Beckwith, Dorman

1958 FINALS

LADDER

Team	W	L	D	For	Agst	%	Pts
Melbourne	15	3	0	1608	1300	123.7	60
Collingwood	12	6	0	1528	1235	123.7	48
Fitzroy	12	6	0	1551	1283	120.9	48
North Melb	11	7	0	1228	1324	92.7	44
Essendon	10	8	0	1519	1365	111.3	40
Hawthorn	9	9	0	1419	1298	109.3	36
Carlton	8	10	0	1158	1260	91.9	32
St Kilda	7	11	0	1340	1454	92.2	28
South Melb	7	11	0	1450	1634	88.7	28
Richmond	7	11	0	1425	1611	88.5	28
Footscray	6	12	0	1401	1440	97.3	24
Geelong	4	14	0	1192	1615	73.8	16

SEMI FINAL September 6 — MCG
Collingwood **4.9.33** v **Melbourne 11.12.78**
Goals: Merrett 2, Gabelich, Weideman

PRELIMINARY FINAL September 13 — MCG
Collingwood 14.12.96 v North Melbourne **10.16.76**
Goals: Brewer 4, Merrett 2, Serong 2, Weideman 2, Bennett, Fellowes, Smale, Turner

GRAND FINAL September 20 — MCG

Collingwood	2.2	7.6	12.9	12.10	(82)
Melbourne	5.1	7.4	7.6	9.10	(64)

Goals: Weideman 2, Brewer 2, Beers 2, Bennett 2, Merrett 2, M. Twomey, Fellowes
Best: Merrett, Turner, Bennett, Fellowes, Serong, Gabelich, Weideman, Harrison, Sullivan
Umpire: Nash
Attendance: 97,956 at the MCG

Grand Final Team
B: R. Reeves, H. Sullivan, R. Gabelich
HB: K. Rose, M. Delanty, P. Lucas
C: B. Gray, J. Henderson, K. Turner
HF: B. Beers, M. Weideman (c), W. Serong
F: M. Twomey, I. Brewer, K. Bennett
R: G. Fellowes, B. Harrison, T. Merrett
Reserves: K. Smale, R. Greve

CHAPTER FIFTEEN

1990

Breaking the drought

'As far as these guys are concerned, they will be written up at Collingwood in letters of gold. They are going to be gods.'

The past can sometimes get in the way of the present. In some cases it can even have a negative impact on the future.

That's the conclusion Leigh Matthews came to within weeks of inheriting the role of Collingwood coach early in the 1986 season. The Hawthorn champion had been pegged as Bob Rose's assistant and the handover was meant to take 12 months. But Rose fast-tracked it after a hat-trick of defeats, waking Matthews up with a phone call on the Sunday morning after losing to North Melbourne in Round 3. Matthews would recall: 'I was curled up in bed when the telephone rang at 7.45 a.m. It was Bob Rose. He said, "Are you going to be at training this morning?" Then he dropped the bombshell: "I've been thinking about things and I've decided to resign."'

With a series of near misses and hard-luck stories and no premiership since 1958, the spectre of the 'Colliwobbles' hung over everyone connected to the black and white – players, coaches, administrators, members and fans. Two incidents shortly after he took over pinpointed to Matthews that the anchor of the past had weighed Collingwood down for too long.

The first came when a social basketball team comprised of Collingwood players lost a game after leading for most of it, and one of them – almost subconsciously – raised the 'Colliwobbles' tag as a defence. It mattered little that this team later won the title. The second came at an even more unlikely venue, Sandown Racecourse. Matthews was there to see a horse in which he had a share run a close placing, beaten only a head by the winner. From nowhere, across an almost deserted track, a voice cried out: 'Bad luck about running second. But you're at Collingwood now, you'll get used to that.' It was the voice of former Melbourne player Noel McMahen, who had captained the Demons to flags over the Magpies in 1955 and 1956.

As different as the moments were, Matthews knew the first battle he had to win at Collingwood had as much to do with perception as performance. He concluded: 'I quickly realised that the place was haunted by the club's grand final record of the past two decades.' An exorcism of sorts was required.

It's not surprising that Collingwood was spooked by what had occurred since

Bob Rose comforts Max Richardson (18), while Con Britt (27) offers a consoling pat to his coach after the 1970 Grand Final loss.

it had wrenched that famous thirteenth VFL premiership out of Melbourne's grasp on a wet, muddy afternoon in 1958. Nine grand finals since, and all they had yielded were eight losses, a draw that simply delayed the agony of defeat for another week, and untold heartache for supporters who wondered whether they would ever get to see a black and white premiership.

The manner of each grand final defeats was different; the pain no less in any of them.

In 1960 Collingwood kicked only two goals – the lowest grand final score in 33 years. Four years later, giant Ray Gabelich stampeded into an open goal appearing to break the shackles, only for Demon back pocket Neil Crompton to follow his opponent up the field and kick the most unlikely of goals to sink the Magpies by four points. It was Rose's first year – and in his first stint – as Collingwood coach. Yet if anything, 1966 was worse. A close encounter of the grand final kind all afternoon, the deadlock was broken when a wobbly

PLAYER OF THE YEAR — Peter Daicos

Of all of Peter Daicos's many and varied achievements over his glittering career, what he achieved in 1990 – with the team and also individually – might well be considered his crowning glory.

To return to the forward line, where it all started for him, and to kick 97 goals in Collingwood's premiership season was a phenomenal effort. It was a remarkable performance for a small forward, playing mainly out of the forward pocket or at half forward, to kick so many goals – emulating his coach, Leigh Matthews, who kicked 91 with Hawthorn in 1977.

Daicos kicked a goal in every one of his 25 games in 1990. His biggest haul was seven against Carlton in Round 2, all of them coming in the second half when he was shifted from defence to attack. There were also five hauls of six goals.

Those goals came from all angles and from all distances – some dribbled precisely from the boundary, others nailed superbly on the run, some kicked around corners. There were even a few trademark long bomb torpedo punts. To watch Daicos's highlight reel from 1990 is to watch one of the best seasons, and some of the best football, a small forward has ever played.

---

punt from St Kilda teenager Barry Breen proved to be the only thing that separated the two exhausted teams. Surely, it couldn't get any worse than that.

At half-time in the 1970 Grand Final, past nightmares were seemingly banished. Collingwood led by 44 points and champagne bottles were uncorked. But somehow, in a defining game for modern football, and a defining match for almost a generation of Magpie people, Carlton and Ron Barassi conjured a miracle to come back and win by 10 points. Seven years later, in the first grand final shown live on television, the club led by 27 points at the last change before North Melbourne staged a revival. Only a late mark and spiral torpedo goal to Magpie forward Ross 'Twiggy' Dunne drew level the scores. Eerily, Collingwood lost the grand final replay by the same margin they had led by at three-quarter time the week before.

There was a sense of injustice about 1979's five-point loss to Carlton. The Blues' last goal had come from Ken Sheldon after he had gathered a tap from Wayne Harmes that many believed had come from over the boundary line. Debate still rages over whether Harmes was in or out. There was no such fine line a year later when Richmond created what was then a record grand final thrashing of 81 points. A third successive grand final defeat followed in 1981, when Collingwood went down to Carlton again.

With all that had taken place and the collateral damage to the club and its psyche, it's not hard to see why Matthews wanted to focus on the future and forget about the past. What happened at Victoria Park pre-Matthews would always be a part of the fabric of Collingwood, but the coach couldn't care less about it. It wasn't going to help win the next flag. He set about trying to change perceptions about Collingwood, and within Collingwood. He put together a bunch of young players unaffected by what had happened in the past, trying to make them compatible with the stars of the present. All he cared about was forming a team capable of burying the Colliwobbles tag once and for all.

Matthews' coaching career started with a win over Geelong at Victoria Park, against the backdrop of a financial crisis that resulted in a 20 per cent pay cut to the players, the sacking of general manager, Peter Bahen, and the resignation of president, Ranald Macdonald. It was the first of 12 wins for the 1986 season, with only percentage separating Collingwood from a finals berth. It came with the bonus of an Under-19s premiership that promised so much for the future.

Then the bottom fell out in 1987, as the coach shuffled the decks, seeking players that suited his purpose and casting off others that didn't. Seven wins saw the Pies finish twelfth, third from the bottom with the lowest percentage in the competition. There were revivals in 1988 (when the club finished the home-and-away season in second spot) and 1989 but the Magpies failed to win any of their three finals from those years. Some forecast that Matthews had done his best with the list because the team lacked leg speed, a potent forward line and the capacity to perform at the highest level. Those things would change in 1990, the first year of the newly named Australian Football League.

That was hardly obvious in the pre-season months that followed Collingwood's almost predictable fadeout to Melbourne in the 1989 elimination final. Two recruits commanded a bit of attention, both of them rovers from South Australia, recruited to inject some pace into what was perceived as a sluggish midfield. One of them was the highly-rated Tony Francis, from Norwood; the other, less feted, was Scott Russell, who hailed from Sturt.

The club culled David Cloke on the eve of the season, as well as pint-sized Matthew Ryan and forward David Robertson. Each fired a few parting shots at the coach, particularly about his less than communicative manner. Robertson famously dubbed Collingwood as 'Hollywood', implying that whatever glittered wasn't always gold, while Cloke could barely believe he had been given his

The Herald

Geoff Poulter on Collingwood's make-or-break year:

Collingwood meets its moment of truth this season. There are no longer any excuses for the Magpies if they don't make a proper fist of it this year. They have the personnel to make the final five again but they have now reached the stage where that achievement is no longer satisfactory. The time has arrived where they must go on from there.

---

marching orders after serving the club well. Don Scott, Matthews' former Hawthorn teammate, took aim in *The Herald* when he mused: 'Perhaps there is a lack of communication between the coach and his players. Perhaps Matthews is capable of getting his message across to some players, but not all.' Scott finished by saying it could be a 'bleak year'.

It looked as if Scott may have had some ammunition when an injury-hit Collingwood fell to old rivals Carlton in the pre-season Foster's Cup. Losing Russell to a broken cheekbone, Michael Christian (who had been training to play forward) to a knee injury and Paul Hawke to a hamstring, the Magpies were never in the hunt. *The Sun* predicted that: 'The Colliwobbles came to VFL Park six months ahead of schedule.' A practice match loss to Footscray at least welcomed back Craig Starcevich, James Manson and Denis Banks, who had had injury-interrupted pre-season. Another defeat followed, to Richmond at Burnie's West Park, with Tigers coach Kevin Bartlett boldly stating that 'we are building for things to happen in the '90s'. The losses had bookmakers turning out the Magpies at 16-1 for the premiership, with Philip Nott, saying 'they appear to be the most vulnerable of the final five sides from last year ... they seem to have the same problems, a lack of a forward and good rovers'.

Matthews had been experimenting in seeking more goals, with classy wingman Gavin Brown spending plenty of the pre-season deep in attack, while Peter Daicos was also slated as a small forward capable of causing headaches.

Leigh Matthews studies the match-ups in the huddle as captain Tony Shaw looks on.

On the roving front, Francis was making an early impression, with captain Tony Shaw declaring him a 'certainty' to make a difference. He did that, for sure – but not, initially, in the way Collingwood selectors had hoped.

Francis's 21st birthday was meant to be a memorable occasion, falling on the day that he would play his debut AFL game, against West Coast at Subiaco in Round 1. But Collingwood was never in the hunt, trailing all afternoon and going down by 46 points. There would be no post-match celebrations. To make matters worse, Francis was reported by three umpires for kicking Murray Rance as the pair went over the boundary line, sparking a five-minute brawl that involved up to 30 players. Francis's explanation at the tribunal hearing was that the sprigs of Rance's boots had brushed his groin. He added: 'As a result, I lashed out with my left leg. At no stage did I make contact. All I wanted to do was to tell Murray that if he was going to kick me in the groin, I can do it, too.'

It didn't help. Collingwood's biggest recruit was suspended for six matches, and the season that Matthews hoped would bring all his plans together was off to a terrible start.

Francis finally got his 21st birthday party at the famous Grace Darling Hotel, a few hours after Collingwood had overcome Carlton in Round 2, a good win that would have an impact on the direction of the season ahead. When the Magpies trailed the Blues in the second term, Matthews reached into his bag of tricks to try and light a spark. He dragged Brian Taylor, who had kicked a century of goals four years earlier, and replaced him with James Manson who ended up with four goals. Taylor was furious, and was banished to the reserves for the time being.

But another move had bigger consequences – Matthews shifted Daicos from half-back into attack. The impact was instantaneous. Collingwood went on to win the game by the same margin as Daicos's number (35 points), and the man himself finished with seven second-half goals. He earned himself three Brownlow Medal votes and Matthews had a template for what his forward line might look like for the rest of 1990.

The win over Carlton was the first of four straight victories. The closest came in the Round 5 clash with St Kilda – the first meeting of these two clubs at the MCG since the 1972 first semi-final, yet another finals loss for Collingwood. It was an old-fashioned arm-wrestle resolved by a piece of Daicos magic late in the game. With the contest in the balance, Daicos's opponent, Kane Taylor, infringed on the Collingwood forward which resulted in a contentious free kick downfield. And Daicos's kick to an unattended Alan Richardson in the goal square at the 27-minute mark of the last term put the Magpies in front.

At the club's Bad Taste Ball: from left, Mick Gayfer, Craig Kelly and Darren Millane.

'We had a go at each other,' Daicos confessed afterwards. 'Sometimes they [the umpires] pay it, and sometimes they don't.'

Best afield was Graham Wright, who had a classic duel with another young tyro in Saint Robert Harvey. Wright had gone the opposite direction to Brown in 1990, and both moves were paying dividends. While Brown had transformed from a state wingman the previous year to a forward, Matthews had changed Wright's role from an opportunistic forward to playing a critical role on the opposite wing to Darren Millane.

Two reality checks came after that narrow win over St Kilda, against Essendon and Hawthorn, teams that had won all but one of the previous seven premierships. Collingwood could manage only 10 goals against Essendon, going down by 26 points, and just 13 a week later in a two-point loss against Hawthorn.

Mick Gayfer blamed himself for the loss to Hawthorn. The reliable defender had a rare brain fade when kicking across goal 10 minutes into the last term. Jason Dunstall intercepted, kicked a goal and sparked a Hawks revival. 'The option was there,' Gayfer insisted. 'But I just didn't kick it hard enough into the wind, and Dunstall really came from nowhere. It cuts pretty deep.'

Graham Wright was best on ground against the Saints in Round 5.

After kicking 23 goals in those two losses, Collingwood booted 43 in its next two games, with big wins over Fitzroy and North Melbourne. Thirteen of those came from Daicos – six against Fitzroy in what was a close contest before '30 minutes of astonishingly lucid forward play' in the last term buried the Lions, and seven against the Kangaroos. Brown also kicked seven in the North game. Two of Daicos's goals that day were audacious banana shots, prompting Matthews to describe them as 'unbelievable ... I wasn't quite sure what I saw. I'm still not quite sure'.' Not a bad effort from a bloke who had spent the previous day in bed, sick with the flu.

In the week leading up to the Round 10 clash with Melbourne, Collingwood lost one of its former players and long-time

Controversial full-forward Brian Taylor controls the ball against Fitzroy.

AFL administrator, Jack Hamilton, who died in a car accident. The message from one of Hamilton's daughters to president Allan McAlister was simple on the day of the game: 'Make sure you win it for Dad.' Both sides wore black armbands and lined up for a minute's silence before the game. Despite the fact that the Demons kicked the first two goals, there was never any danger of an upset. The Magpies kicked five goals to nil in the second term to take a stranglehold on the match. By game's end, the margin had bloated out to 52 points, making the aggregate wins over three weeks 177 points. Daicos did most of the damage with six goals, fending off four opponents. Mick McGuane had 37 touches. Shane Morwood had a career-high 32. And Tony Francis's second AFL game was far less controversial than his first, with a solid display at half-forward.

Collingwood's strong first half of the 1990 season brought with it expectation. Put Collingwood and expectation together, and those outside the club were starting to talk premierships, and perhaps an end to the 32-year premiership drought. Internally, however, it was a different story. Players were coaxed

Above: **Mick Gayfer is tackled in Round 12 against Geelong.**
Below: **Peter Daicos creates another miracle goal out of nothing.**

not to talk about finals or flags when asked by journalists. After the Magpies had beaten Geelong by 11 points in Round 12, the coach was emphatic about putting the premiership genie back in its bottle faster than the speed of his club's midfield. The captain was the same. As soon as he finished belting out 'Good Old Collingwood Forever' with his teammates, Shaw was showered and dressed. 'It's not an occasion, mate, I just want to go and have a beer with the trainers,' Shaw insisted.

Matthews admitted his 'gut feeling' was that this Collingwood was a superior team to the 1989 model, but he added, 'We really can't do anything this year until we make the finals and play well in the finals, and first and foremost, we've got to get there to do that. In all honesty, the hype is built up by the media. It's irrelevant to us.''

Collingwood rolled almost seamlessly through the next month without a blemish, with wins over Richmond, West Coast, Carlton and Sydney. That brought the club's winning streak to nine and took it to the top of the ladder, albeit for one week only. Politicians traditionally love winners, so it was hardly a surprise when the treasurer, Paul Keating, fixed himself on the Magpies, arriving in Melbourne with 12 political journalists from Canberra for the game against Carlton. He enjoyed the win, but liked it even more when he won a crisp $10 note in a bet on the game with Carlton president and Liberal powerbroker John Elliott. 'I have been in one grand final team this year [the 1990 Federal election in March], so I want this to be a second one,' Keating said. 'Collingwood is a sort of natural fit for me. What I enjoy is they don't ever let their enthusiasm wane, they don't give up and they keep trying.'

Then in Round 17, Collingwood's run of wins came to a dramatic end against Footscray at the MCG. The Magpies had nosed their way in front at the 23-minute mark of the last term, having trailed by 28 points at the final change. But just when a tenth straight win seemed a certainty, Bulldog Steven Kolyniuk ruined the party. He took a mark, baulked around Graham Wright, threw down three bounces before driving home the match-winning goal with his left foot. It was doubly frustrating for Wright, who earlier had been penalised for a tackle on Terry Wallace coupled with a 50-metre penalty that resulted in a goal to Darren Davies. Matthews was fuming with the penalty, saying: 'You guys saw it; you have the guts to write it.' He was also fuming over Collingwood's poor shooting for goal – the Magpies had 33 scoring shots for their 12.21 compared with the Bulldogs' 26 shots for 14.12.

Damian Monkhorst and Tony 'Plugger' Lockett exchange pleasantries in Round 18.

Inaccuracy was still a problem a week later against St Kilda, but 16.21 was more than enough to shut out the Saints by 68 points. Collingwood's midfield brigade of Millane, Shaw, McGuane and Russell was damaging, as was Craig Kelly, who restricted Tony Lockett to three goals. Daicos kicked 4.6, before revealing that Matthews had quelled his goal celebrations. He said Matthews 'coaches like he plays – he is cool, highly efficient and does not deal in histrionics. At Collingwood, he has taught us that style. Do the job properly, without fuss, and if you win at the end of September, then go and celebrate.'

The anticipation ahead of the Round 19 clash with Essendon at Waverley was such that Channel Seven opted to cover it live on television. Fearless

The Mightiest Magpies

Right: Darren Millane sends a Bomber flying in the rain in Round 19.
Opposite: The mood in the locker room was subdued after a woeful performance against the Hawks in Round 20.

The Herald
On Essendon's narrow win over Collingwood in Round 19:

As a guide to the premiership, it was not so conclusive; Essendon would have been unlucky to lose and, in turn, Collingwood can consider itself equally unfortunate. And so, in the end, the league heavyweights slugged it out for 100 minutes without gaining an apparent psychological advantage should they meet again in the finals.

football tipster Lou Richards was confident his old side would win and threw in one of this famous dares. 'Tell you what, if Essendon wins, I will appear on the forecourt of the National Mutual building in Collins Street at midday on Monday, and let Paul Salmon dunk me in a tank of water brought especially from the South Pole.'

The game was played on a wet and windy afternoon. In a classic contest, full of desperation and determination. The Bombers opened the game with the first four goals, slowed to almost a walk in the middle stages, then held off the fast-finishing Collingwood to win by six points. Essendon had no luck with injuries; Collingwood had little luck in the run of play. The hard luck story came from a dubious free kick to Michael Long 18 minutes into the final term, which resulted in Essendon's only goal for the term, kicked by David Johnson. One last chance to win the match by Gavin Crosisca was smothered by a desperate Mark Thompson.

But there were lessons learned. Many of the key Magpie players were off their form, and could hardly play as poorly again in the finals. Daicos, in his

200th game, managed only one goal, his equal lowest return of the season. Matthews even used him across half-back for a time. The battle between Millane and Greg Anderson had been anticipated almost as much as the game itself, but the Essendon wingman clearly took the points. Teammates close to Millane knew how frustrated he was with his performance that day. Privately, he told them it wouldn't happen the next time he came up against Essendon – and Anderson. Every Collingwood fan was hoping his teammates felt the same.

But if Matthews could see positives in the gritty comeback against Essendon, there were none to be drawn from Collingwood's Round 20 loss to its old nemesis, Hawthorn. The win was the Hawks' ninth from their previous 11 games against the Magpies. The final margin was 83 points, with the Hawks plundering 26 goals against the normally thrifty Collingwood defence while a mere 12 goals went back the other way. It would be the only time in 1990 that the Magpie back half would concede 20 goals or more. Matthews said: 'We were exceptionally bad; they were exceptionally good. I've got no reasons for the poor performance. Today we were woeful. I know that, you know that, everyone knows that.'

Was it just a blip on the radar or something else? Only the finals would tell. The dilemma for the coach was whether to stick with the players and structures that had taken the Magpies to within striking distance of a flag, or change the plan well beyond midstream. The *Herald* debated: 'Is now the time for Collingwood to bring back Brian Taylor?' Don Scott suggested Taylor might be

PLAYER OF THE YEAR

Darren Millane

It's the image that Collingwood supporters will never forget – Darren Millane tossing the Sherrin in the air as the siren sounds to end 32 years of torment and heartbreak. A year and one day later Millane was dead, killed in a car accident.

The other thing Magpie fans will never erase from their minds is the inspirational qualities Millane displayed throughout that season, particularly after Round 21 when he fractured his thumb in two places.

For some, it would have signalled the end of their season. For Millane, it meant that the intense pain he was suffering was just going to have to be a by-product of chasing the ultimate success. Nothing was going to stop him from playing a role in Collingwood's quest for the 1990 flag.

Millane played 23 games in 1990, gathering 584 touches, including 28 in the grand final. But sheer statistics cannot underpin just how important he was to the Magpies that season. Perhaps the best example was the fact that he was voted by his peers as the AFL Players Association's Most Valuable Player, one of the most fitting tributes of his nine-season AFL career.

The two semi-finals against West Coast were fiery affairs.
Above: Mick McGuane takes on the Eagles.
Opposite, top: Brian Taylor shows Chris Lewis he means business.
Opposite, bottom: Peter Daicos celebrates the remarkable goal that kept Collingwood in the drawn game.

worth a punt, but believed that the centre half-forward position was Collingwood's greatest concern. Fellow columnist Robert Walls disagreed, saying 'I do not think the Magpies should hit the panic button yet. Their style of game is a running, possession style so they cannot afford to have Taylor and [James] Manson on the field at the same time.'

In the end, for the Round 21 game against Fitzroy, Matthews punted on playing Taylor who had been steadily regaining form in the reserves. It was his first senior game since Round 7, but Taylor himself was confident he would deliver and duly did so, kicking four goals as the Magpies annihilated the Lions by 86 points. It was never going to be enough to lock in his spot, but Taylor left Victoria Park that night feeling more secure than he had for quite some time.

The more important issues arising out of the Fitzroy thrashing were injuries to Shaw and Millane. It was said that Shaw's knee injury 'cast a pall of gloom over what would have been a jubilant Magpie social club' that night, with Matthews denying that the skipper had chipped a bone in his knee: 'Hell no, he's strained a medial ligament.' Darren Millane's thumb injury was a much greater concern, and one that needed to be kept secret. The club put out a story that the brilliant wingman had simply dislocated his thumb. He hadn't. He had fractured it in two places and technically, his season could have been over. But Millane played on, pushing himself through the pain threshold, and was not only out there for the next game against North Melbourne, but gathered 30 touches. Pain meant nothing to Millane or Shaw. This Collingwood team was on a mission. Nothing would get in its way.

As much as the players played down what might be ahead for them, the club had to make plans – just in case. The Magpies asked the Liquor Commission for a permit to sell alcohol around the ground on training nights from 3 September to the 28th, scheduled to be grand final eve. This included a wish list for an 'all-night licence' until 7 a.m. on grand final weekend. Local residents were less than impressed. One of them, Don Watson, former John Cain speechwriter and soon-to-be speechwriter and adviser for Paul Keating, started a letterbox campaign to oppose the special licence. 'I'd love nothing more than to see Collingwood win their first flag in 32 years, but I am worried about the possibility of 48 hours of continuous drinking. Allan McAlister may regard us as a "bunch of yuppies" but the club must realise it exists in a residential area.'

Publicly, though, the lid was still wedged tight. Matthews didn't want any talk of flags. And Tony Shaw had seen enough hype and disappointment to know that it was not what the players needed. On the eve of the club's qualifying final against West Coast, after finishing the home-and-away season second to Essendon, he declared that 'the season starts now'.

Embracing the opportunity was the theme of the moment. Matthews arranged sports motivator and media personality Alan Jones to secretly fly in from Sydney to speak with the players. Both Jones's appearance and his message leaked out. When asked about his meeting with the Magpies, Jones suggested the Colliwobbles didn't exist as a concept for this team, saying, 'I know from talking to those blokes and discussing how they approach big matches that it is not a factor with them.' But not everyone was of the same opinion, especially after a dramatic conclusion to Collingwood's first final – a thrilling draw against West Coast that threw the finals schedule into chaos, pushed the season back a week and brought the doomsayers out once more.

It was a remarkable match, one that the *Sunday Herald* described as being 'played like a matter of life and death. In terms of premiership hopes, perhaps it was. It was classic finals football. A contest chock full of nervous fumbles, acts of brilliance, the odd moment of sheer genius.' The biggest margin was 14 points, opened up by Collingwood in the first 10 minutes. Time and again, the scores tightened and the game was in the balance. Collingwood led at every change, though only by two points at the last one. Just before time-on, the Eagles had clawed their way to a 10-point lead and appeared to be the fresher side. Then Matthews took a gamble. Having banished Taylor to the bench in the second term, the Magpies coach gave him one last life line by bringing him on again. Twice within the space of three minutes, Taylor answered the challenge and his two goals regained the lead for a desperate Collingwood.

Then Daicos kicked one of the most remarkable goals of his remarkable career. Receiving a handball from Millane, he made the impossible possible with a checkside kick from the left boundary line that appeared to defy the laws of physics. But the Eagles were not done – a goal to Karl Langdon followed, and when Chris Waterman missed a chance, the difference was back to a point.

PLAYER OF THE YEAR — Graham Wright

Collingwood garnered so many laurels in its famed 1990 season, but there was one narrow miss.

Wingman Graham Wright polled 7 votes in the Brownlow Medal, leaving him outright second and only one agonising vote from the winner, Footscray's Tony Liberatore. Wright polled more best-on-grounds than Liberatore – four to three – and flew home in the count with two BOGs in the last two games.

cast off A series of injuries and illness had hampered the Tasmanian's progress as a small forward since his 1988 debut, but he cast those off to stamp himself as one of the AFL's best wingman in 1990. The centreline trio of Wright, Tony Shaw and Darren Millane proved a near-perfect blend of speed, stamina and strength and it played a significant part in the club's success.

Like Shaw, Wright played every game in 1990. He had 563 touches from his 26 games, more than 200 more than in any other of his 11 seasons at the club. Importantly, he laid 53 tackles, second only to Shaw's 55 at the club that season.

Enter Peter Sumich, West Coast's full-forward, who had already kicked four goals. With 28 seconds left, he marked about 10 metres out on a serious angle. On the wrong side for a left footer, he took his time, but missed the goals. His kick resulted in the first finals draw since the 1977 Grand Final. As Channel Seven commentator Peter Landy said: 'I think the only people rubbing their hands will be at Jolimont [then AFL headquarters].'

While some critics took aim at Collingwood's lost opportunity, Matthews was immediately on the offensive, claiming the draw would actually disadvantage the flag favourites, Essendon. He said, 'One week off is all right, two weeks off starts to be a bit of a problem and some of them [the players] might have had four or five weeks [off].' Still, he conceded the Magpies had to play better. The one great positive for the weekend was that Hawthorn – the team that Collingwood feared the most – was eliminated by Melbourne a day after the draw. Football manager 'Gubby' Allan, who went to the MCG that day with Matthews, walked away confident the Magpies would finally break their long drought.

Collingwood was determined to go on without Taylor. Although he had almost been the hero in the qualifying final, the 1986 Coleman medallist was dumped for the replay. Tensions had been high for some time within the club with Taylor's plan to release a diary on his – and Collingwood's – season after it was all over. This had led to an uneasy relationship with the coach and with a few of the senior players. When told of his axing from the team, Taylor took it on the chin, saying that he would continue to train with the group, but would retire at the end of the season.

Collingwood had little trouble accounting for West Coast in the return bout, so that the Magpies' first finals win since the 1984 first semi came with ease. An eight-goal-to-two first term set the foundations for the 59-point win. Matthews declared the club was well placed in the race for the flag. Asked if they could win it, the coach said, 'I'm confident if we play up to our capabilities we can match anyone in the competition.' Daicos and Brown each kicked four goals in the match, Christian was impressive at centre half-forward, and Wright and Francis were key players. Denis Banks was simply happy to be out there again, after five weeks off with a broken wrist. He knew something special was in the offing.

The next stumbling block was Essendon, a team that hadn't played a game since Round 22. The Collingwood players were quietly confident they would get a different result in the second semi-final than they did in Round 19. Still, the Magpies looked a little nervous early in the match while the Essendon players seemed more than a little rusty. The game was still in the balance when Shaw quipped to Sheedy at quarter time, 'they're looking a bit slow, Sheeds'. Collingwood took a two-goal lead into half-time, but it was tight and tense. No one amongst the 91,555-strong crowd was prepared for what followed. Matthews' men burst from the blocks, clinically compiling a five-goal-to-two third quarter, making the difference 28 points at three-quarter time. But instead of resting on those laurels, and trying to protect the lead, Collingwood whacked its foot on the accelerator. Another five-goal quarter came and this time the Bombers couldn't even manage one major for the term as the final margin bloated out to 63 points. Brown kicked five of Collingwood's 17 goals; Daicos and Doug Barwick three each in what *The Sun* called a 'sledge-hammer demolition'.

Collingwood was into its first grand final in nine years, but Matthews was taking nothing for granted. Speaking after the semi-final win he said, 'After a long seven or eight month build-up, to actually qualify for the grand final ... it's a bit of a dream in a way. But it's great. We are in it! Of course, we can win it. But in two weeks' time, it will be another 50–50 game. That's the way footy works.' Collingwood supporters dared to dream that all the nightmares of grand finals past would be washed away with the first premiership under the banner of the AFL.

Essendon easily accounted for West Coast in the preliminary final, meaning another clash with Essendon to decide the premiership. But the make-up of the Magpies' team for the big game was anything but assured. Alan Richardson had played 18 games for the season and had been an important player for the Magpies' structure. But he had snapped a collarbone in the semi-final and was facing a race against time to be ready. Matthews gave Richardson's shoulder some close attention at the end of the last training session, and it was clear that he was never going to be right to play, even though the Magpies publicly insisted he would. But there was more than one

Shane Morwood and Tony Shaw leave the ground after defeating Essendon in the semi-final.

The Mightiest Magpies

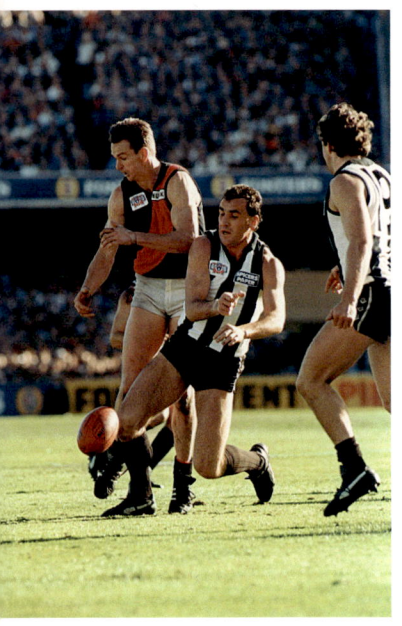

Left: Millane bumps Anthony Daniher out of the way.
Right: Morwood clears the ball to Kelly while Shaw looks on.

hard luck story. Defender Ron McKeown had played 20 games during the season, but had been dropped for team balance in the second semi-final. He, too, would miss out when Collingwood took to the field that famous October afternoon in 1990. The only change from the previous match was Richardson out, allowing Shane Kerrison to come into the team.

Matthews demanded no balloons or streamers were to be placed in the rooms before the game. The only thing that stared down at the Collingwood players as they prepared for the most important game of their lives was the Tigers emblem from the wall of the Richmond rooms they were using. It was just as if this was any other game, except it wasn't. Matthews had his players steeled with a belief that the rest of the world didn't believe they could win . Morwood said later: 'Leigh showed us a video of [boxer] Sugar Ray Leonard before a fight. He had his back to the wall. That's how I felt. I really believed that no one really thought we could do it. I kept telling myself there were a lot of people who didn't believe in us, and I just wanted to stick it up them.' Shaw said that Matthews barely said anything to his team before they ran out on the field. The words plastered on the blackboard were: 'Operation Pressure. First 10 minutes. Numbers to the contest. Long and quick into the forward line.' The words that came directly from the coach were simple: Matthews told his team he was proud of them, regardless of whether they won, lost or drew the game. They ran down the race desperate to make him even prouder.

The fear in the Collingwood camp centred on Essendon's big forwards and the damage they could potentially cause. This seemed justified in the opening term when Paul Salmon kicked the first two goals of the game. It prompted the coach to quickly move Craig Kelly onto Salmon. He reversed it in a matter of minutes, shifting Michael Christian back again. Salmon would not kick another goal for the game. Collingwood needed a lift though. Several flurries forward had failed to produce a goal in the first 20 minutes and the Bombers' forward set-up appeared to be functioning better than the one at the other end of the ground.

Then, almost on cue, Daicos emerged to kick the club's first goal at the 21-minute mark of the first term. It was as important as any of the previous 95 goals he had kicked that season and typically, it was an opportunity created out of almost nothing. A tap-on from Craig Starcevich went out into loose space, as Channel Seven commentator Ian Robertson observed, 'No one can break clear.' But Daicos managed to gain a break on Peter Cransberg, before gathering and kicking from an acute angle from the forward pocket. It seemed to settle the Magpies down a bit, and was followed by another goal from Brown just 20 seconds before the end of the quarter. The Magpies had a three-point lead at the first break.

But if the pent-up emotions of the tight, tense first term had largely been kept in check, all of that changed in the space of a few mad seconds soon after the quarter-time siren had sounded. The spark was ignited soon after Denis Banks ankle-tapped his opponent Keiran Sporn, trying to get a reaction. He got one – Sporn threw a punch at Banks. That's all that Brown saw as headed down to the fight that ensued. He ran from deep in the forward line,

Tempers flare during the quarter-time break in the grand final.

where he had just kicked his first goal, and made heavy contact with Sporn. Terry Daniher, following Brown in, and seeing what he had done to Sporn, floored the Collingwood forward. For a few moments, the brawl raged out of control as players got right into the action. But as they started to calm down and dissolve from the pack, one prostrate figure was left lying unconscious on the ground. It was Gavin Brown.

Meanwhile, another spot fire had ignited near what was meant to be the Essendon huddle. Bombers' runner Peter Power had seen the Brown–Sporn incident from a distance. He exclaimed, 'You ripper!' when he saw Daniher hit Brown in retaliation. That prompted Collingwood football manager Graeme Allan to throw a punch at Power. Years later, Essendon coach Kevin Sheedy admitted that he gave Allan 'a clip over the ears' as he ran out to address his team. Other officials became involved as well in a situation rapidly careering out of control. Finally, a policeman intervened and Matthews arrived and called for calm as the two teams went back to their respective huddles to get on with the business of playing football. In the end, six players would be reported on 13 charges, extended to seven on 16 charges after a trial-by-video investigation. Three officials, including Allan and team manager Eddie Hillgrove, would also be brought before the football judiciary.

When the Collingwood players got to their huddle, Leigh Matthews could see their 'eyes were rolling in the back of their heads'. He ordered them to be calm. He ordered them not to carry on the fight in the second term. He told them that the team that entered the second term with the right approach would win the premiership. It was the perfect call from a coach sensing his team was intent on carrying the brawl and what had happened to Brown with them for the rest of the match. As they headed back into the fray to start the second term, the players were determined to follow their coach's instructions to the letter.

Essendon, not Collingwood, reacted badly when play resumed. Within a minute, the scene was set. Starcevich was awarded a free kick and then a 50-metre penalty which resulted in the first goal of the second term. It was the first of four goals in the space of nine minutes that changed the course of the game. Gavin Crosisca got the next one, after pouncing on a loose ball to slot the goal through on his trusty left foot. Then a super tackle from Scott Russell saw Alan Ezard penalised. That, too, resulted in a 50-metre penalty and goal to the Magpies. Then Crosisca got a second goal after drifting across the pack to mark just over 20 metres out from goal. Russell received another free kick, this time for a push in the back, just before the 10-minute mark of a term that was getting away from Essendon. His goal put Collingwood 34 points up.

Essendon's sole goal for the quarter came at the 24-minute mark when Derek Kickett somehow threw his boot at the ball to score a brilliant goal. But it was followed just as quickly by another one from Collingwood, again off the back of some undisciplined play from the Bombers. This time it was Barwick who got the kick, and another 50-metre penalty brought him into point-blank range. The difference at half-time was 34 points. If any other team had been leading by that margin, at that stage of a grand final, the contest would have been considered over. But this was Collingwood, and fans at the ground and across living rooms all over Australia rested uneasily as the two teams made their way off the MCG and into the rooms.

Still, Matthews wasn't finished. As calm as he was at half-time, he wanted to make a point to Daniher as the two headed towards the adjoining races. He grabbed hold of Brown and led him to the wire where Daniher was about exit. He waited for him to arrive and said, 'He'll be back, Terry.' There were a few other expletives exchanged, but the point was made. Brown was coming back and Collingwood held a massive lead. Essendon was going to have to do something special to change that.

Leigh Matthews, with concussed Gavin Brown by his side, gives Terry Daniher a serve at half-time.

> **THE AGE**
>
> Gareth Andrews on Collingwood's long-awaited success:
>
> What a mighty Collingwood victory. It was a win that released all the raw energy of that home-grown fanaticism best represented by the black and white. Collingwood steamrolled Essendon. They gave the opposition no quarter. They were relentless and ruthless in pursuing their goal and when they saw the ball they decided it was theirs. They were at the bottom of every pack and they chased down their opponents as if there was no tomorrow.

If Daniher had been the subject of some Magpie abuse from across the fence after the Brown incident, he was about to cop even more. Just five minutes into the second half, Starcevich headed in to mark a kick from Jamie Turner when Daniher collected him high. Symbolic of the Bombers' lack of discipline, it earned another 50-metre penalty and goal after Mick McGuane stepped in to take the groggy Starcevich's kick. The margin was out to 40 points. Starcevich was taken off, but just a few minutes later Brown came back on to the roar of the crowd. It was an inspiring effort to get back on the field and he ran up to Daniher to let him know that he hadn't stopped him.

Daicos built on the big Collingwood lead with his 97th and final goal of a remarkable 1990 season. In keeping what with what came before it, he made it a special one, too. A left wobbly boot from Millane bounced fortuitously for Daicos, but he was on an acute angle and running out of room. Just in time, he threw his boot to the ball and it was home. The difference was 46 points.

Almost as soon as the black-and-white faithful started to feel safe, the Bombers bounced back with two quick goals in the space of two minutes, via Peter Somerville and David Grenvold. It was back to 34 points again, and a sense of unease swept over the ground. Surely they couldn't. Could they? Fittingly, it was Brown who eased the tension. Just 16 minutes after coming back onto the field after being heavily concussed, he was composed enough to swoop on an errant handball from Mark Thompson and slot it through the goals. It was a team-lifting goal. The player down and seemingly out earlier in the game had allowed the Magpies to take a 40-point margin to the last change.

The Sunday Sun declared, 'A Collingwood flag was a foregone conclusion at the start of the last term'. But few among the Collingwood supporters in the crowd felt that way. They had been teased and tempted by premature success in previous years and it wasn't going to happen this time until it was officially over. Still, the omens were good. Simon Madden hit the post with a kick for goal in the first minute of the last term. Then, better still, he kicked into the man on the mark, Michael Christian, before the Magpie defence swept the ball away. This final term had become an arm-wrestle and 19 minutes elapsed without either side scoring a goal, which suited Collingwood perfectly.

It was Barwick who broke the deadlock. He gave off to Banks before getting the ball back only 15 metres out and driving it home. The Magpie fans behind the goals rose in unison as Barwick held his arms skyward with a look of euphoria on his face. It was then the crowd began to chant Collingwood, and the realisation dawned on them that they were, indeed, watching history. With six minutes of game time remaining, Channel Seven panned to the boundary line, near the Collingwood race, where former coach Bob Rose was. For someone who had been through so much pain, the moment was not lost on him. As Ian Robertson said of Rose, 'there will be a tear very close to his eye, as there would be for most of the Collingwood army chanting now. Essendon [is] striving, but there's no way known that they will get back into it.' Now, it was simply a matter of counting down time.

Collingwood's best two players on the day, Tony Shaw and Damian Monkhorst, combined for the last goal of the game. Shaw marked 45 metres out, then spotted Monkhorst loose at half forward. The big man did not let him down. Before this, he had kicked only three goals in his career, but the 21-year-old was never going to miss this one. As Shaw was running back to the centre for the next contest, he came across Essendon captain Tim Watson. 'What do you think?' Shaw asked him. Watson said, 'I think you've got us.' The margin was 49 points, and there was less than two minutes left on the clock.

Matthews finally decided to leave the coach's box. Wearing a shirt and tie underneath a Collingwood sleeveless sweater, he was almost mobbed as he made his way through the MCC members to the boundary line. As he reached the ground, he pumped his fist while TV reporter Eddie McGuire looked on, then the coach raised his arms above his head and waved them madly to

Leigh Matthews, with a very young Eddie McGuire in the background, during grand final celebrations at the Southern Cross Hotel.

Right: **Peter Daicos** – minus his false teeth - savours his moment with the cup.
Below: **Tony Shaw**, premiership captain, falls to his knees as the siren goes.

the Collingwood crowd before being embraced by Gubby Allan and James Manson, still wearing the dressing gown. It was a rare showing of emotion from Matthews, who said later that it was only when Monkhorst kicked the goal that he knew Essendon could not stage a comeback.

The Bombers added a point to their tally. McGuane brought the ball back into play, with a short kick to Millane, who had played tirelessly, despite his fractured thumb. But, as Channel Seven's Sandy Roberts said, 'He will feel no pain tonight.' Millane paused to kick the ball, rechecked his options, before waving to his teammates downfield to make a lead for him. Before he got the chance to have his 29th disposal, the siren sounded. It was over, and so, too, was the most lampooned premiership drought in Australian sport. He threw the ball in the air to himself, but was never going to let the Sherrin out of his grasp. In his column in the *Sunday Sun,* Millane would say, 'I have the football, and no one, repeat no one, is going to take it off me.' The poignancy of the moment would not be realised until almost exactly 12 months later when

Millane died in a car accident, but for now his moment in the last seconds of the grand final was etched forever in the minds of Magpie supporters.

Tony Shaw collapsed to the ground in relief as much as exhaustion. He had finally got what he wanted, but there was more to come. Shaw was announced as the winner of the Norm Smith Medal, an appropriate award for a guy who had given his all. Fortunately, he had arranged with official Billy Cook to bring out his two false teeth so that his happy snaps could be savoured for years to come. Peter Daicos wishes he had had the same foresight. 'I am sort of lost for words,' said the skipper who had never been that way before. 'It's a big event. I feel it now because these blokes and the club have been brilliant, and I feel it for the fans, too, because they stuck with us.' It was said that Shaw 'wore the grin of a boy unattended in an ice-cream parlour'.

It was the start of a lengthy period of celebrations, at the ground and elsewhere. Emphasis was placed on the words 'Oh, the premiership's a cakewalk' from the theme song. It blared over and over from the MCG address system and was played ad nauseam in homes across the city, the state and the country. Collingwood's 32-year, 11,704-day wait was over. The team went on their victory lap, sharing the premiership cup with their long-suffering fans. After the game, they seemed to share the spoils with half of Melbourne.

Tony Shaw (22) shows the cup to the fans, on the shoulders of Michael Christian (21) and James Manson (30).

Craig Kelly and Darren Millane show off their handiwork.

Streets were closed in the heart of Collingwood as tens of thousands of fans descended on Victoria Park that afternoon, long into the night and again the next day. Cars were gridlocked for kilometres around the ground, and many of those who had been at the MCG decided to walk back to Vic Park, exchanging high fives along the way with those stranded in their cars. Victoria Park itself was a sprawling, drinking, exultant, black and white mass, and the reception for the players when they hit the stage late on Saturday night defies description. The next day was more benign, as fans gradually accepted that what they'd seen was real. The party continued for weeks. No other VFL/AFL premiership in recent history has come close to sparking such emotions, or such widespread and long-lasting celebrations. It was a moment that Melbourne would never forget.

Former players and supporters openly wept. Former player and 1990 board member Wayne Richardson summed it up when he said of the premiership team, 'as far as these guys are concerned, they will be written up at Collingwood in letters of gold. They are going to be gods.' Lou Richards, who would soon bury the Colliwobbles in a mock ceremony attended by thousands at Victoria Park, heaped praise on Matthews. So, too, did Bob Rose, the man who had given Matthews the green light to coach Collingwood. Rose said it was a 'staggering feeling to have broken the hoodoo after 32 years ... I have a great admiration for the players and for the coach and his tactics and the team spirit. They were working as a team.'

Matthews took great delight in serving up the last rites on the Colliwobbles myth. He reserved his credit for his players, pointing out that 'they are the ones who go out there and do it on the day – they

1990: Breaking the drought

are the heroes. These guys, and the Collingwood guernsey, maybe, have been unfairly given the derogatory 'Colliwobbles' thing for failing in finals. They've played magnificent football over the past month, and it's a credit to them that it's now at an end. They have cut down the folklore of Australian sport.' History aside, the coach couldn't wipe the grin off his face in the rooms after the game, or later that night. 'As for the players, I thank them,' he said. 'Nothing surpasses what those men did today. The satisfaction for me is them justifying the faith I had in them. I thank for them that and will be grateful to them for the rest of my life.' Then he added: 'I'm just happy for everyone who is happy.'

On that basis, Leigh Matthews was happy for a hell of a lot of Collingwood supporters that night. The premiership was, once again, a cakewalk. Magpie fans were sure that, with the monkey finally lifted from their backs, a new era of success was just around the corner. But that was the future, and for the time being they celebrated long and hard. They had every reason to: the most infamous drought in football history was over.

An image that would linger in the fans' minds for the next 20 years: Tony Shaw holding the premiership cup aloft.

The Mightiest Magpies

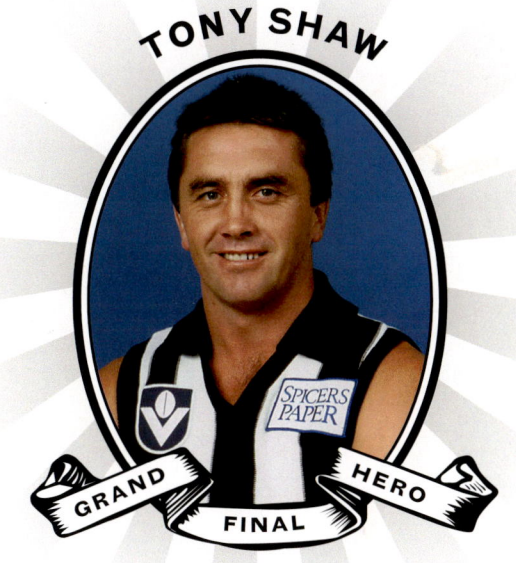

Tony Shaw played more games than any other person in Collingwood's long and celebrated history, 313 in total, but if you ask the man himself only one of them truly mattered. It came on 6 October 1990, at the conclusion of his most consistent season, and it was the game he was almost destined to play.

Dismissed by some early in his career as being too small and too slow, Shaw became the embodiment of a footballer who dragged himself to the contest and simply willed things to happen. He had won a Copeland Trophy in 1984, the year the Magpies finished third, but he had to prove himself all over again when coach Leigh Matthews arrived at the club.

The culmination of Shaw's persistence and hard work came in 1990 when he led Collingwood magnificently, not just in the grand final but throughout the season. Shaw finished with the most disposals in the competition that season (736) and won his second Copeland Trophy.

Yet it was his steady hand and cool head that proved just as important to the team during the season, and especially in the grand final, when he had a game-high 32 touches. That helped Collingwood win its first flag in 32 years, and won him the Norm Smith Medal.

PLAYERS

#	Player	Games	Goals
32	Colin Alexander	4	1
12	Denis Banks	18	9
17	Doug Barwick	23	36
26	Gavin Brown	18	49
21	Michael Christian	16	8
8	Jason Croall	2	0
28	Gavin Crosisca	23	22
35	Peter Daicos	25	97
2	Tony Francis	16	15
3	Michael Gayfer	25	0
37	Athas Hrysoulakis	2	0
14	Terry Keays	6	5
23	Craig Kelly	23	1
44	Shane Kerrison	14	1
30	James Manson	26	33
34	Mick McGuane	22	13
5	Ron McKeown	20	8
42	Darren Millane	23	9
1	Damian Monkhorst	26	3
7	Shane Morwood	26	3
13	Alan Richardson	18	7
29	Scott Russell	26	16
31	Darren Saunders	4	0
22	Tony Shaw	26	7
49	Heath Shephard	2	2
27	Craig Starcevich	15	18
36	Andrew Tarpey	2	1
9	Brian Taylor	6	9
43	Brendon Tranter	1	0
6	Paul Tuddenham	10	14
24	Jamie Turner	26	5
19	Graham Wright	26	12

Club Awards

Copeland Trophy – Tony Shaw
RT Rush Trophy – Darren Millane
J J Joyce Trophy – Scott Russell & Graham Wright
J F McHale Trophy (most courageous) –
   Darren Millane
Harry Collier Trophy (best first year player) –
   Scott Russell and Tony Francis
Jack Regan Trophy (best senior clubman) –
   Craig Kelly
Phonse Kyne Trophy (services to the Club) –
   Mick McGuane
Bob Rose Trophy (best finals player) – Gavin Brown
Joseph Wren Memorial Trophy (most improved) –
   Alan Richardson
Leading goalkicker – Peter Daicos (97)

1990 SEASON

ROUND 1 April 1 Subiaco
West Coast 14.16.100 v Collingwood **8.6.54**
Goals: Taylor 2, Tuddenham 2, Barwick, Brown, Daicos, Starcevich

ROUND 2 April 7 Waverley Park
Carlton **13.9.87** v **Collingwood 19.8.122**
Goals: Daicos 7, Manson 4, Barwick 3, Crosisca 2, Alexander, Russell, Wright

ROUND 3 April 16 Victoria Park
Collingwood 20.8.128 v Sydney **12.21.93**
Goals: Tuddenham 4, Daicos 3, Manson 3, Barwick 2, Crosisca 2, Shephard 2, Banks, Brown, Russell, Wright

ROUND 4 April 21 Victoria Park
Collingwood 14.12.96 v Footscray **11.12.78**
Goals: Daicos 6, Tuddenham 4, Tarpey, Richardson, Manson, Barwick

ROUND 5 April 28 MCG
St Kilda **13.13.91** v **Collingwood 12.20.92**
Goals: Barwick 2, Crosisca 2, Daicos 2, Manson 2, Banks, Richardson, Shaw, Starcevich

ROUND 6 May 5 MCG
Collingwood **10.15.75** v **Essendon 15.11.101**
Goals: Barwick 3, Crosisca 2, Keays, Kerrison, McGuane, Millane, Wright

ROUND 7 May 12 Waverley Park
Collingwood **13.14.92** v **Hawthorn 13.16.94**
Goals: Barwick 3, Daicos 3, Brown 2, Wright 2, Manson, Shaw, Starcevich

ROUND 8 May 19 Princes Park
Fitzroy **9.21.75** v **Collingwood 17.18.120**
Goals: Daicos 6, Brown 3, Manson 3, Tuddenham 2, Crosisca, McGuane, McKeown

ROUND 9 May 26 Victoria Park
Collingwood 26.20.176 v North Melbourne **14.12.96**
Goals: Brown 7, Daicos 7, Manson 3, Russell 3, Richardson 2, Barwick, Crosisca, Millane, Tuddenham

ROUND 10 June 2 Waverley Park
Collingwood 16.14.110 v Melbourne **9.4.58**
Goals: Daicos 6, Francis 2, McGuane 2, Starcevich 2, Millane, Morwood, Russell, Tuddenham

ROUND 11 June 10 Carrara
Brisbane **10.13.73** v **Collingwood 15.17.107**
Goals: Daicos 4, Manson 3, Starcevich 3, Banks, Christian, McGuane, Morwood, Turner

ROUND 12 June 16 Waverley Park
Geelong **12.16.88** v **Collingwood 14.15.99**
Goals: McKeown 3, Daicos 2, Manson 2, Shaw, Starcevich 2, Barwick, Francis, McGuane

ROUND 13 June 30 Victoria Park
Collingwood 14.17.101 v Richmond **5.12.42**
Goals: Daicos 4, Brown 3, Banks, Francis, Millane, Richardson, Russell, Starcevich, Wright

ROUND 14 July 7 Victoria Park
Collingwood 15.12.102 v West Coast **11.10.76**
Goals: Daicos 6, Millane 3, Barwick 2, Brown, Christian, Morwood, Shaw

ROUND 15 July 14 Waverley Park
Collingwood 17.11.113 v Carlton **8.11.59**
Goals: Daicos 5, Brown 3, Christian 3, Banks 2, Manson 2, McGuane, Russell

ROUND 16 July 22 SCG
Sydney **19.9.123** v **Collingwood 21.21.147**
Goals: Brown 3, Daicos 3, Francis 3, Manson 2, Russell 2, Banks, Christian, Crosisca, McGuane, Richardson, Shaw, Turner, Wright

ROUND 17 July 29 MCG
Footscray **14.12.96** v Collingwood **12.21.93**
Goals: Daicos 3, Banks 2, Barwick, Crosisca, Francis, McGuane, McKeown, Millane, Wright

ROUND 18 August 4 Victoria Park
Collingwood 16.21.117 v St Kilda **7.7.49**
Goals: Daicos 4, Crosisca 3, Keays 3, McKeown 3, Barwick 2, McGuane

ROUND 19 August 12 Waverley Park
Essendon **13.6.84** v Collingwood **11.12.78**
Goals: Brown 5, Manson 2, Barwick, Daicos, Francis, McGuane

ROUND 20 August 18 Waverley Park
Hawthorn 26.7.163 v Collingwood **12.8.80**
Goals: Barwick 3, Francis 2, Manson 2, Brown, Christian, Daicos, Keays, Shaw

ROUND 21 August 25 Victoria Park
Collingwood 17.16.118 v Fitzroy **4.8.32**
Goals: Daicos 4, Taylor 4, Turner 3, Monkhurst 2, Barwick, Crosisca, Russell, Wright

ROUND 22 September 1 Waverley Park
North Melbourne **8.19.67** v **Collingwood 23.18.156**
Goals: Daicos 6, Brown 5, Starcevich 4, Wright 3, Barwick, Crosisca, Richardson, Taylor, Francis

1990 FINALS

LADDER

Team	W	L	D	For	Agst	%	Pts
Essendon	17	5	0	2526	1815	139.2	68
Collingwood	16	6	0	2376	1825	130.2	64
WC Eagles	16	6	0	2274	1920	118.4	64
Melbourne	16	6	0	2339	2066	113.2	64
Hawthorn	14	8	0	2414	2002	120.6	56
North Melb	12	10	0	2519	2210	114.0	48
Footscray	12	10	0	2016	2031	99.3	48
Carlton	11	11	0	2277	2187	104.1	44
St Kilda	9	13	0	2328	2313	100.6	36
Geelong	8	14	0	2248	2398	93.7	32
Richmond	7	15	0	1988	2530	78.6	28
Fitzroy	7	15	0	1874	2389	78.4	28
Sydney	5	17	0	1904	2704	70.4	20
Brisbane	4	18	0	1733	2426	71.4	16

QTR FINAL September 8 Waverley Park
Collingwood 13.12.90 v West Coast **13.12.90**
Goals: Daicos 4, Barwick 3, Brown 3, Taylor 2, Manson

QTR FINAL REPLAY September 15 Waverley Park
Collingwood 19.12.126 v West Coast **9.13.67**
Goals: Brown 4, Daicos 4, Crosisca 2, Francis 2, Manson 2, Christian, Kelly, McGuane, Millane, Russell

SEMI FINAL September 23 MCG
Collingwood 17.15.117 v Essendon **7.12.54**
Goals: Brown 5, Barwick 3, Daicos 3, Russell 2, Starcevich 2, Crosisca, Francis

GRAND FINAL October 6 MCG

Collingwood	2.5	8.9	11.10	13.11 (89)
Essendon	2.2	3.5	5.6	5.11 (41)

Goals: Brown 2, Barwick 2, Crosisca 2, Russell 2, Daicos 2, Monkhorst, Starcevich, McGuane
Best: Shaw, Russell, Monkhorst, Millane, McGuane, Francis, Kerrison, Starcevich
Umpires: Sawers, Rich
Attendance: 98,944 at the MCG

Grand Final Team
B: S. Kerrison, M. Christian, M. Gayfer
HB: S. Morwood, C. Kelly, G. Crosisca
C: D. Millane, T. Shaw (c), G. Wright
HF: D. Banks, J. Manson, D. Barwick
F: S. Russell, G. Brown, P. Daicos
R: D. Monkhorst, M. McGuane, T. Francis
Interchange: J. Turner, C. Starcevich

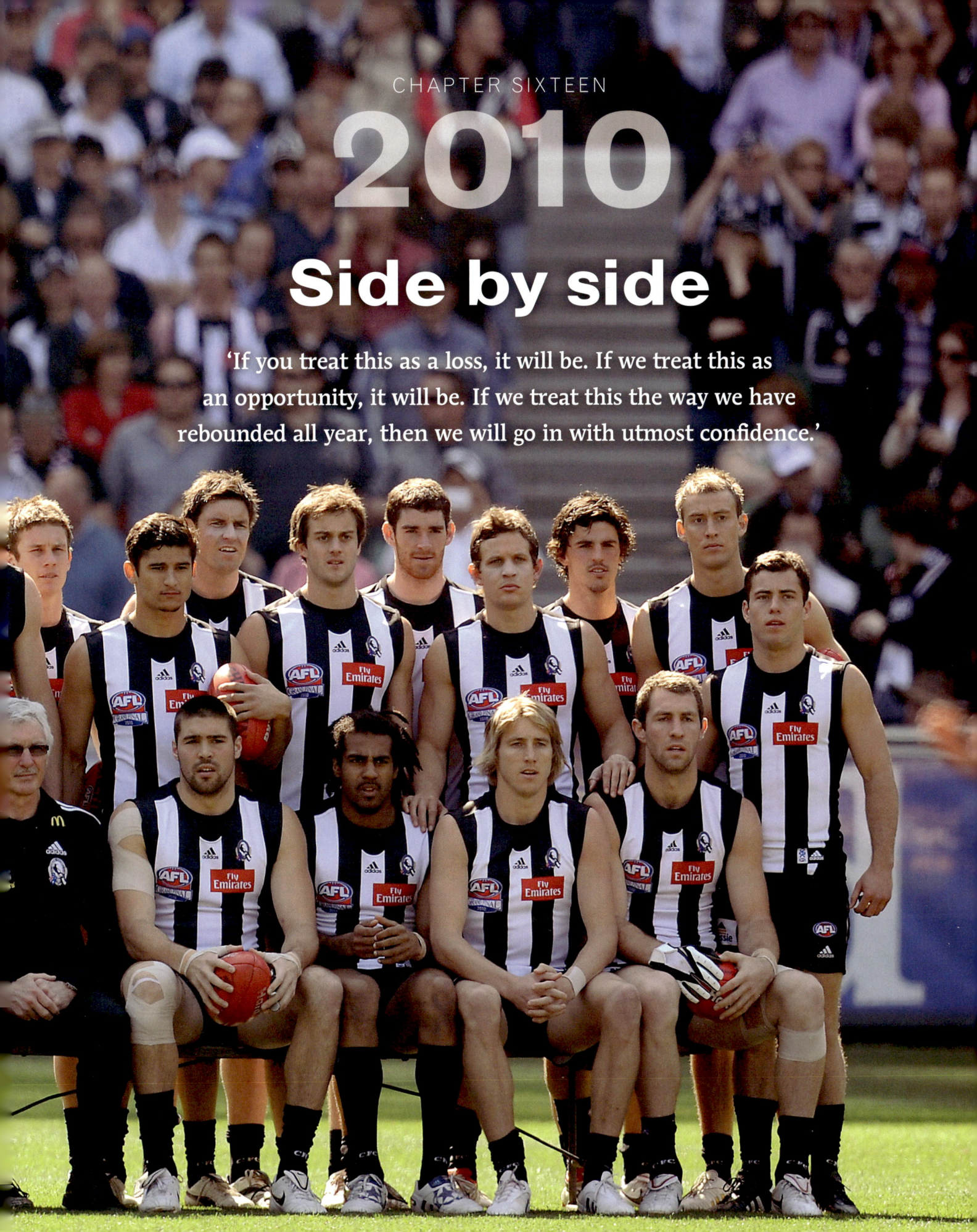

CHAPTER SIXTEEN

2010

Side by side

'If you treat this as a loss, it will be. If we treat this as an opportunity, it will be. If we treat this the way we have rebounded all year, then we will go in with utmost confidence.'

It's just on 11 minutes into the second quarter of the 2010 preliminary final, and a strange quiet has descended on the MCG. Collingwood is in the middle of the best half of football that many of its fans have ever seen, torching the team that has won two out of the past three premierships. The scoreboard shows a scarcely believable 57 to 14. But right now there is a lull in the action, as the players contest a couple of ball-ups in succession, the ball locked between half-forward and wing in front of the Great Southern Stand. Slowly, the half-silence is filled by a rumble that builds to a low, stirring roar. It's the elongated chant of 'Coll-ing-woo-od', the war cry that would become the soundtrack to the final weeks of the club's 2010 finals campaign, coming to the football world's attention.

For those at the ground, it's an amazing sensation – spine-tingling, uplifting and thrilling. It's not immediately obvious where it's come from, or how it started. But it's huge, almost visceral in its impact. Fans turn to each other and grin, or shake their heads. What they're witnessing on the field is out of the ordinary, and now it's being matched by what they're hearing. Even the experienced heads commentating the game for Channel 7 are taken aback. Former Geelong skipper Tom Harley sounds awestruck. 'I've never heard this at a game before . . . this sort of atmosphere and the chant like that,' he says. 'Terrific stuff,' adds Dennis Cometti. The reactions are understandable, because this is no ordinary display of fan fervour. It's the sound of the competition's sleeping giant awakening.

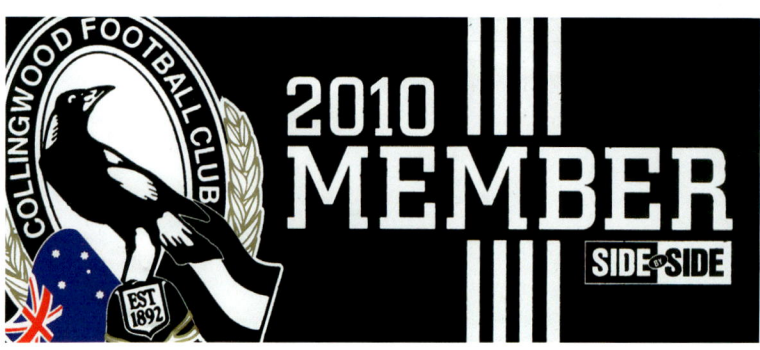

That awakening had been a long time coming. The last time Collingwood fans sang at the MCG with such gusto was on grand final day, 1990. That day ended the club's infamous 32-year flag drought and was meant to signal the rebirth of the Collingwood Football Club. But it didn't. Instead it was followed by the mother of all premiership

2010: Side by side

Mick Malthouse comforts Paul Licuria in the wake of the 2002 Grand Final loss.

hangovers, and the bleakest decade in the club's history. The team missed the finals in 1991, after seemingly only waking up halfway through the season, then was harshly eliminated in the first week of finals in 1992. Then it was eighth, eighth, tenth, eleventh, tenth, fourteenth and – in 1999 – dead last.

That was too much for such a proud club. Collingwood had not won a finals match since grand final day 1990, and hadn't even been near September action for five years. So something had to change. Everything had to change. And it did. Eddie McGuire took over as president in a bloodless backroom coup – that rarest of football occurrences – and brought with him a new board. He also introduced unprecedented levels of professionalism into the club's administration, headed by new CEO Greg Swann. Most importantly, he managed to persuade Mick Malthouse to return east from the West Coast Eagles and take over the coaching reins from Tony Shaw.

Just three years later, the Pies were back in a grand final, and in front in the final quarter. It was an extraordinary achievement by Malthouse and his team of mostly honest battlers. Steinfort, McKee, Betheras, Freeborn: these were not the names that Magpie fans had thought would feature in their next flag after 1990. But 10 minutes into the last quarter that was what looked like happening. That they ultimately fell short to the great Brisbane Lions team was no disgrace. Indeed, Collingwood fans feel nothing but pride for that team, which took them further, and faster, than anyone had thought likely.

The McGuire-Malthouse revolution looked to be on track, and well ahead of schedule. But the defeat in the 2003 Grand Final was limp, and crushing. Two injury-plagued years saw the team plummet to bottom-three finishes, then a first-round finals exit in 2006, as the Pies paid the price for some poor recruiting decisions earlier in the decade. Then came the heroic 2007 campaign that ended with an agonising five-point loss to eventual premiers Geelong in the preliminary final, a semi-final loss to St Kilda in 2008 and another preliminary final loss to Geelong – this time a thumping – in 2009. The Pies kept getting close, but were always falling short. They simply weren't good enough.

In most other ways, by the start of 2010 the rebuilding of the Collingwood Football Club was just about complete. It enjoyed record membership levels, sponsorship deals that were the envy of every other sporting organisation in the country, astronomical TV ratings and huge crowds. It was professionally run and financially sound. In all ways bar one it was a massively successful organisation. But success for footy clubs is ultimately measured by premierships – and it had been 19 long years since Collingwood's last.

Malthouse and recruiting manager Derek Hine had spent years building a playing list that could end that drought, while the coach and his team of assistants developed a game plan they believed could take them all the way. But Malthouse was running out of time. A succession plan had been agreed in 2009 that would see former skipper Nathan Buckley take over as coach in 2012, working as an assistant until then. Many doubted whether the plan, which would also see Malthouse take on a 'director of coaching' role from 2012, could work. But the short-term impact was clear: season 2010 would be Malthouse's second-last crack with the Pies as senior coach, and he knew he had to make it count.

The club first showed it was deadly serious about the 2010 flag in November of 2009, when it traded away valuable picks at the national draft in order to bring in experienced ruckman Darren Jolly from the Sydney Swans. Collingwood had lacked a big, hard-bodied ruckman for years, a weakness that often cost the team in finals, and Jolly seemed perfect for the role. When the Pies then played tough at the negotiating table with St Kilda and grabbed former Saints' skipper Luke Ball through the draft, Collingwood sent a clear message that it believed its premiership window was well and truly open. Jolly was already a premiership ruckman, and Ball, a former #2 draft pick, was an A-grade in-and-under midfielder and ferocious tackler. Now both would start the season in black-and-white jumpers. And even better, the club had been able to hang on to Sharrod Wellingham, Nathan Brown and Tyson Goldsack, all of whom had been touted as trade bait. Magpie fans could scarcely believe their luck – or contain their excitement. Despite a horror draw – the only top-four side of 2009 to have to play each of the other top -four sides twice in 2010 – nothing could diminish the sense of anticipation leading into the season.

But if there was anticipation at Collingwood, there was outright excitement at the Whitten Oval. The Western Bulldogs had won the pre-season NAB Cup in fine style, playing an impressive brand of fast, skilled, attacking football. In ex-Sydney full-forward Barry Hall, they looked to have found the key attacking focus they'd lacked for years. As they headed into the opening round of the season, and a clash against the Pies, their form and confidence were sky high. The Doggies were flying.

Alan Didak turns on the style against the Bulldogs in Round 1 at Etihad Stadium.

PLAYER OF THE YEAR

Dane Swan

So good was Dane Swan's season that the major talking point became the one award he didn't win – the Brownlow. A hot favourite before the count, Swan finished third, again confirming that umpires are unreliable witnesses when it comes to judging best players.

He was voted the season's best player by the AFL coaches, the AFL players, and the judges at just about every media outlet around the country. He was voted best player in the Australian International Rules team. And, most importantly of all, he became only the fourth man in the club's history to win three successive Copelands.

Swan's success was based on relentless, gut-busting running, a brilliant footballing brain and an insatiable appetite for possessions. He averaged about 32 touches a game in 2010, and used most of them expertly. He proved impossible to tag, and even in his quietest games always contributed something important.

The figures and the awards don't lie: despite his ungainly gait Dane Swan is one of the truly elite midfielders in the competition, and one of the best to have worn the black-and-white jumper.

All of which made Collingwood's first quarter of the season even more impressive. The Pies produced a scintillating eight-goal barrage that had the crowd at Docklands roaring. The pace was frenetic from the start, with both sides playing fearless, aggressive football. But the Dogs could find no easy way out of their defensive areas as Collingwood players swarmed all over them, creating opportunity after opportunity. It was a sign of things to come.

A five-goal quarter-time lead represented a dream start for Malthouse's men, but the Dogs came back with great spirit in the second term and closed the gap to just three points early in the third. An hour into the home-and-away season and the Magpies were facing their first big test: could they somehow regain the momentum from the resurgent Dogs? You bet they could. Collingwood kicked nine of the next 12 goals to run out winners by six goals. There was even time for party tricks in the last quarter, when a double-handed over-the-head tap from the otherwise quiet Darren Jolly set up Dane Swan for one of the goals of the day. Small forwards Alan Didak (4), Paul Medhurst (4) and Leon Davis (3) were all superb, but the real drive came from running defenders Harry O'Brien and Heath Shaw, who were dashing and creative all day.

It was as emphatic an opening round win as Collingwood could have hoped for. Magpie fans were already eagerly looking ahead to the big Round 3 clash with St Kilda, knowing that Melbourne – which had been thumped by Hawthorn by more than nine goals in the first week – would provide little more than a heavy training run in between. That was the theory, anyway.

The Collingwood players who ran out in Round 2 looked lethargic, struggling painfully for touch. The Demons were much more impressive than their first round showing had indicated and they led narrowly for most of the game, but there was still a feeling that the Pies would always be able to do enough to win. With just 10 minutes to go in a poor standard game, Melbourne was 11 points up, and crunch time had well and truly arrived. A mark and goal to Jack Anthony followed by a moment of individual magic from Leon Davis put the Pies back in front by a solitary point with just a few minutes left.

The last three minutes of the game were full of high drama. Every contest became critical, and with 90 seconds left the Pies decided to try and run down the clock. But the Demons manned up, forcing

Teenager Steele Sidebottom saves the day by spoiling Ricky Petterd's attempted mark in the last seconds of the Round 2 match against Melbourne.

captain Nick Maxwell to bomb the ball into attack, and Melbourne broke clear. They launched two late attacks on goal, the second of which was a kick to the top of the square with just seconds left. Melbourne's Ricky Petterd flew and got first hands to the ball, but Steele Sidebottom flew with him and did just enough to stop him getting the ball at the second attempt. The siren sounded just as Heath Shaw pounced on the loose ball. What was meant to be a regulation victory had instead turned into a great escape.

The Jekyll and Hyde performances of the first two rounds had left Collingwood fans confused about whether their team was a genuine contender or not. They were no more enlightened after an engrossing Round 3 contest with St Kilda that produced almost as many sensations as it did goals.

St Kilda had become famous through 2008–9 for their so-called 'Saints footy' – an uncompromising, attritional game style that prioritised defence over attack and relied heavily on giving the opposition no time or space and pressuring them into mistakes. They had taken Hawthorn's game plan of 2008 to the next level. Collingwood had struggled badly against both the Saints and the Hawks over the past two seasons, unable to come up with ways through their packed zone defences. For the first half of the game at Docklands, it looked as if Collingwood was taking on the Saints at their own game. Magpie players, especially the forwards, applied huge pressure and closed down their opponents at every turn. Defenders pushed further and further up the ground, making it even harder for St Kilda players to break out of defence and into attack. The match was played in compressed spaces, and Collingwood actually had the better of the opening half, leading by three points at the long break. It was an encouraging start, and a win looked even more possible when star Saint Nick Riewoldt left the ground late in the second quarter with a serious hamstring injury.

But all that promise evaporated after half-time. Collingwood's wasteful first half return of 4.8 became a disastrous final score of 4.17, the team unable to kick a single goal in the second half. Players missed shot after shot, including many direct kicks, some from almost straight in front. It wasn't just the kids either, but senior players as well. The Pies were the gang that couldn't kick straight, and St Kilda eventually ran over the top, kicking the last six goals of the game for a 28-point win. Collingwood still took plenty of heart from the loss: despite their lack of serious scoreboard pressure, they'd actually outplayed the Saints for two-and-a-half quarters.

Collingwood's diabolical kicking for goal was not the only major talking point after the match. There was also Riewoldt's hamstring (it was a bad one, and he would miss three months), and a nasty verbal spat at quarter time involving Mick Malthouse, VFL manager Paul Licuria and the annoying Steven Milne. All three were later fined by the AFL – the incident was an ugly footnote to a game that had been played in poor spirit throughout.

The next five weeks set up Collingwood's season. Hawthorn, Essendon, Carlton, North and Fremantle all looked like winnable matches, but history had shown the Pies didn't always win the matches they were expected to. Instead, for once Collingwood did what good sides do: it won them all, and by big margins – 64 points over Hawthorn, 65 against Essendon, 53 over Carlton, 66 over North and 36 at Fremantle. Only against Carlton was the dominance threatened, when the Blues twice closed to within three points in a pulsating third quarter before the Magpies pulled away again.

All the wins featured what were rapidly becoming two Collingwood trademarks – super-fast starts, and a spread of goalkickers. The team's worst first quarter across those games was 4.2 against Carlton, but the others produced either five- or seven-goal first terms. Collingwood liked to hit their opponents early and leave them shell-shocked. By the end of the season they would be ranked the highest-scoring first-quarter team in the competition. They also liked to spread the responsibility for kicking goals: there were 11 different goalkickers against the Hawks and Bombers, and a staggering 13 against Carlton, North and Freo. Eight rounds into the season, and it was clear that

the Magpies had married the manic tackling and defensive pressure of Saints footy with an attacking philosophy and scoring power that few other teams could match. It was a heady mix.

By now the team's approach had a name – the 'Collingwood press'. That name neatly summed up the way the Magpie defenders pressed higher and higher up the ground, limiting the avenues through which their opponents could get the ball out of defence. Allied with fierce tackling and physical pressure that gave players little time to look for more creative exit routes, the press ensured the ball spent a lot of time inside Collingwood's forward 50. And that meant plenty of scoring opportunities. If opposition teams just tried to bomb the ball out of defence, it was usually mopped up and sent straight back by the likes of Harry O'Brien and Nick Maxwell, who were patrolling the perimeter of the zone. If opponents tried to find a way through with precise kicks or handballs, they were often caught by the intense Magpie pressure and forced into turnovers. Opposition teams had absolutely no room for error.

After eight rounds Collingwood sat on top of the ladder. The question remained, however, whether the Pies and their new game plan were enough to beat the very best sides. They had already fallen short against St Kilda, and in Round 9 they also failed against Geelong. It wasn't a bad performance by any means, and there was only five points in it at half-time. But, as had happened against St Kilda, the Magpies fell away badly in the second half, managing only 2.12 to slide to a six-goal defeat.

That loss confirmed the view of some critics that Collingwood still wasn't quite in the same league as the big two, St Kilda and Geelong. The doubters were given further ammunition the following week, when the Brisbane Lions produced a rare night out in an otherwise poor season to inflict a surprise defeat at the Gabba.

Fears of a mid-season wobble were allayed – albeit temporarily – with another brilliant display against the Bulldogs in Round 11. The first three quarters of this contest saw Collingwood at its absolute best, with Swan, Pendlebury, Didak, Davis, Ball and Thomas all outstanding, and the margin blowing out to eight goals late in the third quarter. It was still 43 points early in the final quarter after Swan roved beautifully and ran in for an easy goal. But then the Bulldogs stormed home, drawing to within nine points with three minutes left, but ran out of time. The win was a good, and important, one, but the late fade-out left fans worried.

That was nothing compared to how those fans felt the next week, after the traditional Queen's Birthday meeting with Melbourne. The Demons had caught Collingwood on the hop in Round 2, and there was no way the Pies

---

THE AGE

Robert Walls on Collingwood's progress:

There is no doubt that while the Saints and Cats will be eyeing each other off between now and grand final week they will also be keeping a close eye on the Magpies. Why? Because the Pies of 2010 are better than 2009, and are a genuine chance of winning the flag. There is a lot to like about this year's Magpies. They are younger, faster, harder and share the ball by hand more than they have in the past. Five regulars from last season are struggling to get a game. Over the past season-and-a-half, six youngsters have been introduced. What Malthouse has been able to do is blend the new with the old to produce a hard-working, highly skilled team that doesn't rely on stars.

would fall into the same trap of over-confidence again, especially given they'd been in a mini-slump themselves. And that's the way the game started, with Travis Cloke, Steele Sidebottom and Leon Davis all grabbing goals inside the first few minutes. But Melbourne fought back, the Magpies lost their radar around goals again and soon the match had turned into the same nip-and-tuck struggle of earlier in the season. There was rarely more than a goal in it after that, and the Demons led late after a Mark Jamar goal until, with just a couple of minutes left, veteran Tarkyn Lockyer marked 40 metres out and coolly slotted one through to level the scores. The last minutes were desperate, as both teams went in search of the score that would win the match, but the siren sounded with the ball yet again in dispute in Melbourne's attack.

The result meant Collingwood had won only one of its past four games, and the apparent resurgence in the first three quarters against the Dogs looked like a false dawn. The team's problems with goalkicking were also now in particularly sharp relief. Inaccuracy had arguably cost the team both of its big games – 4.17 against St Kilda and 6.14 against Geelong – and the deplorable 9.22 against Melbourne had almost certainly cost them the full four points. Travis Cloke was the focus of much of the frustration, with the big forward attracting much praise for his wonderful contested marking (number one in the competition) but regularly driving fans, teammates and coaches to breaking point with his ability to miss the simplest set shots. Cloke's, and the team's, wastefulness, would be big talking points for the rest of season.

Collingwood's mid-season break could not have come at a better time. Given the recent string of results the Pies knew they had to return to winning ways, and regulation victories over Sydney in Sydney, and West Coast in Melbourne (memorable only for Jarryd Blair's debut, and for Alan Didak's outrageous burst of three goals in just under three minutes in the third quarter) followed. The game against Port Adelaide at AAMI Stadium was always likely to be more troublesome, given that it was Mark Williams' last game as Port coach. The Pies trailed by five goals at the first break, but still finished up with a fairly comfortable victory, inspired by Dane Swan's stunning 16-possession second quarter.

Those three wins set up the first of two 'matches of the season' in four weeks – against St Kilda at the MCG in Round 16. Travis Cloke

Dane Swan shrugs off the attentions of his St Kilda opponent at the G in Round 16.

Harry O'Brien marks in front of Nick Riewoldt while Ben Johnson (26) keeps Steven Milne under control.

was suspended after an errant elbow against Port, and skipper Nick Maxwell missed with a calf injury. Nick Riewoldt was just back for St Kilda and still looking rusty. The Magpies were desperately searching for premiership credibility, needing the inner belief that only comes from beating the best. They knew that winning this match, and the one against Geelong in Round 19, was crucial to their chances.

Any way you look at it, this was a blockbuster, and it was played in front of more than 81,000 fans. And right from the opening it looked as if Collingwood wanted to make a statement. The Pies started the game on fire, throwing themselves at the contests, and the Saints were unable to withstand the early pressure. The press was operating at extreme levels. Luke Ball and Heath Shaw set the tone with fierce tackles inside their forward 50 that led to team-lifting goals. Leigh Brown nailed one from the boundary, Chris Dawes – back in the team for the suspended Cloke – marked and goaled, and by quarter-time the Pies had a three-goal break.

The first quarter had been played at a finals-like intensity, and that continued into the second term as Shaw goaled again soon after the restart when he soared for a speccie. Then Leigh Brown stunned his critics by gathering a loose ball, twisting one way, turning the other and sending it straight through with a left-foot bullet from just on 50. Macaffer snapped truly from in close to extend the lead and, even though Riewoldt goaled after the siren, the Pies still led by 26 points.

Collingwood put the game to bed in the third term with four straight goals, while St Kilda could manage only 1.6. It was a complete reversal of their Round 3 clash, except that the Pies were much more threatening in attack than the Saints had been. The Magpies continued to apply the squeeze and the Saints simply had no answers. Four more goals in the final term ended up securing an eight-goal win, leaving the Pies on top of the ladder after Round 16 for the first time since 1990. Even though St Kilda finished with a Collingwood-like scoreline of 6.16, nobody doubted that the Pies had emerged as legitimate premiership contenders.

Even the most optimistic Magpie fans knew such favouritism couldn't be justified until their team had beaten the mighty Geelong. So the contest between the two became an even bigger blockbuster than Collingwood and the Saints had been. The Pies had warmed up perfectly, first with an 82-point rout of Richmond (during which Didak unveiled his now famous 'shimmy'), then with a nine-goal-to-two first half that destroyed Carlton. They were ready for their biggest test of the season.

To say they passed that test with flying colours is a massive understatement. The Pies dominated the first one-and-a-half quarters, so much so that the ball rarely made it out of their forward 50. The press was on in full force, the tackling was ferocious (Luke Ball alone had 14 for the game) and the attacking pressure relentless. Wellingham, Pendlebury, Thomas, Swan and Didak were unstoppable, and there were no passengers. The team had rarely played better. Geelong couldn't find a way out, or around, or through, and only Collingwood's lack of clinical finishing – again – kept the margin to 28 points midway through the second quarter.

Then Geelong showed its class by taking control of the contested possessions and changing the game completely. Before Collingwood knew it, the Cats cut the margin to one point in less than 10 minutes, and when Joel Corey goaled just before half-time they had – improbably – taken the lead. It looked like the same old story: Collingwood dominating, not making the most of their chances, then getting cut down by one of

Below: **Leon Davis is chaired off by Alan Didak and Nick Maxwell after an emphatic win over Carlton in Round 18. Davis is Collingwood's first Indigenous player to play 200 games.**
Opposite, left: **Travis Cloke celebrates a goal against the Cats in Round 19.**
Opposite, right: **Leigh Brown, Heath Shaw and Chris Dawes give the song their all after beating the Cats.**

2010: Side by side

THE AGE

Rohan Connolly on Collingwood's win over Geelong:

That sense of team, that sometimes intangible quality that makes 22 individuals gel seamlessly into an efficient, disciplined unit is for the Pies, these days, profound. It certainly was too much for Geelong on Saturday night as Collingwood proved once and for all it can beat every team in the competition. The Pies are alive, the energy and fervour with which they play palpable, the defensive pressure manic, and the hunger to cash in on it insatiable. Against the Cats, Collingwood was aggressively positive in everything it did. Its defenders were prepared to leave their men to initiate attack. Its entire midfield group was prepared to run hard into attack to become goalkicking options. And the Pies simply refused to let the ball out of the Geelong back line with any ease or system at all, 12 goals to six forced from turnovers the proof. After Saturday night, there's no question now – Collingwood can take on anyone.

Geelong's trademark withering bursts of football. This time, though, the Pies were determined things would be different.

Matthew Stokes grabbed the first goal of the third quarter, and a Steve Johnson goal midway through the term extended the lead to 12 points. That's when Collingwood produced a fightback every bit as thrilling as Geelong's had been. Benny Johnson goaled brilliantly on the run from near the boundary, and Cloke overcame early jitters to tie things up with less than five minutes to go. Then Didak produced a magical, spearing pass from the boundary that set up Thomas alone in the square, and when Beams added a sensational snap out of heavy traffic inside the last minute, Collingwood ended a breathtaking third quarter 13 points to the good. The last quarter was a much more dour affair, but Jolly's snap over his shoulder provided a 20-point buffer and sent the Magpie hordes into rapture.

The final margin flattered Geelong. But the most important thing about Collingwood's 22-point victory was the way the game had been played, with the Cats being thrashed in most of the game's key indicators. They were smashed in contested possessions 144 to 102, 48–26 in clearances and the inside-50s count was a lopsided 66 to 37. Even another bout of wayward kicking (14.23, including five posters) couldn't disguise Collingwood's superiority. With the exception of about 25 minutes in the second and third quarters, the reigning premiers had been completely outplayed.

Dale Thomas has the ball on a string against the Doggies in the first finals outing.

The win installed Collingwood as clear flag favourites. As far as most fans were concerned, the remainder of the season was mainly about players not getting injured. An eight-goal first quarter and 98-point win against Essendon raised barely a ripple, and the only real talking point out of the scrappy narrow escape against Adelaide was that it secured top spot. The significance of Alan Didak's barely-noticed departure with a shoulder injury would become known a few weeks later. Leigh Brown's report that day and subsequent suspension gave Josh Fraser the chance to come back from the seconds and play his 200th game in the final round of the season, a meaningless game against Hawthorn that was lost when a late Dayne Beams shot faded at the last minute and went through for a behind.

So, after 22 rounds, Collingwood sat in top spot on the ladder for the first time since 1977. Those who had been around for a while believed you had to go back even further, to 1970, for the last time the Pies had topped the ladder and also been the best side in the competition. But as everyone at Collingwood understood only too well, the claim to 'best side in the competition' would really only be decided in September. Or so we thought.

The first finals outing was against the Western Bulldogs. The Pies and their fans should have been confident, given the results of the previous meetings between the sides during the year, and the fact that the Dogs had injury worries and were missing important players such as Adam Cooney. But there was still a strange nervousness leading into the game, partly because of the scars of past Septembers, and partly because of the weather. That Saturday night, the sky around the MCG was as ominous and threatening as any seen for years, and there were wild, wild winds: it looked for all the world like the apocalypse was about to hit. Fans stocked up on ponchos, umbrellas and industrial strength wet-weather gear, and everyone wondered whether the storms would reduce the gap between the two teams.

In the end, amazingly, hardly a drop of rain fell on the G. The only storm that hit was one of black-and-white jumpers – and it swamped the Bulldogs. The Doggies were good for the first five or six minutes but after that it was all Collingwood. By the long break the margin was 32 points, and could easily have been twice that such was Collingwood's domination of the game. Once again the team had the yips in front of goal (7.15 at half-time), but there was never any danger of that inaccuracy coming back to haunt them: four more goals in the third term and six in the last saw the Pies canter away to a 62-point win, doubling the Bulldogs' score in the process.

Dane Swan celebrates a goal as the Magpies steam to a commanding lead in the third quarter of the qualifying final.

If a 10-goal finals win could ever be considered routine, this was it. Dane Swan's 39-possession, three-goal game was a talking point, as was Didak's late banana goal on the run from the boundary. But the real jaw-dropper was Leigh Brown's memorable chase back into defence, outpacing Dogs' midfielder Daniel Cross and holding the ball in to create a stoppage. A few minutes earlier Brown had snapped a superb left-foot goal from a boundary throw-in. He was unrecognisable from the player of 2009.

The demolition of the Dogs sent Collingwood straight through to a preliminary final where, for the third time in four years, they would face Geelong. The 2007 contest had ended in tears after a heartbreakingly narrow defeat, and the 2009 meeting was a downright embarrassing 73-point thumping. The Cats had lost narrowly to St Kilda in their qualifying final and were still regarded by many as Collingwood's biggest threat. It would be Collingwood's press, backed by its round-the-boundary approach to goal, against Geelong's high possession, give-and-go, straight-up-the-middle style. Preliminary finals are never less than big, but this one loomed as huge.

And huge is what it proved to be – just not in the way most people expected. Instead of a tight, close contest, the crowd of more than 95,000 was treated to the most exhilarating demolition job that had been performed on Geelong for some time. Collingwood can rarely have played better in any game, let alone a big game, than it did for the first two-and-a-half quarters.

Their superiority was evident from the very beginning, when a period of trademark forward pressure forced Gary Ablett, of all people, into a hurried, misguided kick out of defence. His kick was marked and rebounded by Harry O'Brien, who kicked long and set up a towering Travis Cloke mark. Cloke kicked truly, and the Magpies were away. Scott Pendlebury ran into an open goal after Geelong crumbled under pressure at half-forward, and Chris Dawes marked and centred for Sharrod Wellingham to score. Inside 10 minutes and the Pies led by 18 points.

Travis Varcoe grabbed one back for the Cats, but immediately after the restart the ball broke to Leigh Brown deep inside the centre square, who bombed a long ball forward in hope. It bounced between the goal and behind posts about 15 metres out, took one massive off-break to the right, then took another to tumble through for a miracle goal. Even the most pessimistic Magpie fans began to wonder if this would maybe be their team's night after all. Those hopes were supported soon after when a Leigh Brown miskick was marked by Alan Didak and converted. The Cats were being strangled by the manic intensity of Collingwood's forward pressure, and that pressure produced another goal late in the term when Matthew Scarlett ran into trouble and was fiercely tackled by Dale Thomas. The ball spilled to Dayne Beams, who handballed to Pendlebury, who slotted it home perfectly on his wrong foot from 45, sending the Magpie Army behind the goals into ecstasy. If the roar that greeted that goal was huge (and it was) it was nothing compared to the one that followed three minutes later, when great work from Ben Reid, Tyson Goldsack and Dane Swan repelled a rare Geelong attack and allowed Brent

Scott Pendlebury urges his teammates on after goaling during the first quarter onslaught in the preliminary final against the Cats.

Macaffer and Heath Shaw to set up Ben Johnson for one of his trademark running goals from just inside 50.

Quarter-time came, and with it a standing ovation for a Collingwood team that had delivered a blistering 7.2 to 1.1 first term. Fans of both sides could scarcely believe what they were seeing. The Pies had gone inside 50 an amazing 22 times to eight. Their pressure was phenomenal, with one experienced commentator likening it to 'a tsunami'. Collingwood fans did not want the quarter to end, fearing that the break might also break whatever spell had been cast over their team. They need not have worried. From the very first bounce of the second quarter, more fierce pressure forced Ablett into an errant backwards handball, forcing Joel Corey into a second backwards handball that missed its target. The ball ran free towards Collingwood's goal, allowing Didak to kick off the ground to Cloke, who handballed to Steele Sidebottom for a snapped goal. Less than 30 seconds in, and the Pies were out by 43 points.

That goal broke Geelong hearts, and seemingly much of their resistance. Cloke took a big mark in the square, Beams kicked truly from half-forward and then Thomas was the beneficiary of a Geelong interchange infringement. Dane Swan snapped one of the goals of the game, after a sequence of bone-rattling tackles from Didak, Macaffer and Beams forced first Milburn, then Ottens, into critical spillages. When Dawes added a late major after yet another failed attempt by Geelong to clear the ball from defence, the half-time margin

Magpie fans celebrate the demolition of the Cats, while the players regroup before leaving the ground.

Herald Sun

Mark Robinson on Collingwood's demolition job on Geelong:

Collingwood's pressure is something we haven't seen in the game before. They have forged new territory from St Kilda's zone of 12 months ago. They press space and the man and the support network is like a cavalry charging a besieged fort. It forced handballs, indecision and turnovers. Collingwood's pressure made fools of many Cats players.

THE AGE

Michael Gleeson on Collingwood's preliminary final win:

It was not simply the victory nor the unexpectedly large early margin of this match that made Collingwood a juggernaut charging into this year's grand final, it was the breathtaking manner in which it was done. From the first quarter Collingwood physically squeezed Geelong, forcing indecision and error, harassing the Cats into giving Collingwood back the ball ... It was a game very much in the style for which Collingwood has become known, and created in Geelong a game most unlike that for which it is known. Geelong sought to continue to play a game that looked very 2007, against a younger faster side that was playing a game that was very 2010.

Opposite: In the dying minutes of the first grand final, Ben Johnson plays close as Lenny Hayes's kick bounces clear of Steven Milne and through for a point.

---

was 62 points and the game was as good as over. During the early stages of the third quarter, the Pies led Geelong – one of the all-time great VFL/AFL teams – by a staggering 81 points. But Collingwood players put the cue in the rack after that, not wanting to get hurt and miss out on the grand final, so the final margin was a more respectable 41 points. But when the game was alive, when it counted, the Pies had made the Cats look third-rate.

'They just annihilated us early and we were a bit shell-shocked,' Geelong full-back Matthew Scarlett admitted later. 'I've played for a while and I've never seen a side [apply so much] pressure. They just swarm you and it's like they've got three or four extra players out there. I've never seen anything like it.'

Grand final week was the usual mixture of nerves, anticipation, excitement and fear. The Pies were favourites, and deservedly so, but their fans had been burned too many times before to believe in anything until it had happened. Dane Swan had won every media award on offer during the season and was a hot favourite for the Brownlow, but in the end finished third, with teammate Scott Pendlebury in equal fourth. Training sessions at Gosch's Paddock were joyous affairs, with up to 15,000 fanatics turning out to cheer the players' every move.

The big selection queries in the lead-up centred around Luke Ball, who had cramped in his hamstring in the third quarter against Geelong, Leon Davis, who had been a late withdrawal against the Cats, and Simon Prestigiacomo, the club's veteran full-back who hadn't played since corking his thigh in Round 20. Ball recovered in time, and selectors decided to give Leon one more chance to atone for his disappointing grand final performances in 2002–03, bringing him back in and omitting Tyson Goldsack. Presti, despite his long absence, was passed fit and considered a better match-up for Nick Riewoldt than 21-year-old Nathan Brown.

They were all tough calls, but nothing compared to that which Presti himself made on the day before the game. He'd been chosen in the team, but felt some slight tightness in his groin during the final training session. Nobody else saw anything wrong, but the quiet, self-effacing Presti couldn't live with the idea that he might break down and cost his teammates a shot at the flag,o he went to coach Mick Malthouse in tears and withdrew from the side. It was the ultimate act of selflessness.

So much of that first grand final seems like a blur. There was the dream start, with Darren Jolly goaling on the run inside the first minute. Then Dids' surgical-like precision from the boundary, Daisy's mongrel helicopter punt sailing through from 50 and the fleeting feeling that maybe the footy gods were wearing black-and-white this time. A St Kilda fightback, more goals and missed chances – so many missed chances – in the second. A 24-point half-time lead that should have been much more, and would have been much more had Trav not missed two sitters just before the break. Then the slow, gut-churning realisation that St Kilda were closing the game up in the third quarter and turning it into the kind of attritional contest they love. A goalless third term, with more frustrating misses, and only eight points in front at the last change.

But if much of the first three quarters has become blended together in the memory banks, the last quarter is the exact opposite. Here, every action, every contest, seems in sharp relief. There are the goals, of course, especially Leon's moment of magic that set up a 14-point lead and looked, briefly, to have exorcised his grand final demons. Lenny Hayes's long bomb to bring them back, Milne's hands-in-the-back on Harry, Goddard's huge hanger and the sick-in-the-pit-of-the-stomach feeling that followed. There is also the injustice of the free paid against Harry for throwing, that led to a vital St Kilda point. There is Nick Maxwell's despairing, lunging dive that got a touch on Riewoldt's dribbled kick just millimetres from the line, plus his brave mark that led to the goal that put the

PLAYER OF THE YEAR

Alan Didak

In 2010 Alan Didak gave the Magpie fans yet another reason to love him, apart from his extraordinary skills and Daicos-like ability to conjure freak goals out of nothing. Courage. Didak tore the pectoral muscle in his left shoulder off the bone in the season's penultimate game against Adelaide. Eddie McGuire later described the injury as the kind 'that would put most of us on WorkCover for a year'. But Didak missed just one game, then played through the pain barrier in all four finals. He played so well (even down to tackling and smothering) that few outside the club had any idea how much discomfort he was in.

Didak's season had been outstanding anyway – leading goalkicker with 41 goals, fourth in the Copeland, a spot in the All-Australian team and any number of magic moments. But the bravery he showed in the final stages of the campaign has become part of the folklore surrounding the 2010 flag, evoking comparisons with Darren Millane's legendary efforts in 1990. And it was fitting that, like Millane, the ball was in Dids' hands when the final siren rang in the grand final replay.

STEELE SIDEBOTTOM — GRAND FINAL HERO

Steele Sidebottom was the only teenager on the ground in the grand final replay. But that wasn't his only claim to fame: he was also the only player with more than 11 disposals who did not commit a turnover. In these days where maintaining possession is crucial, that is priceless. Sidebottom, the youngest player on the MCG, had 25 high-quality possessions and didn't once cough up the ball to an opponent.

That underlines Sidebottom's extraordinary composure, his ability to deliver on the big stage and, above all, his sublime skills with hand or foot, on both sides of his body. All had been on display right throughout the season, but never to better effect than in the biggest game of the year.

Sidebottom added to his day's work with two quality goals in the second half, and a couple of vital assists as well. He ended up in second place in the **Norm Smith Medal** voting, just two votes behind **Scott Pendlebury**. It was an amazing performance by a young man who promises to be a key part of **Collingwood** teams for years to come.

Pies back in front when all seemed lost. There is Dale Thomas diving headlong into any number of packs, and Benny Johnson desperately keeping the ball in front of him and the Saints at bay in the final seconds. There's the manic desperation of both sides in the final minutes, and the brief chance to reflect on how sweet a one-point victory to the Pies would be. And then there's that wickedly bouncing ball eluding Johnson and – eventually, thankfully – Milne, tying up the scores for good. The result was only the third drawn grand final in VFL/AFL history.

At the end of it all, nobody knew how to feel. Everyone was utterly drained, punchdrunk from the drama. Stranded on the G with a microphone pointed at him, Maxwell described the absence of extra time as 'a joke'. Nobody except the AFL and the TV broadcasters could face the idea of going through all that again. It was just too painful.

The players had to deal with even more confusion, with sewerage leaks forcing them away from their rooms and over to the other side of the ground. Then, as fans were filing out of the stadium in a kind of stupor, the storm hit – this eerie, wild, burst from nowhere that suddenly turned the G into a bleak, windswept landscape. It was almost like a signal that this game had to be wiped from the minds of both teams. Was this a premiership won or a premiership lost? Nobody knew. It was back to square one.

Of course, everyone looked for signs of which team was coping better. The Saints seemed to regroup more quickly on the ground straight after the match. But that night the two teams took very different paths to the replay – St Kilda cancelled its planned evening function, while Collingwood went ahead with its own. In 1977, the last grand final draw, Collingwood had cancelled its function, while North Melbourne went ahead. Ever

the student of history, Eddie McGuire remembered that, and how beneficial North believed their approach had been. So this time the Magpie players got to unwind a bit, talk with friends and family about the crazy, crazy events they'd just experienced and – hopefully – get ready to move on. The Saints, on the other hand, shut out the world and bunkered down. Weeks later, Collingwood people would point to the decision to proceed with the function as crucial to the team's preparations.

That night, Malthouse gave one of his most important speeches as Collingwood coach. The message he gave was not one of disappointment or opportunities missed. Rather, it was one of praise, and of hope. He congratulated the players for coming back in the last five minutes, when the game seemed lost. 'In those last five minutes you just won yourself through to a grand final,' he said. 'We are in the same place we were eight days ago.' Malthouse then threw down a challenge to those players who hadn't been at their best on grand final day, again disguising it as an opportunity. He reminded them how lucky they were to get a chance to redeem themselves in seven days time. Some players wait years, and others never get the chance at all, he said. Then came the key part of the club's approach to the week ahead. 'If you treat this as a loss, it will be. If we treat this as an opportunity, it will be. If we treat this the way we have rebounded all year, then we will go in with utmost confidence.'

Above, left: **Captains Maxwell and Riewoldt wonder what to do next after the draw.**
Right: **The Auskick kids are not happy with the result either.**

The Mightiest Magpies

Opposite: **Dale Thomas defies gravity to chase down Lenny Hayes in the grand final replay.**

Nick Maxwell and the other club leaders did their best to back up Malthouse's words. It was half-time in the grand final and scores were level. The captain admitted later he was 'absolutely shot' and 'had nothing left', but faked positivity for the sake of his teammates. Players recovered from the numbness and exhaustion in their own ways, but Maxwell and the other team leaders had to force the pace of some of the mental recovery, and soon the optimism and energy began returning. Gradually, under the watchful eye of conditioning coach David Buttifant and his team, the battered bodies began recovering too. By early in the week, there was nothing fake about it – there was a good feeling around the club.

The second grand final week was much more like a normal football week – no Brownlow count, no parade, fewer functions and distractions. And that suited Malthouse and his team down to the ground. There were still selection dramas, however. Patience finally ran out with Leon Davis's failures on the big stage, and he was dropped for Tyson Goldsack. And even though he might have been right physically, the selectors felt Presti was simply too big a risk having not played footy in six weeks. Plus Nathan Brown had done a

PLAYER OF THE YEAR

Scott Pendlebury

magnificent job on Riewoldt in the first grand final. So one of the club's most beloved characters would have to miss out.

There was a better feeling about the second grand final. The weather was just about perfect, with bright sunshine. There were more club supporters at the ground and fewer corporates, less hooplah. Julie Anthony did a better job with the national anthem, and even Lionel Ritchie, mocked beforehand as an out-dated choice for pre-match entertainment, got the crowd going. Plus the game was being played in October, and Collingwood has a happy relationship with October grand finals, having won seven of its pre-2010 premierships in that month.

The game itself started in remarkably similar fashion to the one seven days earlier, with the Pies again set to goal inside the first 30 seconds after a centre clearance from Leigh Brown, a deft tap from Dawes and a precision kick to Cloke from Pendlebury. But before Cloke could take his kick from the square, Swan infringed off the ball and the kick was reversed. For those who look for early omens in matches, or who believe Collingwood is cursed in finals, this was not a good start.

Once again, the Magpies dominated general play. Once again, they couldn't quite make it count on the scoreboard. Goldsack and Johnson goaled from set shots, but they were the only majors in the first three quarters of the term. Then Nick Riewoldt marked on

Scott Pendlebury raised his performances to become one of the game's top midfielders, winning All-Australian selection, the Anzac Medal for best on ground on Anzac Day and finishing second in the Copeland and fourth in the Brownlow. The silky-skilled midfielder didn't have too many quiet days in 2010, but unfortunately one of them came in the drawn grand final. He knew he needed to lift for the replay.

What most didn't know at the time was that Pendles had been ill in the week before the draw, and had lost 6kgs. He still played reasonably well, but his output was nowhere near his regular levels. He rose to the occasion by winning the Norm Smith Medal for best on ground in the replay.

It completed a dream season for the poised, polished left-footer, who won many fans in 2010, including Greg Baum in *The Age*, who wrote: 'In a game that is said to be growing ever faster, Pendlebury plays it either at a jog or a standstill, yet rarely is caught with the ball, and rarely misuses it. He has the gift of awareness and the quality of poise.'

One of the most memorable moments from the 2010 Grand Final replay, Heath Shaw's 'smother of the millennium'.

his own in the square and turned around to boot the Saints' first, a goal that would have cut the margin to eight points. Instead, Heath Shaw sprinted from 40 metres away, snuck in on Riewoldt's blindside and, with a full-length dive, knocked the ball away mid-air as it fell from Riewoldt's hand to his boot. It was one of the greatest individual moments ever witnessed in a grand final, and Magpie fans will cherish forever the sight of Riewoldt's leg flailing at fresh air and the star Saint briefly having no idea what had happened.

Just as importantly, the ball went to the other end of the field after Shaw's kick-in, and Brent Macaffer snapped a beauty over his head to secure a healthier quarter-time lead of 20–2. The Saints dominated much of the second quarter, but developed the jitters in front of goal. Sam Gilbert missed three easy chances, Sam Fisher missed another and only a dodgy free to the impressive Brendon Goddard allowed the Saints to post a major before half-time. Didak goaled against the run of play, but there was still only 15 points in it late in the term. Then Brett Peake's hopeful clearing kick bounced wickedly and evaded Ben

McEvoy. Darren Jolly gathered, also evaded McEvoy, and passed to Macaffer in the square. From the restart, Jolly ran forward to get on the end of a spearing pass from Steele Sidebottom and steered through another.

At half-time it was Collingwood by 27 points – three more than at the same time the previous week. But this time there would be no St Kilda comeback: the 'Collingwood press' saw to that. The next 10 minutes was a snapshot of Collingwood's entire season as, all over the ground, tackle after tackle was laid and the Saints were suffocated. Ferocious pressure in the goalmouth forced an errant handball, which Chris Dawes kicked out of mid-air. Then Wellingham sharked a ruck contest and Swan crumbed beautifully, both running into open goals, and the margin had blown out to 46 points. St Kilda eventually steered one through, but before anyone had even started to worry about a comeback, Didak smothered Blake's attempted clearance, re-gathered and snapped the goal of the day with his right foot from 45. There was no doubt about it – this was going to be Collingwood's day.

A 41-point margin at the final change should have been more than enough, but long-suffering Magpie fans wanted a greater safety net before they really believed. Early final quarter goals to Dawes and Thomas provided it, and the tears started to flow, most publicly from Eddie McGuire. The final minutes of the game were a joyous celebration: both sides wanted the game over, for different reasons, and the Collingwood players started kicking the ball among themselves as they ran down the clock. Every single one of those marks, no matter how simple, was greeted with a huge roar. The last, and loudest, came when the siren rang, with the ball in Alan Didak's hands.

The final result was 56 points, Collingwood's greatest-ever winning margin in a grand final. Over the course of both grand finals, Collingwood players had laid a staggering 176 crunching tackles. In the replay they laid 21 in their forward 50 alone, compared to St Kilda's five. They had 55 inside-50s, well ahead of St Kilda's 39, and won the clearance count 44–25. Scott Pendlebury

The siren sounds and Nick Maxwell sinks to the ground, becoming the eleventh Collingwood premiership captain.

won the Norm Smith Medal, but such was the evenness of the Magpies display that it could just as easily have gone to Jolly (35 hit-outs) or Sidebottom or Thomas. All gained votes from the judges, along with Luke Ball, Dane Swan and Nathan Brown, who kept Riewoldt goalless. The whole finals series, except for the draw, was as emphatic a statement of Collingwood's superiority as you could wish for – 62 points over the Dogs, 41 points over Geelong and then 56 points over St Kilda. Not since 1929 could the Magpies claim such an undisputed rating as the best team in the competition.

That rating was backed up by the stats. The Magpies were the number one team for a raft of important measures, including tackles, inside-50s, contested possessions, time the ball spent inside-50, scores from turnovers and number of goalkickers (nearly 9 per game). They averaged 12 more contested possessions, 13 more tackles and 12 more inside-50s than their opponents per game. They had fewer inside-50 entries against them than any other team. About the only area where the Pies suffered was in free kicks – they received the second fewest frees per game in the competition.

Below: **Simon Prestigiacomo congratulates his replacement in the team, Nathan Brown.**

The celebrations were delirious, and widespread, but somehow gentler than 1990. The club went out of its way to acknowledge not just those who had played on the day, but also those who had contributed throughout the year. Almost by stealth, there had been generational change at Collingwood throughout the season. The team from the opening game included seasoned campaigners Tarkyn Lockyer, Paul Medhurst, Shane O'Bree, Josh Fraser, Jack Anthony, Simon Prestigiacomo and Leon Davis. All of them were, at the time, considered to be in the club's best 22. But none of them featured in the grand final replay. For varying reasons, only Davis would survive into 2011.

The team had been rebuilt not just in search of a flag, but while on its way to one. The addition of Jolly and Ball was vital: the former was a huge influence when it counted, while Ball proved to be the hard-tackling extracting machine the club had hoped for. He finished fifth in the Copeland. Fraser's demise was hastened by the growth of Leigh Brown, who by season's end was playing out of his skin. Anthony found himself pushed aside by the development of Chris Dawes, while the extraordinary progress of Steel Sidebottom (second in the Norm Smith voting) and Dayne Beams (sixth in the Copeland) made life difficult for Lockyer and O'Bree. Jarryd Blair came from the rookie list to play in a flag in just his twelfth game. Ben Reid became a central member of the defence, and Brent Macaffer filled a valuable role up forward. Scott

THE AGE

Rohan Connolly on the more restrained premiership celebrations compared to 1990:

This outpouring wasn't quite so spontaneous. But then neither was this premiership. Indeed, you could argue, it's a triumph that's been more than a decade in the making, from the moment of Eddie McGuire's rise to the Collingwood presidency in 1999, the year the club 'won' its last wooden spoon. The feeling among both those up on the stage and the thousands of fans in front of it was more one of satisfaction than euphoria, of entitlement born of a long-term, unwavering commitment. And rightly so. Collingwood worked long and hard for this flag. What it picked up on Saturday afternoon was no more than it thoroughly deserved.

After playing his third grand final in 12 months, Luke Ball consoles former teammate Lenny Hayes.

Pendlebury joined Swan in the elite category, while Dale Thomas and Sharrod Wellingham were two of the most improved players in the competition. The end result was one of the least experienced premiership-winning teams in history: nine of the premiership 22 will go into 2011 having played 56 games or less – a promising stat for the future.

This was a flag that had been in the club's sights since Nick Maxwell, Eddie McGuire and other club leaders took the bold step of uttering the 'P' word before the 2009 season. Eddie and Mick Malthouse had it in their sights for 10 years before that, when they came to a club at rock bottom and started to turn things around. This flag was more than a decade in the making.

But in some ways it was also 120 years in the making. The 2010 premiership was built on what Malthouse calls 'teammanship' – discipline, selflessness and subversion of the individual to the team. Those are the very same values that captain Bill Strickland and secretary Ern Copeland used to underpin their rebuilding of an ailing Collingwood Football Club back in the 1890s. They are the values on which the club built its success, and they are as strong, and important, now as they were then. Collingwood won the 2010 flag 'side by side'. Even without the slogan, that's how it won its first flag in 1896. And it's how Collingwood will win its next premierships, too.

Long after the crowd has gone, the victorious team returns to the centre of the MCG with the cup to sing the song one more time.

DALE THOMAS
GRAND FINAL HERO

Not too long ago, Dale Thomas was considered by those outside Collingwood to be a flashy footballer who could deliver great highlights but would never be a consistent, four-quarter midfielder.

Those opinions changed radically during Thomas's breakout 2010 season – and especially after both of his grand final appearances. He is now rightly regarded as one of the most dangerous and courageous midfielders in the game.

Thomas drastically improved his stats in 2010, winning more of the ball with far more consistency than ever before – without sacrificing his trademark flair. So good was his season that he finished third in the club's best and fairest.

He was Collingwood's best player in the drawn grand final, where his clean hands, 'mad dog' attack on the football and willingness to throw himself into the fiercest contests – especially in that frenetic final quarter – brought back memories of Gavin Brown at his best. He was also well up among the Magpies' best in the replay. If a single Norm Smith Medal had been awarded for performances over both games, he probably would have won it.

PLAYERS

#	Player	Games	Goals
9	Jack Anthony	7	5
12	Luke Ball	24	7
43	Jaxson Barham	1	0
17	Dayne Beams	25	26
47	Jarryd Blair	12	7
15	Leigh Brown	19	21
16	Nathan Brown	13	0
32	Travis Cloke	24	38
1	Leon Davis	20	27
31	Chris Dawes	20	30
33	Brad Dick	2	5
4	Alan Didak	24	41
25	Josh Fraser	9	5
6	Tyson Goldsack	11	1
26	Ben Johnson	23	7
18	Darren Jolly	26	24
24	Tarkyn Lockyer	11	6
30	Brent Macaffer	21	16
5	Nick Maxwell	22	0
3	John McCarthy	2	0
7	Paul Medhurst	10	12
11	Shane O'Bree	6	3
8	Harry O'Brien	26	6
10	Scott Pendlebury	26	17
35	Simon Prestigiacomo	13	0
20	Ben Reid	21	0
39	Heath Shaw	23	5
22	Steele Sidebottom	25	24
36	Dane Swan	26	24
13	Dale Thomas	26	18
34	Alan Toovey	26	2
21	Sharrod Wellingham	24	15
19	Cameron Wood	4	3

Club Awards
Copeland trophy – Dane Swan
R T Rush Trophy – Scott Pendlebury
J J Joyce Trophy – Dale Thomas
J F McHale Trophy (fourth) – Alan Didak
Jack Regan Trophy (fifth) – Luke Ball
Best Clubman – Nick Maxwell
Best first year player – Jarryd Blair
Leading desire indicators – Luke Ball
Best player in finals – Dane Swan, Nick Maxwell, Dale Thomas (equal)
Leading goalkicker – Alan Didak (41)
Best VFL player – Tom Young
Phonse Kyne Trophy (for services to the club) – Rohan Bownds (trainer)

2010 SEASON

ROUND 1 March 28 Docklands Stadium
Western Bulldogs **13.15.93** v **Collingwood 19.15.129**
Goals: Didak 4, Medhurst 4, Davis 3, Swan 3, Anthony, Cloke, Pendlebury, Thomas, Wellingham

ROUND 2 April 3 MCG
Collingwood 12.14.86 v Melbourne **12.13.85**
Goals: Anthony 2, Davis 2, Lockyer 2, Pendlebury 2, Beams, Cloke, Fraser, Medhurst

ROUND 3 April 9 Docklands Stadium
St Kilda **10.9.69** v Collingwood **4.17.41**
Goals: Beams, Cloke, Didak, Sidebottom

ROUND 4 April 17 MCG
Collingwood 17.21.123 v Hawthorn **8.11.59**
Goals: Davis 3, Thomas 3, Didak 2, Jolly 2, Cloke, Johnson, Macaffer, Pendlebury, Sidebottom, Swan, Wellingham

ROUND 5 April 25 MCG
Collingwood 18.12.120 v Essendon **8.7.55**
Goals: Cloke 4, Fraser 3, Dawes 2, Welingham 2, Beams, Didak, Johnson, Medhurst, Pendlebury, Thomas, Toovey

ROUND 6 May 2 MCG
Carlton **16.6.102** v **Collingwood 24.11.155**
Goals: Ball 3, Dawes 3, Medhurst 3, Beams 2, Cloke 2, Didak 2, Sidebottom 2, Wellingham 2, Jolly, O'Brien, Pendlebury, Swan, Thomas

ROUND 7 May 8 MCG
Collingwood 23.19.157 v North Melbourne **14.7.91**
Goals: Sidebottom 5, Medhurst 3, Davis 2, Dawes 2, Didak 2, Jolly 2, Cloke, Johnson, O'Bree, Shaw, Thomas, Toovey, Wood

ROUND 8 May 14 Subiaco
Fremantle **15.7.97** v **Collingwood 20.13.133**
Goals: Cloke 5, Didak 3, Wood 2, Anthony, Ball, Beams, Davis, Johnson, Macaffer, O'Bree, Pendlebury, Sidebottom, Swan

ROUND 9 May 21 MCG
Collingwood **6.14.50** v **Geelong 12.14.86**
Goals: Beams 4, O'Bree, Swan

ROUND 10 May 29 Gabba
Brisbane 13.10.88 v Collingwood **11.14.80**
Goals: Dawes 2, Didak 2, Sidebottom 2, Anthony, Jolly, O'Brien, Pendlebury, Thomas

ROUND 11 June 6 Docklands Stadium
Collingwood 17.11.113 v Western Bulldogs **16.7.103**
Goals: Davis 3, Didak 3, L Brown 2, Wellingham 2, Beams, Cloke, Fraser, Jolly, O'Brien, Pendlebury, Swan

ROUND 12 June 14 MCG
Melbourne **11.10.76** v Collingwood **9.22.76**
Goals: Dick 4, Cloke, Davis, Jolly, Lockyer, Sidebottom

ROUND 13 June 26 Stadium Australia
Sydney **10.11.71** v **Collingwood 13.18.96**
Goals: Dawes 3, L Brown 2, Cloke 2, Sidebottom 2, Dick, Didak, Jolly, O'Brien

ROUND 14 July 3 Docklands Stadium
Collingwood 20.15.135 v West Coast **7.10.52**
Goals: Dawes 4, Jolly 4, Didak 3, Beams 2, Lockyer 2, Pendlebury 2, Swan 2, Ball

ROUND 15 July 9 Football Park
Port Adel **12.7.79** v **Collingwood 16.9.105**
Goals: Dawes 3, Blair 2, L Brown 2, Didak 2, Thomas 2, Beams, Cloke, Jolly, Lockyer, Swan

ROUND 16 July 17 MCG
Collingwood 15.10.100 v St Kilda **6.16.52**
Goals: Brown 3, Macaffer 3, Beams 2, Shaw 2, Ball, Davis, Dawes, Sidebottom, Swan

ROUND 17 July 24 MCG
Collingwood 19.13.127 v Richmond **6.9.45**
Goals: Davis 4, L Brown 3, Didak 3, Macaffer 3, Jolly 2, Beams, Dawes, Pendlebury, Swan

ROUND 18 July 31 MCG
Collingwood 15.15.105 v Carlton **9.3.57**
Goals: Beams 3, Davis 3, Cloke 2, Dawes 2, Didak 2, Pendlebury, Swan, Wellingham

ROUND 19 August 7 MCG
Geelong **12.13.85** v **Collingwood 14.23.107**
Goals: Beams 3, Cloke 2, Wellingham 2, L Brown, Didak, Johnson, Jolly, Macaffer, Swan, Thomas

ROUND 20 August 13 MCG
Essendon **10.4.64** v **Collingwood 24.18.162**
Goals: Cloke 5, L Brown 3, Macaffer 3, Blair 2, Dawes 2, Didak 2, Jolly 2, Swan 2, Beams, Shaw, Thomas

ROUND 21 August 21 MCG
Collingwood 6.18.54 v Adelaide **7.9.51**
Goals: L Brown 2, Thomas 2, Cloke, Didak

ROUND 22 August 28 MCG
Hawthorn 15.8.98 v Collingwood **13.17.95**
Goals: Blair 2, Davis 2, Jolly 2, Ball, Beams, Cloke, Dawes, Shaw, Sidebottom, Swan

2010 FINALS

LADDER

Team	W	L	D	For	Agst	%	Pts
Collingwood	17	4	1	2349	1658	141.7	70
Geelong	17	5	0	2518	1702	147.9	68
St Kilda	15	6	1	1935	1591	121.6	62
Western Bulldogs	14	8	0	2174	1734	125.4	56
Sydney Swans	13	9	0	2017	1863	108.3	52
Fremantle	13	9	0	2168	2087	103.9	52
Hawthorn	12	9	1	2044	1847	110.7	50
Carlton	11	11	0	2143	1983	108.1	44
North Melbourne	11	11	0	1930	2208	87.4	44
Port Adelaide	10	12	0	1749	2123	82.4	40
Adelaide	9	13	0	1763	1870	94.3	36
Melbourne	8	13	1	1863	1971	94.5	34
Brisbane Lions	7	15	0	1775	2158	82.3	28
Essendon	7	15	0	1930	2402	80.4	28
Richmond	6	16	0	1714	2348	73.0	24
West Coast	4	18	0	1773	2300	77.1	16

QTR FINAL September 4 MCG
Collingwood 17.22.124 v Western Bulldogs **8.14.62**
Goals: Sidebottom 3, Swan 3, L Brown 2, Didak 2, Pendlebury 2, Cloke, Davis, Dawes, Jolly, Thomas

PRELIMINARY FINAL September 17 MCG
Collingwood 18.12.120 v Geelong **11.13.79**
Goals: Cloke 3, Pendlebury 2, Sidebottom 2, Swan 2, Wellingham 2, Beams, L Brown, Dawes, Didak, Johnson, Macaffer, Thomas

GRAND FINAL September 25 MCG

Collingwood	4.2	7.8	7.13	9.14	(68)
St Kilda	3.2	4.2	7.5	10.8	(68)

Goals: Cloke 2, Didak, Macaffer, Jolly, Thomas, O'Brien, Blair, Davis
Best: Thomas, Shaw, Sidebottom, Maxwell, N Brown, Swan, Didak
Umpires: Chamberlain, Ryan, Rosebury
Crowd: 100,016 at the MCG

GRAND FINAL REPLAY October 2 MCG

Collingwood	3.2	6.5	11.8	16.12	(108)
St Kilda	0.2	1.8	4.9	7.10	(52)

Goals: Didak 2, Macaffer 2, Dawes 2, Sidebottom 2, Wellingham 2, Johnson, Jolly, Swan, Thomas, O'Brien, Goldsack
Best: Pendlebury, Sidebottom, Thomas, Jolly, Ball, N Brown, Shaw, Maxwell
Umpires: Chamberlain, Ryan, Rosebury
Crowd: 93,853 at the MCG

Grand Final Team
B: N. Maxwell (c), N. Brown, A. Toovey
HB: H. O'Brien, B. Reid, H. Shaw
C: S. Wellingham, D. Swan, B. Johnson
HF: A. Didak, T. Cloke, L. Ball
F: D. Beams, C. Dawes, S. Sidebottom
Foll: D. Jolly, S. Pendlebury, D. Thomas
I/C: T. Goldsack, L. Brown, B. Macaffer, J. Blair

COLLINGWOOD PREMIERSHIP PLAYERS

Player	Collingwood Years	Named In Premiership Team
ADDISON, Jim	1903–04	1903
AHERN, Charlie	1929	1929
ALDAG, Bill	1930–31	1930
ALLAN, John W	1902–03	1902
ANDERSON, George P	1911–17	1917
ANDREW, C Bruce	1928–32; 1934	1928, 1930
ANGUS, George	1902–11	1902, 1903, 1910
BALL, Luke	2010–	2010
BANKS, Denis	1979–91	1990
BARWICK, Doug	1988–91	1990
BATCHELOR, Keith	1952–55	1953
BAXTER, Tom	1907–11	1910
BEAMS, Dayne	2009–	2010
BEERS, Brian	1958–61	1958
BENNETT, Ken	1957–62	1958
BEVERIDGE, Jack	1926–34	1927, 1928, 1929, 1930
BLAIR, Jarryd	2010–	2010
BOWYER, Percy	1928–38	1929, 1930, 1935, 1936
BREWER, Ian	1956–61	1958
BROWN, Charlie W	1916–23	1917
BROWN, Gavin	1987–2000	1990
BROWN, Leigh	2009–	2010
BROWN, Nathan J	2008–	2010
CALLAGHAN, William	1895–96	1896
CALLESON, George	1896–98	1896
CARMODY, Jack H	1933–39	1935, 1936
CHESSWAS, Harry	1922–31	1927, 1928, 1929, 1930
CHRISTIAN, Michael	1987–95	1990
CLAYDEN, George	1924–33	1927, 1928, 1929, 1930
CLOKE, Travis	2005–	2010
COLECHIN, Bert	1916–21	1919
COLLIER, Albert	1925–30; 1933–39	1927, 1928, 1929, 1930, 1935, 1936
COLLIER, Harry	1926–40	1927, 1928, 1929, 1930, 1935, 1936
CONDON, Dick	1894–1900; 1902–06	1896, 1902, 1902
COVENTRY, Gordon	1920–37	1927, 1928, 1929, 1930, 1935
COVENTRY, Syd	1922–34	1927, 1928, 1929, 1930
CROSISCA, Gavin	1987–2000	1990
CROWE, Jim	1936–37	1936
CURTIS, Harry	1914–23	1917, 1919
DAICOS, Peter	1979–93	1990
DAWES, Chris	2008–	2010
DAYKIN, Richard	1908; 1910	1910
DELANTY, Mike	1957–62	1958
DIBBS, Charlie	1924–35	1927, 1928, 1929, 1930, 1935
DIDAK, Alan	2001–	2010
DOBRIGH, Gus	1914–21	1917
DOHERTY, Vin	1934–39	1935, 1936
DOHRMANN, Herman	1895–96	1896
DOW, Charles	1896–1902	1896
DOWDELL, Harry	1892–1900	1896
DROHAN, Eddie	1903–08	1903
DRUMMOND, Tom	1916–22	1917, 1919
DUMMETT, Alf	1901–10	1902, 1903
EDMONDS, Horrie	1929–34	1929, 1930
FELL, Matthew	1898–1905	1902, 1903
FELLOWES, Graeme	1956–64	1958
FINCK, Jack	1951–54	1953
FLAHERTY, Danny	1893–97	1896
FRANCIS, Tony	1990–98	1990
FRASER, Keith	1933–36	1935, 1936
FROUDE, Fred	1930–39	1930, 1935, 1936
GABELICH, Ray	1955–60; 1962–66	1958
GAYFER, Michael	1986–93	1990
GIBB, Percy	1905–14	1910
GIBBS, Arthur	1896–98	1896
GILCHRIST, Paddy	1910–13	1910
GILLARD, Wal	1896–99	1896
GOLDSACK, Tyson	2007–	2010
GOOCH, Arthur	1950–56	1953
GRAY, Brian	1956–65	1958
GREEN, Jack W	1911–18	1917
GREGORY, Jim	1896–1901	1896
GREVE, Bob	1955–59	1958
HAILWOOD, Frank	1896–1902; 1904	1896, 1902
HALL, Richard	1895–96	1896
HAMS, George	1948–55	1953
HARRIS, John D	1925–29	1927, 1928
HARRISON, Barry	1958–61	1958
HAYSOM, Wally	1919–20	1919
HEALEY, Des	1948–55	1953
HENDERSON, John	1957–66	1958
HUGHES, Les	1908–22	1910, 1917, 1919
INCOLL, Jack	1902–06	1902, 1903
JOHNSON, Ben	2000–	2010
JOLLY, Darren	2010–	2010
KELLY, Craig	1989–96	1990
KERRISON, Shane	1986–95	1990
KINGSTON, Ron	1950–59	1953
KNIGHT, Jack	1934–40	1936
KYNE, Phonse	1934–44; 1946–50	1935, 1936
LAUDER, Albert	1926–31	1928, 1929, 1930
LAXTON, Charlie	1912–21	1917, 1919
LEACH, Arthur	1898–1908	1903
LEACH, Fred	1897–1903	1902
LEACH, Ted	1901–03	1902
LEE, Charlie	1916–19; 1923	1917
LEE, Dick	1906–22	1910, 1917, 1919
LIBBIS, Billy	1925–33	1927, 1928, 1929, 1930
LOCKWOOD, George	1902–04	1902, 1903
LOCKWOOD, Teddy	1902–05	1902, 1903
LUCAS, Peter	1949–59	1958
LUMSDEN, Ernie	1910–12; 1917–20	1917, 1919
MACAFFER, Brent	2009–	2010
MacLEOD, Norm	1927–32	1928
MAKEHAM, Bob	1923–32	1927, 1928, 1929, 1930
MANN, Neil	1945–56	1953
MANSON, James	1985–92	1990
MAXWELL, Nick	2004–	2010
McCARTHY, Con	1915–21	1917, 1919
McCORMACK, Con	1902–03	1902, 1903
MCDONALD, Robert	1896–97	1896
McGUANE, Mick	1987–96	1990
McHALE, Jock	1903–18; 1920	1910, 1917
McIVOR, Duncan	1909–11; 1914	1910
MERRETT, Thorold	1950–60	1953, 1958
MILBURN, Charlie	1923–27	1927
MILLANE, Darren	1984–91	1990
MONKHORST, Damian	1988–99	1990
MONOHAN, Jack	1893–1907	1896, 1903
MORGAN, Leo W	1933–41	1935, 1936
MORWOOD, Shane	1983–93	1990
MURPHY, Frank	1925–34	1927, 1928, 1929, 1930
MURPHY, Len	1928–37	1928, 1929, 1930
MUTCH, Alec	1911–21	1917, 1919
NORRIS, Charlie	1910–11	1910
O'BRIEN, Harry	2005–	2010
OLIVER, Norm M	1909–11	1910
PANNAM, Alby C	1933–43; 1945	1935, 1936
PANNAM, Charlie E	1917–22	1917, 1919
PANNAM, Charlie H	1894–1907	1896, 1902, 1903

Player	Collingwood Years	Named In Premiership Team
PARKER, Jack	1951–55	1953
PEARS, Harry	1902–08	1902, 1903
PENDLEBURY, Scott	2006–	2010
POULTER, Joe	1923–28	1927
PROUDFOOT, Bill	1892–1906	1896, 1902, 1903
REEVES, Ron	1957–65	1958
REGAN, Jack	1930–41; 1943; 1946	1935, 1936
REID, Ben	2007–	2010
REYNOLDS, Pen	1913–19	1917, 1919
RICHARDS, Lou	1941–55	1953
RICHARDS, Ron A	1947–56	1953
RILEY, Lou	1934–38	1935, 1936
ROSE, Bill	1950–55	1953
ROSE, Bob	1946–55	1953
ROSE, Kevin	1958–67	1958
ROSS, R Jack	1931–40	1935, 1936
ROWE, Percy H	1920–24; 1927–28	1927, 1928
ROWELL, Ted	1901–03; 1906–15	1902, 1903, 1910
RUMNEY, Harold	1927–35; 1937	1927, 1929, 1903, 1935
RUSH, Bob	1899–1908	1902, 1903
RUSSELL, Scott	1990–98	1990
RYAN, Dave	1907–12	1910
SADLER, Jim	1908–17	1910
SAUNDERS, Harry	1916–26	1917, 1919
SCADDAN, Joe	1910	1910
SEDDON, Mal	1911–15; 1919–21	1919
SERONG, Bill	1956–61	1958
SHARP, Lerrel	1953–59	1953
SHAW, Heath	2005–	2010
SHAW, Tony	1978–94	1990
SHEEHY, Maurie	1914; 1916–22	1919, 1928
SHORTEN, Jack	1909–10; 1912–13	1910
SIDEBOTTOM, Steele	2009–	2010
SMALE, Ken	1955–58	1958
SMITH, Archie	1892–1902	1896
STACKPOLE, Keith	1935–39	1935, 1936
STARCEVICH, Craig	1987–93	1990
STOCK, F	1893–1896	1896
STRICKLAND, Bill	1893–1897	1896
SULLIVAN, Harry	1955–60	1958
SWAN, Dane	2003–	2010
THOMAS, Dale	2006–	2010
TODD, Ron	1935–39	1936
TOOVEY, Alan	2007–	2010
TURNER, Jamie	1984–93	1990
TURNER, Ken	1956–65	1958
TWOMEY, Bill J	1945–58	1953
TWOMEY, Bill P	1918–22	1919
TWOMEY, Mick	1951–61	1953, 1958
TWOMEY, Pat	1947–49; 1952–53	1953
VERNON, Dick	1909–11	1910
WAITES, Terry	1953–54	1953
WALLER, Neville	1953–58	1953
WALTON, Bill	1918–19	1919
WEIDEMAN, Murray	1953–63	1953, 1958
WELLINGHAM, Sharrod	2008–	2010
WESCOTT, Leo	1922–27; 1929; 1931–32	1927, 1929
WHELAN, Marcus	1933–42; 1946–47	1935, 1936
WILLIAMS, George	1893–1901	1896
WILSON, Ernie	1919–28	1919, 1927
WILSON, Percy	1909–20	1910, 1917
WOODS, Bervin	1935–40	1935, 1936
WRIGHT, Graham	1988–98	1990

ACKNOWLEDGEMENTS

Thanks to everyone who helped me put this book together, and especially to my frequent co-author Glenn McFarlane, whose work on the 1927–30 chapters in one of our previous books, *The Machine*, formed the basis for the modified versions that appear here. Glenn also helped out with some photo and other research, and I can't thank him enough for his help.

To my publisher at Penguin, Andrea McNamara, a huge shout of 'Tooooovs' by way of appreciation for all her enthusiasm, professionalism hard work and support. It's been great working 'side-by-side' on a Collingwood project with a publisher who shares my passion for all things black-and-white, and who also wants this book to be everything it can. Andrea, I hope you're as happy with the results as I am (and I hope Nan and Emily like it too). Thanks also to the rest of the team at Penguin, especially Cameron Midson, who has done a terrific job with the design.

As always, Col Hutchinson at the AFL was outstanding with his statistical information and records, while Tamara Bell and Donna Bishop at the Herald & Weekly Times were a great help when it came to finding photos. Peter Furniss, Pat Overend, Tom Wanliss, Bernie Murphy and the rest of the team at the Collingwood Football Club History and Archives Committee were wonderfully helpful, and good company, during the research process. Thank you also to the following, all of whom have helped in one way or another: Gary Diffen, Kate Holmesby (your dad will hate this), Nick Place, Isabel Smith, Will Smith, Michael Winkler and my match-going Magpie mates, Murray, David, Brayden and Scott. And a special, heartfelt thank you to Belinda Byrne, whose practical assistance was invaluable, and whose love and support kept me sane (well, close anyway) during what was a particularly rugged period of time. You are a true Collingwood legend.

And finally, to the Collingwood Football Club, for providing – through that unforgettable 2010 season – the perfect inspiration to dust off an idea that had been in my head for ages. Let's hope we have to add another chapter to this book before too much longer.

PICTURE CREDITS

Every effort has been made to contact the copyright holders of original source material contained in this book. Where the attempt has been unsuccessful, the Publisher would be pleased to hear from the copyright holder to rectify any omission.

The majority of photographs in this book have been sourced from private collections, with the following exceptions:

Herald and Weekly Times Ltd: pages ii, iv, viii, 246–247, 265, 267, 268, 280, 281, 282, 283, 284, 285, 286, 287, 288, 289, 293, 295, 297, 298, 299, 301, 306–07, 309, 311, 313, 316, 317, 318, 319, 320, 321, 322, 323, 325, 327, 328, 329, 330, 331, 332, 333, 334

Collingwood Football Club: pages vi, 291, 292, 298, 300, 302

State Library of Victoria: pages 59, 195, 211, 212, 213

Australian Gallery of Sport and Olympic Museum Collection: page 11, The First Grand Final (1896), kindly donated by Rod Oborne (1989.2084).

MICHAEL JOSEPH

Published by the Penguin Group
Penguin Group (Australia)
250 Camberwell Road, Camberwell, Victoria 3124, Australia
(a division of Pearson Australia Group Pty Ltd)
Penguin Group (USA) Inc.
375 Hudson Street, New York, New York 10014, USA
Penguin Group (Canada)
90 Eglinton Avenue East, Suite 700, Toronto, Canada ON M4P 2Y3
(a division of Pearson Penguin Canada Inc.)
Penguin Books Ltd
80 Strand, London WC2R 0RL England
Penguin Ireland
25 St Stephen's Green, Dublin 2, Ireland
(a division of Penguin Books Ltd)
Penguin Books India Pvt Ltd
11 Community Centre, Panchsheel Park, New Delhi – 110 017, India
Penguin Group (NZ)
67 Apollo Drive, Rosedale, North Shore 0632, New Zealand
(a division of Pearson New Zealand Ltd)
Penguin Books (South Africa) (Pty) Ltd
24 Sturdee Avenue, Rosebank, Johannesburg 2196, South Africa

Penguin Books Ltd, Registered Offices: 80 Strand, London WC2R 0RL, England

First published by Penguin Group (Australia), 2011

10 9 8 7 6 5 4 3 2 1

Text copyright © Michael Roberts 2011
The moral right of the author has been asserted

All rights reserved. Without limiting the rights under copyright reserved above, no part of this publication may be reproduced, stored in or introduced into a retrieval system, or transmitted, in any form or by any means (electronic, mechanical, photocopying, recording or otherwise), without the prior written permission of both the copyright owner and the above publisher of this book.

Cover and text design by Cameron Midson © Penguin Group (Australia)
Typeset in ITC Mendoza by Cameron Midson
Colour reproduction by Splitting Image, Clayton, Victoria
Printed in China by Leo Paper Products Ltd

National Library of Australia
Cataloguing-in-Publication data:

Roberts, Michael, 1961–
The mightiest Magpies : the story of every Collingwood premiership season / Michael Roberts.
9781921518775 (pbk.)
Collingwood Football Club – History.
Australian football teams – Victoria – Collingwood – History.

796.336099451

penguin.com.au